CW01067195

AGAINST THE BOMB

AGAINST THE BOMB

The British Peace Movement
1958–1965

RICHARD TAYLOR

CLARENDON PRESS · OXFORD
1988

Oxford University Press, Walton Street, Oxford OX2 6DP
Oxford New York Toronto
Delhi Bombay Calcutta Madras Karachi
Petaling Jaya Singapore Hong Kong Tokyo
Nairobi Dar es Salaam Cape Town
Melbourne Auckland
and associated companies in
Berlin Ibadan

Oxford is a trade mark of Oxford University Press

Published in the United States
by Oxford University Press, New York

©Richard Taylor 1988

All rights reserved. No part of this publication may be reproduced,
stored in a retrieval system, or transmitted, in any form or by any means,
electronic, mechanical, photocopying, recording, or otherwise, without
the prior permission of Oxford University Press.

British Library Cataloguing in Publication Data
Taylor, Richard.—1945–
Against the bomb: the British peace
movement, 1958–1965.
1. Great Britain. Nuclear disarmament
movements.
I. Title.
327.1'74'0941
ISBN 0–19–827537–4

Library of Congress Cataloging in Publication Data
Taylor, R. K. S. (Richard K. S.)
Against the bomb.
Based on the author's thesis.
Bibliography: p.
Includes index.
1. Antinuclear movement—Great Britain—History.
2. Nuclear disarmament—Great Britain—History.
I. Title.
JX1974.7.T32 1988 327.1'74'0941 87–34969
ISBN 0–19–827537–4

Typeset by Litho Link Limited, Welshpool, Powys
Printed and bound in
Great Britain by Biddles Ltd,
Guildford and King's Lynn

To the memory of my parents
Jeanne and Ken Taylor

PREFACE

This book is based upon my Ph.D. thesis, and my greatest debt is to my supervisor, friend, and colleague David Coates, who provided initial and continuing encouragement, advice, and guidance.

I am also very grateful for their support and advice to my friends Jill Liddington, Colin Pritchard, Luke Spencer, and Nigel Young. Details of primary and other sources consulted are given in the Bibliography, but thanks must be given here to all those leadership figures in the Peace Movement who consented so readily to the in-depth interviews which form an important primary source for the study; to April Carter and the late Hugh Brock for the loan of the DAC archive for consultation; to Arthur Goss for the loan of the NCANWT archive for consultation; to numerous individuals who were active in the Peace Movement for the loan of private collections of papers; to the British Library of Political and Economic Science, London School of Economics and Political Science, University of London, for access to the CND archive, and to numerous Movement pamphlets, relevant newspapers, etc.; to the Modern Records Centre, University of Warwick; to the Librarian at the Commonweal Collection, housed in the J. B. Priestley Library, University of Bradford; to the Library at the University of Hull, where the *Daily Worker* and other Marxist source material was available for consultation; to Peter Cadogan for permission to consult the Committee of 100 press cuttings collection and numerous other papers relating to the Committee; to the research section of the City of Leeds Central Library, for access to various periodicals; and to the Inter-Library Loan staff at the Brotherton Library, University of Leeds.

I am also very grateful to Liz Dawson for typing the final manuscript so quickly and efficiently.

This book deals with issues that are still contentious and with perspectives that, in some respects, are sharply divergent. It may be, therefore, more than usually necessary to emphasize that the full responsibility for the views expressed, and for any inaccuracies or infelicities that remain, is mine alone.

R.T.

Leeds
February 1987

ACKNOWLEDGEMENTS

I am grateful to the following for their kind permission to reproduce extracts from published sources: A. D. Peters and Co. Ltd. for extracts from Christopher Driver, *The Disarmers*, London, Hodder & Stoughton, 1964; Allison & Busby for extracts from Peggy Duff, *Left, Left, Left,* London, 1971; Manchester University Press for extracts from Frank Parkin, *Middle Class Radicalism*, Manchester, 1968.

CONTENTS

INTRODUCTION

The Nuclear Disarmament Movement of the late 1950s and early 1960s was one of the largest extra-parliamentary movements in modern Britain, and arguably the most significant. Moreover, politically and socially it marked the divide between the immediate postwar years of austerity and optimism, followed by the consensual, Keynesian growth of the 1950s, and the unsettled, questioning decade of the 1960s. Perhaps most important of all, it articulated the growing fear and anxiety amongst many thousands of people, from a wide variety of backgrounds and beliefs, about the seemingly inexorable arms race, and the potential horror of nuclear war.

In all these ways the Movement is significant for our times. The shadow of the nuclear threat hangs over us all, and unless and until world-wide nuclear disarmament takes place, peace movements focusing upon these issues will persist in one form or another. The Movement analysed in this study was the first such mass movement to arise, and its experiences, its history, and its politics are of relevance to later movements and, more generally, to later generations who have to come to terms with the nuclear issue.

The first and primary purpose of this study is to describe and analyse the development of the British Nuclear Disarmament Movement from its origins in 1957–8 through to its decline and disintegration in the mid-1960s. There is a particular focus on the complex ideological composition and orientations of the main strands within the Movement. Whilst these were neither discrete nor bound by their organizational location, they were concentrated in particular organizational formations (which themselves changed and developed through time). The approach here is thus not chronological but analytical. Each of the major organizational components of the Movement is analysed, politically and historically, but above all ideologically, in order to attain an overall analysis of the Movement, its various objectives, and its political and other problems.

Thus there is discussion of the single-issue, apolitical, moralistic perspectives in the context of CND; and of the Direct Action, extra-parliamentary perspective in the context of the Direct Action

Committee and the Committee of 100. In relation to the directly socialist sections of the Movement, there is similar analysis both of the Labourist and generally 'reformist' perspective which dominated an important stratum of the Movement, and of the various Marxist positions.

The emphasis in this study is thus political and analytical rather than directly historical. The approach is based upon the analysis in depth of the dominant groups in the Movement and the ideologies and strategies they adopted, rather than upon an all-embracing historical account of the Movement as a whole (and this explains the virtual omission of some important areas: there is, for example, no extended discussion of the youth movement of CND, nor of the local, regional, or indeed Scottish and Welsh movements).

Yet this study will be concerned to pursue a detailed historical record of a kind, for a number of reasons. To begin with, the themes just outlined cannot be explored in a vacuum: they must be discussed in the context of actual, historical events. Similarly, the Movement cannot be discussed without reference to the substantial defence and foreign policy issues which were at the heart of the specific politics of the Movement.

Moreover, there is independent and legitimate justification for the considerable historical detail entered into, because the views and analyses of the Movement's leaders, previously unrecorded, constitute an important resource for analysis of the Movement and its politics. And, ultimately, the real political workings of the Movement—its policy disputes, its strategies, and its internal conflicts—can only be analysed properly by looking in detail at the historical record at first hand.

The book is divided into three sections. Part I deals with the mainstream movement of CND itself. Part II analyses the direct action wing, the focus for the Movement's radicalism. Part III is concerned with the 'socialist dimension' to the Movement, both the Labour Party and the various shades of Marxist grouping. And the brief Postscript discusses the legacy of the Movement for subsequent generations.

PART I

THE MAINSTREAM

CND IN EMBRYO

The National Council for the Abolition of Nuclear Weapons Tests

THE Nuclear Disarmament Movement had diverse roots. Radical pacifism was of central importance; and, to a much lesser degree, the extra-parliamentary left had its distinctive role.[1] The 'orthodox' mainstream of the Movement, however, originated elsewhere. To some extent the impetus for opposition to nuclear weapons came from the Labour Movement, as the creation in July 1957 of the Hydrogen Bomb Campaign Committee signified.[2] It was, however, from the outset the reflex action of the formal (and, especially, the parliamentary) Labour Movement in response to the widespread surge of popular protest against nuclear weapons. The Committee never had the grass-roots support of 'ordinary people', outside the orthodox political party activists, which was later to characterize CND.

There were, however, genuinely popular, though very much minority, movements of protest against nuclear weapons and their testing which arose in 1957, largely outside the Labour Movement. One of these, the Direct Action Committee, had its origins within the pacifist movement and is discussed in detail in Chapter 4. The other, the National Council for the Abolition of Nuclear Weapons Tests (NCANWT), was the principal forerunner of CND itself in both organizational and ideological terms, and is the subject of this chapter.

The NCANWT had its origins in the Golders Green and Suburb

---

[1] See chs. 4, 5, 7.

[2] The Hydrogen Bomb Campaign Committee was a creation of the Labour left, and had as its objective the adoption by the Labour Party of a policy of unilateral nuclear disarmament. Among the 30 or so MPs giving their support were Frank Allaun, Emrys Hughes, Fenner Brockway, and Konni Zilliacus. There was considerable constituency support and, in Sept. 1957, a demonstration of approximately 4,000 in Trafalgar Square. However, with Bevan's disavowal of unilateralism at the 1957 Party conference, the Campaign disintegrated, and it disbanded in 1958, merging into CND to become, subsequently, the Labour Advisory Committee.

Women's Co-operative Guild.[3] At the beginning of 1955 the Guild
convened a meeting of various local bodies 'to discuss what we
could do together in our own area to help towards the banning of
the H-Bomb'. The immediate actions of this group were, first, to
send a message to the Prime Minister:

We ask our Government to do all in its power at the forthcoming Four
Power Talks, to reach agreement on the vital matter of banning nuclear
weapons and ending the present experimental explosions: and to work
towards a progressive disarmament programme for the preservation of
peace.

and, secondly, to

appeal to all local organizations and groups to help us in our continued
efforts for the above policy in defence of humanity.[4]

As a result of this appeal the Golders Green Joint Committee for the
Abolition of Nuclear Weapons was formed, following a meeting on
11 July 1955. By December 1955, Miss Gertrude Fishwick, a
retired civil servant and former suffragette, had established the
Hampstead Joint Committee for the Abolition of Nuclear Weapons
as an 'offshoot of the Golders Green Joint Committee'. By this stage
the Golders Green Committee consisted of

representatives from the Society of Friends, T U Branches, Labour Party
Wards, The Finchley and Friern Barnet District Trades Council, the
Fellowship of Reconciliation, Co-operative Women's Guilds, and has the
support of the Women's International League, and local Branch of the
United Nations Association and similar bodies.[5]

Those active in these two organizations[6] provided the nucleus for
the NCANWT organization. Arthus Goss, a Quaker active in peace

[3] Similar organizations arose elsewhere at around this time. Laurens Otter,
for example, was chair of a group in Guildford. But it was the Golders Green
and Hampstead groups which provided the essential catalyst for subsequent
development.
[4] Quotations are from a circular letter from Mrs A. Simpson, Chairwoman of
Golders Green and Suburb Women's Co-operative Guild, 24 June 1955, NCANWT
archive.
[5] Circular letter from Miss Gertrude Fishwick calling a meeting to establish The
Hampstead Joint Committee for the Abolition of Nuclear Weapons, 2 Dec. 1955,
NCANWT archive.
[6] Miss Fishwick was perhaps the foremost of these in terms of her commitment,
enthusiasm, and hard work. Christopher Driver has claimed with some justification
that it was Miss Fishwick who triggered off 'the chain reaction which ended in CND'
(*The Disarmers*, London, 1964, p. 31). Miss Fishwick died two days before the

movements, and proprietor of the weekly *Hampstead and Highgate Express*, became chairman of the new Hampstead group, and these two relatively small but active groups (Golders Green and Hampstead) worked closely together, sometimes acting formally as a Joint Council for the Abolition of Nuclear Weapons.

Through 1955 and 1956 the nuclear testing of the major powers increased,[7] and the public concern over radiation dangers grew rapidly. At the suggestion of Miss Fishwick the National Peace Council, an umbrella peace body with an eclectic but fundamentally liberal pacifist outlook, took the initiative of calling a meeting to discuss nuclear weapons tests. Pressure had also been mounting from elsewhere, including the Science for Peace group, a Communist Party-influenced body.

The resulting conference, held in the Alliance Hall, Palmer Street, London on 29 November 1956, was in effect the founding meeting of the NCANWT. The meeting, although successful, was rather confused. It had been called to make recommendations to the Council on the appropriate action to be taken to oppose further testing of nuclear weapons by Britain. However, because of the length of the discussion, caused by the large number who wished to contribute, 'the final resolutions had to be taken in some haste,[8] and this, perhaps, explained why, without appreciating that the resolutions were presented as alternatives, delegates warmly supported both of them. The resolutions and votes were as follows:

1. To ask the National Peace Council to give assistance in the initial stages to inaugurate an independent *ad hoc* organization with the purpose of urging that the British Government should:
   (*a*) announce its decision not to test nuclear weapons;
   (*b*) work determinedly for international agreement to bring the testing of these weapons to an end.
   (For: 41   Against: 3   Abstained: ?16)
2. That an organization for the abolition of the testing of nuclear weapons should be set up at once by the members of this meeting.
   (For: 32   Against: 4   Abstained: ?24)[9]

launching of CND in Feb. 1958. Others prominent in these early days included Vera Leff, Ianthe Carswell, Ann Meeling, Arthur Goss, Peggy Darvell, and Ernest Kay.

[7] The USSR tested the largest bomb to date on 23 Nov. 1955; Britain carried out a series of tests in the Monte Bello Islands in May and June 1956, and in Australia in Sept. and Oct. 1956; the Christmas Island tests, which took place in May and June 1957, were announced in 1956.

[8] 'Conference on Nuclear Weapons Tests, 29 Nov. 1956, A Summary', NPC Paper NC 9859, NCANWT archive.   [9] Ibid.

Miss Fishwick and Arthur Goss decided that the second of these resolutions should be acted upon, in part because this was a positive decision of the meeting whereas the first was a request for advice and assistance from a separate organization. More important, however, was the enthusiasm of the sixty or so who attended for immediate and decisive action.[10] An *ad hoc* Committee was established, under the new NCANWT title. Arthur Goss became chairman and Dr Sheila Jones, a physicist and a member of Hampstead Labour Party, secretary. Other members of the Committee were Ianthe Carswell (Hampstead Committee), Gertrude Fishwick (Golders Green Committee), and Sydney Hilton (Science for Peace). Letters in the Press announcing the campaign 'brought us a great volume of support from all over the country'.[11] By the time the National Peace Council executive committee met to decide what action to take on the first resolution from the November conference, the *ad hoc* committee had already established a presence, and the NPC wisely decided to leave the matter there.

The central thrust of the campaign was apparent from the outset.

Our aim is to canalize the large volume of support among the general public in favour of the cessation of nuclear weapon tests. We regard it as of major importance that Britain should halt, or at least postpone the forthcoming tests on Christmas Island, to give a moral lead to Russia and America to reach agreement on the banning of all further tests.[12]

Both the Golders Green and Hampstead Committees retitled themselves as Committees against nuclear weapons *tests*, and the movement took a conscious decision to broaden its appeal by focusing on the specific issue of nuclear testing. The Committee began immediately to canvass support from public figures. From the outset Arthur Goss and the Committee were convinced that the

[10] Ibid. According to Sydney Hilton, then active in Science for Peace, the NPC 'had called the meeting, to see how people felt and then really tried to dampen it down. And so I asked whether all the people who had spoken in a similar sense to myself might care to meet in the hall when the meeting had closed, to decide what we might want to do. . . . And that was why I found myself with the people from the North West London group against nuclear weapons . . . and that was when I met Arthur Goss.' I am indebted for this information to Fred Barker of the University of Manchester, who interviewed Professor Hilton in May 1982. This extract is from the unpublished MS of that interview. The organizations represented at the meeting included some local trade union and Labour Party branches as well as Church and peace groups.

[11] NCANWT information sheet, n.d., NCANWT archive.   [12] Ibid.

NCANWT should attempt to mobilize public opinion on a non-party basis: 'we are a non-party organization, and welcome the support of all who wish to help in the campaign (except proscribed organizations)'.[13] The tone of the campaign was moral—a human protest against the evil of nuclear weapons testing and, implicitly, of nuclear weapons themselves, and the NCANWT saw its primary role as being that of awakening and informing the general public of these tremendous dangers. A central part of this function was to mobilize the public support of as wide a range of prominent and weighty personalities as possible. The NCANWT experienced considerable problems in attracting such support. Although Professor Barbara Wootton, Dr Donald Soper, and E. M. Forster all agreed readily to lend their names as sponsors, both Canon Collins and Bertrand Russell declined. Russell replied to the NCANWT in January 1957, stating that he was

finding it rather difficult to make up my mind whether to support your memorandum or not. I have undertaken to do, in the near future, a careful discussion of the whole question and, on the whole, I prefer to make no pronouncement meanwhile, although I expect I shall arrive at conclusions very similar to yours.

Within two months, however, Russell had joined the list of NCANWT sponsors.

Some senior political figures and scientists were also loath to commit themselves publicly to this new and untried campaign. Anthony Greenwood, for example, having previously agreed by telephone to become a sponsor, declined because of pressure of work; and Professor Bronowski wrote that, whilst he was opposed to both the testing and making of nuclear weapons, he felt that he could voice this opposition 'more effectively on informal occasions than at a formal public meeting'.[14]

Nevertheless the NCANWT did manage, within a few months, to gather together a very impressive list of sponsors, which was to form the basis of CND's own list in 1958.[15] But it was the

---

[13] Ibid.
[14] Letters from Greenwood, 10 Jan. 1957, and Bronowski, n.d., NCANWT archive.
[15] NCANWT list of sponsors by late 1957: John Arlott, Lord Boyd Orr, Benjamin Britten, CH, Ritchie Calder, Jim Campbell, the Bishop of Chichester, Count Michael de la Bedoyere, Bob Edwards, MP, Dame Edith Evans, E. M. Forster, CH, Gerald Gardiner, QC, Dayan Dr I. Grunfeld, Professor Alexander Haddow, D.Sc., Ph.D.,

unexpectedly large response of ordinary men and women to the NCANWT, and the letters which appeared in the national Press publicizing its programme, that was of most importance. More than 1,000 letters were received within a week of the publication of letters in the *News Chronicle* and the *Guardian*.[16] Local groups were rapidly established and, within four months of its inauguration, a total of seventy-five had come into existence.[17]

Many of the local groups devoted considerable energy to propagandizing for the Harold Steele trip to the testing area in the Pacific, which marked the inauguration of the DAC in the summer of 1957.[18] This indicates the intertwined and fraternal relationship which existed in the first few months between the embryonic organizations of the new Movement. In the localities there was a general feeling, which persisted at least partially through the years of splits and dissension, that everyone was campaigning for similar objectives and that differences of methods and 'style' were far less important than the unity which existed around the central nuclear issues. Even at this early stage, however, there were marked differences in ideology and priorities between the NCANWT (at leadership level) and the DAC. The National Council was concerned primarily with exercising political pressure in two ways: first, by lobbying MPs, circulating constituency Labour Parties and undertaking other, similar party political pressure; and secondly, by organizing peaceful and legal demonstrations of protest to mobilize public opinion. The NCANWT estimated that several thousand letters had been written to MPs by the end of March, and at a lobby of the Commons on 18 March, arranged to coincide with the opening in London of the 1957 session of the Disarmament Subcommittee of the United Nations, cards were sent in for eighty MPs. The NCANWT subsequently claimed much of the credit for the Labour Party's decision in April to call for the suspension of the British Test series, and for similar resolutions from the Liberals,

Barbara Hepworth, Dr Julian Huxley, FRS, Rose Macaulay, Sir Compton Mackenzie, The Rt. Rev. George F. MacLeod, Denis Matthews, Henry Moore, CH, Ben Nicholson, Sir Herbert Read, Flora Robson, CBE, Earl Russell, OM, FRS, The Rev. Dr Donald Soper, Michael Tippett, Vicky, Professor C. M. Waddington, Sc.D, FRS, Barbara Wootton, Miles Malleson (NCANWT archive).

[16] According to David Boulton, in an unpublished MS account of the origins of the NCANWT, NCANWT archive.

[17] Ibid. (according to the NCANWT *Newsletter* of July 1957 there were several other groups in existence too.)

[18] See ch. 4.

the British Council of Churches, and the Free Church Federal Council.

The NCANWT, however, was intent from the outset on keeping itself non-aligned politically, and exclusively concerned with the single issue. It saw its task as raising the consciousness of the general public over the issues, rather than becoming involved in party political arguments. This necessarily involved, so it was argued, appealing to Liberals and Conservatives, and indeed the mass of apolitical citizens, on the nuclear issue, and not confining the appeal to those active in the Labour Movement. Arthur Goss put this point of view forcefully: 'we wanted one objective only, the abolition of nuclear weapons . . . we're *all* agreed about nuclear weapons—we will *not* agree about anything else. . . . It's a *campaign*, not a more general political organization.'[19]

Given this determinedly non-aligned stance, though, it was essential for the NCANWT to make a major impact through public demonstrations (or 'public witness', as many of the Quaker supporters of the Council preferred to describe it). The NCANWT did in fact organize a successful demonstration against the Christmas Island test, in which 2,000 women—many clad in black sashes—marched through central London in torrential rain on 12 May 1957 to a well-publicized rally in Trafalgar Square, addressed by Dr Edith Summerskill, Vera Brittain, Diana Collins, and Sheila Steele. It was as a result of the upsurge of public support following this demonstration that the NCANWT decided to employ Peggy Duff as full-time secretary[20] in order to cope with the administrative and organizational work of the rapidly expanding movement. A further indication of public concern over the tests was the support received by the NCANWT from the United Nations Association. The UNA had been becoming more involved in the peace issue under the secretaryship of David Ennals. In October 1956, the UNA had proposed that the Christmas Island tests should be suspended as

[19] Arthur Goss, in conversation with the author, Jan. 1978
[20] Peggy Duff had been involved in numerous single-issue, progressive campaigns, including the National Campaign for the Abolition of Capital Punishment, of which she had been secretary. With the announcement of a two-year moratorium on the death penalty, this post had come to an end and she was thus available for the NCANWT secretaryship. She went on to become organizing secretary, later secretary, of CND, from 1958 to 1967. Subsequently she was secretary of the International Confederation for Disarmament and Peace (ICDP) until her death in 1981. The full story of her political life, up to 1970, is told in her autobiography *Left, Left, Left*, London, 1971.

long as other nations suspended theirs. By March 1957, this quali-
fication had been dropped, partly as a result of representations from
Ritchie Calder, science correspondent of the *News Chronicle* and a
UNA executive member.

In June 1957 David Ennals joined the NCANWT Committee: in
David Boulton's view this was seen as 'a far bigger catch than either
the Labour or Liberal parties, since UNA's Honorary Presidents
were Sir Anthony Eden, Earl Attlee, and Lady Violet Bonham
Carter, with Sir Winston Churchill as First Patron'.[21]

Although welcoming the creation of local NCANWT committees, the national committee never envisaged the campaign as orientated towards mass movement and demonstration: its strategy
depended on élite influence rather than mass support. And this was
considerably more than a strategic disposition: it reflected the
fundamental liberal élitism of the NCANWT's ideological assumptions. The most fundamental of these was the notion that the
nuclear issue was separate and autonomous, and could be
campaigned for *and* 'solved' without reference to other political
(and socio-economic) questions. And this liberal, single-issue orientation, combined with the strong emphasis on the moral as opposed
to the political rationale for the campaign, subsequently characterized CND as much as the NCANWT.

This central division—between those who believed that nuclear
disarmament was an autonomous single issue, and those who
argued that the issue of the bomb was connected politically,
economically, and culturally with the wider structure of society—
formed one of the most fundamental characteristics of the
Movement and is a recurring theme of analysis throughout this
study. Similarly, the sharp divergence in both ideology and tactics
between those who favoured a purely moral approach and those
who saw the Movement as essentially political, underlay a considerable amount of the tensions in the Movement, and again forms a
major analytical theme in the context of the Movement as a whole.

As a part of this overall approach, the NCANWT—and later
CND, both leadership and rank and file—made the implicit

---

[21] Boulton, op.cit. An approach from the NCANWT to Canon Collins's Christian
Action organization suggesting a joint campaign against the tests was, however,
rejected by the Canon. Although in favour of the idea, Canon Collins was too busy
with the South African Treason Trial Defence and Aid Fund to become involved
with the NCANWT.

assumption that a swing in public opinion on nuclear issues would result automatically in a change of nuclear policy.[22]

Three other specific ideological aspects of the NCANWT are also worthy of note, particularly because of their impact on the subsequent development of CND. There was, first, the attitude of the NCANWT to 'orthodox' pacifism. Although Arthur Goss, and many of the others involved in the NCANWT, were themselves pacifists, the NCANWT was adamant from the outset that it must appeal to a wider constituency than existing pacifists. Even more importantly, the NCANWT was convinced that the issue of nuclear weapons *per se* must predominate, whereas the pacifists in and around the Peace Pledge Union (PPU) argued forcefully that there was qualitatively and morally no difference between nuclear war and 'conventional' war, and that therefore *all* war must be opposed, *all* weapons abolished. Thus, many pacifists believed that the implication of the NCANWT (and, again, later of CND) was that conventional war was 'acceptable'. Both the Society of Friends and the Fellowship of Reconciliation (FoR), for example, were reluctant initially to become involved in the Movement; and Sybil Morrison and others in the PPU mounted a long campaign of opposition.[23]

However, it is clear that the NCANWT leadership was intent on creating a non-pacifist body, campaigning exclusively on the specific issue of nuclear weapons and their testing. The leadership was thus not prepared to make any concessions to the pacifist groups in order to secure their support.

The second ideological aspect of the NCANWT worthy of comment was not, however, subject to any such ambivalence. From the outset the NCANWT was absolutely opposed to involvement with Communism and the Communist Party. (Although there were individual Communists and 'fellow travellers' involved in the NCANWT they were in a small minority and never exercised

---

[22] The ideological view associated with such a position has long characterized the major part of the British left in the Labour Party. For critical analyses see Tom Nairn, 'The Nature of the Labour Party' in Perry Anderson and Robin Blackburn (eds.), *Towards Socialism*, London, 1965; and Ralph Miliband, *Parliamentary Socialism*, 2nd edn., London, 1973

[23] It should be noted that the radical pacifists of the DAC had, of course, a very different perspective; and that the opposition of the Society of Friends and the FoR, unlike that of the PPU, was very short-lived—the Society of Friends, in particular, becoming centrally involved with CND.

control.) Ostensibly apolitical, the NCANWT was in reality deeply anti-Communist, as its propaganda and public statements made abundantly clear. Arthur Goss's attitude was especially uncompromising: 'I was and always have been non-Communist, perhaps I should say anti-Communist: they seem to be as dictatorial as Fascists.'[24] For the NCANWT the question of Communist involvement was hardly a problem as the Communist Party (CP) at this stage, although opposed to British nuclear tests, was pursuing a firmly multilateralist (and implicitly anti-unilateralist) policy, as is discussed in Chapter 7. Moreover, although the Movement grew rapidly through 1957 it was not of sufficient size and importance prior to the establishment of CND to attract the serious attention of the CP. Such problems for CND as there were in this context came during and after 1959–60.

The final ideological dimension of importance in the NCANWT was its attitude towards direction action. Despite the local, rank-and-file sympathy for the DAC and its campaigns that was noted earlier, there is no doubt that the NCANWT leadership was fundamentally opposed to the DAC and to direct action politics in general. In part this resulted from the NCANWT's primary concern with creating a climate of public opinion favourable to nuclear disarmament and its emphasis upon the importance of attracting 'big name' support; given this approach, there was a natural hostility to direct action which, it was argued, would alienate both 'ordinary people', *and* respectable public figures who might otherwise have been sympathetic.

There was, however, a disagreement *in principle* with direct action which rendered any real co-operation between the leadership of the two wings of the Movement ultimately impossible. Arthur Goss has summarized this position clearly:

I was opposed, *totally* opposed, to this Direct Action business. . . . I believe I am a *true* democrat—our objective was to *persuade* our fellow citizens that nuclear weapons should not be tested; (and) . . . that Britain should renounce unilaterally its nuclear weapons—not to *force* them to do it, which is an absurd notion anyway. . . . I took the view that to snarl up all the traffic in Trafalgar Square . . . got you a lot of publicity but did you a great deal of harm. Why annoy the rest of the Londoners by snarling-up their traffic? And if you're serious in what you're saying, are you really suggesting that the British Government, whatever colour it is, is going to

[24] Goss, in conversation.

alter its foreign policy or its arms policy because a group of people snarl up the traffic? It's so ludicrous, absurd . . . But let's suppose . . . you *could* force the British Government to take a different line of action—that's the very thing I'm fighting against, I'm fighting for a world where you don't *force* your opponent to do something contrary to his will, you *persuade* him to. And the idea of winning by force is what war is all about. . . . Direct Action is therefore a total abnegation of what we're working for.[25]

This clear and forceful argument has its ideological roots firmly in liberalism: a belief in reasoned argument and persuasion, an implicit acceptance of the institutional and political framework as a viable vehicle for achieving change, an avowal of the consensual basis of society, and a similar rejection of a politics based upon class conflict (or indeed any other conflict). This liberalism underlay the subsequent CND leadership's ideology. Indeed, in some respects the NCANWT had a more firmly anti-direct action attitude than Canon Collins and the CND leadership.

The sum of all these ideological and organizational considerations was quite clear and unambiguous. The NCANWT provided the basis from which CND itself grew. The formation, the priorities, the policies, and the projected image of CND—at least in the early days—derived directly from the NCANWT. There were, of course, several factors specific to the rise of CND which were not extant at the time of the NCANWT's formation, but the basic orientation at leadership level remained constant between the two organizations. At the organizational level the dovetailing was remarkably close, and the merger of the NCANWT into CND was a relatively smooth transition. At CND's inauguration the NCANWT handed over not only its assets and contacts, but also its premises at 146 Fleet Street (and these were given rent-free to CND by Eric Baker, General Secretary of the National Peace Council). This was in large part because of the congruence of the two organizations' objectives and the fact that, although the NCANWT *maintained* its support through the latter part of 1957, its 'period of mushroom growth was undoubtedly in its formative three or four months'.[26] Arthus Goss and the other NCANWT leaders were convinced of the need for a larger and more prestigious initiative if the Movement were to succeed.

This harmony was further enhanced by the NCANWT's

[25] Ibid.
[26] Boulton, op. cit.

decision, in November 1957, to adopt what was in effect a policy of British unilateral nuclear disarmament in addition to its continued opposition to nuclear testing. The response from NCANWT supporters to this suggested policy change, according to an opinion poll circulated with the NCANWT Bulletin, had been overwhelmingly (99.5 per cent) in favour.[27] And, by mid-December, 'only one of the sponsors had so far objected to the broadening of the campaign, Mr E. M. Forster'.[28]

Not all was sweetness and light, however. There was a bitter dispute between members of the NCANWT committee and the new CND executive committee about the appropriate NCANWT representation. Linked to this dispute, but separate from it, was the equally bitter argument about Peggy Duff's role as the organizing secretary of the new CND organization. On the first matter, the new CND executive agreed that two representatives of the NCANWT should be included on the new committee. The initiative for the merger had come, as far as the NCANWT was concerned, from Arthur Goss and Sheila Jones, and they formed part of the new CND executive from the outset. The NCANWT was not, however, altogether happy with this cosy arrangement. At its meeting on 24 January 1958 the executive committee of the NCANWT decided to put forward Mrs MacGregor and Dr Hilton as its representatives. The CND executive blandly deferred consideration at both its February and March meetings, and thereafter quietly dropped the proposal.[29]

In part this reflected the élitism and 'club' mentality of CND's leadership. But it is also significant that both MacGregor and Hilton were thought to have CP connections (Hilton was an active member of Science for Peace), and Arthur Goss and Canon Collins were determined to avoid any Communist 'contamination'.

The dispute between Arthur Goss and Sheila Jones on the one hand and Peggy Duff on the other was somewhat more straightforward, but none the less significant. There had been mounting tension between Sheila Jones, as secretary of NCANWT, and Peggy Duff, as organizing secretary. This resulted eventually in Peggy

[27] Information as given in a letter from NCANWT to sponsors, 6 Dec. 1957, NCANWT archive.
[28] NCANWT minutes, 17 Dec. 1957, NCANWT archive.
[29] Arthur Goss remained an active and centrally important figure in CND for many years (although Sheila Jones resigned, for political as well as personal and professional reasons, shortly after CND's establishment: see ch. 2).

Duff threatening to resign her position at the end of 1957 in the light of Sheila Jones's criticisms. In the event Arthur Goss dissuaded Peggy Duff from resigning. But, in private notes written at the time, he made it clear that he sympathized with Jones's position and felt that Duff had taken to herself executive powers. He added that Duff was 'a hard worker ... but should be kept to the job of *organizing* secretary. Later she did succeed in becoming the Secretary of CND: a mistake in my view. The Executive Committee ought to have appointed a topline person as Secretary and retained Peggy Duff as organizer not spokesman for CND'.[30]

This whole episode is indicative of a number of factors. First, as was seen during CND's years of expansion, Peggy Duff could be a rather difficult character to work with, especially for those unused to the rough-and-tumble of Labour Movement politics.[31] Moreover, she had both a strong bureaucratic/organizational concept of how the Movement should work *and* an equally strong, and by no means incompatible, attachment to linking the Peace Movement with the left of the Labour Movement and Labour Party in a quasi-populist radical alliance. Secondly, it indicated the emphasis which Arthur Goss and others wished to place upon a respectable, almost genteel image, and the need to have the important office of secretary occupied by a 'big name'. Thirdly, Peggy Duff was not trusted by Arthur Goss because of her suspected involvement with Mrs MacGregor and Dr Hilton, as correspondence from the time makes clear.[32] Finally, in this episode as in others, the desire to preserve and present an *apolitical* image was apparent. Peggy Duff was not only rather too prickly and aggressive on a personal level for the NCANWT leaders; she was also a politically committed and decidely non-middle-class activist. The tensions which existed on these grounds in the NCANWT were magnified and exacerbated in the larger and far more prestigious CND, and it is no small tribute to Canon Collins's political and diplomatic skill that, despite numerous tensions, Peggy Duff remained on relatively harmonious terms with the CND executive for most (though not all) of her long period of office.

There were thus significant tensions and problems within the

[30] Annotations in longhand by Goss to a letter from Duff to Goss, 9 Jan. 1958, NCANWT archive.

[31] Peggy Duff was described by David Boulton (op. cit.) as 'a cross between Margaret Rutherford gone to seed and Violet Carson as Ena Sharples'.

[32] Correspondence from 1957 and 1958 in the NCANWT archive.

NCANWT/CND relationship, and the handover from one organization to the other took place at the leadership level neither as smoothly nor as harmoniously as is often claimed, or as appears to be the case on first examination. However, there can be no doubt that, despite these problems, it was the NCANWT that formed the basis of the new CND Movement. The problems and divisions, as much as the strengths and appeal, of the NCANWT were a microcosm of the environment within which CND itself was to operate.

2

FORMATION AND ADVANCE
The Early Years of CND, *1958–1960*

THE organizational groundwork undertaken by the NCANWT (and the inherited resources) certainly eased the process of bringing CND into existence; and the continuing concern over the hazards of nuclear testing remained a powerful mobilizing factor through CND's early years. But CND's genesis had other components also: there were several specific events in the autumn of 1957[1] which acted as the final precipitants.

October saw the launching of the Russian sputnik, an undeniable challenge to American missile supremacy and a further tightening of the screw in the nuclear arms race. In November, Professor George F. Kennan, the former US Ambassador in Moscow, delivered the Reith Lectures on the theme of 'Russia, the Atom and the West', in which he argued against the cold war orientation of American foreign policy, and outlined the real dangers of nuclear confrontation between East and West. Both these events took place in the wider context of the shift in political consciousness and the growing unease with the conservative *status quo*, both nationally and internationally, occasioned by the twin political crises of Suez and Hungary in 1956. It was in this unsettled climate that the Labour Party conference of 1957 took place. Aneurin Bevan profoundly shocked the left of the Party by his powerful and

---

[1] There had been other events of some importance earlier in the year. Most notable of these was Duncan Sandys's 1957 Defence White Paper, which for the first time made explicit Britain's reliance upon nuclear weapons and committed the Government to the use of such weapons in response to a conventional attack. Moreover, the White Paper admitted quite openly that there was no adequate protection against nuclear attack and that widespread devastation would occur in the event of nuclear war.

Another event of importance in the spring of 1957 was the attempt by Harold Steele to journey into a nuclear testing area in the Pacific. It was to support this project that the Emergency Committee for Direct Action was originally formed. This is discussed further in ch. 4.

unequivocal denunciation of the unilateralist position at the conference. (This whole episode was of crucial importance in the context
of Labour Movement involvement in the unilateralist movement,
and is analysed in Chapter 6.) But it also resulted in a *general* revulsion against nuclear policies. In particular it led many to feel, with
J. B. Priestley and Jacquetta Hawkes, 'overwhelmingly that no-one
was speaking for this point of view which, as far as we were
concerned, . . . had lasted ever since Hiroshima'.[2] The result was
that, 'in the heat of this emotion',[3] J. B. Priestley wrote his seminal
New Statesman article, 'Britain and the Nuclear Bombs',[4] which, as
Canon Collins has recalled, acted as 'the real catalyst' which
brought CND into being.[5] The huge response from the *New Statesman*'s readers prompted Kingsley Martin, the editor, to call
together at his flat the 'rather famous little gathering'[6] of the
'midwives of CND'.[7] Among those attending were Bertrand
Russell, J. B. Priestley, Jacquetta Hawkes, George Kennan, Professor P. M. S. Blackett, and, somewhat incongruously, Denis Healey.[8]
Martin, whose journal had been campaigning against nuclear tests,
proposed that 'an all-out disarmament campaign' should be
launched, and all those present (except Denis Healey) agreed.[9] The
following day Martin telephoned Peggy Duff and the NCANWT/
CND linkage was formed. However, not only were there problems,
albeit secondary, as far as the NCANWT was concerned: the
Martin/Priestley group also had misgivings about building a
major new organization on the foundations of the minuscule
NCANWT.[10]

Nevertheless, despite such misgivings on both sides the merger
took place and CND came into being. That this was accomplished
with such speed and with so few problems was due primarily to the

[2] Jacquetta Hawkes, in conversation with the author, Jan. 1978.
[3] Ibid.
[4] *New Statesman*, 2 Nov. 1957.
[5] Canon L. John Collins, *Faith Under Fire*, London, 1966, p. 302.
[6] Hawkes, in conversation.
[7] Collins, op. cit., 303.
[8] According to Hawkes, Healey told the group that they 'were all being foolishly Utopian—this produced rather a hostile atmosphere' (Hawkes, in conversation).
[9] David Boulton, unpublished MS account of the origins of CND, NCANWT archive.
[10] 'For Priestley the NCANWT committee was made up of well-meaning non-entities who hardly measured up to the stature required (for a major national campaigning organization)', Boulton, op. cit.

commitment and skills of two very different, but complementary, activists involved: Peggy Duff and Arthur Goss. And it was Duff, with Martin, who was responsible for the triumphant inaugural meeting held at Canon Collins's home at Amen Court, on 16 January 1958.

J. B. Priestley and Kingsley Martin agreed to become sponsors of the NCANWT, the NCANWT was persuaded to take part in the founding meeting of CND in January 1958, and, again as a result of an approach from Peggy Duff (in December 1957), Canon Collins agreed to become involved—and to hold the meeting at his house. The NCANWT had previously decided to call its sponsors together at a public meeting to discuss the policy and structure of the new campaign but, according to Sheila Jones's account, Kingsley Martin persuaded the NCANWT to merge their meeting with that which was to take place at Collins's house.[11]

The NCANWT had also invited Ritchie Calder to chair the sponsors' meeting, in the hope that he would be elected chairman of the new campaign. But Martin told them that it had already been arranged that he would chair the 16 January meeting. Assuming that Martin himself would thus be proposed for chairman of the new campaign, the NCANWT canvassed support for Ritchie Calder. However, the Martin/Priestley group outmanoeuvred the NCANWT. At the 16 January meeting, 'people were asked to suggest who should be on the Committee. Not many names were volunteered, and in the end Kingsley Martin read out a list of people he thought might serve. . . . it was obvious that Collins was going to take command.'[12] As Driver has claimed, there was 'little doubt that the composition of the new Executive had been effectively decided beforehand among the Martin/Priestley group'.[13] Those who accepted nomination to the executive committee were Ritchie Calder, James Cameron, Canon L. John Collins, Howard Davies, Michael Foot, Arthur Goss, Sheila Jones,[14] Kingsley

---

[11] Sheila Jones, interviewed by Alasdair MacIntyre and cited in Boulton, op. cit.

[12] Ibid.

[13] Christopher Driver, *The Disarmers*, London, 1964, p. 43.

[14] Sheila Jones and Arthur Goss had not known beforehand that they were to be included on the Martin/Priestley list for the new executive committee: 'presumably this was our reward for having agreed to play [i.e. cancel their proposed sponsors' meeting]. That was what we decided afterwards because we were rather surprised to find that we were included on the list of the new executive' (Jones, quoted in Boulton, op. cit.).

Martin, J. B. Priestley, Professor Rotblat, Lord Simon of Wythen-shawe, and Peggy Duff.[15] At the first meeting of the executive committee on 21 January 1958 it was agreed to ask Bertrand Russell to become president of the new campaign and Lord Simon, treasurer. CND was now formally launched.

CND'S FIRST YEAR OF EXISTENCE: 1958

The second meeting of the newly elected executive took place at Amen Court on 28 January 1958.[16] A number of important decisions was taken at this meeting. Canon Collins was elected chairman of CND, proposed by Michael Foot and seconded by J. B. Priestley; Ritchie Calder became vice-chairman and Peggy Duff, organizing secretary. Lord Simon was asked to be treasurer but requested time to decide.[17] Canon Collins[18] and Peggy Duff were to remain the dominant figures in the CND leadership throughout the years of CND's success.[19]

---

[15] Among those who declined the invitation to join the executive committee were the Bishop of Chichester and Sir Julian Huxley.

[16] Those attending were Ritchie Calder, Canon L. John Collins, Howard Davies, Michael Foot, Arthur Goss, Sheila Jones, J. B. Priestley, Professor Rotblat, Lord Simon of Wythenshawe, Peggy Duff. (Apologies were received from James Cameron.)

[17] The executive committee in fact had considerable difficulty in securing a suitable treasurer. Lord Simon declined the invitation (although he accepted membership of the committee). After some confusion, and interchange of letters, as to whether or not he was a unilateralist, Lord Wilmot eventually took on the post in June 1958. Lord Wilmot resigned, because of ill health, in Oct. 1958. Ted Bedford then took over and, for the first time, the executive had an efficient and committed treasurer: Bedford remained in office until May 1960. Laurie Kershaw followed and remained until Apr. 1963, to be succeeded by Dick Robinson. (Information taken from various CND executive committee minutes, from 1958 to 1964, Modern Records Centre, University of Warwick.)

[18] Canon L. John Collins, rather unkindly described by Boulton (op. cit.), as 'a churchman with a worldly taste for gracious living and whisky, a Christian socialist who sent his sons to Eton', was chairman of CND from its inception until his resignation in 1964. Born in 1905, he became Canon of St Paul's Cathedral in 1948, following various Church of England appointments, including Priest-in-ordinary to the King, Chaplain in the RAF, and Dean of Oriel College, Oxford. Apart from his major commitment to the Peace Movement, Collins had a lifelong concern with the politics of southern Africa, primarily through the work of the organization which he created in 1949 and of which he remained president, Christian Action. Collins died in Dec. 1982.

[19] The hostility between Peggy Duff and Sheila Jones, and to a lesser extent Arthur Goss, persisted, and resulted in Jones's resignation from the CND executive in June 1958. She objected to Duff's increasing role, and also to the 'socialist slant'

It was agreed that the executive committee itself 'be constituted as the Campaign for Nuclear Disarmament'. This was to remain the formal, organizational structure of CND for several years, until the pressure for a more democratic structure became too strong to resist. This was a strongly held élitist view. As Arthur Goss put it: 'we didn't want membership—either people supported us or they didn't support us ... this is the campaign *we* are running, ... there's nothing wrong with being self-perpetuating.'[20]

The committee also, in the euphoria of its youth, adopted a conciliatory, albeit patronizing attitude to the DAC: it was agreed that CND should 'give its blessing to the emergency Committee's plans, and should publicize them, but should make it clear that at this stage of the campaign they could not be very closely involved'. This caution was to turn rapidly into hostility between CND and the DAC: although in part organizational, there was also a deep-rooted ideological difference of view. Throughout the DAC's existence this difference deepened and, with the creation of the Committee of 100, the split between the constitutionalists and the direct actionists became, at least at national level, total. At this early stage, however, the CND executive committee hoped that the DAC could be 'loosely affiliated', and hence brought under executive committee control. Subsequent overtures from the executive to DAC along these lines were spurned, not surprisingly.

Evidence of the executive's firm intention to exercise control over the rapidly growing Movement was also apparent in its decision that, at all public meetings held to promote CND's cause, 'the Campaign should insist that a resolution supplied by them should be put to the meetings'. In return for help with speakers and finance for publicity, the executive committee would 'require the local committee to hand over 50 per cent of any profit made on the meeting'. Public meetings were planned for big cities such as Oxford, Cambridge, Leeds, Manchester, Liverpool, and Bristol, and were without exception well attended and successful. The

which Duff gave to CND. Both she and Goss continued to press, unsuccessfully, for the appointment of an honorary secretary to the executive. No 'honorary secretary' was ever appointed and Duff assumed this role *de facto*. (Immediately after Jones's resignation Goss wrote, to Lord Simon of Wythenshawe, that he felt a 'lone watchdog' on the executive committee. Collins asked Goss to take on the post of honorary secretary, but he declined. Source: NCANWT archive.)

[20] Goss in conversation with the author, Jan. 1978.

inaugural public meeting in London planned for Central Hall on 17 February 1958 was, however, to be the first major event for the new campaign.

Before moving on to discuss this meeting and its repercussions note must be taken of three other important aspects of the discussion at this, the first real business meeting of the executive committee. Russell, as has been noted, had been elected president, but there was perhaps some indication of the concerns, even unease, later to become very explicit, that the executive committee felt about Russell's attitude. It was agreed, at this meeting, that 'a good churchman should be enrolled as President with Earl Russell'.[21] A more tangible and perhaps more important aspect of policy was the executive committee's decision not to adopt a membership system. This policy persisted through the years of CND as a mass movement, membership being introduced only in 1966. There were two basic reasons for this policy: first, that by maintaining a loose structure of supporters rather than members, the executive committee leadership was able to continue its policy of élite control and resist pressures for democratization (and, to be fair, avoid the dissipation of energies on internal organizational discussion and bureaucratization); and second, that CND would have run the risk of proscription by the Labour Party had it become a formal membership organization. Strong arguments were advanced, of course, against the policy of élite control as the Movement grew, and these pressures became eventually too strong to resist, as is discussed below. But the demand for a membership organization was never very strong, and was not really an issue until CND began to decline. (This was in part because of the second argument given above, but also because of the pervading, albeit nebulous, commitment to a quasi-libertarian, anti-bureaucratic ethos).

Finally, and most important of all, the executive committee decided upon a final draft of the policy statement:

The purpose of the Campaign is to demand a British initiative to reduce the nuclear peril and to stop the armaments race, if need be by unilateral action by Britain. As a first step towards a general disarmament conven-

---

[21] No action was ever taken on this matter, but it is interesting to speculate on the effect that a 2–1 Collins majority in a triumvirate leadership would have had on the later, turbulent history of the Movement. (Not that another churchman would necessarily have sided with Collins, of course: Rev. Michael Scott was, after all, the co-founder with Russell of the Committee of 100.)

tion, Britain should press for negotiations, at top level, on the following issues:-

1. the stopping of all further tests of nuclear weapons;
2. the stopping of the establishment of new missile bases;
3. the securing of the establishment of neutral and nuclear free zones;
4. the securing of the abolition of the manufacture and stockpiling of all nuclear weapons;
5. the prevention of the acquisition of nuclear weapons by other nations.

In order to underline the sincerity of her own initiative, Britain should be prepared to announce that, pending negotiations:-

(a) she will suspend patrol flights of aeroplanes equipped with nuclear weapons;
(b) she will make no further tests of hydrogen bombs;
(c) she will not proceed with the establishment of missile bases on her territory;
(d) she will not provide nuclear weapons for any country.

As Peggy Duff has commented, although the statement mentioned a unilateralist initiative, it was 'ambiguous. It was not entirely unilateralist.'[22] The reasons for the tone and content of this statement were debatable. In part, undoubtedly, the 'moderation' of the policy was due to the executive committee's concern that the UNA's support for CND should be secured. Whilst the NCANWT group were anxious to avoid an explicit unilateralist commitment for this reason, the *New Statesman* group were keen to make a dramatic stand on a unilateral initiative. Over and above this, however, it may reasonably be surmised that, quite simply, the executive committee was not fully aware of the immense popular appeal of unilateralism, nor of the need to crystallize the general demand for nuclear disarmament around a specific and simple policy objective. The leaders of the executive committee were, on the whole, a cautious and relatively conservative group (of which more later), but the initial policy statement was as much the result of an understandable political uncertainty as it was of political conservatism.

Nevertheless, even given these qualifications, many of the major objectives of subsequent CND policy were apparent in this early statement. *Missing*, however, were several crucial aspects of subsequent policy: in particular, of course, the absence of any emphasis upon the necessity for a British unilateralist initiative.

[22] Peggy Duff, *Left, Left, Left*, London, 1971, p. 123.

Moreover, there was no call for the ending of the *existing* US presence in the UK. And there was certainly no indication of the later policy commitments adopted by CND of Britain's leaving NATO and adopting a neutralist foreign policy. Finally, and significantly, there is an absence in this statement of the general condemnation of the society and social structure which, arguably, had produced the existing nuclear arms race and its dangers. In contrast to some extent with later CND statements—and certainly with both DAC and Committee of 100 policy declarations—the initial CND policy statement was indicative of the predominantly single-issue, liberal pressure group role which the executive committee saw CND fulfilling.

The net result of this inevitable compromise on policy was unsatisfactory to both parties. The NCANWT/UNA group was suspicious of what it regarded as the covert advocacy of fullblooded unilateralism; and the *New Statesman* group took the same ambiguity to indicate a retreat from unilateralism.

The Central Hall meeting

The Central Hall meeting on 17 February was to settle the issue. The meeting was a tremendous success. Five thousand people packed not only Central Hall but three overflow halls, and even then 1,000 were turned away. £1,700 was collected for CND funds. There was a wide range of extremely effective speakers, including Bertrand Russell, A. J. P. Taylor, Canon Collins, Alex Comfort, Michael Foot, J. B. Priestley, and Sir Stephen King-Hall; and the overall tone was emotive, militant, and uncompromising. There was no doubt, following the meeting, that a mass Movement was in the process of creation and that only a strong and explicitly unilateralist policy would satisfy the demands of the rank and file. A delegate conference from nuclear disarmament organizations had been planned by the executive committee for the day following the Central Hall meeting, at St Pancras town hall. At this meeting, 'the policy statement agreed by the Executive came under heavy attack as highly ambiguous and unnecessarily cautious. Glad to have their own point of view backed so strongly from outside, Canon Collins, Kingsley Martin, and J. B. Priestley prepared what they called a "clarification" of the statement, and, without waiting for full executive approval, issued it to the Press.'[23]

[23] Boulton, op. cit.

The text of the revised statement ran as follows:

The purpose of the Campaign is to press for a British initiative to reduce the nuclear peril and to stop the armaments race.

We shall seek to persuade the British people that Britain must:

(a) renounce unconditionally the use or production of nuclear weapons and refuse to allow their use by others in her defence;

(b) use her utmost endeavour to bring about negotiations at all levels for agreement to end the armaments race and to lead to a general disarmament convention;

(c) invite the co-operation of other nations, particularly non-nuclear powers, in her renunciation of nuclear weapons.

In pressing for this unconditional renunciation by Britain the Campaign realises the need for action on particular issues, pending success in its major objectives, and we believe that Britain must:-

(a) halt the patrol flights of aeroplanes equipped with nuclear weapons;

(b) make no further tests of nuclear weapons;

(c not proceed with the agreement for the establishment of missile bases on her territory;

(d) refuse to provide nuclear weapons for any other country.[24]

This was a very much stronger version of CND's policy and amounted virtually to a new policy position. Instead of calling on the government to 'press for negotiations' it demanded unconditional renunciation of the use or production of nuclear weapons, plus a refusal 'to allow their use by others in her defence'. Immediate action was called for, with no reference to 'negotiations', to 'halt' (no longer 'suspend') H-bomber patrol flights, to stop tests, to reverse the decision to accept missile bases, and to refuse to provide nuclear weapons for other countries.

The aftermath of the Central Hall meeting (and the delegate conference meeting on 18 February) was also significant. Immediately following the Central Hall meeting a sit-down demonstration of several hundred at Downing Street took place and five were arrested.[25] This was a portent of direct action divisions to come—'gentle breezes, which later were to develop into storms and hurricanes', as Collins has put it[26]—and, in conjunction with the revision of the policy statement, discouraged 'moderate' support for the campaign. Press coverage of the Central

---

[24] CND archive, British Library of Political and Economic Science, London School of Economic and Political Science, University of London.

[25] Mervyn Jones, Ernest Rodker, John Eustace, Denis Hunt, David Epstein, and Owen Evans. All were fined. (*Daily Worker*, 19 Feb. 1958.)

[26] Collins, op. cit., 306.

Hall meeting was minimal, only the *Daily Worker* carrying a comprehensive and headline report. Most of the press concentrated neither on the Central Hall meeting, nor on the policy objectives of CND, but rather on the Downing Street sit-down. *The Times* maintained a total silence on the whole episode, much to the indignation of the executive committee.

From this moment on, CND became a national Movement, with considerable and visible support. Nevertheless, the immediate result of the various events was to create something of a crisis in the new executive. The new policy statement and the aggressively militant tone and actions of the new Movement resulted in Howard Davies (the UNA treasurer) resigning from the executive committee a few weeks later and official relations between CND and the UNA being severed. As previously noted, Sheila Jones also resigned from the executive committee, in part for these political reasons. Professor Rotblat withdrew from the executive committee (although not until November), but agreed to remain a sponsor; Professor Haddow withdrew his name from the list of sponsors; and Lord Wilmot, although willing to become treasurer, stated that he was not in favour of unilateral nuclear disarmament, and the executive committee therefore declined his offer (although he later changed his position and became, briefly, treasurer, as noted earlier). As Collins has written somewhat ruefully, from this time onwards 'I do not remember a time when the struggle for power within the Campaign was abandoned'.[27]

The campaign, however, had now achieved the invaluable asset of a single, central, and realistic campaigning demand which mobilized support and gave CND its distinctive character as a *unilateralist* campaign. The price that the executive committee paid for this success was to broaden the campaign, irreversibly. It was to become a *mass movement* rather than an élite pressure group; and the corollaries of this were that the politics of CND, in terms both of objectives and of tactics, were to be shifted towards the more militant wing of the Movement, and that consequently the backing of some of the more 'moderate', élite sections would be lost.

The Aldermaston March

The executive committee had a continuing problem, central to this whole question of orientation, concerning the DAC's proposed

[27] Ibid., 310.

march from London to Aldermaston scheduled to take place over Easter 1958. It was DAC activists who had originated the Alder-maston March idea (and who indeed had carried out protests there as early as 1952), and, although the NCANWT had previously agreed to give its support,[28] there was considerable opposition among the CND leadership to the idea of the March (especially from J. B. Priestley[29]). Others in the leadership, such as Kingsley Martin, supported the March, and the executive committee thus found itself in a dilemma. Canon Collins was reluctant to commit CND to the March. Hugh Brock has recalled that he and Frank Allaun had had 'a terrible job to persuade Canon Collins to come and speak in the Square when the March moved off'.[30]

The executive committee was thus somewhat nonplussed by the success of the March. The initiative had in one way been taken away from them by the DAC. The executive committee's decision to 'fudge' its policy towards the March was an understandably 'political' reaction, especially given the opposition of such an important figure as Priestley. Nevertheless, as a result of the success of the March, the executive committee had no alternative but to give its backing—albeit belatedly—to similar protests.[31]

Other CND activities in 1958

Numerous activites were organized by CND in the summer of 1958. The first of these—a mass lobby of Parliament held in May —was a qualified success. The organizers had hoped for 12,000: in the event approximately 9,000 materialized, and 7,500 attended a meeting in the evening. On 22 June CND organized a 'March on

[28] Pat Arrowsmith, the organizing secretary of the Aldermaston March commit-tee, wrote later, on 8 Apr. 1958, to Arthur Goss 'just to say a big thank you . . . for all you did—to help organize the March and make it the success that it appears to have been' (NCANWT archive).

[29] Priestley argued that the Movement was too small to make such marches impressive; and, anyway, they attracted 'the wrong type of publicity' (letter from Priestley to Sheila Jones, July 1958, cited in Boulton, op. cit.). Jacquetta Hawkes (in conversation with the author) confirmed that this had been Priestley's view.

[30] Hugh Brock, in conversation with the author, Mar. 1978.

[31] There were undoubtedly tensions between DAC and CND over the latter's assumption that it alone should be responsible for national demonstrations. However, according to April Carter, over the specific issue of CND's taking over the Aldermaston March the DAC felt no resentment. 'My definite recollection is that we [DAC] were delighted—we had succeeded in making CND more activist and we certainly had not contemplated organizing a second march ourselves' (April Carter, letter to the author, 12 Dec. 1982).

London'—a project the DAC had originally planned and which was taken over by CND only after considerable dispute between DAC and CND. (Feelings still ran deep more than twenty years later. Both Michael Randle and Pat Arrowsmith recalled that the CND leadership had acted unscrupulously.[32]) In the event it was poorly publicized, and a rather disappointing 2,000–3,300 took part in the demonstration and final rally: the event 'was virtually ignored by the Press'.[33] It seemed as though CND was unable to harness and articulate the popular protest that had been apparent at the inaugural meeting—and above all during the DAC's Aldermaston March. Canon Collins and the executive committee took the opportunity to play down the role of mass demonstrations, and Collins, writing in the *Manchester Guardian*, argued that the most important task was 'the slow background work of persuasion of the people who make opinion in this country, in particular the TUC and the three Party Conferences'.[34] And, in the same newspaper a few days later, it was claimed that

> the prevailing mood had changed to a dour, even pessimistic, determination rather than lighthearted optimism. . . . Each [demonstration] has on the whole looked more housewifely and less flamboyant—and also smaller—than the last. . . . The Campaign will hold no more of them, but the smaller group of pacifists who are committed to direct action is thinking of carrying on.[35]

An academic analysis of CND's first year, written in 1959, could thus quite reasonably conclude that by the end of 1958 there had been 'a change of emphasis (in the CND leadership) and a gradual transition from the attempt to create a mass Movement to the formation of a pressure group which would exert its influence on and within other organizations'.[36] With the hindsight of even a few years it was of course clear that this judgement was wholly mistaken: the Campaign had become, by late 1959, irrevocably committed to mass movement politics. The point to note here, however, is that by late 1958 it seemed as though the initial impetus in this direction was on the wane.

[32] Michael Randle and Pat Arrowsmith, in conversation with the author, May and Jan. 1978 respectively.
[33] R. A. Exley, *The CND: Its Organization, Personnel and Methods in its First Year*, MA (Econ.) thesis, University of Manchester, Sept. 1959, p. 141. Canon Collins estimated numbers at 3,300, the *Daily Telegraph* at 2,000.
[34] *Manchester Guardian*, 20 June 1958.
[35] 'London Letter', *Manchester Guardian*, 23 June 1958.
[36] Exley, op. cit., 143.

This was exemplified, and corroborated for many in the CND leadership, by the successful Women's Conference in June 1958— 'Women against the Bomb'—where the focus was strongly upon the medical, scientific, psychological, and above all *moral* aspects of nuclear weapons and nuclear war. A controlled, intellectual emotionalism pervaded the conference—both audience and platform speakers (Dr Antoinette Pirie, Dame Peggy Ashcroft, Dr Winifred de Kok, Marghanita Laski, and Jill Balcon amongst them).[37]

Thus, by late 1958, an intensity and an urgency permeated the Campaign, and the 'nuclear issue' dominated the lives of many activists (and such intensity was stronger, if anything, in the DAC and later, the Committee of 100). This mood, though, was overwhelmingly 'moral' rather than 'political' in nature, for most activists. The bomb was a moral issue—and a moral outrage—not a political problem. This was an understandable, albeit simplistic and indeed fallacious view, and it was one held by large numbers of people at both leadership and rank and file levels *throughout* the years of mass activism.[38]

The development of the Movement through 1958, and its varied attempts to articulate opposition to nuclear weapons, resulted also in the creation of several specialist groups. The scientists' group, which produced a detailed technical publication, *Scientists' Bulletin*, was invaluable in Peggy Duff's view,[39] although Professor Joseph Rotblat was the only scientist to become a prominent CND campaigner. A press and publicity group under the chairmanship of J. B. Priestley was established, and succeeded in having Priestley's play *Doomsday for Dyson* screened by Granada Television. But Priestley was not a good public relations or press liaison officer, and the group was dissolved in June 1958, and replaced by a publicity committee, chaired by Ritchie Calder. Other groups included the women's group (which produced some of CND's best literature,

[37] Jacquetta Hawkes has recalled the extraordinary impact of meeting: 'the fact that people were beginning to die of radiation many years after the Hiroshima and Nagasaki bombings . . . gave a lot of moral drive to it . . . [we] had a series of letters written by a man who was dying of radiation sickness to his wife, and Jill Balcon read these out and everybody was in floods of tears, including Jill Balcon. . . . an extraordinary meeting—women came up to me with gold watches—and pressed me to take them and do what we could' (Hawkes, in conversation).

[38] See Richard Taylor and Colin Pritchard, *The Protest Makers: The British Nuclear Disarmament Movement of 1958–1965, Twenty Years On*, Oxford, 1980, pt. ii, for detailed empirical evidence on this point.

[39] Duff, op. cit., 158.

including Antoinette Pirie's *Tomorrow's Children*); and the Labour Advisory committee, replacing the H-bomb Campaign committee as the CND contact group with the Parliamentary Labour Party and the trade union leadership.[40]

From the outset there was considerable support for CND in the universities and colleges. These student groups exercised considerable influence in the New Left[41] and they produced many of the most creative thinkers and policy-makers that were to emerge in CND's later years (e.g. Stuart Hall, Alan Shuttleworth, John Slater, John Gittings, Richard Gott, and Nigel Young). However, these groups operated semi-autonomously and informally, and Colleges and Universities Campaign for Nuclear Disarmament (CUCaND), though it held yearly conferences and, later, represented student opinion on the Campaign's committees, was never a powerful voice in the organization.[42] Youth CND was considerably more important than any of these, however, and developed later into a semi-autonomous movement with its own paper, *Youth Against the Bomb*, its own policy priorities, and certainly its own style. The youth campaign mobilized many thousands of active and committed adolescents, but, although it was increasingly critical of the CND leadership, never became heavily involved in the direct action/CND dispute. Similarly, YCND, though containing many left-wing socialists, never openly challenged CND's leaders on *political* grounds.

The organizational policy of the executive committee in 1958

In 1958 this took two primary forms: the continuing attempts to incorporate the DAC into CND's structure, and the creation of the co-ordinating committee in an attempt to provide a discursive, but

[40] Oddly enough, given the strong Christian presence in the Campaign, the Christian group was not formed until 1959, following a major rally at the Albert Hall organized by Christian Action and the Friends' Peace Committee. The initiative was then taken by Francis Jude, a Quaker, and the group produced some useful pamphlets, and organized both demonstrations and pilgrimages to Canterbury, Winchester, and Porton.

[41] See ch. 7.

[42] CND's influence on a whole generation of students should not be underestimated, however. Peggy Duff has recalled that John Slater 'told me that he had never met one [ex-student] who had changed his political views or his opposition to the bomb since those days in the late fifties and early sixties when CND was the biggest political stimulus in the universities' (Duff, op. cit., 161).

powerless, forum for discussion for the whole Movement. Through early 1958 the executive committee made various overtures to the DAC and there was considerable enthusiasm by the executive committee for the merging of direct action activities into the general programme of the Campaign. Through the summer and autumn, however, the executive's view hardened as it became clear that the DAC were unwilling to be 'co-opted'.[43] By the end of 1958, therefore, it was clear to all concerned that the DAC was a separate, and in some senses a hostile, organization. Moreover, as will be discussed below, DAC supporters and sympathizers were at the forefront of the campaign to 'democratize' CND which gathered momentum in 1959. The establishment of an executive committee hegemony over the Movement, which had been Collins's objective at the outset, was always an ambition unlikely to be fulfilled.[44] By the end of 1958 this objective, to all intents and purposes, had been abandoned.

The co-ordinating committee was seen as the key instrument in the executive committee's attempt to establish for itself a link with the constituent bodies of the Movement, through which information and discussion could be passed in both directions, between the executive committee and the various groups and regions. This scheme had the political advantage, as far as the executive committee leadership was concerned, of providing an organizationally coherent framework for the Movement, whilst leaving the power of decision-making totally in the hands of the executive committee. To an extent this worked well, in 1958. There were over 200 local groups by the end of 1958 and these were organized on a regional pattern which was to remain largely unchanged through CND's years as a mass movement.[45] These formed the basis of the representative structure for the co-ordinating committee, which, by the year end, also included representatives from the whole range of affiliated

[43] See the executive committee minutes for 18 Mar. 1958, 6 May 1958, 29 June 1958, and Jan. 1959, CND archive.

[44] And some, like Arthur Goss, thought Collins had been far too conciliatory. 'I would rather have said . . . right at the beginning . . . "we're totally opposed to this method . . . please clear off and leave us alone" ' (Goss, in conversation).

[45] The following regional groups were established in 1958: London, East Anglia, Scottish Council, North East, North West, Midlands, Yorkshire, Wales, South West, South East, Southern. Most followed the London Region pattern of organization, where each of 91 local groups were entitled to send one delegate; the full Council then elected an executive committee (with the power to co-opt members). (CND archive, and Exley, op. cit.)

groups, including the DAC. And yet by the end of 1958 the whole idea of the co-ordinating committee operating as the central organizational focus of the Movement had been discarded and its role downgraded. In part this was because of the independent role of the DAC, but also because it had become clear that some real democratization would have to take place. The 1958 conference, although rejecting proposals for democratization, had given indications that the rank and file was unwilling to accept the paternalistic style of campaign government favoured by the executive committee: 'A number of rank and filers are not prepared to be general hewers of wood and drawers of water without some representation on the executive committee' was one delegate's view of the 1958 conference, and it fairly summarized the position of a substantial and vociferous section of CND supporters.[46]

Thus by the turn of the year CND, although growing rapidly and with its peak of support and its major political successes still to come, was already entangled inextricably in organizational problems which had their fundamental roots in *ideological* differences within the Movement. Before we move on, there are two further developments in CND during 1958 which must be noted briefly. We will then be in a position to review some of the distinctive ideological features of CND which lay at the heart of its existence.

First, no mention has yet been made of CND's sponsors, who not only were invaluable in giving the Campaign publicity and credibility, but also provide some sort of index of the Campaign's national appeal. By the end of the year CND had secured sponsorship from an impressive list of national figures with representation from the arts, the Churches, and the universities. The significant point, however, is that the sponsors came almost exclusively from the liberal establishment, and reflected very much the perspective of the executive committee itself. Secondly, and related to this, although details were given earlier of the composition of the early executive committee, there were important changes during 1958. Nineteen people were at one time or another members of the executive committee during the year, the following being co-opted at various times: A. J. P. Taylor, Jacquetta Hawkes, Sir Richard Acland, Frank Beswick, and Benn Levy. Of the nineteen, four resigned

[46] Jim Roche of Leeds at the 1958 conference, annual conference report, CND archive.

during 1958: Lords Simon and Wilmot, Sheila Jones and Professor Rotblat. (Frank Cousins was invited to join the executive committee and declined. Subsequently, through the key years of Labour Movement involvement, 1959–61, Cousins kept his distance from CND.) A brief glance at the nineteen reveals their impeccable liberal establishment credentials. Thirteen of them were listed in the current *Who's Who*; four were journalists, at least twelve were authors, and almost all had at one time or another contributed to newspapers and journals; most were 'associated with the Labour Party, and the remainder were fairly sympathetic towards the Party'.[47] Almost all were in the 45–65 age range. The importance of this 'cultural homogeneity' amongst the executive committee was enhanced by the organizational structure—that is, by the fact that the executive committee, in 1958 at any rate, was beholden to no rank-and-file pressure and operated as an autonomous ruling group. It is important, finally, to note the changing power balance among the individuals on the executive committee during the year. By the close of 1958, apart from those who had resigned, both J. B. Priestley and Kingsley Martin had receded somewhat in importance. Canon Collins and Peggy Duff were key figures in policy-making and strategy, as well as in administration. And, of the others, Jacquetta Hawkes, Arthur Goss, Michael Foot, and A. J. P. Taylor played particularly forceful roles. The net result of this, in terms of policy approach, was to reinforce Collins's own ideological direction, and thus strengthen the twin approaches of a fundamentally moral basis complemented by a firm and unequivocal belief in the Parliamentary Labour Party as the vehicle for achieving the Campaign's aims.

PROFILE OF CND AT THE END OF 1958

The leadership's commitment to the Labour Party tactic is explored in detail in the context of the overall relationship between the Nuclear Disarmament Movement and the Labour Movement to which the whole of Chapter 6 is devoted. Here, the concentration will be upon the predominantly non-political basis of CND. It must, however, be borne in mind throughout this discussion that, at least for the politically astute among the CND leadership (and this

[47] Exley, op. cit., 206. Both Collins and Hawkes, in conversation with the author, confirmed this.

most certainly included both Canon Collins and Peggy Duff), the moral thrust at the core of the Movement was complemented by an equally insistently emphasized belief in winning over the Labour Party, as the means of putting these beliefs into political practice.

Having made this qualification, however, attention can now be turned to the analysis of the deep-rooted moralistic basis of the Movement.

CND's rank and file: The dominance of 'moral protest'

Thus far, attention has been directed almost exclusively to the leadership of CND. But what of CND's rank and file? An empirical survey of over 400 'core activists' from the nuclear disarmament Movement of 1958–65 has yielded a detailed profile of the rank and file of the Movement.[48]

What emerges from this survey of the rank and file? Above all, perhaps, it reinforces the overall impression of a highly variegated, eclectic, and ideologically nebulous Movement, typical, at one level, of the middle-class radical movements of which, Parkin has argued, CND was the principal example in twentieth-century Britain.[49] The unity of the Campaign was genuine and total on the issue of unilateral nuclear disarmament, but, on everything else, Movement supporters were deeply divided. In the early years of the Campaign this diversity was on balance a strength, as it brought into the Movement a very wide range of individuals and groups from the community. There is much truth in Dick Nettleton's recollection of the wide appeal of CND.

[CND was] more or less accurately a cross section of the community. It was incredible: you could call a meeting in some small town and there was a vicar, and a few 'posh' middle class people, a few trade union people, the odd anarchist etc. . . . even with fairly small committees in CND . . . you always got this kind of cross section of people. . . . CND was stamped in some way with middle class ideas—if you're comparing it with say the Labour Party or trade unions or some other left organization. But by and large it represented a good cross-section.[50]

[48] This survey forms one of the bases of Taylor and Pritchard, op. cit. The sample was self-selected via letters to the Press, etc. (Details are given in Taylor and Pritchard's Appendix I.)

[49] See Frank Parkin, *Middle Class Radicalism: The Social Bases of the Campaign for Nuclear Disarmament*, Manchester, 1968.

[50] Dick Nettleton, in conversation with the author, Jan. 1978.

In the early years it was the moral commitment, the felt urgency of the issue, the optimism and enthusiasm of a *new* movement, and above all the dramatic and continuing growth of the Movement through the early years, which pulled people together and more than compensated for the fundamental ideological diversity that was inherent in the Movement. As time passed, and as the frustrations of the Movement's failure to attain its objectives became greater, so, inevitably, the diversity changed to being a key factor in the bitter divisions and internal conflicts which contributed so much to the eventual decline and disintegration. But in the early years this moral commitment swept along the diverse ideologies in what appeared to be a common cause of overriding importance. Emotional, committed, sincere, internationalist, liberal, and above all convinced of the urgent moral imperative of nuclear disarmament, the rank and file marched and demonstrated in their tens of thousands through 1958, 1959, and 1960, and beyond in the (no doubt simplistic) belief that 'the world' could not ignore their call for sanity and morality. It was not to be, of course; but whilst they thought it was possible—or probable, even certain—the Campaign went from strength to strength, despite the inherent divisions and complexities of both the Movement and the issues themselves.

The Christian influence among the rank and file of the Movement was strong and its distinctive contribution should be noted here. Of course, virtually all those involved in the Movement shared an abhorrence of nuclear weapons on generalized humanistic and moral grounds. But, within the 'moral protesters' context, what if anything was distinctive about the *Christian* position? For Canon Collins the Campaign was based 'on moral principles uncompromisingly'.[51] But were these distinctively Christian? Elsewhere, Collins had written:

the real issue, when all is said and done is the moral question: the preparation for and the implied use of nuclear weapons are the hideous denial of all the best in the human tradition—for myself I should want to add and the hideous denial of Christianity despite whatever the Church may say.[52]

This does not get us very much further, however: in what ways does this deny Christianity?

Walter Stein, an academic and a Roman Catholic peace activist,

[51] Collins, in conversation with the author, Jan. 1978.
[52] Collins, in Philip Toynbee (ed.), *The Fearful Choice*, London, 1958.

has given one of the fullest and most reasoned answers to this and related questions.[53] Stein's central submission was that

nuclear defence cannot provide security. . . . secure or insecure, however, there is now no *moral* alternative to an unconditional renunciation of the 'deterrent'. . . . in essence, the plea is very simple indeed:
  (i)   that some things are intolerable, irrespective of circumstances; that total war is thus absolutely intolerable; and that nuclear 'defence' means total war;
 (ii)   that the mere willingness to *risk* a nuclear war that could annihilate civilization, poison the whole of this planet, and for ever violate the life of the future, if life survives, is a wickedness without parallel, a blasphemy against creation; and
(iii)   that the policy of 'deterrence' involves a conditional willingness to unleash such a war—and is therefore not only wicked in what it risks, but in terms of implicit *intention*.[54]

Thus, what is involved in deterrence 'not only involves risks of [nuclear weapons'] eventual use but hypothetically commits us to murder, here and now',[55] and murder is, of course, against God's law. For Stein there is a qualitative moral shift involved in the nuclear situation, a qualitative moral change as a result of this massive quantitative increase in destructive potential.

According to another Roman Catholic writer, E. I. Watkin, it was not necessary to accept this qualitative change, however.

According to the traditional moral theology of the Catholic Church, there are seven conditions which must *all* be satisfied if a war is to be just, that is, morally justifiable. . . . It is, I submit, certain . . . that the major war against the Communist bloc . . . could not fulfil [the] three last conditions of a justifiable war (i.e. (1) Only right means may be employed in the conduct of the war. The employment of immoral means renders it unjustifiable. (2) There must be a reasonable hope of victory. (3) The good probably to be achieved by victory must outweigh even the probable, *a fortiori* the certain, evil effects of the war) . . . No cause, however just, however important the issue, however great the value to be achieved by victory, can justify such diabolism, or should we rather call it criminal lunacy. No end however excellent can justify means so flagrantly immoral.[56]

---

  [53] See Walter Stein, (ed.) *Nuclear Weapons and the Christian Conscience*, London, 1961; and Walter Stein, *Peace on Earth: The Way Ahead*, London, 1966.
  [54] Stein, *Nuclear Weapons*, 23.
  [55] Ibid., 125.
  [56] E. I. Watkin, 'Unjustifiable War', in Charles S. Thompson, (ed.), *Morals and Missiles: Catholic Essays on the Problems of War Today*, London, 1959.

Not all Christian campaigners followed such exclusively doctrinal arguments, however. In particular those—primarily but not exclusively Anglicans and Nonconformists—who had a strong social and political motivation, pursued rather different lines of argument. Trevor Huddleston, CR, for example, argued that

[The Christian must] meet fear with faith . . . [and] renounce nuclear weapons because *they are essentially evil* . . . [and] meet the needs of the have-not countries by *voluntarily* accepting a lower standard of life for ourselves. . . . [The Christian must] say to the Communist 'we have a religion which can withstand all attack and which in spite of our own failures in the profession of it, has an eternal validity, therefore we are not afraid of yours.'[57]

For the Christian rank and file of the Nuclear Disarmament Movement, however, the problems of Christian commitment frequently appeared less complex, more easily resolvable, and much more a black-and-white, 'are you for or against sin?' type of question. Olive Krause, minutes secretary of Bradford CND and a committed Christian CND supporter, expressed typical frustrations. Of forty-five letters written to Yorkshire clergy in the spring of 1961 only four replies had been received and only one of these was sympathetic. 'It would seem', wrote Olive Krause to Diana Collins,

that the Church of England are mainly against us. Some of the Methodists and Congregationalists are with us but are afraid to do anything active. . . . I have come to the shocking conclusion that they [the Archbishop of York and the Bishop of Bradford] are so involved in theological and scholastic muddle they do not know the true meaning of Christianity which was so simply put by Jesus in the Sermon on The Mount that a child can understand.[58]

Why then were the Church hierarchies—and for that matter a considerable proportion of the ordinary clergy and laity—either hostile or apathetic to the issue of nuclear disarmament and the policies advocated by CND? That the establishments of the Churches were of this view is undeniable.[59] Despite the prominent

[57] Trevor Huddleston, CR, 'Meet Fear with Faith', Fellowship of Reconciliation, n.d. (?1959).
[58] Olive Krause, open leter to Diana Collins, quoted in *Christian Action Newsletter*, spring 1961. Loaned by Olive Krause to the author, with other private papers.
[59] The hierarchy of the Church of England has remained steadfastly opposed to unilateral nuclear disarmament from the 1950s to the 1980s. The Archbishop of

and articulate Christian clergy who were involved with the Movement—Canon Collins, Rev. Michael Scott, Rev. Dr Donald Soper, among others—none of the official organs of the Churches (with the exception of the Quakers, the Methodists, and the Unitarians) committed themselves either to support for CND or other Movement organizations, or to support for unilateralism in principle.

Whilst the issue remained on the somewhat abstract, moral plane the Church was willing—indeed eager—to condemn nuclear weapons. On a basis equivalent to denouncing sin, the Church felt quite secure in declaring itself against the indiscriminate use of nuclear weapons. Thus 'the doctrine of massive retaliation was found by Churchmen to be difficult to reconcile with their value systems'.[60] There was thus a general consensus in the Church to

Canterbury, replying to a letter from Miss Fishwick of 24 Dec. 1955, stated the position clearly: 'You say to me: "It is clear that the H-Bomb could only deter if it were known that in certain circumstances it *would* be used." I do not agree. It could deter also if it were known that in certain circumstances it might be used. The deterrent effect lies precisely in that uncertainty whether it would be used or not. I think it is very unhelpful to ask the Government to remove that uncertainty which thereby removes the deterrent effect, until the efforts to get a reliable international agreement about armaments and about coexistence have been achieved. It is to that end that Christians should devote their energies and their prayers' (letter from Archbishop of Canterbury to Miss Fishwick, 29 Dec. 1955, NCANWT archive).

On 14 Mar. 1981, the Archibishop of Canterbury commented on unilateralism as follows, on the Radio 4 phone-in programme, 'Person to Person': 'I've come to the conclusion that I cannot support that [i.e. unilateralism], but that's not to say I am complacent. . . . I believe that we must work all the time to reduce the arms race and that we must work through indirect means—such as understanding between nations, a readiness, particularly on the part of Christians, to cross political frontiers, not to impute wrong motives or to make use of lies and propaganda or to stir up polarization and hatred and vindictive attitudes. Now I take with seriousness and respect the sincerity of those who believe that we should set an example by abandoning nuclear weapons. But I believe if we were to do it, it would certainly destabilize a balance which had undoubtedly contributed to the peace of Europe for thirty-five years. I doubt the exemplary power of this gesture which would be made, as we still expect in the foreseeable future to be sheltering under the American nuclear umbrella. . . . I think we have got to be realistic and practical and work systematically towards peace through nuclear disarmament. So I am a multilateral disarmer' (transcript of broadcast (extract), *South Yorkshire Bulletin for Nuclear Disarmament*, 2 May 1981, p. 10).

Since then the archbishop's opposition to unilateralism has hardened and become more explicit. See especially his speech at the Feb. 1983 Synod, at which the unilateralist resolution was heavily defeated. (Nevertheless it should be noted that, in the 1980s, there has been a far greater official commitment to the Peace Movement from the Non-Conformist Churches.)

[60] A. J. R. Groom, *British Thinking About Nuclear Weapons*, London, 1974, p. 460.

favour the Gaitskell rather than the Sandys line on nuclear weapons, although it was rarely articulated in such explicitly party political terms. However, the central point is that 'as the protest movement became politically active so the Churches, as institutions, stood back from it'.[61] Politically the Churches are, after all, as much a coalition as are the political parties themselves. For the hierarchies to have committed themselves to a clear *political* policy on any issue, however major and however clear a moral dimension it might have, would thus have provoked considerable conflict. The dominant style of government in the Churches, as in the wider political sphere, in late twentieth-century Britain, has been that of consensus. Despite the insistence by some Christian activists— Walter Stein for example, as previously cited—that the nuclear issue was an overwhelmingly *moral* issue and must therefore be judged within terms of Christian *moral* precepts, there were many influential Christians, both in the Church itself and in national political life, who were absolutely unwilling to accept the political consequences of such moral absolutism.

An important subsidiary cause of this attitude on the part of the Christian Churches was the relative weakness of Christian CND in the Movement.[62] Christian CND was 'not very active as a separate unit'[63] primarily because most of the leading Christian activists— Canon Collins being the prime example—concentrated their activities in CND as a whole rather than in Christian CND.

The net effect was that whilst the Christian presence was strong in the rank and file, and whilst the Churches as a whole were strong in their general condemnation of nuclear weapons and in their general support for disarmament,[64] the Christian influence on the political direction of CND, at the rank and file level, was minimal.

---

[61] Ibid.

[62] Christian CND was established by Francis Jude, as noted above. Among its sponsors were Sir Richard Acland, John Braine, Professor Herbert Butterfield, Robert Davis, Dom Bede Griffiths, Rev. Trevor Huddleston CR, the Bishop of Llandaff, Rt. Rev. George F. MacLeod, Archbishop Roberts, Rev. Michael Scott, Rev. Dr Donald Soper, the Bishop of Southwark, Fr. Franziskus Stratmann, Dame Sybil Thorndike, Rev. Dr Leslie Weatherhead, the Bishop of Woolwich, and Rev. Austen Williams.

By 1963 there were 16 religious pacifist groups working for nuclear disarmament, according to *Houseman's Peace Diary*, 1963.   [63] Groom, op. cit., 463.

[64] Groom (op. cit.) notes that the one issue which continued to excite the Churches was the question of nuclear testing and the need to secure a test ban treaty. In this area at least 'morality' and 'politics' walked hand in hand.

The leadership perspective

At the leadership level of CND, however, the combination of a Christian-based moralism and a hard-headed and astute political commitment to the 'Labourist tactic' was dominant. The major thrust of the leadership's campaign was to publicize the moral case against nuclear warfare. For Jacquetta Hawkes and J. B. Priestley the unilateralist case 'was almost entirely moral'.[65] Although Collins himself, and some others in the leadership,[66] were pacifists they, unlike the DAC, were very clear that they did not want CND to be seen as a *pacifist* group. The focus was thus on moral outrage at nuclear weapons, rather than on a full-scale pacifist rejection of the immorality of war *per se*. This may have alienated the 'traditional' pacifists of the Peace Pledge Union (PPU), but it was essential for providing the basis of the Campaign's strategy. Just as full-scale pacifism would have greatly diminished the Campaign's appeal, so would a thoroughly political orientation. It was Collins's nice sense of tactical possibilities, at least as much as his principled moral commitment, which kept the campaign on the moralistic/ Labour Party strategy. It was only the generalized moral basis that could bring in the wide support, stimulate public interest and concern, appeal to the Labour Party, and act as a unifying platform.

What then constituted the two interrelated aspects of the executive committee's policy: the moralistic approach, and the Labourist strategy? Of all the early leaders of the campaign it was perhaps J. B. Priestley and his wife Jacquetta Hawkes who best exemplified the content and the tone of the moral approach. Priestley appealed to the common sense of the 'ordinary people', and was contemptuous of the 'VIP—Highest-Priority-Top-Secret-Top-People class, men now so conditioned by this atmosphere of power politics, intrigue, secrecy, insane invention, that they are more than half-barmy'.[67] Combined with the populist appeal to common sense was the firm rejection of pacifism. 'This [unilateralism] is not pacifism. There is no suggestion here of abandoning the immediate defence of this island.'

Still less was Priestley concerned with left politics; he explicitly

[65] Hawkes, in conversation.

[66] e.g. Arthur Goss, Donald Soper, Sir Richard Acland. However, relatively few of the executive committee were pacifists.

[67] This and the following quotations are taken from Priestley's article, 'Britain and the Nuclear Bombs', *New Statesman*, 2 Nov. 1957.

accepted that Britain was, and should continue to be, allied with the Americans against Russian communism, and he implicitly accepted the existing political structure. What was envisaged was rather the creation of a morally based, popular movement of public opinion gathering strength from all sections of the community (with the exception of those Priestley described as the 'few uncertified lunatics' who were in control of the military machine). This was a populist concept, *par excellence.* Priestley, whose radio appeals had been so effective in capturing the national mood during the crisis years of the war, was attempting to harness a similar national upsurge of popular support for unilateralism in 1958. He presented the issue starkly: to rid Britain of nuclear weapons, and thus lessen the dangers of 'universal catastrophe and apocalypse', required, it was argued, a change of policy on the one specific issue—nothing more, nothing less. To him—and to some extent to the CND leadership as a whole,[68] at least in the early years—it was a simple message: unilateralism was the only sane policy: to rely on the British nuclear deterrent was immoral, irrational, and suicidal. As A. J. P. Taylor has observed: 'one of the difficulties was that we were all so absolutely convinced that unilateral nuclear disarmament was sensible, morally right, wise—we simply could never make contact with our opponents, who seemed to be thinking in old-world terms.'[69]

This was thus the morality of common sense. It was neither socialist in its foundations and implications, nor Christian. Still less was it concerned with the details of defence and strategic arguments. Rather, it represented the bluff, good-hearted, non-intellectual, common-sense approach of the man-in-the-street: a populist moralism in fact.[70]

Closely entwined with this moral rejection of nuclear weapons was the affirmation of Britain's potential role as a world leader

---

[68] Although to some, especially Canon Collins and Peggy Duff, the political complexities were always very apparent.

[69] A. J. P. Taylor, in conversation with the author, Apr. 1978.

[70] In this sense Priestley presented almost a music-hall version of the no-nonsense Yorkshireman, which co-existed a little uneasily perhaps with the metropolitan urbanity which characterized the rest of the executive committee. And yet Priestley's image *was* largely an image, not a reality. For many years Priestley had lived in opulence in the South (and latterly near Stratford-upon-Avon), travelling internationally and living a highly cosmopolitan life. More importantly, his own intellectual interests and abilities were extensive, and well appreciated by others on the executive committee.

through moral example. In one important sense the campaign was the last fling of those who wanted to see Britain occupying world power status: if Britain could no longer rule by force then surely she might exert moral and cultural, and therefore political, influence. The early leadership laid great emphasis upon Britain's unique position as the third nuclear power who could make the unilateral gesture and thereby encourage multilateral disarmament, whilst making Britain less likely to suffer nuclear attack as a result of having no nuclear bases. In the article already referred to, Priestley stressed this aspect of unilateralism:

there is nothing unreal in the idea of a third nation, especially one like ours, old and experienced in world affairs, possessing great political traditions, to which other and smaller nations could look while the two new giants mutter and glare at each other. . . . our bargaining power is slight; the force of our example might be great.

Unlike the more radical supporters of the Movement, the CND leadership accepted the general theory of deterrence, and was loyal to the NATO alliance: the leadership was, in essence, arguing about a *specific policy commitment*, and not a whole structure and style of politics. The implicit, and conservative, assumption was made that the existing political and strategic framework was given and almost immutable, and that the unilateralist campaign involved no more than a change of mind (and heart) on the part of the existing political leadership.

The central emotive appeal of Priestley's original article set the tone—and it was that rallying call to the British people that brought out so many of the previously non-political thousands behind CND's banners. It was the ability of CND to provide the mixture of moral indignation, response to fear, humanitarian concern, and above all a single, simple solution to an increasingly urgent problem, that fired the enthusiasm of so many.

And yet it would be wholly incorrect to see the CND leadership as an inexperienced, apolitical, and somehow pure group which was led astray or overwhelmed by the political hardliners and the 'wild men' of the Left.[71] Most of the leading figures were veteran campaigners on humanitarian causes dear to the heart of the

---

[71] Stuart Hall made this point forcefully: 'the notion that it was a kind of "pure" thing, which was sullied by us politicos, is not really [correct]: it's not as simple as that!' in conversation with the author, Apr. 1978).

moderate Left—capital punishment, foreign affairs issues in the
1930s, anti-apartheid movements, and so on. As Stuart Hall has
observed, 'they were people who knew how to lobby, how to
influence people in the Labour Party and/or Government. . . .'[72] The
early leaders had intended to keep CND firmly in this small
pressure group role: 'to make it an issue and then build a Fabian-
style infiltration . . . feeding Royal Commissions with the right sort
of evidence and talking to the right sorts of people and mobilizing
the majorities'.[73] There is here a difference of emphasis, perhaps
even of perception, between the predominantly emotive and
popular approach of Priestley, and the more *realpolitik* perspective
of Collins: and it was the latter approach which dominated the
executive committee after the initial enthusiasm of the early months
of CND.

What *was* common to both was their conception of CND as a
pressure group; and they were thus at a loss when it became
obvious that a huge *mass movement* was developing. As such
diverse authorities as Stuart Hall and Lord Home[74] have pointed
out, the élite pressure group, which CND was at the very beginning,
always works more effectively 'from the inside', rather than on the
streets. The executive committee was quite unable to control the
developing mass movement, which was viewed by the executive
committee with a mixture of distaste, horror, and incomprehen-
sion. As Jacquetta Hawkes rather wistfully recalled:

as far as the leaders of the campaign at that early stage [were concerned]
when it really was a compact sort of little campaign it depended very
considerably on friends. . . . we all knew one another. . . . for some time it
did keep that sort of atmosphere, and it had a very good middle period
when it was coherent, cohesive and friendly but large—and then it began
to disintegrate.[75]

The élite nature of the early Campaign leadership was inextricably
linked to an espousal of the *moral* basis of its perspective. And yet
working through the Labour Party was certainly accepted by the
executive committee leadership from the outset. For Collins and
the executive committee this was seen entirely in terms of the

[72] Ibid.
[73] Ibid.
[74] Ibid., and Lord Home, in conversation with Colin Pritchard, May 1978.
[75] Hawkes, in conversation.

Parliamentary Labour Party and, a little later, the trade union bloc votes as exercised at Party conference. However, it is important not to confuse this commitment to translating CND's moral campaign into political reality with any allegiance on the part of Collins and the executive committee to a wider, more socialist ideological stance.[76] They certainly did not envisage a mass movement—and neither did they have any such sympathy with the concomitant radical foreign policy changes, which, for both the conventional Labour left and, even more, for the New Left were logical and necessary consequences of unilateralism (i.e. principally, British withdrawal from NATO, and the establishment of a neutral bloc involving Britain as a central member). Thus both the growth of the mass Movement from 1959–60 and the developing leftward slant of CND policy were achieved against executive committee wishes, and, together with the equally unpalatable process of democratization which took place in CND from 1959 onwards, were embarrassing, distressing, and, ultimately, unacceptable to the original executive committee leadership.

There were, as Stuart Hall has said,[77] two styles of politics operating, conveniently symbolized by the front and the back of the March. The only intersection of these two perspectives lay in the issue of the bomb itself. But this unanimity on the issue was more

[76] Peggy Duff, alone of the executive committee, must be excepted. In her autobiography she makes her deep and lasting allegiance to socialism very clear. Her involvement on the left both pre-dated and post-dated her CND involvement (she was active in the International Confederation for Disarmament and Peace (ICDP) and European Nuclear Disarmament (END) until her death in 1981). It was because of CND's inability to broaden its concerns to the 'more immediate and urgent concern' of the Vietnam War that she left the organization in early 1967 (Duff, op. cit., 207). For her the bomb was a 'symptom and not a cause . . . the real threat to peace lay in the hegemonies of the super-powers, and especially of the United States' (ibid.). In the conclusion to her autobiography Duff was bitterly cynical about the Labour Party: the Labour Left is 'far worse than it has ever been' (265); the aim of the Labour Party is 'to run capitalism a little more efficiently, a little more humanely, than the Conservatives' (266). For her, a purely single-issue campaign was 'a form of escapism' (271). Radical change would come only through a movement which can link the issues—of war, imperialism, exploitation—and struggle, against the whole capitalist system. What is needed is 'a mass refusal to conform' (271). ' "No man", wrote John Donne, "is an island". That goes for CNDs too' (276).

Such socialist, extra-parliamentary radicalism differentiated Peggy Duff from all other members of the executive committee. Her continued hard work, enthusiasm, and activism in the cause of the Peace Movement testified to her commitment.

[77] Hall, in conversation.

apparent than real. In essence, those in the leadership saw the bomb, enormously important though it was, as a monstrous mistake by a society that was fundamentally sound in structure and attitudes: what was needed, therefore, was a change of policy on this particular issue. (As the obverse of this, of course, the 'back end of the March', so to speak, enormously varied though its ideology was, saw the bomb as the final, absurd, and obscene product of a society which was based on irrational if not insane assumptions.)

The ideological gap was reinforced by both a social class and a generation gap. In a revealing private letter from Diana Collins to Jacquetta Hawkes, the antipathy between the executive committee leadership and the Movement's activists was graphically illustrated. Referring to a social event organized by the London regional committee of CND, Diana Collins wrote: 'the thought of spending a social evening organized by our long-haired bearded friends instead of an evening with you and Jack [J. B. Priestley] fills me with such despondency and gloom that I can hardly bear to contemplate it. However John [Collins] says that as he is Chairman he thinks perhaps he *ought* to put in an appearance.' . . .[78]

Those on the early CND executive were at the height of professional and public life, and, as Collins has recalled, mixed socially with the highest in the land: 'I knew Hugh Gaitskell quite well—and Wilson and Callaghan—[and] I would say in some senses that Gaitskell was a man of lively character, and a person that I found myself drawn to—excepting on this [CND] issue'.[79]

The CND leaders, as they claimed, based their arguments and their campaign on the moral issues and the moral arguments; but equally important were their conservative, single-issue ideological assumptions, and the natural élite nature of their leadership grouping. As Canon Collins implied, on all important criteria the CND leadership tended towards the Gaitskellite establishment and had little in common with the inherent radicalism of the mass Movement which, almost unwittingly, they had been instrumental in creating.

CND thus emerged from its first year of existence as a strong mass Movement, growing rapidly and with considerable potential.

[78] Letter from Diana Collins to Jacquetta Hawkes, 16 Feb. 1959 (private collection of J. B. Priestley).
[79] Collins, in conversation.

However, the ideological and political problems which were to escalate in the years immediately following were already apparent.

CND IN 1959–1961: THE PEAK OF SUCCESS

Successes for the Campaign

By early 1959 there was no doubt that the Movement was making a considerable public impact. Not only was media coverage extensive, the evidence of the opinion polls was encouraging for CND. Those agreeing with the central, unilateralist policy of CND increased from 22 per cent in February 1958 (with 58 per cent disagreeing and 20 per cent 'don't knows') to 30 per cent in June 1959 (with 50 per cent disagreeing and 20 per cent 'don't knows'). And, amongst Labour voters, opinions were evenly divided (40 per cent agreeing with the unilateralist position, 40 per cent disagreeing, and 20 per cent 'don't knows') by June 1959, despite the clear opposition of the Party's leadership.[80]

The years 1959 and 1960 were seen in retrospect by the executive committee leadership of CND as the peak of success. Canon Collins, for example, has recalled: 'it was Aldermaston 1959 that lives most in my memory, that stands out as justifying my being there rather than in the Cathedral during Easter weekend. . . . From Aldermaston 1959 till the Autumn of 1960 was the period of the Campaign's greatest success.'[81]

What exactly *was* achieved in these years? And what was happening inside the Campaign? 1959 began very positively for the executive committee. At its meeting on 2 January Michael Foot proposed, and it was unanimously agreed, that a 'second' Aldermaston March should be organized by CND for Easter 1959. At its meeting on 3 January the co-ordinating committee endorsed this proposal and promised its full support. Active support was thus ensured from the outset from the Friends' Peace Committee, Christian Action, Victory for Socialism, Universities and Left Review, and the DAC (although, according to Canon Collins, the DAC was initially against a repetition of the 1958 March). The important decision to reverse the direction of the March was also made by the

---

[80] Summary of detailed Gallup Poll information as cited in Exley, op. cit., 102–8.
[81] Collins, op. cit., 312–15.

executive committee, at the suggestion of Jacquetta Hawkes, according to Canon Collins.[82] This symbolized 'our determination to present our case positively to those responsible for our nuclear defence policy, and not negatively, against those whose livelihood depended upon their work at the Aldermaston establishment'.[83]

The March, organized by Roy Shaw[84] with Michael Howard as chief marshall, took place shortly after the annual conference in March (which is discussed below in the context of 'democratization'), and was a great success.[85] CND had expected 'many hundreds' at Falcon Field on the first day: in the event 4,300 gathered at the start, according to the *Guardian*. This had increased to 5,000 by the time the March had reached Reading (according to *The Times*—but only 2,000 according to the *Daily Telegraph*), and there were 3,000 at Slough (according to the *Observer*). On the last day there were 15,000 on the March and 20,000–25,000 at the final rally in Trafalgar Square. The *Guardian* reported that 'the speakers were lyrical in their delight'.[86] Moreover, the Press not only gave full coverage of the March, but was on the whole sympathetic to, if not supportive of, the objectives of CND.[87]

[82] Ibid. (confirmed by Collins, in conversation).

[83] Ibid. The DAC of course had a very different view of the purpose of the March (and of other demonstrations too). As Collins noted, the DAC 'always wanted to walk the other, original way; they never believed in the political strategy' (Collins, in conversation).

[84] Roy Shaw was at that time a member of the Department of Adult Education and Extramural Studies, University of Leeds. After a period as the first Warden of the Department's Centre for Adult Education in Bradford, he left to become Professor of Adult Education at the University of Keele. In 1978 he became secretary of the Arts Council of Great Britain, and he was knighted in 1980.

[85] It was described by the *Daily Mail* as 'the biggest single demonstration since the war', cited in CND annual report for 1959, CND archive.

[86] Speakers at the final rally were Michael Foot, Rev. Donald Soper, Antoinette Pirie, Rev. Joseph McCulloch, and Sir Richard Acland.

[87] *The CND Bulletin*, Apr. 1959, carried the following extracts, under the headline, 'Aldermaston to London—1959, without Prejudice':

I am writing this sitting on the grass verge of a country lane in Berkshire. During the past forty five minutes nearly 5,000 people in a marching column three miles long have trudged past on this, the first, day of the anti-H-Bomb march from Aldermaston to London. These marchers—men, women and children—have come from all over Britain and many parts of Europe and the Commonwealth. And late this evening it looked like developing into the biggest single demonstration since the war. . . . (*Daily Mail*, 28 Mar. 1959).

The column took the road again heading for Maidenhead. . . . few marchers could feel that they were part of a small illicit band of near-martyrs. Those not marching seemed the outsiders. (*Observer*, 29 Mar. 1959).

During 1958 over 250 major public meetings had taken place all over Britain. Two hundred and seventy-two groups had been formed and vast quantities of CND literature/propaganda produced. Following these successes, and the huge Aldermaston March, the executive committee was keen to consolidate its strength at the grass roots and 'planning started on the next big event . . . "Nuclear Disarmament Week" . . . as soon as the March was over'.[88]

In the event, although 'a considerable number of new supporters were enrolled and about twenty new groups were formed . . . it was not entirely successful'.[89] In fact, this was an understatement: the whole project proved to be a major disappointment to CND.

This was in part due to the general election. The election in fact dominated CND activities and tactics from Easter onwards in 1959, and in the long term had a far greater importance than undermining the potential success of what had been planned as

---

The third day of the march—sixteen miles from Slough to Chiswick—has been tough, but although each was tired the morale this evening was higher than it had been at any time. From noon the rain beat down relentlessly. . . . But the more unpleasant it became the higher rose the spirits of the marchers. 'They must take us seriously now,' said a sixteen-year old boy. 'No one can say any longer that we are a lunatic fringe.' (*Evening News*, 30 Mar. 1959)

London saw a different kind of Easter parade yesterday—the end of the four-day 'Ban-the-H-Bomb' March from Aldermaston. The four-mile procession drew in an oddly-assorted cross-section of the British public. There are not many occasions, one would have thought, that would bring together archaeologist Jacquetta Hawkes, Canon John Collins, Goon Show creator Spike Milligan, and left-wing firebrand Michael Foot. But the Campaign for Nuclear Disarmament did it. Besides them and besides the young and weirdly clad, there marched a lot of ordinary, anonymous men and women in ordinary clothes. And the thousands who watched them recognized that something very different in the way of processions was passing through the London streets. (*Daily Express*, 31 Mar. 1959).

[88] Executive committee report, 1959, CND archive. Plans included: a 'model programme' for local groups (suggestions were made for pickets, Church involvement, leaflet distribution, theatre production, meetings with the trades council, women's organizations, etc., and a 'march of young people around town followed by dance'); and various national events (e.g. *Stars in Your Eyes* at the Royal Festival Hall, with among others, Michael Redgrave, Peggy Ashcroft, Jill Balcon, Benjamin Britten, Sybil Thorndike, Gerard Hoffnung, and Cecil Day Lewis); and a Downing Street picket for 24 hours through the seven days. There were two final national rallies on Saturday 20 Sept., in London and Glasgow.

[89] CND annual report, 1959. Only 12,000 attended the final rally in Trafalgar Square, according to CND. However, local groups reported an increase in membership totalling 2,109 (and at this stage only 94 groups had reported, so the eventual total may have been higher) (executive committee minutes, 4 Dec. 1959, CND archive).

CND's major event (after Aldermaston) of the year. Indeed, from Easter 1959 until the general election in the autumn the leadership of CND failed to maintain momentum. This may have been consistent with the predominantly Labourist perspective of the CND executive, in that it subordinated the Campaign *per se* to the absolute requirement to work for a Labour victory in the election; but it seriously weakened the Campaign in the whole range of its extra-parliamentary presence and activities through the crucial period of mid- to late 1959.

However, CND's relationship with the Labour Movement certainly became closer in 1959. Following the CND annual conference in March, the Labour advisory committee was divided into three subcommittees covering the House of Commons, the constituency Labour Parties, and the trade unions. Frank Beswick (MP up to the 1959 election when he lost a marginal seat at Uxbridge[90]) remained chairman of the main committee and of the parliamentary committee. John Horner and Olive Gibbs became respectively chairman of the trade union and constituency Labour Party subcommittees, and agreed to serve on the co-ordinating committee.

Considerable advances were made in the Labour Movement by CND in 1959 (see Chapters 6 and 7). Both the Transport and General Workers' Union and the General and Municipal Workers' Union moved considerably closer to CND policy (the latter only temporarily, however). Effective propaganda information was produced by the subcommittees mentioned above, and the number of resolutions advocating unilateral nuclear disarmament submitted to the Labour Party's annual conference was indicative of the high level of Labour Movement support for unilateralism by mid-1959. (The conference never took place, of course, because of the election; but the rising tide of unilateralist opinion was certainly a portent of the dramatic 1960 conference.)

The 1959 general election and CND's problems

As soon as the general election campaign began, CND groups were sent a list of candidates fighting marginal seats who supported CND policy. The CND questionnnaire survey ascertained that 211

[90] Frank Beswick had been asked to join the executive committee on 27 Oct. 1958, and had accepted. Another important addition to the executive committee was Rev. Dr Donald Soper, who joined in late Feb. 1959 (executive committee minutes, CND archive).

Labour, 37 Liberals, 20 Welsh Nationalists, 2 Scottish Nationalists, 9 Communists, and 7 others supported CND policy.[91] A handful of new MPs supporting CND was elected: Judith Hart, Archie Mannel, Laurie Pavitt, and Alan Brown; but several CND-supporting members lost their seats, including Frank Beswick, Lena Jeger, Ian Mikardo, Tom Williams, Edward Evans, Maurice Orbach, and Percy Morris. According to CND, the new Parliament contained forty-nine MPs who supported unilateralism. Thus, although the subcommittees had been active—and had indeed helped to lay the foundations for the unilateralist victory which was to come at the 1960 conference—the net result of the general election of 1959 was bad for CND, as indeed it was disastrous for the Labour Party.

There had been widespread disillusionment, and not only on the left, about the 'unsocialist' way in which Gaitskell had run the election campaign. For those who expected a moral lead (on defence as on other major issues) from the Labour Party, just as much as for those who hoped for a vigorously asserted socialist alternative politics to emerge from the Party, the 1959 election marked a nadir.

The election destroyed the buoyant optimism of CND. It was not only that Labour's emphatic defeat destroyed CND's (or at least the executive committee's) belief that the successful culmination of the short, vigorous campaign originally envisaged would be accomplished with the election of a Labour government. A second major factor, at least for many of the activists, was the *manner* in which the Labour Party had fought the campaign, and the marginality of defence issues in that campaign. The survey of the 1959 election carried out by David Butler and Richard Rose makes the point succinctly: 'Despite its "special week" from 13 to 19 September, the CND drew very little attention in the election.' A footnote adds: 'strangely little was made of the announcement by CND of the names of seven Labour candidates who were prepared to defy the party Whip over the H-Bomb and of seventy-two more who favoured unilateral renunciation of its use.' Further, 'one of its leading members, a Labour candidate, remarked sadly that he got no reaction at his meetings, so that he had had to switch his fire to the Rent Act.'[92]

[91] Annual report, 1959.
[92] David E. Butler and Richard Rose, *The General Election of 1959*, London, 1960, p. 65. The authors added evidence from a Gallup Poll, held the week after the

The cancellation of the Blue Streak project shortly after the election, combined with Labour's defeat, produced a new environment in which CND had to operate.

While the political assumption that CND could gain power through winning control of the Labour Party had been destroyed by the election, CND's military assumption was altered by this abandonment of Blue Streak. . . . if Britain had no means to deliver her weapons, she was no danger to any prospective enemy. Therefore, according to the logic of the CND argument, she was in no great danger of direct attack, provided American bases in Britain were removed.

Once Britain turned to a US-linked deterrent, it became 'clear to many in CND that British unilateralism would have little effect in ending the Cold War. That goal could only be achieved by some change in the basic conflicting alliances. Accordingly, in the early part of 1960, CND turned its attention more closely to NATO.'[93]

The significance of this change, for CND, can hardly be over-estimated. No longer was the simple, emotive, morally based slogan of 'Ban the Bomb' a sufficient response to the complexities of the situation. Indeed, those on the political left of the Movement, especially on the New Left, had been arguing from the outset that a break with the alliance system and with American-dominated capitalism, and the establishment of a neutral, 'third way' socialist bloc, was the logical, as well as the politically desirable, development of CND's unilateralism.

For the leadership of CND all this was most unpalatable, of course: 'I think quite a number of us really quite strongly disapproved once the Labour Party and further left had weighed in and it became a *neutralist* thing' (Jacquetta Hawkes).[94] For that proportion of the rank and file that was outside the politicized wing of the

dissolution of Parliament on 15 Sept., about the issues which most concerned the electorate. 92 per cent were 'especially concerned' with economic issues, whilst only 20 per cent were 'especially concerned' with foreign affairs. Moreover, of this 20 per cent, only 8 per cent were concerned primarily with the H-bomb issue. Only 55 per cent of Labour supporters thought that a Labour government would be better able to handle foreign affairs (ibid., 71 ff.).

[93] Frank E. Myers, *British Peace Politics: The Campaign for Nuclear Disarmament and the Committee of 100, 1957–1962*, Ph.D. thesis, Columbia University, 1965, pp. 123–4. A. J. R. Groom, arguing from within a strategic studies perspective, has made a similar point: 'The protesters never fully grasped that the real unilateralist act was to leave the alliance system and that this had nothing to do with giving up nuclear weapons, which are only a strategic disposition' (Groom, op. cit., 408 ff.).

[94] Hawkes, in conversation.

Movement—the 'moral protesters', who were a substantial section, as has been seen—the essential message of the Movement remained the unambiguous moral clarion call to unilateral nuclear disarmament. This was further complicated by the separately based ideological approach of the DAC and related activists who, quite justifiably by their own terms of reference, rejected all such 'politicking' as irrelevant to the basic pacifist cause.[95]

From 1960 onwards, therefore, there developed a continuing and increasingly bitter debate in the Movement over ideological orientation and strategic disposition. This division has been characterized as being between those

who saw CND as a rebellion against political activity, with its bargaining and compromising, and those who concentrated on CND's role as a foreign policy pressure group with mass support. The former opposed any political strategy except a demand for British unilateral nuclear disarmament, CND's original policy aim. The latter argued for a more detailed and flexible approach.[96]

Whilst there is some truth in this, the reality was more complex. Spanning this 'moral/political' division was the spectrum of radicalism/conservatism. Thus, the former, 'moralist' group included not only the relatively conservative 'moralists' of the CND leadership (Jacquetta Hawkes, Arthur Goss, *et al.*), but also the militant radicals of the DAC (Pat Arrowsmith, April Carter *et al.*). Similarly, and even more importantly, the latter 'political' group included not only 'trimmers' (like Canon Collins) and orthodox Labour left supporters (like Frank Allaun and Ian Mikardo), but also radical neo-Marxists (most notably those of the New Left—in particular Stuart Hall and Edward Thompson).

Moreover, to complicate the division still further, it is important to note not only that the Labourists and Marxists were opposed to each other's perspectives and strategies on ideological grounds, but also that both contained within them important strands of 'moralism'. Thus, in the Labourist context, the moralism of the

[95] For example, Pat Arrowsmith was dismissive of this aspect of policy: 'I could never get worked up about this [i.e. withdrawal from NATO and the adoption of a neutralist foreign policy]. As a pacifist I could never see it as a problem really. I was opposed to NATO, of course, because it was equipped with nuclear weapons. I could see no argument whatever for being in: the argument for getting out seemed a part of the argument for getting rid of the bomb really. But I never wanted to emphasize it particularly—after all, the bomb itself was the issue, the central issue' (in conversation with the author, Jan. 1978). [96] Myers, op. cit., 124

Independent Labour Party (ILP) tradition was a major influence, whilst the quasi-populist moralism of Thompson in particular played a significant role in the ideological stance of the New Left. Whatever the rights and wrongs of the dispute, there is no doubt that the initiative and the politically creative policy-making emanated from the political strata of the Movement. This was perhaps hardly surprising, given the more complex and increasingly *political* nature of the new situation in which the Movement found itself. Stuart Hall's[97] pamphlet 'NATO and the Alliances'[98] put the case clearly for combining unilateralism with withdrawal from NATO:

So long as [CND's] basic principles are opposed by the major political parties, it is correct for the campaign to steer clear of any direct commitment in narrow political terms. But in every other sense, CND must, it seems to me, either now become more political than it has ever been before, or watch its case proved obsolescent by the march of events. . . . it is clear that CND cannot afford to base itself upon a policy of 'clean hands for Britain' alone. . . . we must be careful to insist that Britain must unilaterally disarm, not merely to salve her own conscience, not merely to cut the cost of defence to the taxpayer, but in order to *use that renunciation as a political lever.* . . . The point would be that Britain, *disencumbered of both Bomb and Alliances*, would then be free to act as a rallying point outside both nuclear alliances—the Warsaw Pact and NATO: a focus for all those other nations, within and without both alliances, which could be persuaded by the weight of international opinion, to join an offensive for disengagement and disarmament.

Whereas the 1959 national conference had 'left the impression that the Campaign did not envision a Britain outside of NATO',[99] the 1960 conference adopted a resolution embodying very similar

[97] Stuart Hall was one of the leading members of the first New Left (see ch. 7), editor of *Universities and Left Review*, and the first editor of *New Left Review*. From 1959 onwards (following the general election), he was a major influence on CND policy-making, and from 1960 became perhaps the most important single figure in CND's 'think-tank'. An independent Marxist of some influence in a number of academic fields, Hall was Director of the Centre for Cultural Studies at the University of Birmingham from 1972 to 1979, when he became professor of sociology at the Open University. He has published widely, and his pamphlets for CND were amongst the most influential in the Movement. He was a tireless worker and public speaker for CND, especially in the early 1960s.

[98] Stuart Hall, 'NATO and the Alliances', CND pamphlet, London, spring 1960. Interestingly, Hall, in an earlier CUCaND pamphlet, 'Breakthrough', Oxford, 1958, had argued for Britain pursuing a neutralist policy, but remaining inside NATO.

[99] Myers, op. cit., 121.

proposals to those made in Hall's pamphlet, cited above: after reaffirming unilateralism as a basic aim of CND, the resolution, from Croydon CND, argued that 'this aim cannot be achieved so long as this country remains a member of NATO which is committed to reliance on nuclear weapons for the so-called defence of the free world'.[100] The 1960 policy statement included a commitment to withdrawal from NATO: 'The British Government would inform NATO and SEATO that as she has renounced nuclear weapons she cannot continue to be a member of any alliance that is based on the use of these weapons.'[101] Such sentiments were to be pushed considerably farther at subsequent CND conferences, culminating in the controversial 'Steps Towards Peace' statement prepared by Stuart Hall in 1962 (see Chapter 3). Here, it is sufficient to note that this series of developments shifted the balance of emphasis in CND and indeed, in the long term, changed the whole nature of the Campaign.

There were, however, other important events in 1960 which were to have a profound effect on the subsequent development of the Movement. Two in particular were crucial: the unilateralist victory at the 1960 Labour Party annual conference, and the massive Aldermaston March of 1960. The Labour conference victory, and its aftermath and implications, are discussed in Chapter 6. In this context it need be noted only that this somewhat unexpected success was not an unqualified blessing for CND. Of course, it increased considerably CND's prospects for attaining its political objectives via the Labour Party. And it brought into still greater public prominence the controversy surrounding the Campaign and its objectives. On the other hand it deepened the divisions within the Movement over 'moral versus political' principles, strategies, and tactics which had been evident throughout 1959 and 1960 as the support from Labour Movement organizations increased. The Movement, in other words, was beginning to disintegrate even at the very height of its success. When it came to the supreme test, in Labour Party terms, over whether CND was strong enough to *hold* the Party to the 1960 decision in the face of the 'sharpened . . . hostility of the Press and of all those opposed to our aims',[102] it

---

[100] Reported in *CND Bulletin*, Mar. 1960, CND archive.

[101] CND annual conference statement for 1960, CND archive.

[102] Collins, in a letter to CND group secretaries, 8 Oct. 1960 (Goss's private papers).

became apparent very quickly that CND was, at least at that particular juncture, unequal to the task. Not the least of the reasons for this failure was the unwillingness of the mass of CND supporters to become heavily involved in Labour Party politics. The subsequent effects of this long-drawn-out battle (during which Gaitskell shrewdly emphasized the neutralist implications of CND's anti-NATO policies) were indeed profound—both for the Labour Party and, more particularly, for CND. In 1960, however, it seemed as though CND was riding the crest of the wave and that 'carrying the Labour Party' was the penultimate pinnacle of success—with 'only' the translation of a *party* commitment into a *government* policy remaining.[103]

An important aspect of the build-up of the Movement's self-confidence was the success of the 1960 Aldermaston March. *The Times* was fulsome in its coverage. The March had begun with 10,000 at Falcon Field and had grown to 20,000 by the time it reached Slough. The final day was an impressive triumph for CND, with between 60,000 and 100,000 in Trafalgar Square, and a wide range of organizations (and opinions) represented.

Press coverage was widespread and, generally, favourable.[104] Following the March, support for CND increased considerably in the heightening tension internationally surrounding the U2 incident and the subsequent collapse of the summit conference. Large meetings were held in Central Hall, Westminster (26 May), and in the Free Trade Hall, Manchester (13 May), and later in the year, a national march, orginally organized by London Region but taken over by National CND, took place from Edinburgh to London, beginning on 3 September and finishing on 24 September, and involving large regional marches in the north-west and the Midlands.

However, even these 'demonstration successes' contained considerable problems for CND's leadership. As George Clark has

[103] Although, even after the Labour conference vote, CND was still eager to pursue its formally non-party political policies. Thus, in Canon Collins's letter of 8 Oct. 1960 (ibid.), reference was made to the need to 'achieve the same support in the other political parties. The unilateralist motion moved by Lt. Col. Lort-Phillips was heavily defeated at the Liberal Conference this year. No effort must be spared to increase support there during the coming year.'

[104] *The Times*, the *Observer*, and the *Daily Mirror* were generally favourable to CND and the March's objectives, although some reservations were expressed; the *Daily Herald* and the *Daily Worker* were wholly supportive; and the *Daily Telegraph*, the *Daily Mail*, and the *News Chronicle* were wholly opposed.

noted, the power balance in the Movement changed markedly in 1960.

In the early days they [the CND leaders] had a confidence behind which they could hide because nobody who was going to challenge their assumptions had any troops in the field. And it wasn't until the 1960 March that it became clear to them that they weren't in charge any longer. Then you could say there was a major gap. . . . 1960, although it was a repetition of 1959, was not their March.[105]

Allowing for Clark's somewhat partisan stance on the whole issue, it is true that 1960 marked the watershed for CND as a movement. Prior to Aldermaston 1960 the élite leadership, basically unchanged in orientation and only marginally different in personnel, retained control of CND. From Aldermaston 1960 this was no longer possible. It was not only the massive size of the Movement that caused this break (though size itself was an important factor in creating the self-confidence, self-assertion, and fundamentally anarchic character of a *mass* movement). From this time, also, there sprang a greater radicalism, a greater desire to operate outside the conventional parliamentary arena, to create a *new* politics with its own style and its own priorities. It was the sense of the 'power of the March' which acted as the catalyst for the lurch to radicalism, and this in turn was one of the causes underlying the creation of the Committee of 100. Thus, the success of the Aldermaston March of 1960 presaged the split which was to occur with the inauguration of the Committee of 100, and which was to be a major cause of dissension and bitterness in the Movement from 1960 onwards.

It is thus perhaps not too much to claim that the major successes of the Movement in 1960 contained the twin germs of the Movement's failure: the inability to hold Labour to its policies, let alone its wider political objectives; and the split between the traditional constitutionalists of the CND leadership and the radicals of the Committee of 100, occasioned primarily by the growth and self-confidence of the mass Movement.

[105] George Clark, in conversation with the author, Jan. 1978. George Clark was one of the leading activists in CND and, later, in the Committee of 100. Although initially associated with *Universities and Left Review* he became involved with DAC Gandhian politics, and was a tireless organizer and campaigner in London Region CND. He was chief marshall of the early Committee of 100 demonstrations and founded the Caravan Workshops. Since his Peace Movement activities he has become involved in community activism, and has been an independent councillor in West London.

These problems were reflected in both the structure and ethos of CND in the latter part of 1960. Despite wide-ranging and significant activity on a number of fronts,[106] the 'golden days' of élite rule of the Campaign had gone forever. No longer was it, nor could it ever again become, Jacquetta Hawkes's 'compact sort of little campaign (which) depended very considerably on friends'.[107]

Changes in CND's structure and organization

The pressure for changes in the structure of CND throughout 1959–60 reflected both the growing politicization of the Movement and the demand of the rank and file for more control over what it regarded as its Movement. The moves towards democratization were essentially a part of the process of change from the temporary, pressure-group campaign envisaged by the early leadership, to the mass Movement of 1960 and beyond. By 1961 Collins and the leadership had been forced to concede a democratic constitution.[108]

[106] There was considerable activity in the parliamentary sphere. In February, Frank Allaun tabled a motion calling for the renunciation of nuclear weapons but, although signed by 40 MPs, this was not enough to have the motion debated. On 1 Mar. 1960, 43 Labour MPs abstained from voting for the Labour Party's official defence motion. A public meeting took place on the eve of the reassembly of Parliament in October, and, generally, the parliamentary group co-ordinated the efforts of unilateralist MPs and worked hard to put CND's viewpoint in the Parliamentary Labour Party and on the floor of the House of Commons.

Other meetings in 1960 included a successful and well-reported Central Hall rally on 15 Feb. 1960 at which speakers from the Sahara project of DAC appeared with a range of new supporters from public life: John Osborne, John Braine, Cliff Michelmore, Humphrey Lyttleton, and James Robertson Justice.

In Jan. 1961, CND's *Bulletin* was replaced by the more ambitious and large-scale Campaign newspaper *Sanity*, and the propaganda/educational role of CND was also furthered by the establishment in London Region CND of several study groups in June 1960.

Finally, during 1960 the CND executive committee was strengthened by the addition of Antoinette Pirie, John Horner, and Laurie Pavitt, although, as noted, the increasingly 'mass movement' ethos meant that the executive no longer played such a central role.

[107] Hawkes, in conversation.

[108] Collins has made it clear subsequently that the CND executive resisted such changes for as long as possible: 'If we were to keep the interest and enthusiasm of the campaign alive, [we had] despite dangers of infiltration and a slowing up in tempo, to provide some means of communication and expression of personal responsibility. . . . [up to 1960] we dealt with this problem first by setting up an Advisory Co-ordinating committee, with no executive power, . . . and, secondly, by calling an Annual Conference to which every regional and sectional set-up and every group of CND was asked to send representatives. . . . at least we bought time during which CND was able to get on with its work' (Collins, op. cit., 315–16).

Although this maintained some sort of unity it 'certainly slowed up the Campaign . . . and lost us the active involvement of some distinguished writers and speakers'.[109] A. J. P. Taylor certainly agreed with Collins's last point:

> . . . there was, of course, a great drive, especially from some village Hampdens, for it to be run on a democratic basis. And ultimately . . . they carried this. . . . And at that the National Committee [the executive committee] dropped out. . . . There was a gradual drop-off and I left when it became *democratic*. It was this *far* more than the Committee of 100 which reduced the CND to the sort of level [that it reached post 1965].[110]

In what did these changes consist? At the 1959 conference a suggestion from Russell that elections for the executive committee should be held, and a membership scheme introduced, was rejected by the executive. At conference a much more moderate reform—to increase the members of the executive committee to provide for direct representation of the local groups, through a representative nominated by each regional council[111]—was carried and implemented (i.e. twelve representatives, one from each regional council). However, no major change of policy, or indeed of leadership control, resulted.

At the 1960 conference, proposals for a fully democratic constitution were defeated but the executive committee 'saw the writing on the wall, and tabled proposals for a fully democratic constitution for the 1961 Conference'.[112] The proposals presented to the annual conference on 4–5 March 1961 marked a radical departure from previous CND/executive committee practice and represented a virtual surrender by the executive committee leadership. A pyramid power structure was proposed, with local groups as the base and the executive committee as the apex. CND policy was to be laid down by annual conference, which was to be held in the spring (this was changed to the autumn from 1963). The annual conference was to be composed of one delegate from each local group and each specialist section.[113]

[109] Ibid.
[110] Taylor, in conversation.
[111] Conference report, 1959, CND archive.
[112] Duff, op. cit., 155. Duff goes on to note that a subcommittee of the executive committee was established in Apr. 1960 to draft a new constitution (but that it was 'largely my [Duff's] brainchild').
[113] A local group was defined as one having at least 20 members or locally registered supporters, which accepted CND policy, and which held at least one meeting

The national co-ordinating committee was abolished, and replaced by a national council, which was to be responsible, between conferences, for the overall policy and strategy of the campaign. The new constitution provided for a chairman, a vice-chairman (later three of them), a treasurer, and ten individuals to be elected by the annual conference to the national council. There were also to be three representatives from the Labour advisory committee, one from each regional council, one from each specialist section, and up to twelve co-options, at least four of whom should be regional representatives. From the national council, an executive committee was to be elected which should include four representatives of the regions (and later one from YCND). The executive committee had power to co-opt, but only to a maximum of three, and these had to be confirmed by national council. Finally, at the executive committee meeting on 30 April 1961, it was reported that a liaison committee, with representation from CND, DAC, and the Committee of 100, had been established.[114] However, the committee had no executive power and was, quite literally, restricted to matters of liaison (over the Aldermaston March, the DAC Holy Loch demonstration, etc.).

The results of the elections produced both a national council and an executive committee not strikingly different in composition from the previous hierarchy of CND.[115] However, the changes were significant: they gave formal expression to the fact that the control of CND had passed to a large extent out of the hands of its original élite leadership.

CND *and the creation of the Committee of* 100

All these changes and the problems they signified were overshadowed by the dramatic division in the Movement

per year, for all members, at which delegates and officers were elected. Local groups were to pay a minimum of £5 per annum to the national campaign. Specialist groups were designated as those recognized by the national council as having specialized knowledge and associations in a particular field (e.g. the Scientists and Christian groups).

[114] Representation was: four from CND, two from DAC, and two from the Committee of 100 (executive committee minutes, 30 Apr. 1961).

[115] On the national council of 29, Collins remained chairman, Ritchie Calder vice-chairman, and Laurie Kershaw, treasurer. Other 'old stalwarts' included James Cameron, Michael Foot, Arthur Goss, Jacquetta Hawkes, Kingsley Martin, J. B. Priestley, and A. J. P. Taylor (CND annual report, 1960–1, CND archive).

occasioned by the creation of the Committee of 100 in September 1960. For Canon Collins, the advent of the Committee was a disaster.

It was at the height of this mood of optimism [i.e. immediately prior to the 1960 Labour conference], just when CND seemed to be flourishing like a green bay tree, that the winds of dissent blew into a gale, and the storm broke. With the advent of the Committee of 100 came bickerings, misunderstandings, irreconcilable attitudes and strained loyalties which inevitably reduced the effectiveness of the Campaign. . . . in my view, particularly coming at the time it did, the launching of the Committee of 100 was a serious blow to the Campaign, and one from which it never fully recovered.[116]

Certainly, the events surrounding the emergence of the Committee of 100 could hardly have been more dramatic, and the Press had a sustained opportunity for the sensationalized 'personality clash' journalism at which it excels.

The unfolding relationship between Bertrand Russell and his supporters, and the CND executive in general and Canon Collins in particular, was both complex and confusing. Memoranda, statements, and mutual recriminations were issued at frequent intervals and crisis meetings abounded. Inasmuch as this related to the origins and birth of the Committee of 100, the analysis is most appropriately left until Chapter 5. The point here is to note the effect upon CND. At one level, there is no doubt that the whole affair was blown up grossly out of proportion by the media, and, indeed, by the two 'prima donna' participants themselves. There is considerable evidence that Russell, at this time aged ninety, was heavily under the influence of Ralph Schoenman, the originator of the Committee of 100 idea, and was not perhaps fully responsible for all that was carried out in his name. Nevertheless, there is no doubt that Russell was a most prickly character, in the context of the Nuclear Disarmament Movement, and that his single-minded determination to bring home the urgency of the situation as he saw it would tolerate no interference, or even qualification, from the CND executive. Canon Collins, on the other hand, had hoped from the outset that Russell would be 'a sort of figurehead to be trotted out on occasions, whereas Russell really wanted to be in charge'.[117]

---

[116] Collins, op. cit., 318.
[117] Duff, in conversation with the author, Jan. 1978.

Collins was, according to Arthur Goss, 'very publicity conscious.
. . . he is among those who also personally enjoy being a "figure"
and being in the news and the limelight.'[118] And, according to Peggy
Duff, 'John Collins always wanted to bring the tablets down from
on high';[119] in her opinion, both Collins and Russell were 'quite
impossible'[120] during the furore over the creation of the Committee
of 100, and the whole business seemed to her 'extraordinarily
childish'.[121] There was thus much pent-up frustration between the
two men who had been almost vying for power within the
Movement for some time: the ferocity of the dispute owed
something to this powerful personality clash. However, despite its
profound effect on both the CND leadership, which is discussed
below, and the Movement as a whole, it is important to note that at
the activist level the division was by no means total, and was
regarded by many as being a tiresome irrelevance. As Peggy Duff
has pointed out:

one of the problems was that the ordinary rank and file people just didn't
want to have to choose between Canon Collins and Russell. . . . They
didn't distinguish between Committtee and Campaign. . . . for them it was
all part of the Campaign against nuclear weapons. Those who could sit,
sat, and those who couldn't went along and cheered them. And everybody
marched. And the relationship at grass roots level was always pretty good.
It was always at the top that they fought.[122]

Dick Nettleton[123] put the same point even more strongly.

The division was at the centre – in London between the few individuals at
the centre of the Campaign. But everywhere else, in the regions, in the rank
and file – in fact in the proper Movement – amongst the people who
actually carried out the work of the Campaign – everyone worked quite
harmoniously together.

[118] Letter from Arthur Goss to Donald Pennington, 28 Sept. 1961 (Goss's private
papers).
[119] Duff, op cit., 164.
[120] Duff, in conversation.
[121] Duff, op. cit., 173.
[122] Duff, in conversation.
[123] Dick Nettleton, in conversation with the author, Jan. 1978. Dick Nettleton,
who had been a long-standing activist on the Labour left, a trade union branch
secretary, and a town councillor, was organizer of North-west Region CND from
1963–7, before moving to London to succeed Peggy Duff as secretary of CND in
1967. He remained CND national secretary until 1973, and was also secretary of the
British Council for Peace in Vietnam. From the mid-1970s he was involved in work
with the elderly in a sheltered homes project in Oxfordshire.

Nevertheless, and despite his personal annoyance, Collins was correct, from his 'Labourist perspective', in his belief that the adoption of civil disobedience by the Movement would not only be a diversion, but counter-productive because it would alienate the Labour Movement, and confirm the already current notion that the Movement was extreme, 'cranky', and not a serious political phenomenon.

Collins, however, being an astute and tough political operator, was eventually able to weather the storm of 1960 and early 1961, though his control over the Movement declined continuously and progressively from 1961 onwards. For other, less politically experienced, executive committee members, the creation of the Committee of 100 was a profound shock from which they never recovered. (Jacquetta Hawkes, for example, felt that the creation of the Committee of 100 destroyed the Movement.)

From the CND leadership's point of view Russell had certainly acted in bad faith. Russell *had* informed Canon Collins that he intended 'to say something in a respect for those who practise direct action'[124] at the rally to mark the end of the Edinburgh–London March on 24 September in Trafalgar Square, and Russell had been persuaded to postpone (but not abandon) his action. However, no mention was made at this stage of the proposal to establish a new 'Committee of 100'. Meanwhile leaflets were sent out by Russell and Rev. Michael Scott to potential members of the new committee, and rumours began to circulate, culminating in the notorious 'leak' to the *Evening Standard*, which headlined the plans for a new committee, on 28 September.[125]

The CND leadership was thrown into confusion, not surprisingly.[126] Following the *Evening Standard* story on 28 September Canon Collins telephoned Russell and 'was glad to find that he shared my distress at this premature disclosure of his plans'.[127] Collins then issued a press statement on behalf of CND reiterating

[124] Letter from Bertrand Russell to Canon Collins, 3 Sept. 1960, cited in Duff. op. cit., 170.

[125] This is discussed in some detail in ch. 5.

[126] Jacquetta Hawkes, for example, knew nothing of the plans for the new Committee: 'The first thing we heard was from Marghanita Laski who rang up and said "What's this about our getting involved in illegal action—I don't want to do that", and so on—and we said "What are you talking about?"—we didn't know at all!' (Hawkes, in conversation).

[127] Collins, confidential chairman's report to the executive committee of CND, n.d. (Nov. 1960), CND archive.

Formation and Advance, 1958–60 65

the policy of legal demonstration, but rejecting and sympathizing with those who felt bound by conscience to undertake illegal civil disobedience action. (He also issued a personal statement opposing civil disobedience and making clear his annoyance at Russell's action.) Russell offered to resign as president 'should the Executive pass a resolution to that effect'.[128] Collins called an emergency meeting of the executive in response to requests from 'several members'.[129] This was a 'brief and very badly attended meeting'[130] and, understandably, somewhat chaotic. Although the majority of the executive committee was unable to attend,[131] as many as possible were contacted by telephone and consulted about the issue of a Press statement. The statement, which made it clear that not all members of the executive committee were present, was explicit in its criticism of both Russell's actions and its general rejection of civil disobedience.

According to Collins, he 'informed those present, as well as those contacted on the telephone of Earl Russell's offer of resignation should the Committee pass a resolution asking for it. I urged that no such resolution be put, and this was agreed.'[132] However, the *Daily Mail* of 30 September reported that this meeting had called for Russell's resignation. Both Collins and Duff subsequently refuted this absolutely.[133] Whatever the truth of the matter (and it seems almost certain that Collins's account is, in this respect, accurate), the damage was done, and Russell and Rev. Michael Scott issued an angry and highly critical statement to the Press on 30 September. Events now degenerated into petty and childish low farce. Collins and Russell had four meetings in the week beginning 3 October 'to try to clear the matter up'[134] but Russell insisted on witnesses being present. Peggy Duff and Kingsley Martin were 'blackballed by Lord Russell',[135] but eventually Arthur Goss and Michael Howard (for Collins and Russell respectively) were agreed. Tape recordings of all these conversations were made,[136] such was the suspicion engendered by the events of the previous few weeks.

[128] Ibid.   [129] Ibid.   [130] Duff, op. cit., 171.
[131] There were only four executive committee members present, plus Mervyn Jones, according to Austin Underwood (letter to secretary of London Region CND, 2 Oct. 1960, CND archive).
[132] Collins, confidential report.
[133] Ibid.; and Duff, op.cit., 171.
[134] Collins, confidential report.
[135] Duff, op. cit., 172.
[136] These are housed in the Russell archive, McMaster University, Canada.

A number of draft statements were discussed and 'eventually a statement of Amity was agreed on the evening of Thursday, October 6th'.[137] The statement was brief and to the point:

> The President and Chairman of the Campaign for Nuclear Disarmament wish to make it clear that they will continue to work together in amity for nuclear disarmament, and they hope that in due course a joint statement will be issued by them concerning the subject of the recent press controversy.
>
> They hope that all members of the Campaign for Nuclear Disarmament, those who support civil disobedience and those who do not, will continue as during the last three years to work for the common end.
>
> Signed: Russell (President)
>   L. John Collins (Chairman)[138]

This brought only temporary relief to the beleaguered Campaign, however. Whilst Collins was away on holiday, Scott issued a seven-page statement giving his version of the events. When Collins returned home he received, on 24 October, a copy of a letter sent by Russell to all members of the executive tendering his resignation as President:

> I cannot countenance the chairman of an organization of which I am president permitting the policy of that organization to be misstated in public statements which are said to have come from him and have not been publicly repudiated by him.[139]

In Scott's view this was the inevitable result of Collins's persistent failure to endorse CND's eclectic and tolerant view of the individual campaigner's right to support civil disobedience. The problem, in Scott's view, was that statements attributed to Collins in the Press, to the effect that the executive felt they must 'warn' Russell that CND was 'bound by the decision of the Annual Conference to use only legal and democratic methods of persuasion',[140] had never been repudiated by either Collins or the executive committee. This does not appear to tally with the facts, however. The *Daily Mail* of 25 October certainly did repeat its allegation concerning the executive committee's 'warning' to Russell, first

---

[137] Collins, confidential report.
[138] CND archive.
[139] Cited in Duff, op. cit., 173.
[140] Scott's statement, CND archive.

made on 30 September. But Collins's letter to the *Daily Mail* repudiating this statement was published on 27 October.[141]

The full meeting of the executive committee, held on 5 November 1960, and attended by twenty-six of the twenty-seven members, was faced with an additional and heightened crisis. Russell had arranged with the *Observer* for a statement by him to be published, and there was no doubt that the statement — 'certainly contentious, possibly libellous'[142]—would have damaged the Campaign considerably. The executive committee was thus very concerned to secure a retraction of Russell's article. A lengthy resolution was passed *nem. con.* (with three abstentions) indicating a conciliatory attitude to direct action but reaffirming CND's policy, and expressing 'unreserved confidence' in Collins as chairman. The resolution also accepted 'with regret' Russell's resignation and recorded its 'great appreciation of his past services' to CND. A Press statement embodying this resolution was then drafted.

This statement was never released, however. A telephone call was made (according to Peggy Duff, by John Dennithorne, secretary of the Welsh council of CND of which Russell remained president[143]) to Russell who, having been informed that the executive committee had passed the resolution noted above, agreed to withdraw his article from the *Observer,* provided that the resolution was amended. The following resolution was then passed:

The Executive Committee regrets that false statements, purporting to come from the Chairman, about CND policy and concerning the President's actions, have been made in the Press.

The following Press statement was also agreed:

The Executive Committee of the Campaign for Nuclear Disarmament met

[141] A slightly abridged version of the following letter from Collins appeared in the *Daily Mail,* 27 Oct. 1960: 'On September 30th you reported that Lord Russell had been warned by me and members of the Executive Committee of the Campaign for Nuclear Disarmament to abandon his plans for civil disobedience or resign his Presidency.

While I was not able to repudiate this statement immediately because I had left London for the north of England, I informed one of your reporters who contacted me at King's Cross on October 2nd on my return that this was untrue and asked for a correction to be made. In spite of this, I note that you have repeated this false statement in today's issue. I trust, therefore, that as you have twice misinformed your readers on this matter, you will kindly publish a correction' (CND archive).

[142] Duff, op. cit., 173.

[143] Ibid., 174.

on November 5th and agreed to issue the following statement in connection with the resignation of the President, Earl Russell:

1. The Executive passed an unreserved vote of confidence in the Chairman, Canon L. John Collins.
2. It regrets that false statements, purporting to come from the Chairman, about the Campaign for Nuclear Disarmament's policy and concerning the President's actions have been made in the Press.

Finally, the Executive appealed to all groups

as stated in the Press Statement agreed by the Executive Committee 'to look only to the future and the work that has still to be done to lift the shadow of nuclear war', to seek any further information they may require from their next Regional Meeting, and to hope, as we all do, that it may be possible for Earl Russell to return as our President.

The extremity of the crisis had thus been avoided but a rift had been created which was never to be healed. The notion that the failure of the Movement was to be attributed exclusively, or even primarily, to this split is wholly untenable. But there can be no doubt that the creation of the Committee of 100, and the furore surrounding its birth, had a highly deleterious effect on CND, even though, arguably, it 'made considerable impact, [and] aroused enthusiasm'[144] in the wider Movement. As has already been noted, there is considerable evidence that Russell was heavily under the influence of Ralph Schoenman at this time, and this may explain something of Russell's behaviour. However, Peggy Duff was probably correct in arguing that it was Russell himself who had misinterpreted both the feelings of the executive and the feelings of the Movement as a whole:

He probably expected and hoped that the Executive would repudiate the chairman and beg the president to come back. They did not do this, partly because Lord Russell's tactics had been unwise, had laid him open to charges of bad faith, and had enormously helped the canon; partly because the great majority of campaigners were quite unreasonable. They did not want to choose between the president and the chairman. They wanted them both.[145]

Whatever the motivations, the impact of the divisions and conflicts was profound and longstanding. At the most obvious level, Russell refused the repeated requests to return as CND presid-

---

[144] Ronald Clark, *The Life of Bertrand Russell*, London, 1975, p. 582.
[145] Duff, op. cit., 174.

ent, and the Campaign was thus robbed of its most prestigious and charismatic leader. The existence of two organizations which were portrayed as being, and to some extent were in reality, in conflict gravely weakened the Movement. For the CND leadership one of the most depressing and worrying aspects of this division was the change of focus away from the moral campaign against nuclear weapons and towards a more politicized conception of campaign activities.[146] Above all, though, the conflict resulted in a concentration of Movement energies on the *internal* disputes over the tactics, strategy, policies, and politics of the Movement itself. 'To sit with Russell or stand with Collins' was not entirely a media-created question: it did reflect a basic division in the Movement which went beyond the question of whether or not civil disobedience could be justified in a 'democratic society'. From late 1960 onwards all the political, cultural, ideological, and generational divisions which had always been inherent in the Movement came to the surface and boiled over into explicit and public conflict. The organizational division between CND and the Committee of 100, and the tactical difference over civil disobedience, served both to symbolize and to articulate this range of conflict. The Committee of 100 thus acted as a negative catalyst as far as the CND leadership was concerned, and marked a qualitative rise in conflict, differentiated from the CND/DAC problems which Canon Collins had always felt could be contained.

Of more immediate importance, as far as the CND leaders were concerned, was the effect on the attempt to consolidate, or more accurately defend, the recent victory at the Labour Party conference. The Committee of 100 weakened gravely CND's prospects in four crucial ways: first, it alienated Labour Movement leaders, and in all probability a large proportion of working-class Labour voters, because extra-parliamentary, direct action politics (particularly when linked in to the quasi-revolutionary rhetoric of many of

---

[146] The Committee of 100 also claimed, of course, and with some justification, that it too based its perspective and strategy upon fundamentally moral considerations. But, for the CND leadership, the Committee's insistence upon civil disobedience and associated militant tactics diverted attention away from the essentially moral and single issue message of the Campaign. This in turn, it was felt, led to the whole Movement being perceived by both 'the public' and the decision makers as essentially *revolutionary* in orientation. (And this was in fact the ideological position of important sections of the Committee.)

The ideological orientations of the various sections of the Committee are discussed in detail in ch. 5.

the Committee's leaders and spokesmen) offended the most central principles of the Labour Movement's parliamentary socialist ideology.[147] Secondly, partly because of this alienation, it made CND's arguments over the issue of unilateralism more difficult to put over in the Labour Party: there was more concern with the wider politics of the Movement, and the issues involved in whether civil disobedience could be justified. Thirdly, there was a strong feeling, which had a considerable basis in reality, that the politics of the Movement overall was moving, if not lurching, to the left; this made it far easier for Gaitskell and the Campaign for Democratic Socialism to point to the links between unilateralism and neutralism, Communist and pacifist influences, and anarchistic tendencies in the Movement (this was a particularly effective part of the 'smear campaign' mounted by the CDS in 1961 prior to the Labour Party conference). Finally, and most important of all, it had a disastrous effect on the leadership's attempts to focus CND's whole attention on the Labour party: for many of CND's activists this was always a distasteful, 'political' option anyway, as has been seen, and the creation of the Committee of 100 strengthened considerably the direct action, extra-parliamentary wing of the Movement for which Labourism *per se* held few if any attractions.

This combination of factors effectively destroyed whatever chance CND might have had of holding the Labour Party to its unilateralist decisions of 1960. Closely related to this, however, and perhaps even more important, was the loss of direction and control which the CND leadership experienced from early 1961 onwards. 1961 was definitely the 'Committee of 100's year', in terms of Movement success, prominence, and creativity, whilst CND floundered and lost its sense of purpose.

The fact that CND passed so quickly from a position of seemingly irresistible and progressive success to one of frustration, disillusionment, and failure was neither coincidence nor accident. Of course, much of the specific unfolding of events can be traced to particular circumstances, juxtapositions, and personal conflicts and relationships. But, fundamentally, the factors that brought success to CND contained also the seeds of CND's problems in 1961 and beyond.

From approximately November 1960 it can be seen, with

[147] All the Labour Party figures interviewed in connection with this study confirmed this view (Michael Foot, Olive Gibbs, Frank Allaun, and Ian Mikardo).

hindsight, that CND was in decline. The peak of CND's achievement[148] was undoubtedly to be found in the period from the huge Aldermaston March of 1960 through to the triumph of the Labour Party conference in the autumn. Much of importance occurred in the Movement in general from 1961 to 1965, but, in overall terms, it was a story of decline and dissension, particularly in relation to CND. It is to an analysis of this decline, and the varied issues which characterized the Movement in these years, that attention is now turned.

[148] This decline was not apparent at the time. Indeed, as is discussed in ch. 3, in terms of the number of groups and the size of Aldermaston Marches, CND was *growing* in 1961 and 1962. However, in *political* terms CND had reached something of a dead end by early 1961.

3

PROBLEMS AND DECLINE
CND 1961–1965

ALTHOUGH the analysis here will be concerned largely with the decline of the Movement, it must be borne in mind that this decline was by no means apparent to the mass of activists (or indeed to the leaders). As late as 1963–4 many in the Movement still believed that the Campaign was growing, that the unilateralist cause would eventually prevail—in short, that the Movement would succeed. Moreover, there was considerable justification, in terms of numbers of activists involved in groups, and of numbers on the Aldermaston March, for this contention, at least in 1961 and 1962, and arguably as late as 1963.[1] And it must be remembered that although *CND* may have been in relative decline, 1961 was a year of dramatic *success* for the Committee of 100, as already noted. Moreover, despite a series of major set-backs in 1962, there was a renewed growth of activism and support for the Committee in 1963, around both the 'Spies for Peace' initiative, and the demonstrations organized to protest at the visit of Queen Frederica.[2]

None the less, for CND, 1961–2 saw a continuation of the problems which had dogged the organization in 1960. Reference has been made above to the 1961 CND conference and the demo-cratization proposals which were adopted. This conference also

[1] This was confirmed by the public pronouncements of many of CND's leaders and committees, as was to be expected. The evidence of increased support was also striking, however: the Aldermaston Marches of 1961, 1962, and 1963 were all massive (1962 probably being the largest of all CND's demonstrations in this period). The support also manifested itself in increased financial contributions to the Campaign which enabled CND to move, in 1961, from Fleet Street to Carthusian Street. In 1962, the Campaign increased the accommodation available in these premises (the ground floor and basement were acquired). More importantly, extra staff were taken on in 1962: an office manager with increased clerical support staff, and two part-time staff—Stuart Hall as literature officer, and Bruce Reid as press officer (with David Boulton already part-time editor of *Sanity*). (CND annual report 1961–2, CND archive.)

[2] See ch. 5.

moved CND closer to the Committee of 100 and civil disobedience.
CND, DAC, and the Committee of 100 must be regarded, stated
one successful resolution, as 'three techniques in a united attack on
preparations of nuclear war'; moreover, the Committee of 100 was
to be congratulated on the timeliness of its first demonstration,
and full co-operation between the Committee and the Scottish
campaign on anti-Polaris actions was to be encouraged.[3] However,
the executive did manage to maintain CND's clear differentiation
from the Committee of 100 on the policy level. There was, though,
a move to invite Russell to resume the presidency of the campaign.
The possibility of a damaging and bitter debate was avoided by the
prompt action of Alasdair MacIntyre, who moved that a vote be
taken on the resolution without any discussion. The resolution was
carried by a large majority, and 'those who stood for conciliation
rather than confrontation heaved a sigh of relief'.[4] But this did leave
a ticklish problem for CND's leaders. The new constitution did not
provide for a president—and J. B. Priestley, long since disillusioned
with the way CND was going, had used this as a convenient excuse
for resigning as vice-president. Collins eventually wrote to Russell,
on 13 April, more than a month after the conference, asking him
whether he would be willing to serve as president 'regardless of
whosoever they may elect to the other offices'.[5] Russell replied on
15 May at some length, stating his view on the need for civil
disobedience, and arguing that it would not be feasible for him to
be president of both the Committee of 100 and CND, given the
disagreements over strategy and tactics. In his reply, Collins took a
firm, some would say intransigent, line. It was the attempt to run
two mass movements, at the same time and to the same end, he
argued, which presented a great danger.

Actions such as those which are from time to time undertaken by Direct
Action involving a small number of people with supporting demonstrations
by the Campaign itself, are, I am sure, welcomed by all. But it was quite
clear at the Annual Conference of CND that the vast majority in the
Campaign does not desire that the Campaign as such should involve itself
during the next twelve months in civil disobedience.
I have on more than one occasion stated in public, and on many
occasions to the Executive of the Campaign, that I would be quite happy to

[3] CND annual report 1961–2, CND archive.
[4] Peggy Duff, *Left, Left, Left,* London, 1971, p. 175.
[5] Ibid., 176.

work with you again should you come back as President. I am still of the same mind.[6]

The final opportunity for reuniting, under a broad umbrella structure, CND and the Committee of 100, was thus lost. As Peggy Duff has commented, had Russell's reply gone, not to Collins as the (re-elected) chairman of the council and executive, but to the conference, 'there is every likelihood that the campaign would have insisted that there was no reason why the president of the committee should not also be president of the campaign.'[7] Probably, the political and ideological differences had developed too far to make this a realistic prospect. But the tension between these two powerful personalities (in Russell's case reinforced by the advice and influence of his closest advisers, Ralph Schoenman and Rev. Michael Scott) ensured that the two organizations could not be brought together. By the time of the next CND Annual Conference, in May 1962, the moment had passed. The Committee was past its peak, and was anyway falling far more under the influence of anarchist ideas and becoming more radical in its overall political perspectives; Ralph Schoenman had been allowed to remain in Britain only if he took no part in organizing demonstrations; and Russell himself had begun to lose interest in the Nuclear Disarmament Movement *per se,* and was turning his extraordinary energies and talents to other related, but separate, political activities.

As a postscript to this discussion of the Collins/Russell relationship it is worth noting, briefly, the views of each man on the other. In his autobiography, Canon Collins has given a not unsympathetic, but not uncritical, summary of his opinion of Russell's role in the Movement.

On personal grounds I was, and remain, sad at the loss of a relationship I enjoyed. Lord Russell is an aristocrat to his finger-tips, and has all an aristocrat's impatience with democratic ways. He is a man for whom I have great respect and high regard. A little vain, perhaps; but he has much to be vain about. ... Whatever differences of opinion or personal difficulties have arisen between us—and regrettably they have—I think every human being ought to be grateful to Lord Russell, grateful to a man who was not prepared to sit back and rest upon his achievements and his prestige, but who has devoted himself by every means in his power to expose and to

[6] Letter from Collins to Russell, 19 May 1961, CND archive.
[7] Duff, op. cit., 178.

resist the folly and immorality of nuclear weapons and other means of mass destruction, and of all that is associated with a defence strategy based upon them.[8]

In a private conversation Collins was rather more explicitly critical, however:

The story of our meetings [i.e. between Collins and Russell—see ch. 2] is really fantastic if the truth were to be told. . . . During the discussions Russell would go upstairs, and it was quite obvious that Schoenman and Michael Scott were there to advise him—he would come down and go back on what we had agreed—again, obviously at their instigation. So we went on and on and on. We got to an agreement [i.e. the statement of Amity]—and then he *completely* broke the agreement as soon as I left England . . . this wasn't Russell, unless he'd been worked on, and Russell was a very vain old man, a great man, a very great man, but a very, *very* vain man. . . . vanity grows with age. . . . I think he just adored having those two adoring younger people around him and he was getting ga-ga, getting near it. . . . a pathetic figure being pushed around in a bath chair with Michael Scott and Schoenman blowing his nose periodically for him.[9]

There are no such explicit (or lengthy) summaries of Russell's view on Collins either in his autobiography or in Ronald Clark's very full and authoritative biography.[10] Nevertheless there can be no doubt of Russell's dislike of and even contempt for Collins.

By the summer of 1960 Russell had come to the conclusion that 'the voice of the Church militant, epitomized by Collins's

---

[8] Collins, op. cit., 325. It is also instructive to note the tension that existed between Canon Collins and Rev. Michael Scott. Although both radical Anglican Churchmen, pacifists, and committed to the unilateralist Movement, they differed sharply over their approach to the strategy and priorites to be adopted. As early as 1958 they had disagreed over the correct approach of the Movement to the Labour Party (with Scott rejecting any form of co-operation or liaison with the political parties). (Canon Collins, in conversation with the author, Jan. 1978.) Moreover, Scott was from the outset a leading activist in the DAC, and opposed to CND's whole approach. Collins has described Scott, rather disingenuously one suspects, as being 'a sweet and lovely man in many respects but . . . easily led astray' (ibid.). There is probably much truth in Peggy Duff's observation: 'I don't think he [Scott] likes John. They both, you see, operate on Africa' (in conversation with the author, Jan. 1978). There was certainly an element of political and professional jealousy over the African connection (and a measure of disagreement in that Scott favoured more than did Collins a non-violent direct action strategy in Africa), in addition to the specific and explicit differences they had in the context of the Nuclear Disarmament Movement.

[9] Collins, in conversation.

[10] Ronald W. Clark, *The Life of Bertrand Russell*, London, 1975.

chairmanship of CND, was becoming little more than a whisper in
the parish magazine',[11] and by the autumn this opinion had hardened into the conviction that 'I could not continue in my position
as President of the CND, which necessitated work with its chairman'.[12] Russell's antipathy to Collins appears to have related
entirely to personal and political matters, and not to have had any
religious dimension to it.[13] Rather, Russell saw Collins as an essentially trivial man, a small-scale, unimaginative, and small-minded
man. Above all, however, it is quite clear from the correspondence
noted above that Russell regarded Collins as devious, unreliable,
and domineering.

Which, if either, of them was correct is a debatable question. But
whatever the truth, the fact remains that the Movement was
weakened considerably by the whole affair and the aftermath of
bitterness which persisted.

THE CAMPAIGN IN 1961–1962

Despite all the dramatic political happenings in the hierarchies of
the Movement, a wide range of campaigning activities also took
place during 1961. For the first time the Aldermaston March of
Easter 1961 was divided into two separate marches, one beginning
from the NATO base at Wethersfield and the other from Aldermaston, coming together 'precisely on time in Parliament Square on the
afternoon of Easter Monday' and marching 'side by side up
Whitehall to Trafalgar Square'.[14] This decision had been preceded
by considerable discussion in the Movement, with the executive
committee eventually deciding in favour of the two-pronged march.

In the event the March was a reasonable success, although
perhaps lacking the excitement and dynamism of 1960. This was
due in part to the dominance of the Committee of 100, in part to
the realization that the battle for the Labour Party was in all probability lost, and in part to the growing ritualization of the whole
process. This last point was of some importance in the overall
context of CND. The Campaign had, by 1961, begun to 'run out of
steam', and out of ideas and originality.[15] CND never solved this

[11] Ibid., 575.
[12] Bertrand Russell, *Autobiography,* vol. iii, London, 1969, p. 111.
[13] All the interviewees who were asked about this (Peggy Duff, Canon Collins, Jacquetta Hawkes, Arthur Goss, among others) confirmed the complete absence of any Christian/atheist tensions.   [14] CND annual report 1961–2.

problem of course—either in general or specific terms—and the attempt to vary the pattern in 1961 must in that sense be judged a failure.

In conventional terms, however, the March *was* a success:

In spite of torrential rain on all four days of both marches, the numbers continued to increase as in previous years. While it is not possible accurately to estimate the numbers taking part on the final day,[16] nearly 7000 left Aldermaston on Good Friday and the March from Wethersfield was as big.

The international section was also far larger than in previous years, mainly due to the large contingent from Western Europe organized by the European Federation Against Nuclear Arms.[17]

Other activities in 1961 were dominated by three groups of factors: the success of the Committee of 100, the failure of CND to maintain and consolidate its success in the Labour Party resulting in the defeat of CND policies at the 1961 conference, and the worsening international situation. The first two of these factors have been discussed in some detail already. The international situation, against which background all the Peace Movement's activities took place, was of course ultimately of far greater significance. The Berlin crisis was followed by the announcement of the Soviet decision to resume nuclear testing, and this in turn was followed by

[15] In the specific context of the Aldermaston March, the point was well put by G. H. Petch. Although the March provided the opportunity 'for a good kick . . . at the Establishment, at the abstract image of authority . . . at respectable conventions in general, [and was thus] a release, a satisfaction . . . [the net result was to serve] as a safety-valve-release [which] serves the Establishment . . . by reducing pressure of frustration, by making easier and more likely mass acceptance of the Establishment, for the rest of the year. We have expressed our feelings. We have protested. We go home. We resume the normal round. . . . The March becomes a part of the Establishment; what is more, necessary to it . . . that it may continue . . . unchanged. . . . It is an urgent immediate priority for the CND that the Aldermaston March image of itself in the public mind—of a mass governed by emotion—be replaced by the image and the reality of "minds working against nuclear war" ' (G. H. Petch, 'The CND and Public Opinion: Methods and Principles of Practice', duplicated discussion document, June–July 1960, Arthur Goss's private papers, loaned to the author).

[16] According to *Peace News*, 31 Mar. 1961, there were 40,000–50,000 in Trafalgar Square for the final rally, and, in addition to the international contingent noted in CND's report, there was a significant working-class presence. (This latter point is partly explained by the CP prominence on the March following their 'change of line'. Peggy Duff, in conversation, has recalled that in 1961, the CP 'flooded the thing with banners. And the Canon was on pretty good terms with the Communists——he handled them quite cleverly; he complained about 1961 and the next year they disciplined the number of banners on the March.')

[17] CND annual report, 1961–2.

the American announcement of a resumption of testing. On all
these fronts CND was active. 'Very early in the Berlin crisis [CND]
issued a statement . . . to the Press. It was, of course, ignored by the
majority of newspapers.'[18] It was also issued as a leaflet, which was
widely distributed by Campaign groups, and on 10 September
CND organized a Trafalgar Square rally on the Berlin issue.
Protests against the tests took the form of a march from the
Embankment to the Russian Embassy on 3 September, followed by
various protests until the series finished, and a similar march and
deputation were organized to the American Embassy following the
announcement of the Christmas Island tests. The 1962 Aldermaston March also finished with a silent demonstration in Grosvenor
Square on Easter Monday, and on the following Thursday, after the
announcement of the American test series, mass distribution of
individual letters to the Embassy was organized by the London
Region in co-operation with the national Campaign. Following this
a vigil outside the Embassy was mounted. Finally, a mass lobby of
Parliament, on the two issues of Berlin and the resumption of
nuclear testing, was organized on 18 October in co-operation with
a number of other organizations. Six thousand people took part,
finishing with a torchlight march to the Russian Embassy. The net
effect of all this on the Campaign was, in parochial terms,
extremely beneficial. There was a considerable upsurge of public
interest and support following on from the heightened international
tension.

   It was in the light of this growth in support that the executive had
changed its mind about the format for the Easter demonstration in
1962. It had been intended to organize a token Aldermaston March
of 100–150, with interim local group activity taking place at
various locations in a ten-mile radius from central London, with a
big march into central London on the final day culminating in a
rally in Hyde Park. Given the increased support, however, and
bearing in mind that 'the Council was also aware that Easter
Marches were already being planned, not only in many European
countries but all over the world and that Aldermaston has become
an international weekend for demonstrations against nuclear
weapons . . . the Council accepted the logic of events',[19] and recom-

[18] Ibid.
[19] Notes from Groups incorporating decisions of the national council and
national executive committee, 24 Nov. 1961, CND archive.

mended to the executive committee that 'a traditional March from Aldermaston' be organized for Easter 1962. In the event the 1962 Aldermaston March was, according to most sources, the biggest of the period, with approximately 150,000 at the final rally in Hyde Park. As noted earlier, following the huge rally there was a final march through Whitehall, and an impressive silent demonstration in Grosvenor Square. Easter 1962 was

also notable for the fact that many other marches and demonstrations took place all over the world, and for the delegations which were sent from the March to the United Nations in New York and the Disarmament Committee in Geneva. Easter demonstrations have become an integral part of a world nuclear disarmament movement.[20]

This did not appear to be a movement in decline: and there were other manifestations of success and growth in 1961–2. The annual report recorded 'a tremendous increase in the sales of literature and of badges. . . . Extra staff have been taken on to deal with invoicing and packing.' The executive committee accepted a proposal that CND should publish 'a quarterly magazine for discussion on a high level of issues involved in nuclear disarmament'. The circulation of *Sanity* rose markedly during the year: it had risen by September 1961 to 15,000, and by May 1962 it fluctuated 'about the 30,000 mark'. Plans were in hand to double its size (to eight pages), and 'in the not too distant future to publish the paper more regularly than once monthly'. (By 1963 sales of *Sanity* had risen to about 40,000).

In terms of the specialist groups the annual report noted that 1961–2 was also a year of considerable activity. The Christian group 'organized a number of activities including the Armistice Day Service in Trafalgar Square on 10 November . . . a conference of students . . . and . . . [later in 1962] sent a deputation to meet the Archbishop of Canterbury'. The Scientists' group proved particularly important in the context of the resumption of nuclear testing, and the *Scientists' Bulletin* increased its circulation. Again, following the resumption of testing, the Women's group, which since 1960 had ceased to operate as a separate unit in CND,

became very active again. A Women's Meeting at the Central Hall, Westminster, on January 15 and the Day for Peace on March 7 were carefully planned and effective and included a new type of demonstration —a Mime performed on the steps of St Paul's Cathedral. A number of

[20] CND annual report, 1961–2.

deputations were sent to organizations such as the British Council of Churches, and on March 14 a deputation . . . spent an hour with the Prime Minister. They have also co-operated with a number of women's organizations abroad. . . . Diana Collins, Dr Antoinette Pirie, and Mrs Pat Horner went to Geneva with a delegation of about fifty women from this organization to lobby the Disarmament Committee. On their return a reception was arranged at the House of Commons and a small meeting at the Conway Hall.

Perhaps most important of all for the CND leadership, 1961–2 saw considerable advances on the international front. In June 1961 it was reported to the executive committee that Lord Simon of Wythenshawe had donated £2,000 to CND on the specific understanding that it be 'earmarked for work in connection with the European and International Movements'.[21] The European Federation Against Nuclear Arms became more influential and more active. In 1961–2 a very active European movement had developed and a number of joint initiatives took place.[22] The Federation was representative of many European countries, but the CND leadership was firmly in control: Canon Collins was one of two presidents (the other being Heinrich Buchbinder from Switzerland) and Peggy Duff one of two secretaries (the other being Christian Mayer-Amery of the Munich committee).

Canon Collins organized a successful international conference in London in September 1961. Following this meeting the possibility of establishing an 'international organization (in reality, an organization of peace groups from the West and the non-aligned states) was discussed, but, in the absence of funds and a secretariat', it was agreed 'to appoint a small committee of three to promote continuing contact and co-operation between organizations'.[23]

Finally, the Accra assembly, which took place on 21–8 June 1962, was an important further attempt by President Nkrumah of

[21] Executive committee minutes, 30 June 1961, CND archive.

[22] For example: 'pressure on Governments to send an affirmative reply to the United Nations Organization concerning willingness to join a non-nuclear club, as proposed in the Unden Place and in the resolution accepted by UNO in the autumn of 1961. In Norway and Denmark this pressure was particularly effective.' (CND annual report, 1961–2.)

There was also widespread co-operation on Easter marches. Frank Allaun, Fenner Brockway, and Pat Arrowsmith, for example, took part in three West German marches.

[23] CND annual report, 1961–2. (The subcommittee consisted of Collins, Buchbinder, and Dr Homer Jack of the American organization SANE.)

Ghana to mount a joint peace initiative with Western peace leaders in order to achieve both nuclear disarmament (especially the removal of European nuclear weapons from Africa), and the mobilization of an anti-imperialist African Unity movement.[24] This was an important initiative and showed CND—and Canon Collins personally—making a serious commitment to the neutralist policies of the Campaign, at least at the formalized and 'safe' governmental level.

However, for various reasons most of these initiatives were relatively short-lived. The ambitious initiatives in the non-aligned world, in particular, were dealt a series of death blows by the fall of Nkrumah, the developing pattern of African and Asian nationalism, and a whole complex of factors affecting the pattern of ideological, political, and economic structures in the Third World (Asia and South America as well as Africa).

PROBLEMS FOR CND

All this was on the 'plus side' as far as CND's executive committee was concerned. But, as has been seen, 1961–2 was overwhelmingly a troubled time for CND's leaders. In addition to the factors already discussed, two areas of crucial importance marked 1961–2 irrevocably as a period of political crisis and ultimately decline for CND: the controversy over INDEC (the Independent Nuclear Disarmament Election Committee) which ended not so much in bitterness as in indecisive and untidy failure; and the 'successful' resolution of the Cuban missile crisis in late 1962, which had profound effects on both the politics and the psychology of CND's campaign.

The Independent Nuclear Disarmament Election Committee

From the early summer of 1961 it was apparent that the 1961 Labour conference would reject unilateralist policies. CND's triumph of 1960 was thus certain to be short-lived, and the leadership's central strategy of winning over the Labour Party suffered a

---

[24] Far from being 'an entirely new venture', as CND's annual report claimed, this was very much an attempt by Nkrumah to follow on from the ultimately unsuccessful DAC-inspired protest against the French nuclear tests in the Sahara, which had been based in Ghana. For a full discussion of DAC involvement, see ch. 4.

major and irreversible set-back. Indeed, from mid-1961 onwards
this whole strategy lacked credibility. By the time the conference
took place a considerable body of opinion had built up inside CND
which was opposed to working through the Labour Party and
favoured an independent political initiative. Indeed, the eventual
Labour Party situation was even worse than CND's leaders had
feared: not only did the conference reject unilateralist policies, 'the
Parliamentary Labour Party [failed] to accept even the resolutions
on Polaris and German troops'.[25] As the CND's annual report
noted, 'it was perhaps inevitable that [these defeats] . . . would
produce doubts in the Campaign about the efficacy of advance
through the Labour Party'.

In the Orpington by-election, which the Liberal Party won from
the Conservatives with a major electoral swing, some members of
London Region CND (including Nigel Young, Michael Craft, and
Laurie Kershaw) had been keen to put forward an independent
nuclear disarmament candidate. The idea did not materialize,
however, and London Region had to be content with organizing an
intensive propaganda and leaflet campaign in the constituency. But
this episode was indicative of the ground-swell of opinion in the
Movement in support of independent nuclear disarmament candidates some time prior to the formal inauguration of INDEC.

The first formal attempt to commit CND to this new radical
stance took place at the meeting of the national council of CND on
29 October 1961. At this meeting an executive statement was
proposed:

That CND should:

(1) undertake intensive activities in constituencies, using election
techniques but without a candidate: (*a*) during by-elections and
(*b*) also at other times in constituencies selected by the National
Executive in consultation with Regions;
(2) and should not, for the time being, put up candidates at by-
elections.

Two amendments were proposed to this. The first, from Laurie
Kershaw, urged a straightforward reconsideration of CND's
exclusive allegiance to the Labour Party:

That this Council urges the National Executive Committee to have the
question of nominating CND candidates at selected by-elections

[25] CND annual report, 1961–2.

thoroughly discussed throughout the movement and that the possibility of such nominations be kept before the NEC as a possibility for future action.[26]

The second amendment, from Michael Howard, although more provisional and hedged around with qualifications, urged a similar reconsideration.

Both these amendments were lost, however, and the substantive resolution was agreed by a large majority.[27] The meeting then agreed that the Labour advisory committee (LAC) be asked to submit a report on political activity 'including their views on a question put by Laurie Kershaw: what advice should CND give to supporters in a constituency where there is an independent candidate supporting the policy of the Campaign?'[28] The LAC complied with this request and produced the following guide-lines which were submitted to the national council on 3 December 1961: 'That the Campaign should obtain answers to a questionnaire from all candidates, that it should publicise the answers widely both to supporters and to the Press, and that it should campaign objectively for its own policy during the by-election campaign'. A recommendation that CND should give no positive advice to supporters as to how they should vote was rejected and referred to the executive committee.

On 17 December the executive committee agreed the following proposals:

(*a*) that the Executive Committee should draw up a suitable questionnaire during the Weekend School from January 5th–7th;
(*b*) that the questionnaire should be sent out to all candidates by the National Office;
(*c*) that the Executive Committee should decide whether, in their opinion, any candidates were genuine supporters of the policy of the Campaign;
(*d*) that Groups be advised to support any candidates considered to be genuine supporters of CND, but to pay due respect to, and recognise the existence of the party allegiances of individual members.[29]

This was approved by the national council on 18 March 1962, subject to annual conference decision.

[26] National council of CND minutes, 29 Oct. 1961, Modern Records Centre, University of Warwick.
[27] Ibid.
[28] Ibid.
[29] CND annual report, 1961–2.

The CND leadership thus maintained its Labourist strategy, if not intact, at least only modified in its essentials. This was another moment of considerable importance for CND. The whole political and strategic policy of the leadership of CND hinged on its conviction that its policy objectives could and would be achieved only via the Labour Party. By 1961 this strategy lacked credibility, as we have seen. The alternative to this, within that section of the Movement which believed in orthodox parliamentary political activity, rested, at least in the short term, on persuading the Movement to adopt a bold political alternative which would challenge Labour and enable the popular strength of the Movement to be articulated in *political* terms. The problems inherent in this strategy were both numerous and formidable. The strength of both the CND leadership and the Labour Movement (especially the 'Tribunite' left in the Labour Party) in CND ensured that the Labourist strategy would be very difficult to overturn. Even more importantly, the 'radical wing' of the Movement—to be found largely in the Committee of 100—was predominantly hostile to any kind of Labourist strategy, and was uninterested in, even positively hostile to, orthodox parliamentary or socialist politics.

The burden of arguing for the alternative strategy therefore rested largely with the activists of the New Left, who occupied an influential position in CND by 1961–2. But there was a central ambivalence in the New Left position. Had the New Left argued unanimously and forcefully for a break with Labourism and the Labour Party, then there might have been a chance of formulating a new socialist party, or at the least an autonomous and identifiable New Left movement based on CND support but encompassing wider humanistic socialist concerns. The New Left was *not* unanimous on this, however. Edward Thompson and Stuart Hall were enthusiastic in their advocacy of 'electoral interventions' to defeat Labour, and were supported by Peggy Duff. But the fundamental ambivalence of the New Left was demonstrated by the unwillingness of the *New Left Review* board to endorse proposals along these lines in October 1961.

Michael Foot denounced the proposal to put up occasional independent CND candidates at by-elections, as 'poison',[30] and

---

[30] Duff, op. cit., 195. At the meeting immediately following the Labour Party conference decisions at Blackpool, Stuart Hall ('in a state of dormouse-like torpor'

remained steadfast in his desire for unity. The issue of endorsement of independent candidates came up at a closed NLR editorial board meeting in late October with Foot present. No decision was taken and Foot's strong opposition to independent candidates had much to do with this impasse. Thompson in a private letter declared that a majority had favoured independent candidates before the meeting.[31]

Thompson also stated that Foot had dissuaded a number of them at the meeting. Nevertheless, a group of people in CND did persist with the idea. One of the key initiators was Michael Craft, chairman of London Region and a member of CND national council. In 1962 the new organization, INDEC, was established. In its statement of aims Michael Craft argued that

the Campaign has now reached the position of a quasi-political movement which has a greater potentiality for reshaping the traditional structure of British politics than any movement for half a century. With its group and regional structure, its considerable educational programme, its capacity to raise finance and produce literature, and above all its flair for finding new methods of publicity, it has become a force to be reckoned with in politics.

The document went on to argue that independent CND candidates would bring the issue of unilateralism to the fore and enable CND supporters to vote. Moreoover, it was argued rather optimistically that it would strengthen CND's position in relation to the Labour Party because the Party would be in danger of losing votes if it did not support unilateralism.

In a subsequent document INDEC made a somewhat shrewder and more realistic political statement. Arguing that 'we should all join the Labour Party and Trade Unions and thus transform them', INDEC went on to claim that

whilst it remained very important to continue and win the struggle in the Labour Party . . . it is now pointless to pretend that victory is just around the corner or that this should be the *sole* element of our political strategy.

through lack of sleep) and Peggy Duff confronted the Labour CNDers on this issue. 'The meeting to a man was wholly opposed to the proposal. . . . It was rather like going to a meeting of catholic fathers and putting forward a proposal for free and unlimited abortion. We really got thrashed.'

[31] David R. Holden, *The First New Left In Britain, 1956–62*, Ph.D. thesis, University of Wisconsin-Madison, 1976, p. 319. The sources for this statement were: private papers loaned by Michael Barratt Brown; minutes of the *New Left Review* editorial board, 21–2 Oct. 1961; and a letter from Edward Thompson to Michael Barratt Brown, 2 Nov. 1961.

... The purpose of INDEC is to provide the beginnings of this in an efficient and organized fashion. It is *not* forming a new Political Party but proposing a new tactic, and its job will cease when it has forced the issue onto the hustings and away from the suffocation of the party machines. This additional weapon in the armoury of the CND movement will help to force unilateralism as a priority issue in the labour movement. ... All groups will know that there are many individuals who will neither march nor sit, but are in sympathy and, given the opportunity, will vote ... we believe that selected political intervention in by-elections to be a viable *additional* tactic in the fight against nuclear weapons.

Such arguments were not convincing, however. They had neither the radical appeal of the New Left stance of Thompson *et al.*, in which the INDEC idea was linked to the positive neutralism and humanistic socialism which might have formed the basis of a genuinely new politics, nor the realistic possibility of securing Labour Party support for unilateralism through exerting the political pressure of a mass of voters backing only unilateralist candidates. INDEC in fact argued *within* Labourist assumptions and thus failed to create a new mood, or a distinctive presence. Thus the INDEC initiative was 'not very successful'.[32] And, for the New Left, it 'was the crowning failure ... to achieve a viable fusion of old and new radical politics that would enable the New Left to act simultaneously within and apart from traditional Labour movement and socialist channels'.[33] Although Edward Thompson supported the idea of INDEC, neither he nor John Saville joined the INDEC board (although Stuart Hall, John Rex, and Mervyn Jones did). Equally important, Peggy Duff, although very keen on the idea, 'had to recognise that I could not continue with my private campaign for candidates and remain the general secretary. It seemed more important to stay, so I did.'[34] Pat Arrowsmith resigned from INDEC only a month after its creation, because she believed that only mass industrial action would secure nuclear disarmament. (It is rather surprising that she had ever become involved in such an orthodox socialist electoral body, given her own clearly identified political perspective).

INDEC was proscribed by the Labour Party before CND's 1962 conference took place, but this led to no spirited left-wing defiance, and the CND conference had no hesitation in backing the executive

[32] Duff, op. cit., 196.   [33] Holden, op. cit., 323.
[34] Duff, op. cit., 195.

resolution, which was moved by Michael Foot on behalf of the Labour advisory committee. It attempted to turn back the campaign clock to the earliest days, when the élite leadership had envisaged CND as a high-powered pressure group exerting influence and pressure Fabian-style through the conventional political system. This, of course, bore no resemblance to CND's real political position in 1962. The élite pressure group had long since given way to the mass extra-parliamentary movement. Nevertheless, the conference gave overwhelming backing to the resolution, and rejected equally heavily a resolution from Twickenham CND (where Michael Craft stood in the 1964 general election—and lost heavily[35]) proposing that CND 'give earnest consideration to sponsoring their own candidate where no other unilateralist is standing'.[36] Conference, however, did pass a further resolution which put INDEC on the same footing as the Committee of 100: 'CND did not do it, but campaigners were free to do as they please and could, as individuals, support any candidate'.[37] This was, typically, a tolerant, practical, and sensible stance for CND to take. It enabled the umbrella movement to continue. Rather than INDEC being ostracized, leading INDEC activists continued, more or less happily, in CND. Laurie Kershaw remained CND treasurer; and Michael Craft remained chairman of London Region and a member of CND national council.

After 1962 INDEC faded from prominence, and not until 1966, when Richard Gott fought Hull in a by-election on the issue of the Labour Government's support for America in the Vietnam war, was the original idea of an independent electoral presence really to make any sort of impact (and even here the actual result was very disappointing for the left). Part of the explanation of this failure lies, of course, in the profoundly conservative political culture of twentieth-century Britain. Moreover, on the more practical level, modern Britain is characterized in its political organization by a conservative electoral system which discriminates heavily against minority parties, and favours the two party system and the status quo.

Given this, and given the specific context of INDEC in CND and

---

[35] The Twickenham general election result in 1964 was: R. Gresham Cooke (Cons.): 27, 427; W. E. Wolff (Lab.): 15, 231; J. Woolfe (Lib.): 12,306; M. H. Craft (Ind. ND): 1,073; Cons. majority 12,196.
[36] CND annual conference 1962, cited in Duff, op. cit., 196.
[37] Duff, op. cit., 196.

the wider Movement, it is not surprising that the whole enterprise foundered. Nevertheless, in the circumstances of late 1961, with Labourism at such a low ebb, and the Nuclear Disarmament Movement gaining strength and becoming more politicized, there was a chance for a new political initiative on the British left to make a significant impact. The fact that INDEC was such a swift and ignominious failure was due, at least in part, to its inability to make a decisive and explicit ideological and political stand. The whole affair was chronically, but understandably, mishandled. Delay and confusion was followed by a half-hearted and unsuccessful attempt to appeal to a broad cross-section of the Movement, which resulted in fact in the alienation of a wide range of potential support.

The INDEC episode marked an important watershed. Perhaps the only alternative to the Labourism (and/or moralism) of the CND leadership, or the quasi-libertarian, quasi-revolutionary, extra-parliamentary activism of the Committee of 100, had lain in an independent, New Left socialist political initiative. The failure of INDEC thus had dire consequences both for the New Left and for the Nuclear Disarmament Movement.

The Cuban missile crisis

In the important but relatively narrow context of the development of the contemporary British left, the INDEC episode was certainly significant. On the world scale, however, the Cuban missile crisis of late 1962 dwarfed such seemingly parochial political concerns. Here, it seemed, was the holocaust so long predicted and campaigned against: the inevitable result of the mutually suicidal arms race. For a week, the Nuclear Disarmament Movement, in common with the bulk of the British, and indeed the international, community, prepared itself as best it could for what was to come.

The concern here is not to follow the fascinating and incredible role played by Bertrand Russell in the whole affair,[38] and still less to provide any account of the history and politics of the confrontation and its eventual resolution. Rather, concentration will be upon the nature of the response made by CND to the crisis, and its aftermath in terms of the effect upon the Movement.

Demonstrations were organized throughout Britain, on a fairly spontaneous, *ad hoc* basis, to protest against the confrontational

[38] See Bertrand Russell, *Unarmed Victory*, London, 1963.

attitudes of the super-powers over the Cuban missile crisis and the possibility of nuclear war resulting. In London, both CND and the Committee of 100 organized demonstrations—on the Sunday and Saturday of 'Cuba week' respectively. According to *Peace News* about 5,000 attended both demonstrations. The tenor was predominantly anti-American. Bertrand Russell set the tone with his telegrams and subsequent 'negotiations' with the USA and USSR leaders. His pronouncements, which were heavily influenced by Ralph Schoenman,[39] laid the burden of blame upon the USA.[40] *Peace News* noted that the demonstration at the US Embassy in Grosvenor Square was marked by chants of 'Cuba Si, Yanqui No', and only a small minority agreed to proceed to the USSR Embassy to make a similar protest there. For a time 'it looked as if there might be a fight between the anti-Americans and the Against-all-Missiles group'.[41]

This marked a growing anti-Americanism in both CND and the Committee of 100. To some extent this was obviously due to the objective situation in which the USA was taking aggressive action, rightly or wrongly, to defend what it saw as its essential interests. It was also due, however, to the increased left influence in the Movement—the New Left, the Communist Party, and the radical libertarians of the Committee of 100, rather than the Labour Party left. Many of these groups, particularly in the New Left, were enthusiastic supporters of Castro, Guevara, *et al.*, in broader ideological terms. From this time, the anti-American strand in the Movement became more and more dominant, culminating in the anti-Vietnam War movements and the second (British) New Left of 1967–8 and beyond.[42]

Even more important in Movement terms was the sudden loss of self-confidence, and the deadening feeling of powerlessness and

[39] See Clark, op. cit., 595–601.

[40] Ibid. Two of Russell's telegrams, sent on different days during 'Cuba week', illustrated this attitude: (Russell, *Unarmed Victory*, 31 and 46 respectively).
To President Kennedy: 'Your action desperate. Threat to human survival. No conceivable justification. Civilized man condemns it. We will not have mass murder. Ultimatum means war. I do not speak for power but plead for civilized man. End this madness.'
To Prime Minister Khrushchev: 'May I humbly appeal for your future help in lowering the temperature despite worsening situation. Your continued forebearance is our great hope. With my high regards and sincere thanks.'

[41] *Peace News*, 26 Oct. 1962.

[42] See Nigel Young, *An Infantile Disorder? The Crisis and Decline of the New Left*, London, 1977.

irrelevance that the crisis brought to activists. Richard Boston noted in his 'Cuba Diary' in *Peace News* of 2 November 1962: 'I went down to the American Embassy this evening. But the sense of futility was so great that I felt I was demonstrating more out of force of habit than because anything was being achieved.'

The national council of CND passed two resolutions calling on the 'British Government to denounce the blockade of Cuba' and declare Britain to be neutral in the event of war. Further, it urged the 'TUC to resolve that, in the event of an armed attack upon or invasion of Cuba the TUC would, if the British Government did not oppose such action, call for a General Strike'. In the light of the 'Proteus' having left Holy Loch, CND asked 'the Prime Minister to seek an immediate assurance from President Kennedy that "Proteus" will not return to British waters'.[43]

Militant sentiments these may have been, but it was quite obvious, both at the time and subsequently, that Britain's ability to influence the course of events was virtually non-existent. If this was the case—and if Russell's typically wry denials of any influence are also accepted[44]—the inability of the Movement to make any impact whatsoever on anything of relevance to the crisis was abundantly clear.[45]

With the resolution of the crisis, the intense *urgency* which had characterized all Movement activism evaporated. When all was said and done, the crisis had *not* resulted in nuclear holocaust; the deterrent arguments as far as 'ordinary people' were concerned,

[43] National council of CND minutes, 27 Oct. 1962, Modern Records Centre, University of Warwick.

[44] Russell is reported to have said to a friend in Penrhyndeudraeth, when the crisis was over: 'I do not consider that I have altered the course of history by one hair's breadth' (cited in Clark, op. cit., 600).

[45] This dramatic loss of credibility was apparent to activists too, as the notorious 'Flight to Ireland' by Pat Arrowsmith and Wendy Butlin dramatically made clear. Explaining their actions in a letter to the *Guardian,* they wrote: 'Last Tuesday night . . . the news . . . clearly indicated that the nuclear deterrent was on the point of failing—a point we had been making in public for five years. Within twenty four hours when there was practically certain to be a confrontation between Soviet missile-carrying ships and the United States blockade, it seemed almost inevitable that nuclear war would break out. It seemed to us that nothing useful could be achieved by ordinary people within 24 hours to avert this event. We therefore decided to go as swiftly as possible to a place where we might conceivably survive a nuclear war—the west coast of Ireland. . . . As the confrontation did not lead to nuclear war we returned to London on Saturday morning and joined in the action in Trafalgar Square that afternoon' (letter from Arrowsmith and Butlin, *Guardian,* 31 Oct. 1962).

had been vindicated. George Clark, although speaking impressionistically, and for himself rather than the Movement as a whole, has put the point well:

up until Cuba in '62 I think it's true to say that the nuclear issue superseded *everything,* but just everything. . . . Of course, Cuba changed all that: they could actually manage the thing intelligently . . . sooner or later they would make a mistake and the thing would go up. . . . *But* it was not within the decade: I think we could well go on living like this for two or three hundred years. . . . The whole kind of frenetic politics of total disaster of that period is difficult to recall.[46]

Despite the protestations of CND's leaders to the effect that the Cuban crisis has exacerbated the cold war, brought nuclear war nearer, and thus made the unilateralist case even more persuasive and urgent, there was no doubt that the prevailing mood, of both the country *and the Movement,* was one of relief that nuclear war had been avoided, and a lessening of tension and urgency on the nuclear issue. As far as the Movement was concerned the Cuban missile crisis thus marked a crucial downturn in activism. The spark had gone; activists breathed a sigh of relief, and devoted rather more time to ordinary life and rather less to campaign activities.[47]

From this time on, the Movement figured less in media reports (although there were exceptions in 1963, as will be discussed below), numbers on demonstrations began gradually to decrease, and the general level of Movement activity also began slowly but surely to decline. A qualitative change in the nature of the Movement thus took place following the Cuban missile crisis. This is not in any sense to argue that the crisis was the *sole* reason for the Movement's decline, but rather that it was a major contributory factor in a decline that was already in process as a result of a complex of quite other factors.

'Steps Towards Peace'

This is not the end of the story of the effect of the Cuban missile crisis upon the Movement, however. In addition to these negative political and psychological results, the crisis precipitated a

[46] George Clark, in conversation with the author, Jan. 1978.
[47] Clark recalled that '*dozens* of secretaries [of CND groups] told me they had to get back to ordinary life: there was no way they could go on at the same pitch of activity' (ibid.).

fundamental shift in CND policy. Again, it would be mistaken to ascribe this change entirely to the Cuban crisis. In Stuart Hall's opinion (and his opinion is significant as he was the chief architect of the new policy statement), the 'Steps Towards Peace' policy emanated from two contexts:

one was really an awareness that we had lost the 1960–61 battle and that as far as a Labour government was concerned they would not, having efficiently defeated it, make any concessions at all—so it was thinking, as it were, was there a minimal programme through which we could keep the issue alive, on the front bench as well as the back bench; secondly, it was undoubtedly a major response to Cuba—at that point I began to lose confidence in the proposition that a movement by Britain would have very significant international repercussions. What Cuba really said was that what really governs the nuclear balance is principally the Soviet or American naval strength; they would go to war or not go to war, blow you out of the ocean or not . . . depending where they were at![48]

The purpose of CND's new policy was to widen the basis of support for a unilateralist initiative.

Irresponsible actions by the USSR and the USA . . . have created many doubts about Britain's part in the arms race. . . . But those who have been led to doubt, but who nevertheless do not feel able to accept the full CND programme, must be encouraged to act, for two alternatives now exist. Either there will be a new intensification of the arms race, or, at last, a move towards disarmament. . . . The new programme . . . is a programme of *immediate steps*. CND will continue to campaign for total renunciation of nuclear weapons by Britain, and a withdrawal from nuclear alliances; but new emphasis will now be given to campaigning for more limited ends, in conjunction with individuals, organizations and newspapers which support these limited ends without feeling able to go all the way with CND.[49]

The new policy proposals, whilst unequivocally advocating the renunciation of British nuclear weapons, tests, and bases, also gave prominence to a range of other initiatives: disengagement in central Europe and the withdrawal of all nuclear weapons to the territories of the USA and USSR, opposition to a European nuclear deterrent, the establishment of 'nuclear free zones' on an ambitious basis (and including 'outer space'), and a new priority for support for the

[48] Stuart Hall, in conversation with the author, Apr. 1978.
[49] CND press statement, 'CND's New Three-point programme', 27 Nov. 1962, CND archive.

UN.[50] The objective behind the policy, as far as the politically sophisticated and radical drafters—notably Stuart Hall—were concerned, was to salvage the Movement from its impasse and to give it some realistic chance of exerting pressure within the Labour Movement, and within the wider, and greatly changed, political environment. There was no intention of reneging on the unilateralist commitment. The crucial point, however, was that this was not apparent either to Movement supporters or to the wider general public interested in the Movement. Moreover, the CND leadership accepted the proposals with some alacrity, in part because it appeared to be part of a process of reconverting the mass movement to a pressure group.

Reaction within the Movement was generally hostile. *Peace News* perhaps represented the criticisms of many activists when it claimed that the programme was too complex and detailed to appeal to the mass of supporters. Moreover, it was argued, the policy rejected the non-violent approach and effectively integrated the Movement into conventional politics. Peggy Duff replied: 'it is time that the disarmament movement in Britain realised that it is not operating in a vacuum and that it must concern itself with the realities of the political situation in the world.' There was thus a need to intervene in a situation where there is a 'total change in the arms race and the Cold War' after Cuba.[51]

The radical wing(s) of the Movement would have none of this, however. For a wide spectrum of CND supporters unilateralism was seen as the *sine qua non* of the Movement and the new policy

[50] According to Peggy Duff, the original idea for the 'Steps Towards Peace' proposals came from Stuart Hall, who thought that 'in the aftermath of the crisis, Governments might be sufficiently shaken to consider at least some steps towards a reduction of tension, to a lessening of the nuclear danger. He came to see me and suggested that CND should launch an interim programme for a few initial steps along these lines. It seemed eminently reasonable to me.

We sold the idea to the canon. Then we took it to the Executive Committee and Council. It was there that the mistake was made. They insisted on enlarging the initial steps from our original three which comprised withdrawal of nuclear weapons from all territories outside the USA and USSR, a test ban treaty and priority for the UN, to almost all the policy of CND with only one exception, withdrawal from NATO. It was this that did the damage, for 'Steps Towards Peace' came to be seen in the campaign as a deep-laid plot to drop the issue of NATO' (Duff, op. cit., 204).

But whilst the NATO issue was important for some CND supporters, it was the issue of unilateralism *per se* which was paramount. As is argued elsewhere in this study the NATO issue was seen as important only by the socialist elements in the Movement.

[51] Duff, *Peace News,* 7 Dec. 1962.

reneged, or appeared to renege, on that commitment. Moreover, the 1961 conference had adopted the 'Crewe resolution' which advocated unilateralist policies for *all* States, including the USA and USSR, which the policy statement implicitly rejected. The CND leadership had been at pains to play down, and where possible to ignore, this commitment,[52] but it remained CND policy. 'Steps Towards Peace' certainly accepted *multilateralism* and argued that CND's role should be to to take positive actions to bring about *multilateral* disarmament. Thus the new policy marked, for many, more than a shift of emphasis, more than an adjustment to the new, post-Cuba, real world of international politics. It reduced 'CND objectives to a series of platitudes, acceptable to even the leaders of the political parties. . . . The writing is on the wall. We call on all who value the ideals which originally inspired them to join CND to act, before it is too late. To win the support of ordinary people CND must be opposed to *all* bombs.'[53] For a great many activists, unilateralism was 'a principle and not merely a tactic'.[54] Peggy Duff, and others, disagreed with this: 'some of the people in the Campaign made unilateralism a sort of religion and any moves on disarmament that weren't unilateral were no use . . . whereas it was really a tactic.'[55]

But the emotive pull of unilateralism was what held the Movement together. The simple, dramatic appeal to 'Ban the Bomb' was always at the heart of the Campaign, and the complexities inherent in the new strategic disposition advocated in 'Steps Towards Peace' offended against the very spirit of the Movement. The furore over the new policy was thus only in part political. More fundamentally, the 'Steps Towards Peace' proposals represented a profound psychological blow to the Movement. It removed the ordinary campaigner's sense of certainty, of there being a central, immovable core to the Campaign which, despite all the splits, divisions, and setbacks, had remained constant, identifiable, credible, and sacrosanct. From this time on the Campaign became directionless, the central thrust of unilateralism was downgraded, and the Movement lurched into a steeper decline.[56]

[52] See Malcolm Pittock, 'Is CND Unilateralist?', *Peace News*, 20 July 1962.
[53] *Solidarity for Workers' Power*, 2.7.
[54] Witney CND leaflet, cited in 'Opposition to CND', *Solidarity for Workers' Power*, 2.9.   [55] Duff, in conversation.
[56] In retrospect both Canon Collins and Stuart Hall have agreed that the adoption of the proposals was a mistake for CND. Canon Collins wrote in *Sanity*, May 1964: 'we must never seem to be departing from our basic policy. It was, perhaps, our

Industrial action

Finally, in the context of 1962 and the new policy, it should be noted that the proposals brought to the fore a range of simmering discontents in the Movement, and exacerbated already existing tensions between CND leaders and a section of the rank and file. In particular, the decision of the 1962 conference to support industrial action had not been implemented. The conference resolution had called unambiguously for an immediate campaign to engage trade unionists in 'both token and direct industrial action, including the blacking of work, on the issue of disarmament'.[57]

The national council had agreed, in July, to establish a series of 'factory weeks', but following this meeting Canon Collins made a statement to *The Times* in which he expressed disagreement with the whole notion of industrial action.[58] As a result Pat Arrowsmith and Rev. Michael Scott resigned from the national council, describing Collins's statement as 'showing a flagrant disregard for the declared wishes of CND at its Annual Conference'.[59]

CND IN 1962–1964

All this interacted with the conflict over the 'Steps Towards Peace' proposals to produce a mood of bitterness, suspicion, and general depression in the Movement. At its root lay the failure of the Campaign to achieve its objectives. As time passed and frustrations grew, so the divisions became greater and more bitter.

failure in this respect which led to the poor reception by the bulk of the campaign of the 'Steps Towards Peace' programme.'
    Stuart Hall was even more definite: 'in terms of the psychology of the movement the 'Steps Towards Peace' proposals were a very bad mistake—*very* bad. . . . in terms of the mass movement it was a very bad judgement. . . . it was not defensible' (in conversation).

    [57] CND annual conference 1962 report of resolutions agreed, CND archive. The resolution was moved by Jimmy Jewers, secretary of the docks group, Committee of 100, and supported by Pat Arrowsmith of the Merseyside trade union committee of CND. For further discussion of the industrial campaign in the Movement, see ch. 4.

    [58] Indeed, Collins had already distanced the CND leadership from the notion of industrial action. In a letter to the *Guardian* on 20 June 1962, Collins wrote: 'the basic policy of the Campaign remains as it was before the Conference. We are still committed to the use of only legal, constitutional and democratic methods of persuasion in all our activities. . . . The particular resolution to which you referred is somewhat ambiguous. It must therefore be interpreted in the light of our basic policy and our approved methods. . . . We have too much political nous to think we can or should dictate or interfere with the trade unions.'

    [59] *Guardian*, 13 Sept. 1962.

Although CND conference endorsed 'the right of the Executive Committee to issue statements providing a set of interim objectives, while reaffirming CND's fundamental opposition to nuclear weapons everywhere',[60] the Movement did not recover from the 'Steps Towards Peace' debate—nor indeed from the other problems discussed above.

In fact the divisions on policy issues became even greater: from 1962 onwards the Committee of 100 became more heavily involved in libertarian politics and came under anarchistic influence, and thus grew even less sympathetic to the political/strategic approach of CND as embodied in the 'Steps Towards Peace' programme. CND, on the other hand, came increasingly under the influence of those who followed the new policy line and its implications. Thus a CND discussion pamphlet by John Gittings and Richard Gott, 'Nato's Final Decade', was held by the purist unilateralists in the Movement to be a further attempt to backslide on the commitment to take Britain out of NATO (though this had not been the authors' intention). This process culminated in the establishment of the disarmament and strategy group of CND in 1963, as a 'think-tank' to formulate the detailed political and strategic advice needed to inform CND policy.[61]

But many of the leading campaigners saw this as yet another stage in the subversion of the Movement from its proper objectives: and several key campaigners, notably George Clark,[62] withdrew from Movement activism.

Civil defence

Nevertheless, there were several areas of CND's activities in 1962–4 that were both important and positive. Not least among these was CND's increasing concentration upon exposing what it regarded as the fallacy and fraud of the Government's civil defence prepara-

[60] Duff, op. cit., 205. (But criticism was made of the way in which the 'Steps Towards Peace' statement had been issued.)

[61] The group included John Gittings, Richard Gott, Terence Heelas, Professor Bill Wedderburn, John Westergaard, Sheila Oakes, Douglas Gill, David Boulton, and Peggy Duff.

[62] In his statement of resignation from the national council in May 1964 George Clark wrote: 'attempts are being made, more particularly by the Disarmament and Strategy Group (Terence Heelas, Sheila Oakes, etc.) to change the principled stand that the campaign has been taking against all nuclear policies during these past six years. This group has the sympathy of the Executive, the General Secretary, and the Editor of *Sanity*' (cited in Duff, op. cit., 206).

tions. The most important CND activity in this field was the ambitious 'Fallex '63' campaign, mounted in the autumn of 1963, but planned in great detail for a considerable time prior to that. This was given a considerable fillip by the revelations of the 'Spies for Peace' group who, during the Aldermaston March of 1963, released hitherto secret information concerning the location of one of the Regional Seats of Government (RSG6) at Warren Row, near Reading, Berkshire. This important event belongs properly to the analysis of the Committee of 100 and this is undertaken in that context in Chapter 5. But it is appropriate here to note the reactions of the CND executive to these events over Easter 1963.

On the March itself the 'Spies for Peace' revelations threw the CND leadership and march organizers into confusion. Peggy Duff was to be seen in the March attempting to dissuade marchers from splitting off to demonstrate at Warren Row, and the initial intention to include extracts from the 'Spies for Peace' leaflet in *Sanity* was vetoed by the leadership because of concern over the security aspects (the back page of *Sanity* had to be torn out, because of this, before distribution). In press and television interviews during and immediately after the March, Canon Collins was less than enthusiastic about the whole exercise.[63] Nevertheless, the executive committee did subsequently acknowledge the publicity value and importance of the revelations. A statement was agreed by the executive committee at its meeting on 29 April 1963 and released to the Press.

The Executive Committee welcomed the enormous public interest created by the revelations concerning the secret Regional Seats of Government and the results of Fallex 1962 and the growing public concern. It was all the more shocking that these preparations have been made without any reference to Parliament or debates on the subject.[64]

If the executive committee was somewhat ambivalent about the 'Spies for Peace' episode—as well it might be, given the explicit political extremism of the individually anonymous but ideologically identifiable group that planned the operation—the revelations

---

[63] *Peace News* in its editorial of 19 Apr. 1963 was highly critical of Collins: 'it was quite understandable that CND should not support a demonstration at the RSG in Berkshire, as it clearly involved the risk of breaking the law. But to denounce the pamphlet as Canon Collins did was almost unbelievable. He was reported on the BBC News to have said that "of course, everyone understands that the Government has to make preparations such as this" '.

[64] Executive committee statement, 29 Apr. 1963, CND archive.

undoubtedly gave a big publicity boost to CND's 'Fallex '63' campaign. The original idea for this ambitious project came as a result of NATO's 'Fallex '62', a simulation exercise which predicted that nuclear war would leave fifteen million dead in Britain. The objective was to link civil defence to CND's wider political and strategic objectives: 'It makes our case against a nuclear divided Europe in dramatic, forceful language. So while we push the issue of civil defence we relate to the whole case against deterrence, against tactical nuclear weapons, against NATO, and for disengagement and neutralism.'[65]

The campaign built up, on a local and regional basis, through the summer, using the detailed and authoritative pamphlet, 'Civil Defence and Nuclear War'. In this, the pattern of 'Fallex '62' was followed as closely as possible, and the effects of a relatively small nuclear attack (one to half a megaton each) on sixty military targets and large towns was calculated. The effectiveness, or rather the total inadequacy, of civil defence preparations in this context was then analysed. The objectives of the campaign were worked out in a series of stages:

First stage: Local groups will approach their authorities in the manner suggested below, and will build up as detailed a picture as possible of local civil defence arrangements.

Second stage: Local groups will pass this information on to the Civil Defence Planning Group, which will thus build up a national picture.

Third stage: The Planning Group will use this information to mirror the local group's activity on a national scale, leading into 'Fallex '63'.

Throughout the three stages, the objectives of local groups will be to get local authorities responsible for civil defence to publish information about nuclear war and their preparations for it, or to express their failure to do so.[66]

Following on from this CND argued that its policy—'of closing down nuclear bases, putting on the pressure for disengagement in Europe, and stepping out on the road to neutralism and disengagement from military alliances'—was the only relevant and practicable alternative to the impending nuclear holocaust which was the likely consequence of existing government policy.

[65] Civil Defence Campaign and Fallex '63, CND document n.d. (? June 1963), CND archive.   [66] Ibid.

An enormous amount of local group work went into preparing and carrying out this programme in each and every region of the country. Certainly the objective—'that every city, town, and village should be clearly informed about what would happen to them if there was even a fairly small nuclear attack on Britain'[67]—was accomplished. The propaganda job was effective—and it annoyed civil defence and government officials considerably.[68] Public consciousness was alerted to the whole issue of civil defence, which had previously been shrouded in mystery. The uncomfortable facts of wholesale human destruction which would inevitably follow a nuclear exchange were made known on a very wide scale, and for the first time.[69]

All in all, therefore, CND had good reason to be satisfied with its civil defence protest. It was left to Peter Watkins, who made the remarkable TV film *The War Game* in 1965, to bring home to an even larger audience CND's message concerning the futility of civil defence and the horrors of nuclear war.[70]

Campaign Caravan

A related series of initiatives, centring on the enthusiasm and commitment of George Clark, was the fieldwork and Campaign

[67] Ibid.

[68] The response of Brighton's civil defence officer, Major General C. M. F. White, was typical: 'I only attack CND's outlook and actions because their policies include attacks on Civil Defence, the attempt to undermine our defences and our will to resist attack physically and morally, and to give to our potential enemies the secret and confidential information on our defence. By so doing they seriously weaken our power to defend ourselves against the powers of evil and oppression. CND talk so glibly of upholding democracy, but in their ignorance, real or assumed, are jeopardising all we normal British people put so much pride and store in' (Report in *Brighton Evening Argus*, photocopy located in CND archive; n.d., but probably Aug. 1963).

[69] It is also worth noting that this was an exercise in which CND and the Committee of 100 co-operated and complemented each other, at least at the local level. CND groups were ideally suited in many cases to undertake the painstaking questionnaire and analysis work involved and to ensure that the local media gave adequate coverage to the campaign. The Committee of 100 was able to make equally effective, and highly dramatic, contributions. The journal *Solidarity for Workers' Power*, for example, contained reports from several places where local council meetings had been interrupted repeatedly by demonstrators demanding an end to civil defence preparations.

[70] Watkins's film was not shown, of course, on BBC TV, although it was commissioned by them. This refusal to screen the film was a long-standing issue of contention between the BBC and the Peace Movement.

Caravan activities which took place from 1962 through to 1964–5. The history and development of these initiatives is complex, and is interwoven with the personal and political conflicts which permeated Clark's own relationship with CND leadership, the New Left, and the Committee of 100. Underlying the whole process, however, was the conviction that it was the rank-and-file activists in the localities who really mattered: without them the Movement would disintegrate. It was because of Clark's conviction, after Cuba, that the Campaign's grass roots needed re-stimulation that the idea was developed. Prior to this Alec Leaver had been appointed national groups officer, but this tended to be a centralized administrative and co-ordinating post. In 1962 Clark established, on his own initiative, 'Campaign Caravan', which toured the country, using the local group as a base for turning outwards to the community. Throughout this four-month tour 'the headquarters of the Campaign remained hostile . . . [and] it was not until the Caravan returned to London that it was informed of the goodwill of the National Council'.[71] The Caravan returned convinced of the need for far greater communication and liaison between the centre and the groups, but 'rather disillusioned about the state of democracy in the country, and the general hope of getting the thing moving'.[72] The executive committee recognized the value of this development and appointed Clark as mobile team organizer; he then undertook a pilot community based project in Coventry. (Although this initially worked well, Clark was recalled to help plan the Aldermaston March.)

It was the evidence of the huge, unruly, divided, and unpredictable Aldermaston March of 1963 that finally convinced the executive committee that the fieldwork function was a necessity if the Movement were to survive. Thus, on 20 May 1963 the executive committee accepted Clark's report in principle and agreed to his appointment as field secretary, although Peggy Duff was asked to draft specific terms of reference for the appointment and to indicate the financial and administrative implications, and its relationship to Alec Leaver's post. Clark, however, resigned his appointment on 31 December

because he felt that the only way of implementing some of the changes which were being pressed for was to serve as a member of the National

[71] Memorandum from George Clark, 'Notes on the Fieldwork of CND', 3 Apr. 1964, CND archive.   [72] Clark, in conversation.

Executive to which he had been elected. Also at that time, he had knowledge that the state of the Campaign at the local level was considerably worse than in September and it was obvious we were running into a financial crisis. He therefore felt that a lead should be given in cutting out overall administrative expenses. The resignation was accepted without comment.[73]

From this time on, despite much to-ing and fro-ing between Clark and the CND leadership, the fieldwork element in CND's work decreased as Clark himself became more disillusioned with the ethos of the Campaign and its general decline. Nevertheless, in addition to the original Caravan tour, four experimental projects had been established. The first was a 'broad campaign' in Somerset which demonstrated that a viable campaign could be sustained in country areas when a huge meeting packed Wells Cathedral. The second was aimed at strengthening an already active group in Welwyn Garden City; but neither this, nor the third project—in Wellingborough, where the aim was to pressurize the local Labour Party—achieved its objective. The final project—to establish an industrial group in Oldham—had just been established when Clark 'went to prison again—over the Queen Frederica visit!'[74]

These, and the original Campaign Caravan, were ultimately the only concrete achievements of the fieldwork campaign of George Clark. Despite a detailed and ambitious series of proposals submitted in 1964, the initiatives were never taken further. It was, perhaps, too late in the Movement's history, and too much against the prevailing structure and ethos of the Movement's leadership, for such an initiative to have succeeded. However, in small-scale terms, and in terms of the potential that was shown to exist for further developments, these campaigns must be accredited successes.[75] Moreover, this whole experience was part of the shift towards a more libertarian ideology in the Movement as a whole. Clark's perspective of beginning from where people were, focusing on their existing concerns and interests, and thus building a movement from below rather than from above, has much in common with the quasi-populist socialism of the 1970s and 1980s, and is indicative

[73] Clark, memorandum.
[74] Clark, in conversation.
[75] Mention should also be made of 'Operation Peanuts'—so-called because of Gaitskell's slighting reference to unilateralist hecklers at a Scottish Labour Party meeting in Glasgow which he addressed in 1961. This, too, although a small-scale programme, had the intention of stimulating local group activism and achieved some revitalization in a number of areas in 1962–3.

of the continuities between the Peace Movement in the two periods.

Another highly significant feature of the Campaign was the changing nature and the considerably more militant, divisive, and unruly spirit of the Aldermaston Marches from 1962 onwards. Peter Cadogan has noted that, as was argued above, the demonstrations over the Cuban missile crisis marked a qualitative change in the nature of the Movement's demonstrations. However, this was not only because of the strident anti-Americanism which henceforth characterized the Movement's activities. There was also a far more highly developed *confrontational* aspect to Movement events.[76] The US Embassy demonstration was the first time that a police cordon was broken: 'There was no violence, only a firm push . . . the war threat had reached the point of actual confrontation and the response to it was of like kind.' By the time of the Greek demonstrations of 1963 (see Chapter 5) 'the last remnants of the DAC tradition of action went by the board. There were scrum downs against police cordons. . . . What had been the Peace Movement was moving Left and into confrontation.'[77]

This new mood of confrontation certainly found expression on the Aldermaston Marches from 1962 onwards. As Peggy Duff has noted: the Aldermaston March

failed to get what it wanted either through marching, through the Labour Party, through civil disobedience, through Voters' Veto, through independent candidates, through any of the strategies marchers advocated. Frustration turned in on itself. It ran furiously across roads, shouted at itself, barred its own passage, trumpeted at MPs who tried to speak, and yet persisted long after many of the early marchers and most of the big names had stopped turning up.[78]

This frustration began in 1962 when there was a violent clash between a minority of marchers on a splinter march to the US Embassy following the rally in Hyde Park. (Despite the fact that this was the biggest ever Aldermaston March—150,000 in Hyde

[76] This was noted, too, with considerable concern by the DAC in its last months of existence and by the non-violent direct actionists' wing of the Committee of 100.
[77] Peter Cadogan, 'From Civil Disobedience to Confrontation', in Robert Benewick and Trevor Smith (eds.), *Direct Action and Democratic Politics*, London, 1972.   [78] Duff, op. cit., 143.

Park according to CND—all the national newspapers headlined the relatively small numbers involved in the violence in Grosvenor Square and at Savile Row police station.) In 1963 the Aldermaston March was a considerably more anarchic affair. This was due in part to the 'Spies for Peace' initiative and the ensuing Warren Row/RSG6 demonstration, and in part to the defection of virtually all the leading Labour MPs in the build-up to a new unity under Harold Wilson, prior to the imminent general election. Above all, however, it was a result of the mounting frustration of a still powerful mass movement deprived of any realistic possibility of attaining its objectives through the orthodox political machinery, and consequently rejecting its no longer credible leaders in favour of a more explicitly libertarian and populist politics. The leadership had lost control, and credibility, and the Gandhian pacifism of the DAC, whilst not extinct, had been largely overwhelmed by a variety of quasi-anarchistic ideologies which had come to dominate the Committee of 100 by late 1962 and early 1963.

Confrontational politics was the dominant mood of the 1963 March. A *Peace News* editorial stated that 'this Aldermaston March—the sixth and almost certainly the last—was the most confused and divided ever. The worst sign of change was the increasing tendency to violence and mob politics.'[79] Thus, despite the large numbers involved,[80] and despite the publicity generated, the 1963 March demonstrated, both to the leaders of CND and to the originators of DAC-style demonstration politics, that the Movement had reached a point where the Aldermaston March was counter-productive and must be discontinued.[81]

[79] *Peace News*, 19 Apr. 1963. The editorial went on to deplore the political hooligansim of the marchers who 'obstructed traffic, brushed against cars and shouted. The police, who looked frightened, were called "fascists". . . . The police violence seemed at least understandable to onlookers.'

[80] According to *Peace News* (19 Apr. 1963), 11,000 gathered at Aldermaston on Good Friday; there were between 6,000 and 17,000 marching on Saturday (including 1,000 who demonstrated at RSG6); by Monday numbers marching had grown to 30,000 and approximately 70,000 attended the final rally.
    A section of the March occupied the full width of the road after leaving Hyde Park, and 72 arrests were made. Perhaps more indicative of the mood and aspirations of the majority of marchers was the collection of 6,500 tins of dried milk for Algeria—a successful attempt to symbolize the connection between nuclear disarmament and humanitarian objectives.

[81] Somewhat ironically, 1963 saw a greater than ever imitation of the Aldermaston Easter demonstration in a variety of other Western nations. *Peace News* (26 Apr. 1963) recorded the following numbers on marches and demonstrations at Easter

The Easter demonstration over the next few years took various forms. In 1964 there was a one-day March, beginning from various parts of London and converging in the centre prior to a rally in Trafalgar Square. There was also a Committee of 100 sit-down demonstration at Ruislip USAF base on Easter Saturday. As Adam Roberts noted, 'both demonstrations were, barring a few incidents, dignified, but they were neither particularly large, nor outstandingly effective.'[82] There was a generally downbeat, *passé* atmosphere to the whole event. Despite the presence of an estimated 20,000 in Trafalgar Square (and a brief, small, and abortive demonstration at the RSG thought to be located in Monck Street), Canon Collins was undoubtedly voicing the general view when he said, in a BBC radio interview: 'this year we are in the middle of a changeover, and this year's demonstration was an interim demonstration . . . we have not found the equivalent to the Aldermaston March. . . . It is ridiculous to say that CND is dead; but it's changing, and I'll be surprised if there isn't much soul-searching in CND now.'[83]

Nevertheless, the 'original' Aldermaston-to-London format was returned to in 1965 (by which time Canon Collins had resigned as chairman—see below). It was a modest, but not altogether unsuccessful affair: 'the Campaign has not grown, as one might once have hoped, and a lot of Aldermaston veterans were not there this year; but . . . there were enough to fill Trafalgar Square to capacity.'[84] CND was moving into its 'post mass Movement', pressure group phase. But, on both this demonstration and the three-day (High Wycombe-to-London) 1966 march, there was persistent disruption from anarchists. Although many of the Movement's activists would themselves have described their ideological stance as broadly anarchist, they had no time for what they regarded as violent and negative action which detracted from the essential peace message of the March. As *Peace News* commented, the anarchists' tactics of 'leading and blocking the Easter March had no apparent point . . . they were a considerable nuisance. . . . The Anarchists have done neither themselves nor the Peace Movement

1963: Germany, 23,000; Switzerland, 1,000; Austria, 1,600; Denmark, 1,000; Holland, 1,500; Australia, 3,500; New Zealand, 800.

[82] Report by Adam Roberts, *Peace News,* 3 Apr. 1964.
[83] Collins, cited in ibid.
[84] *Peace News,* 23 Apr. 1965.

any credit over Easter.'[85] Similarly, in 1966 anarchist hecklers in Trafalgar Square succeeded in disrupting the final rally.

More significant than all this, however, were the two central points relating to the Easter demonstrations from 1962 onwards. First, the demonstration, whether an Aldermaston March or some other demonstration or march format, declined rapidly, after 1963, in terms of numbers, influence, and importance. Second, in part cause and in part effect of this and the general decline of the Movement, the issue of unilateralism itself—and the general concern over nuclear weapons and the danger of nuclear war— faded from the public consciousness. And, on the left, the Vietnam issue came to dominate politics. By the time of the 1966 demonstration, which was dominated by the giant puppet show depicting the US/British collusion over Vietnam, the Movement's opposition to American policy, and Harold Wilson's support for that policy, had become the dominant theme. CND was soon to be all but swallowed up in the mounting national and international protest movement against US involvement in the Vietnam War.

The overall picture by 1965–6, then, was of a substantial decline in CND as a mass movement—and this decline found its most dramatic expression in the virtual demise of the Aldermaston March, the symbol *par excellence* of the mass movement and of Movement power. Most of the factors in this decline have been analysed above, but, before moving on to note the resignation of Canon Collins which, perhaps rather paradoxically, marked the effective end of CND as a mass movement, brief mention must be made of three other areas of importance in this period: the constitutional changes in the campaign; the Partial Test Ban Treaty of 1963; and the growing international dimension of the Movement's activities from 1962 onwards.

CONSTITUTIONAL CHANGES

At the beginning of 1963 the executive committee agreed to a major reform of its structure and practice, as a result of a subcommittee report. A new subcommittee, consisting of the officers plus three members of the executive committee and national council, was established, in effect to act as a management committee, but with

[85] Ibid.

no executive powers.[86] It was also agreed that, at long last, Peggy Duff should become the general secretary and not the organizing secretary of the Campaign. The importance of these decisions was twofold. First, it strengthened the already significant drift towards centralized control of the Campaign. Second, and of more note, was the absence from any real involvement in the Campaign's central direction of almost all the public figures who had initiated the campaign. Of the new subcommittee only Canon Collins, Peggy Duff, Ritchie Calder, and Arthur Goss remained from the 1958 executive committee. Of these, Ritchie Calder had long been an infrequent attender, Canon Collins was to resign in 1964, and Peggy Duff in 1966–7. Thus, by 1963–4, almost all the original leadership of CND had departed, or were shortly to do so.

Eventually, at the end of 1966 'CND gave up the hard struggle to remain something different, adopted membership at last, and became an organization rather than a campaign'.[87] For many of the remaining mass movement activists this was the final blow and they ceased active participation in CND. For George Clark,[88] for example, 'a membership basis spelt the same path the political parties had trod and all that that meant', and he thus never took up membership.[89]

THE PARTIAL TEST BAN TREATY OF 1963

In addition to all the internal, ideological, and psychological factors relating to the decline of the Movement, a number of external events were of considerable importance. Of these the two most important were the Cuban missile crisis—discussed above—and

[86] This proposal was carried by 7 votes to 3, with the chairman abstaining. A quorum of 4 was agreed, with at least one officer and one member to be present. Members of the subcommittee were: chairman, vice-chairman, treasurer, general secretary, Arthur Goss, Anthony Greenwood, and Michael Howard.

A full executive committee meeting was to be held once a month. A proposal that subcommittee meetings should be open was defeated by 7 votes to 4. (Executive committee minutes, 26 Jan. 1963, CND archive.)

[87] Duff, op. cit., 225.

[88] Clark, in conversation.

[89] CND membership took some time to achieve even a modest respectability. According to executive committee minutes in 1967, membership figures were as follows: 221 (plus 300 CND bank standing orders) in Feb.; 800 in Mar.; 1,195 in Apr. 1967; 1,549 in June 1967. Membership fluctuated between 1,000 and 2,000 through the 1970s before rising very rapidly, and to greater levels than ever before, in the early 1980s.

the Partial Test Ban Treaty of August 1963. This treaty, signed on 5 April 1963 by the foreign secretaries of the USA, the USSR, and Britain, represented the first major breakthrough in the negotiations between the nuclear powers to move towards disarmament. (Yet, despite its achievements, the Treaty did not include *underground* tests; and neither France nor China was willing to become a signatory.)

Nevertheless, there is no doubt that the impact of this agreement upon public opinion, in Britain as in the USA, was considerable: the Conservative Party made good propaganda use of the Treaty (notably with a poster showing a demonstrator sitting down, with a placard, and a caption reading 'meanwhile the Conservatives signed the Test Ban Treaty'). Much of the initial support for CND had come from those who worried—as parents, scientists, or citizens—about the harmful effects of nuclear testing. The easing of world tension after Cuba, and the signing of the Treaty, allayed many of these fears and a substantial section of CND support gradually evaporated—not because of any direct disagreements on policy, but because a partial victory seemed to have been achieved and the issue no longer seemed so overwhelmingly urgent and important. And, as Jacquetta Hawkes has pointed out, the Treaty provided a good excuse for both leaders and rank-and-file activists, exhausted after five years of hard campaigning, to cease active work for the Movement: 'We did contribute to the nuclear Test Ban—and I'm afraid that's another factor that encouraged the break-up, we felt "we've done something". . . . So that made a sort of excuse for those of us who were apolitical to wander off!'[90]

INTERNATIONAL INVOLVEMENT 1963–1965

Perhaps partly in response to problems in the domestic Movement, CND—and especially Canon Collins and Peggy Duff—became more involved internationally from 1963 onwards. Collins and others were involved in both the Accra and Moscow conferences in 1962.[91]

[90] Hawkes, in conversation.
[91] The Labour Party NEC, in an ill-thought out manoeuvre, tried to expel both Lord Russell and Canon Collins from the Party because of their sponsorship of the Moscow conference. The attempt was greeted with derision and incredulity, not only by the left but the Press. The NEC rapidly withdrew its objections and no more was heard.

In September 1962 the European Federation (see above, p. 80) met to consider proposals, emanating from the Accra and Moscow conferences and from Quakers in the USA, for the establishment of a new international. Out of the consequent Oxford conference of January 1963 emerged—after much wrangling, principally over invitations issued to World Council of Peace representatives—the International Confederation for Disarmament and Peace (ICDP).[92]

Subsequently, the ICDP performed a significant co-ordinating and initiating role in the international Peace Movement—and acted as a non-aligned representative organization able to negotiate with, and where appropriate co-operate with, the World Council of Peace.

All these international contacts and developments, however, were at the bureaucratic, leadership levels, and were in that sense a further example of the CND leadership's organizational and hierarchical perspective. From the viewpoint of the late 1980s the contrast with the contemporary Movement is very marked. Whereas in the earlier period the Movement was predominantly insular in outlook, the 1980s Movement has been genuinely transnational. Moreover, the 1980s Movement has been characterized both by the *activist* involvement at international level (the European conventions organized in the early 1980s, for example), and by a determinedly libertarian and non-bureaucratic ethos.

The failure of the earlier Movement to extend its 'internationalism' to the mass of its supporters and involve the rank and file in a genuinely international co-operative movement ensured that, whatever other factors there may have been, the international Movement remained bureaucratic and leadership-dominated, with, ultimately, little relevance to the real life of the British Nuclear Disarmament Movement.

THE CAMPAIGN IN DECLINE, 1963–1965

The net result of all the processes that have been analysed above was that, by 1963, following the Aldermaston March, it had

[92] On her resignation as secretary of CND at the end of 1966, Peggy Duff became secretary of ICDP, in which post she worked with consistent enthusiasm, efficiency, and a measure of success until her death in Apr. 1981. (ICDP was created in 1962/3 with Gerry Hunnius, from Canada, as its first secretary.) Collins was opposed to the establishment of the ICDP, in Duff's view because he wished to retain and expand 'a small, restricted group, like the European Federation against Nuclear Arms from which activist, direct action groups were excluded' (Duff, op. cit., 244).

become clear to the whole Movement that a state of crisis existed. No longer was there the expansion and success of earlier years to mask the deep divisions at every level and along every dimension in the Movement. Moreover, those divisions had themselves deepened considerably and the Movement was thus faced with an unpleasant and depressing combination of circumstances: a decline in support and in public concern on nuclear issues; increasing division and ideological conflict within the Movement; and a strategic and tactical impasse.

It was in an attempt to resolve these and related problems that a conference was called in June 1963. At the centre of the whole discussion was the question of the 'umbrella' movement. For most in the Movement the umbrella concept was central—and always had been. The CND leadership may have rejected both the DAC and the Committee of 100 from the beginning, but the rank and file had not. In the more difficult circumstances of 1963 the issue had become central.

The net result of the conference was to confirm, formalize, and expand the umbrella concept, and to launch the 'Tell Britain' campaign—the most notable part of which, 'Fallex '63', has been discussed above. CND produced a brochure outlining the whole project and its approach, the emphasis of which was upon the concerted effort of the *whole* Movement, acting in unison, to oppose nuclear policies: 'No wing will denounce or renounce another. The distinction between "official" and "unofficial" will be forgotten.'[93]

This was a marked departure both from previous CND policy and from the 'tone' of Campaign statements. Predictably, Canon Collins did not like it. He considered resigning at this stage. In his autobiography he has outlined his reasons. Apart from the fundamental disagreement with the umbrella policy, he also felt that neither he nor the majority on the executive was backed by the headquarters staff of CND.[94] Collins also felt that support for CND was waning and that, with the departure of his former colleagues, the Campaign was now characterized by increasing hostility and dissidence. The old comradeship of the executive committee had

[93] Extract from Duff's contribution to the conference, cited in Duff, op. cit., 222.

[94] In this he was correct, as Duff later confirmed in her autobiography, op. cit., 208–25. And others at the centre of CND politics at this period (Stuart Hall *et al.*) undoubtedly supported her views. The 'kitchen cabinet' of CND in 1964, in addition to Duff, included Hall, John Gittings, and Richard Gott—all of whom had views broadly similar to Duff's.

long since disappeared. And, on the practical side, the Campaign was running into debt, and its public image, thanks to the Committee of 100 and the disruptive and violent antics of the anarchists, had suffered considerably.

However, Collins was persuaded to remain as chairman because his departure would have 'rocked the boat' and further lowered morale. At the 1963 CND conference he was opposed by Michael Mitchel Howard, but was elected by a comfortable (*c.* two-thirds) majority. In a statement he outlined his conditions for agreeing to stand again for election: that 'CND should abandon its umbrella policy and thereby clear its own public image'; that 'it should concentrate upon putting an intelligent case for nuclear disarmament by Britain, and should do so by every legal means available'; and that 'majority decisions of the elected council and executive, and the self-disciplines asked for, should be respected'.[95] However, the conference also passed the 'Tell Britain' programme of umbrella campaign activity, and the policy of CND through 1963–4 continued markedly to reflect this approach.

Following the very modest 1964 Easter demonstration, Canon Collins decided that the time to go had arrived. As his comments on the 1964 March, cited earlier, made clear, he was convinced (rightly) that CND, at least in its existing form, was declining as a major political force and this, combined with his previously expressed reservations concerning the organization's problems, persuaded him to resign.[96] Canon Collins chaired his last executive committee

[95] CND annual conference report, CND archive.

[96] His resignation statement was of some length, but the essential points are contained in the extracts which follow (CND archive):

'On grounds of political realism as well as moral conviction, I believe it to be the duty of the Campaign, so long as there is hope in the present British political and constitutional democracy—however open to criticism it may be—to try to win the majority of the British people to its point of view.

And if there is no hope in the future of British democracy, CND is not, in my opinion, and ought not to be, the organization through which to effect a successful revolution. . . . the rule of law in international affairs is unlikely to be furthered by the breakdown of the rule of law in national life. . . . the work of the Committee must be judged on expedient grounds. And on expedient grounds I am convinced that the setting up of the Committee of 100 has done more harm than good to the cause which it and CND jointly espouse. . . . Let me list some of what I believe to be the more important changes needed:

(a) CND supporters pressed for a democratic constitution. But too often supporters have proved unwilling to accept majority decisions. This makes a farce of democracy. . . .

meeting on 7 March 1964 and his resignation took effect from 12 April 1964. The spring of 1964 thus marked the end of an era. Although the departure of Canon Collins was not in itself of *decisive* importance, it did symbolize the end of the initial phase of CND. With the general decline of the Movement, and the distinct withdrawal of Labour left figures from 1963 onwards as they rallied to Harold Wilson in the lead-up to the general election, the original leaders of CND gradually became disillusioned and drifted out of active campaigning. After Canon Collins went, only Peggy Duff remained. (And Peggy Duff never really left the Movement: she merely moved into a different part of it—the ICDP—where her commitment to socialist radical internationalism was combined more easily with her specific peace commitments than was the case in the new-style pressure group and information service organization that CND became after 1964–5.)

(b) A fresh attempt should be made to define CND's attitude to civil disobedience in general and to the Committee of 100 and other similar organizations in particular. . . .

(c) There ought to be a complete repudiation of non-Tolstoian anarchy within CND.

(d) Ways should be found to bring back into service of CND those "intellectuals" whom we have lost. . . .

(e) The work of the "grass roots" needs to be taken more seriously.

(f) We need to take account of the realities of the present political situation in Britain and to adjust our tactics accordingly. It is not necessary to sacrifice principles in order to take advantage of the fact that the return of a Labour government at the General Election would be better than the return of the Tories.

(g) A realistic assessment of the international role of CND is required. . . .

(h) I do not think it wise or prudent that the General Secretary of CND should be the Treasurer of the (ICDP). . . .

(i) Provisions to ensure that *Sanity* is the organ of CND as such need to be seriously considered. . . .

(j) The administrative "set up" should be examined carefully in order to ensure that it services CND adequately, efficiently, and economically. The paid officers, including the General Secretary and the Editor of *Sanity,* should be strictly answerable to a strong and functioning executive. But too much should not be asked of any particular officer—I think the General Secretary, who has worked ceaselessly and devotedly for CND during the last six years should be given a holiday, with pay, for six months (or three at the very least); and she should be made to take it! . . .

I am sad at having to resign, particularly at a time when we seem to be at a crossroads and our future less clear than it has been in the past . . . Because for the next three months at least I can no longer spare even the amount of time and energy I have previously given to the affairs of CND and because the confidence which used to exist between Headquarters and myself as Chairman seems to have grown less, I have come to the conclusion that someone else must take my place. I shall, of course, continue to give my support to CND and its aims in any way I can.'

Thus by the 1964 general election CND had faded from national prominence. Indeed, as in 1959, CND's 'presence' faded in the lead-up to the general election, and for much the same reasons. Ironically, and not for the first or the last time, it was the Conservative Party rather than the Labour Party that tried to make defence and disarmament an election issue.

Throughout 1964 Sir Alec Douglas-Home tried almost single-handed to keep the retention of the British deterrent in the forefront. But only . . . seven per cent of the Gallup sample saw defence as the single most important issue; and only thirteen per cent of NOP sample put the nuclear deterrent in a list of particularly important issues. On the other hand, it was an issue on which public opinion favoured the Conservatives; their policy was preferred to Labour's by thirty-seven per cent to twenty-one per cent according to the Gallup Poll.[97]

Whilst the Committee of 100 ventured even further into the wilderness of libertarian politics, CND's decline as a mass movement accelerated, and by 1965 it was regarded by almost all as a spent force. The Movement, which had begun with such high hopes and such massive support in 1957–8 and had grown rapidly into the largest and most important mass movement of recent British times, had been at its peak in 1959–61. From 1962 onwards it was in crisis and slow decline, and, by the end of 1963 that decline can be seen with hindsight to have been irreversible. By 1965 it was apparent to all that the first mass movement against nuclear weapons was dead.

[97] David E. Butler and Anthony King, *The British General Election of 1964*, London, 1965, pp. 129–30.

PART II
THE RADICALS

4

THE DIRECT ACTION COMMITTEE
Gandhian Pacifism and the Nuclear Issue

THE radical wing of the Nuclear Disarmament Movement was dominated by direct action politics from the outset. Indeed, the theoretical formulation and the political practice of Direct Action both pre-dated and post-dated the mainstream mass CND Movement. From April 1957 to 1960–1[1] the Direct Action Committee against Nuclear War (hereafter DAC)[2] was the main organizational and ideological focus for direct action politics. To analyse the nature of the DAC and its important role in the Movement we must begin by discussing its origins and its relationship with the pacifist movement in Britain.

Since the 1930s, the pacifist movement in Britain had been centred on the Peace Pledge Union (PPU).[3] The PPU, which had attracted a large following in the 1930s, emphasized the importance of the *individual's* commitment to pacifism. This tradition has a link with the core radical individualism of at least a section of the British working-class movement, which in the late nineteenth and early twentieth centuries found its most important articulation in the Independent Labour Party.[4] (In some respects, indeed, some DAC activists saw their movement as centrally in this tradition. As Hugh Brock has said, 'the left and the Peace Movement have

[1] The Committee of 100, which was formed in Sept. 1960 and had its public inauguration in Oct., rapidly came to dominate the direct action wing of the Movement, and had considerable overlap in terms of activists, ideology, and objectives with the DAC (see ch. 5). The DAC co-existed with the Committee of 100 throughout late 1960 and early 1961 but took the decision to disband following the Holy Loch demonstration in May 1961 (see below).
[2] Originally entitled the Emergency Committee for Direct Action Against Nuclear War. (It later became known as the Direct Action Committee Against Nuclear War —DAC.)
[3] For detailed historical and political analysis of the twentieth century pacifist movements in Britain, see Martin Ceadel, *Pacifism in Britain 1914–45*, Oxford, 1980.
[4] For the history of the ILP, see David Howell, *British Workers and the Independent Labour Party 1888–1906*, Manchester, 1983.

always been together in these upsurges— the ILP, the No Conscription Fellowship, and the PPU.')[5]

However, the Second World War destroyed the ideological and organizational basis of the PPU: few were prepared to espouse its full pacifism in the face of the horrors of Nazism.[6] The individualist pacifism of the PPU was 'dealt the death blow' by Hitler.[7] After the war, deserted by many of its former adherents,[8] it lost its influence, though not its zeal and fervour. The policies advocated through the 1940s took account of the new and mounting menace of atomic and later hydrogen bombs and embodied many of the later CND policies,[9] but 'they attracted little public notice'.[10] Even after the rise of the mass Nuclear Disarmament Movement the PPU continued its separate, and often sharply divergent, existence, and continued to hold to its fundamental belief that 'the personal rejection of violence and refusal to take part is in itself an effective *social* weapon for ending war and violence'. By the 1960s the PPU, although surviving 'as a name and an organization . . . [had] lost its guts and its drive. It [was] a ghost that survived.'[11]

Yet it was in the ailing PPU that the movement which eventually resulted in the DAC had its origins. On 5 November 1949 the PPU convened a conference in London with the theme 'Steps to Peace'. At this meeting several study groups were established, one of which was a non-violence commission whose brief was to examine both the philosophy and practical application, in the British context, of non-violent principles.

This development signified the emergence of a permanent split in the PPU between the old guard and the new direct action radicals who were to form the nucleus of the DAC. The inspiration for this group was in part derived from the perceived irrelevance and ineffectiveness of the traditional PPU orientation. But the divisions went far deeper than mere strategy: there were to be other

[5] Hugh Brock, in conversation with the author, Mar.1978.
[6] Although it should be noted that its membership increased up until 1941, and fell sharply only after 1945 when the full horror of Nazism became generally appreciated.
[7] Michael Randle, 'Towards a Social Non-violence', *Peace News*, 14 July 1961.
[8] Including many of the 'big names', e.g. Bertrand Russell, Ellen Wilkinson, Professor C. E. M. Joad.
[9] e.g. a policy of neutrality, disarmament—unilateral if necessary—the abolition of conscription, and the creation of a Ministry of Peace, was advocated in *Peace News*, 6 Jan. 1950.
[10] Frank E. Myers, *British Peace Politics: The CND and the Committee of 100, 1957–1962.* Ph.D. thesis, Columbia University, 1965, p. 39.   [11] Randle, op. cit.

influences in the later 1950s on the DAC itself, but even at this stage the Gandhian tradition was of central importance.

At the core of Gandhi's philosophy was the notion of *Satyagraha*: 'an ethic-principle the essence of which is a social technique of action'.[12] In a society where conflict persists and appears endemic, *Satyagraha* 'supplies the processes whereby constructive solutions may yet be achieved'. Equally central to Gandhi's thought, however, was the notion of non-violence: although he believed that absolute truth existed, he maintained that human knowledge of it was always relative, and that this ruled out any right to use violence in pursuit of the fulfilment of any ultimate objective. Linked to this was the notion of *ahimsa*—action based on the refusal to do harm—which was seen, too, as a central principle. Thus, for Gandhi, the creed of non-violence had nothing to do with 'passivity or submission to evil': it entailed 'the pitting of one's whole soul against the will of the tyrant'. Both a socially defined and a militant pacifism are therefore central to the Gandhian tradition. An ancillary aspect of Gandhi's philosophy, which is of crucial importance in the DAC context, is the emphasis laid upon 'means' rather than 'ends'. In the West, political theory has failed, so it is claimed, to deal adequately with the question of means: anarchism, for example, has developed no constructive techniques for actually achieving an anarchist society, whereas liberal democracy has been concerned 'with mechanism, not with action, with form rather than performance, with instrument and not techniques . . . it relies ultimately upon violent force'. The Gandhian view is that only through a philosophy of action which is linked to the actual practice and structure of the desired 'peaceful society' can a meaningful movement be built. There must thus be a fusion of theory and practice, of means and ends; in conceptual, though not of course in substantive, terms this notion is not dissimilar to the Marxist concept of 'praxis'.

Gandhian philosophy[13] combined two major ingredients necessary for the successful development of a radical pacifist movement: an emphasis upon the need for a social, collective, and militant non-violent campaign; and a reiteration of the centrally moral basis of

[12] Gene Sharp, reviewing Joan V. Bondurant, *The Conquest of Violence: the Gandhian Philosophy of Conflict*, Princeton, USA, 1959, in *Peace News*, 28 Aug. 1959. The subsequent citations in this paragraph are from the same source.

[13] In the 1940s and 1950s influential explications of Gandhian philosophy were Richard Gregg, *The Power of Non-violence*, London, 1936, and Bart de Ligt, *The Conquest of Violence*, London 1938.

pacifist belief. Moreover, the whole philosophy was contained
within an intellectual and ethical framework which had coherence,
relevance, and profundity—qualities perhaps lacking in the traditional PPU orientation.

It is within this context that the PPU's non-violence commission
of 1949, and its subsequent development, must be seen. For
approximately two years this small group met to discuss the
history, philosophy, politics, and implications of Gandhi's campaigns. At a meeting of the commission held on 12 December 1951,
Hugh Brock[14] proposed the formation of 'Operation Gandhi', with
the following objectives:

1. The withdrawal of American forces at present in this country.
2. The stopping of the manufacture of atomic weapons in Britain.
3. The withdrawal of Britain from NATO.
4. The disbanding of the British Armed Forces.

Those taking part in 'Operation Gandhi' had to be willing to face
imprisonment, loss of income and other hardships.[15]

Although there were some misgivings, it was agreed to establish
'Operation Gandhi' along the lines proposed, and in January 1952
a demonstration outside the War Office in Whitehall was planned.
The accompanying statement made clear the Gandhian/Quaker
orientation of the group. There was a stress upon the need for
radical symbolic action, total non-violence, *and* total openness
about the group plans to the police, and a willingness to accept
legal penalties for civil disobedience.[16]

In the event the response for the demonstration was very poor:
only thirteen were arrested following the sit-down outside the War
Office.[17] The significance of the demonstration in the context of the

---

[14] Hugh Brock was a key figure in the development of Gandhian-inspired direct
action politics. He was involved with *Peace News* as deputy editor from 1946 and
editor from 1955 to 1964. (Allen Skinner, also influential in the Gandhian pacifist
movement and subsequently active in the DAC, was editor of *Peace News* from
1951 to 1955.) Brock was instrumental in the establishment and subsequent
development of the DAC and succeeded both in building *Peace News* into *the* paper
of the Peace Movement and in creating a commercially and politically successful
newspaper. He died in 1985.

[15] Non-Violence Commission of PPU minutes, 12 Dec. 1951, DAC archive.

[16] Press statement, 'Operation Gandhi', 11 Jan. 1952, DAC archive.

[17] There were, in fact, ten demonstrators originally arrested: Constance Gibbs
arrived late and, after squatting in the War Office doorway, was arrested. Pastor
Dawe, who had been leafleting and had not intended arrest, and Derek Eveleigh,
who had been due to conduct the press conference and who 'had ventured too near

DAC's development, however, can hardly be overestimated. Not only did the style and strategy of the demonstration set the pattern for future action, but the reporting of the sit-down drew into the Movement activists who were later to be of central significance—in particular, Michael Randle. Randle heard about the demonstration at the London CO tribunal and asked the *Peace News* reporter to put him in touch with the new group. Subsequently he became perhaps the most important single figure in the direct action politics movement—chairman of the DAC, and, later, secretary of the Committee of 100.[18]

In terms of action and personnel, therefore, this demonstration marked the beginning of the direct action movement in Britain. Immediately, the group planned its next action: a 'protest against the decision to manufacture atom bombs in Britain. Someone had heard that a factory was being erected for the purpose in a remote Berkshire village'.[19] One of the group, Hugh Brock, visited the establishment early in 1952, and, as a result, a demonstration was planned for 19 April 1952. Thus was the first Aldermaston demonstration planned.[20] Both this, and a second demonstration on

the War Office and been caught in the net', were also arrested. Eveleigh was discharged by the Bow Street magistrate and the others were fined 30s.

[18] Michael Randle was chairman of DAC from 1957 to 1960 and secretary of the Committee of 100 from 1960 to 1961. Among very many Peace Movement activities he spent a year in Ghana working with the Sahara protest team (see below), has been actively involved on the council and executive of War Resisters' International since 1960, and was chairman from 1966 to 1972. He has spent considerable periods in prison as a result of his civil disobedience activities—notably following the Official Secrets Trial in 1962 (see ch. 5). Among other political activities he was involved in establishing the Campaign Against Racial Discrimination (CARD) and the British Withdrawal from Northern Ireland Committee. Since 1979 he has been full-time secretary of the Alternative Defence Commission.

[19] Brock, *Peace News*, 5 May 1961.

[20] At this stage Aldermaston was an Atomic *Energy* Research Establishment: but it was already known that it was shortly to be changed to an Atomic *Weapons* Research Establishment (see Hugh Brock, 'The Evolution of the Aldermaston Resistance', *Peace News*, 9 Jan. 1959). Brock wrote later that his first visit to Aldermaston 'was an unforgettable trip. . . . It was the vast stacks of bricks and piles of girders which most imprinted itself on my mind. This was at a time when people were crying out for schools and hospitals, for rebuilding after the bombing of World War II. . . . Here was a "crash programme" being carried out of which almost everyone in Britain was ignorant' (*Sanity*, Good Friday ed., 1962). The first demonstration involved 20–30 demonstrators from London and 4 or 5 others, including Austin Underwood. Neither in this nor in the second Aldermaston demonstration was civil disobedience practised. According to Brock this was so that 'as many pacifists as possible could take part' and those who were 'feeling their way towards public action' would be encouraged to participate (*Peace News*, May 1961).

26 September 1953 at which Stuart Morris of the PPU spoke at St Mary's Butts, Reading, following the Aldermaston protest, were modest successes. Relatively few people were involved, and, as Brock noted, there was 'no widespread publicity or support'.[21] Other demonstrations were organized, along similar lines, at the US base at Mildenhall in Suffolk on 28 June 1951, and at Porton (the 'germ warfare' research centre) on 14 March 1953.[22]

The movement, although active and developing its ideology and its strategy,[23] had minimal public impact. In the summer of 1952 'Operation Gandhi', although remaining wholly Gandhian in outlook, changed its name to the Non-violent Resistance (NVR) Group, in response to advice from Gandhian activists in India who pointed out that Gandhi had been firmly opposed to any 'personality cult'.

There were other initiatives in the direct action movement through 1954 to 1957: one, the 'Congress of England', was convened on 3 April 1954 at the instigation of Tom Wardle (with the support of many of the NVR Group's leading members, and with Hugh Brock in the chair). The programme was *neutralist* as well as pacifist, and called for national economic 'independence' as well as decentralization and workers' control. Following on from this a conference was called for 3 July 1954 to create a 'Third Camp Movement', whose primary purpose was to mobilise an internationalist, neutralist, and democratic movement to oppose the Cold War and its ideology.[24]

At a somewhat more mundane, but perhaps more realistic, level, the NVR Group continued its locally based action campaigns from 1953 to 1956.[25] Significantly, however, there was little if any attempt to put Gandhian civil disobedience into practice; nor was there any upsurge of public interest or support. Far too few people were involved for there to be any chance of building a real movement. By the winter of 1956–7 the NVR Group seemed to be

[21] Ibid. See also *NVR Group Newsletter* 12, 5 Dec. 1953, DAC archive.

[22] At Mildenhall 15 sat down outside the main gate of the base. Nobody was arrested. Other local demonstrations were held in 1952 and 1953.

[23] e.g. Michael Randle's open letter on 'The Use of Civil Disobedience in a Democracy', *NVR Group Newsletter* 10, 10 July 1953, DAC archive.

[24] This was organized by Tom Wardle and Allen Skinner. Similar conferences were held in the USA, Holland, and France. The Third Camp conference report, 3 July 1954, DAC archive.

[25] The *NVR Group Newsletter* 18, 24 Feb. 1955, reported that 'objective peace' demonstrations were planned for Ipswich, Bromley, Southend, and Portsmouth.

running out of enthusiasm and ideas: the minutes for 1 December 1956 refer to the fact that the group had 'ceased to be active'.

During 1956 a series of lectures, under the title 'Non-Violence and Social Change', attended by approximately thirty people, was given by Gene Sharp, the American Gandhian pacifist who worked as deputy editor of *Peace News* through the late 1950s and early 1960s. Out of this experience developed the '1957 Committee', which had a more radical and sophisticated programme than any of the preceding organizations in the direct action tradition. In the course of a long report on the foundation meeting, the committee stated that it was agreed

that non-violent resistance should be related equally to ending war and to bringing about radical social changes. These two should be regarded as inextricably interwoven, and attempts to neglect either should be resisted. ... We agreed that social aims in the United Kingdom hinged around the decentralisation of the bureaucratic, managerialist and militaristic features of State Socialism and State Capitalism experienced today. Constitutional means where available should be used to the greatest extent possible. But we realised also that the polarisation of power in two main political parties, and the refusal of such fundamental rights as access for minorities to broadcasting, together with the capitalistic monopolisation of mass newspapers, set severe limits to the spread of revolutionary ideas of any sort. Widespread material contentment, and a feeling of impotence in face of the one threat that might stir people [the H-bomb], made dramatic unorthodox means of spreading ideas more and more necessary. Clear distinctions were needed between constitutional action, non-violent unconstitutional action, and violent revolution. We were interested in the first two.[26]

Here, and elsewhere in this and subsequent lengthy discussion documents, was articulated the authentic politics of the DAC. Since 1949 the direct action movement had come a long way ideologically and strategically. But there had been little sign of any mass movement arising to put these ambitious programmes into practice: and yet, without such support, the politics of direct action became, in practical terms, merely symbolic.

THE FORMATION OF THE DAC

This failure to mobilize support for direct action politics must be related to the general political and ideological climate which

---

[26] The 1957 Committee foundation meeting. The phraseology of this report indicates the initial closeness of the direct actionists and the New Left.

prevailed in the late 1940s and 1950s, and which militated not only against direct action politics but against constitutionalist, CND protest too.

The specific catalyst which led to the establishment of the direct action movement was the attempt by Harold Steele (and initially, other volunteers)[27] to sail into 'the Pacific in order to challenge the right of the British Government to carry out the proposed tests with nuclear weapons'.[28] This project had its origins, according to Hugh Brock, in 'a meeting in my room probably towards the end of March 1957—there must have been Reg Reynolds, Arlo Tatum, Allen Skinner and myself'. In 1957, with the imminence of nuclear tests, 'we were wondering what could be done to stop it . . . and somehow this idea came up of sending someone (or a group of people) to Christmas Island; and I think at this meeting we said we would call ourselves the Emergency Committee for Direct Action against Nuclear War'.[29] The original Committee consisted of Skinner, Brock, and Tatum, but this was soon enlarged to include, among others, Michael Randle (who became chairman), April Carter, Pat Arrowsmith, Rev. Michael Scott, and Will Warren. The Committee also approached various eminent public figures to become sponsors, and by 1958–9 had gathered together an impressive list, including Alex Comfort, Doris Lessing, A. J. Muste, Linus Pauling, Sir Herbert Read, Sydney Silverman, Rev. Donald Soper, and Bertrand Russell.

The original purpose of the Committee—to organize and finance Harold Steele's voyage—was not fulfilled because of the difficulty of obtaining a boat to sail into the area. Steele's trip to Japan in May 1957 was, however, a great propaganda success. During the autumn the DAC established itself and was in a sound position to launch a major campaign by the end of the year. A conference of DAC members and supporters on 23 November 1957 agreed to set up an Aldermaston March committee to organize a four-day Easter protest march to the Atomic Weapons Research Establishment

[27] Originally, it was intended that Sheila Steele, Reginald Reynolds, and other volunteers should accompany Harold Steele.

[28] A letter outlining the plan, announcing the establishment of an 'Emergency Committee for Direct Action Against Nuclear War', and appealing for funds, was published in the *Manchester Guardian* on 12 Apr. 1957. (The letter was signed by J. Allen Skinner, Alex Comfort, Lawrence Housman, Bertrand Russell, Ruth Fry, Spike Milligan, Horace Alexander, Peggy Rushton, John Hoyland, Arlo Tatum, and Hugh Brock.)   [29] Hugh Brock, in conversation.

(AWRE).[30] The committee consisted of Frank Allaun, Hugh Brock, Michael Randle, Walter Wolfgang, with Pat Arrowsmith as organizing secretary. The 'first' Aldermaston March was a tremendous triumph for the committee, and for the Movement in general. Between 5,000 and 10,000 took part and the March received very wide press coverage. From this time onwards there was no question but that the Movement (though never the DAC *per se*) was a *mass* movement. There are several significant points to note about this success. The first is that it was very much a DAC affair: the CND, and others, may have supported, aided, and abetted, but the demonstration was conceived from the outset in DAC terms as a militant, non-violent protest and public witness to the evils of nuclear weapons, within the Gandhian/Quaker direct action tradition of political action.[31]

After the March's success the CND leadership was keen to co-operate with the DAC over future action—or, if a more Machiavellian view is taken, the CND leadership, realizing that the DAC was a force to be reckoned with and that it could thus prove politically disruptive and therefore dangerous, decided that it must be incorporated, integrated, and thus made 'safe'. It is possible to put either interpretation upon Collins's letter to Pat Arrowsmith following the March. After thanking her for her work in making the March such a success—'largely [due] to the inspiration . . . and admirable work you put in'—Collins went on: 'I am only too delighted that it has been so closely associated with the National Campaign for Nuclear Disarmament; and I hope very much that you will continue in the closest possible liaison with us. Indeed I would very much welcome the complete fusion of what one might call the "Direct

[30] Frank Allaun became interested after hearing of the 23 Nov. meeting, and the plans therefore gained press coverage. Both CND and the *Universities and Left Review* group gave support and, later, Michael Howard came in as chief marshall. Lawrence Brown was at the head of the march itself, 'fittingly . . . [because] he was the NVR group member who had joined in the planning of the earlier demonstrations at Aldermaston, Porton, and the Mildenhall bomber base' (Hugh Brock, 'The Evolution of the Aldermaston Resistance', *Peace News*, 9 Jan. 1959).
The Aldermaston March committee was also supported by the Hydrogen Bomb Campaign committee, and its 38 sponsors included 18 MPs (all Labour).
[31] Moreover, there is evidence that, initially at least, the hierarchy of CND was opposed to the whole idea (see ch. 2, p. 29). In a letter to Pat Arrowsmith on 12 Feb. 1958, Collins had declined the invitation to participate: 'unfortunately, however, I am committed to so many engagements that I fear I shall be unable to be with you' (DAC archive).

The Radicals

Action" section of our common effort into the campaign as a whole.'[32]

The second point of importance to note is the significance of the March being *from* London *to* Aldermaston: on all subsequent occasions (when the March was organized under the auspices of CND) the direction was reversed. The AWRE was a 'symbolic spot':[33] and as Pat Arrowsmith, representing one prominent view within the DAC, has emphasized, 'this indicated the orientation of the DAC: the people on it, some of them anyway, were anarcho-pacifists, and certainly saw that power lay with the people and one went to grass roots, to workers, and invited them to consider downing tools on moral issues like nuclear weapons'.[34] The 1958 Aldermaston March marked the real beginning of the divergence not only between constitutional/legal and extra-parliamentary/direct action politics in the Movement but also between an élite pressure group structure and a mass, populist movement.

The third point was, quite simply, that the numbers involved provided the numerical basis on which to build a meaningful direct action movement. The problem which had plagued the Movement since the 1940s—its lack of a base in the community—was not solved by the Aldermaston experience, but at least there was now the realistic possibility of building up a viable organization. This task was made considerably easier by three other factors: the growing public concern over nuclear dangers; the wide media coverage obtained by the whole Movement; and the existence of the larger and more respectable and prestigious CND which acted, at one level, as a recruiting ground for the DAC.

Finally, the March was linked to direct action politics in a logical and direct way. It had been the intention from the outset to mount a vigil at the AWRE following the March,[35] to link together the polit-

[32] Letter from Canon Collins to Pat Arrowsmith, 8 Apr. 1958, DAC archive. In further letters, from Peggy Duff to Hugh Brock and to Pat Arrowsmith, on 15 Apr. 1958, it was suggested that Pat Arrowsmith take the job of assistant secretary of CND 'with particular responsibility for Direct Action projects', a special advisory committee of CND being set up to consider direct action. This was rejected out of hand by the DAC (DAC archive).

[33] *Peace News*, 14 Mar. 1958.

[34] Pat Arrowsmith, in conversation with the author, Jan. 1978. Indeed, there was discussion at the time of obstructing, blockading, or even invading the AWRE.

[35] However, as Pat Arrowsmith has recalled, this was 'toned down because the Labour MP Frank Allaun and the prospective Labour Party candidate Walter Wolfgang did not want to alienate the workers there—we called it a vigil, although

ical message of the March with the direct moral implications for the workers and scientists at the AWRE. Following this week-long vigil after the Aldermaston March, the DAC decided to mount a nine-week 'picket-cum-vigil' beginning on 20 July and ending on 22 September. The declared aims of the picket emphasized both the moral basis of opposition to nuclear weapons and the need to confront those most directly involved in the manufacture, testing, etc. of nuclear weapons in as dramatic and direct a way as possible. Significantly, it was on this latter issue that the DAC first parted company with many of its most important supporters and sympathizers on the Labour left (Frank Allaun, for example). This difference went far deeper than strategy: was the movement about taking the fundamentally moral and pacifist message of nuclear disarmament to the people and building up a non-violent campaign of civil disobedience in opposition to nuclear weapons, or was it ultimately concerned with pressurizing the Labour Movement, and thus the next Labour Government, into supporting a unilateralist defence policy and implementing this through the established constitutional channels? These positions were irreconcilable, and, from this time on, the DAC, although receiving some 'sympathy and admiration'[36] from the Labour left, effectively lost the support of the large majority of Labour left activists, at both parliamentary and rank-and-file levels.

About 170 people took part in the nine-week picket. Some modest success was claimed: thirty workers signed a petition urging the Government to use the AWRE for peaceful purposes only; and a number of workers and lorry-drivers either signed anti-nuclear petitions or stated that they would never again work in nuclear weapons-related occupations. Factory gate meetings were held and canvasses of local housing estates were carried out by DAC supporters. The climax was the sit-down demonstration which took place in the forecourt of the AWRE at the end of nine weeks. The DAC took the decision to organize this demonstration in the light of the four-times-repeated refusal of Sir William Penney, the director of the AWRE, to meet a deputation.

On 22 September 'twenty seven people risked arrest by marching

effectively it was a picket: and this lost us one member of the Committee, Lawrence Brown—who disapproved of toning it down to be a vigil, and we retained Frank and Walter!' (Arrowsmith, in conversation).

[36] Frank Allaun, in conversation with the author, Jan. 1978.

into the forecourt at Aldermaston and sitting down by the main gates'.[37] Despite repeated attempts to arrange an interview with either the director or his deputy, Dr Levin, the demonstrators made no progress. It was therefore decided to mount a week-long sit-down demonstration in the forecourt. Among those taking part were Rev. Donald Soper, Harold Steele, Pat Arrowsmith, April Carter, and Michael Randle. No arrests were made and the demonstration thus proceeded unimpeded by official reaction, but their demands for an interview continued to be refused consistently. At the end of the picket 'fifty took part in the final demonstration outside the plant', and the group dispersed quietly.

The picket exposed many of the fundamental problems which the DAC was to face in subsequent years. Little impact had been made on the Aldermaston workers, and the project had been both small-scale and, in terms of its immediate objectives, unsuccessful. However, it had established a style and a vehicle for non-violent direct action (NVDA) which was to acquire considerable significance in the Movement as a whole over the next few years. And it indicated, too, the substantial differences in approach between the DAC and CND.

(It was not only the Aldermaston picket which pointed to the growing distance between the CND and the DAC: over the summer the two organizations had had some sharp interchanges over the 22 June 'March on London', as was noted in Chapter 2.[38])

DAC DEMONSTRATIONS AND CAMPAIGNS

The Missile Base protests

Late 1958 and early 1959 saw two of the most important of the DAC's campaigns: important both in themselves and because they exemplified the DAC's politics with a new clarity. The first of these were the missile base demonstrations at North Pickenham, in East Anglia, in the winter of 1958–9.

[37] Lengthy DAC report entitled 'Attempt to See the Director at Aldermaston', n.d., DAC archive.
[38] See ch. 2, p. 30. There were other rather petty squabbles too: e.g. A. J. P. Taylor accused the DAC, at a meeting in Sept. 1958 in Cambridge, of organizing the Aldermaston picket demonstration on 22 Sept. to clash deliberately with the CND scientists' meeting, to steal the limelight. DAC replied to this accusation in a letter, in rather hurt tones, to Canon Collins on 7 Oct. 1958 (DAC archive).

In common with its principles and strategy the DAC had been determined, following the Aldermaston March and vigil, to extend its direct action campaign to other key military installations. It became evident in the last few months of 1958 that the Government was moving ahead very quickly with the construction of missile bases for the US Air Force in East Anglia. By November five such Thor bases had been identified in East Anglia, at Feltwell, Tuddenham, Shepherds Grove, Mepal, and North Pickenham. The first three of these had been virtually completed by early November, and Mepal nearly so. There had been a march to Mepal on 24 August organized by the Cambridge Labour Party and Trades Council with the co-operation of local CND groups, but no other public protest had taken place. The DAC thus argued that it was 'vital that a really intensive effort is made to prevent work continuing' on the North Pickenham base which was 'due to be finished in six or seven weeks'.[39] The demonstration was scheduled for the weekend of 6 and 7 December and, prior to that, an intensive campaign had been carried out under the direction of five DAC 'field-workers',[40] to try to persuade the local community, the building contractors, and the Government to cease work on the base. This activity was reasonably successful, at least at the local level: the East Dereham Labour Party gave unanimous support to the campaign; the executive of the Wisbech Labour Party passed a resolution in support; an East Dereham joint meeting of the Amalgamated Engineering Union (AEU) and the building trade workers also expressed support as did various branch meetings of other trade unions, including the woodworkers in Swaffham, and the Transport and General Workers' Union (TGWU) in Wisbech. A number of trade union secretaries and Labour Party agents gave assistance to the DAC in organizing the campaign, and several open-air public meetings were held in local towns and outside factory gates. Persistent efforts were made to 'win over' workers at the base, but there were only modest successes. At the national level, a petition signed by 3,500 opposing the construction of the rocket sites was presented by the DAC to the Prime Minister on 4 December.

[39] DAC archive.
[40] Pat Arrowsmith, Will Warren, Liesl Dales, Frances Edwards, and John Weston Wells. (Initially, April Carter helped Pat Arrowsmith carry out a reconnaissance of the bases.)

The demonstration, led by Pat Arrowsmith, took place on Saturday 6 December with the aim of 'obstructing work on the base as much as possible . . . the group will attempt to walk right into the base and sit round the concrete mixer, which is the focal and most important part of the base whilst it is under construction'.[41] Fifty (forty-six according to *Peace News*) people 'decided to risk the consequences of marching right into it and attempting peacefully to hold up work'.[42] For fifteen to twenty minutes the group obstructed a lorry loading up with gravel, by sitting down: workers on the site gathered to watch and 'to throw mud and insults at us, and we were again showered with a hose'. Eventually the demonstrators were ejected, by RAF personnel and police. A subsequent attempt to re-enter the base later that evening was blocked by the RAF. However, on the Sunday morning at dawn the demonstrators again entered the base and sat down near (or, in one case, inside) the concrete mixer. RAF personnel dragged the demonstrators away 'a great deal less courteously than the civilian police had the day before. Two of us were dumped in pools of icy concrete sludge.' Eventually, after a meeting outside the gates, the demonstrators dispersed: no arrests were made.

The DAC decided to return to the base two weeks later—on 20 December. The first demonstration had received considerable press coverage and questions had been asked in the House of Commons about the way in which demonstrators had been treated. The authorities were thus better prepared on 20 December: a security fence around the base had been completed and a large force of police protected the base. The demonstrators, again numbering approximately fifty accompanied by eighty supporters, were led on to the base by April Carter, Michael Randle, and Rev. Michael Scott. 'Demonstrators were dragged, in a gentlemanly fashion, off the site by the police. They formed up, re-entered and attempted to hold up lorries. One by one they were arrested for obstruction and driven off in police vans to Swaffham. This went on well into the evening, and again the next morning.' Forty-five demonstrators were arrested and those refusing to be bound over (thirty-one) were

[41] DAC briefing for North Pickenham demonstration, 25 Nov. 1958, DAC archive.

[42] Pat Arrowsmith, 'Report on the North Pickenham Rocket base demonstration', n.d., DAC archive. Subsequent quotations describing this demonstration are taken from this document.

given a week to decide whether or not to agree to be so bound: twenty-two refused bail and spent Christmas in jail. Subsequently, thirty-seven people were given a two-week prison sentence.

Why were these demonstrations significant? First, they created a large wave of publicity, in the press, and on radio and television, for both the general cause of nuclear disarmament and for the DAC in particular. More press coverage was given to the North Pickenham demonstration than to any other nuclear disarmament event since the Aldermaston March: moreover, it was almost all favourable—not in the sense of agreeing with the policy objectives of DAC, but in the sympathy and respect shown for the commitment and sincerity of the protesters. Also, it brought the 'nuclear question' onto the agenda: there were numerous discussion articles and editorials concerning nuclear issues, and DAC sympathizers were given invaluable press space to expound their views (most notably the article 'Our Aims at Swaffham' by Rev. Michael Scott in the *Observer* on 11 January 1959). Secondly, and related to this, it enabled the DAC to bring to public attention the philosophy of its Gandhian pacifist politics. From this time on the DAC and its methods became synonymous in the public mind with the Movement as a whole (much to the CND leadership's distress). Thirdly, with these demonstrations the DAC established a successful direct action style of politics: its subsequent activities were to be based largely on the North Pickenham model. Fourthly, the 'success' of this demonstration enabled the DAC to keep alive the movement's dynamism—an essential ingredient in the high-pressure existence of a militant organization characterized by its sense of urgency.

The final reason for North Pickenham's importance lay in its role as a catalyst for opening up the deep-seated differences within the wider pacifist movement, over the proper roles, functions, and strategies for pacifists in the nuclear age. Michael Randle outlined in *Peace News* the reasons justifying direct action of the type carried out at North Pickenham.[43] The fundamental aim of the demonstration was not to attract publicity or demonstrate martyrdom. 'It was an experiment in a new technique (new to Britain at least) to bring home to the workers on the site and the general

[43] Michael Randle, 'The Case for and against Non-violent Obstruction', *Peace News*, 19 Dec. 1958.

public just what the consequences would be of making nuclear weapons and nuclear bases. . . . It presents the challenge of conscience in a meaningful, human way.' The two objections to direct action were that it was coercive, and that 'while there might be situations where it would be right, it ought not to be used by a political minority in a democratic society'—it was in effect an attempt by the minority to impose its will on the majority. Randle's answer was that, *in extremis*, intervention is a duty—and that there can be no more extreme threat than that of nuclear annihilation. On the second point, Randle challenged the notion that the existing society was 'democratic'. 'Democracy implies freedom of choice by the public. But the public cannot exercise this freedom if essential facts and arguments are effectively withheld from it. If . . . the effective media of information are in the hands of a biased minority, freedom of choice and hence democracy are illusions.' Direct action had 'at last managed to break through the barrier of official silence and contempt'. Moreover, even if there were a completely democratic society, direct action politics would retain an essential role because 'majority rule must always operate within the limits imposed by the need to respect human rights'. Where such rights were infringed—as, for example, in Nazi Germany—it is the individual's duty to 'oppose and actively obstruct' the State. This is the case in relation to preparations for 'mass genocide'. The existence of a 'pressure group prepared to use non-violent obstruction against the elected Government whenever it threatens to deprive people anywhere of their basic rights is essential for a healthy society'.

Randle's argument therefore put direct action at the centre of politics, in terms not only of strategy but also of wider principles. Far from being *un*democratic, direct action politics was at the heart of the democratic process, because, echoing J. S. Mill, Randle regarded the protection of both minority opinions and basic human values as the fundamental corner-stone of democracy.

Allen Skinner, in the same issue of *Peace News*, disagreed fundamentally with Randle's position.[44] Whereas he agreed that passive resistance to an occupying power was wholly justifiable, he

---

[44] Allen Skinner, in *Peace News*, under subheading 'There can be no short-cut'. Critical though he was of NVDA, Skinner remained an active and influential member of the DAC, and indeed spent two months in prison, with other DAC activists, in 1959–60.

regarded direct action politics such as that at North Pickenham as coercive and therefore undemocratic, and thus *a priori* unacceptable to pacifists.[45] However, even if this argument were dismissed because of the overriding urgency of the nuclear threat, there was, Skinner contended, a more practical and equally important point. Leaving aside the democratically expressed will of the electorate, however misguided that will might be in relation to nuclear weapons, there could be justification for such action 'only if it is likely to succeed. Now, we know, in fact, that there is no possibility of it succeeding; and if we recognise that, it puts our action in the category of propaganda; what is, in effect, an "advertising gimmick".' Only through an appeal to reason can the advance to a better society be achieved: 'of all people it is the pacifists who must recognise that there can be no coercive short-cut.'

The division thus went beyond the immediate issues of strategy and revealed fundamental disagreements on the nature of modern British society in general, and the degree of democratic structure in particular. The subsequent correspondence in *Peace News*[46] and discussions in the Movement generally, supported Randle's argument, but a significant minority—including several of the older and more experienced radical pacifists—was alienated, from the DAC.

'Voters' Veto'

This polarization was considerably exacerbated by the 'Voters' Veto' campaign. Moreover, this campaign was of considerable

[45] That is, these actions were 'not a refusal to accept coercion; they were an attempt to coerce. . . . [at North Pickenham the demonstrators] were not asserting a freedom: they were seeking to coerce a truck-driver, to deprive him of his freedom to proceed with what he conceived . . . to be his duty' (ibid.).

[46] This included letters from Rev. Donald Soper and Harold Steele. The latter wrote a long and thoughtful private letter to Pat Arrowsmith on 17 Dec. 1958, ostensibly to say that he was unable to take part in the second North Pickenham demonstration on the grounds of ill health. However, his disapproval of the whole direct action politics approach was made explicit in the course of the letter. For him, such actions were always guaranteed to 'provoke . . . in response, vile-tempered violence'. It was in that sense an 'incitement to violence . . . [which was] always a defeat for pacifism'. The aim of the DAC should always remain to 'establish contact with opponents, feeling only compassion for them where they may seem to be in error, indeed only loving them—damn all that stuff about "hampering" and "delaying" and "hindering" ' (DAC archive). (Bertrand Russell, on the other hand, gave his full support to the North Pickenham demonstration, in a letter to Hugh Brock on 19 Dec. 1958.)

embarrassment to the CND leadership, striking as it did at the very heart of CND's Labourist strategy and approach.

The campaign was occasioned by the death of the MP for South-west Norfolk in a car crash, and the consequent by-election. There had been a strong anti-Labour feeling in the DAC for some time. Both April Carter and Michael Randle have testified to the DAC's firm belief that 'the way forward was not through the Labour Party'.[47] Rev. Michael Scott, an influential figure in the DAC,[48] was particularly vociferous in his opposition to any Peace Movement reliance on Labourism,[49] (although according to Michael Randle Allen Skinner was a stronger influence in the DAC's critique of Labourism, and was the driving force behind 'Voters' Veto'). *Peace News* also took a firmly anti-Labourist line, arguing that there were no significant differences between the Labour and Conservative parties over the nuclear issue.[50]

By June the *Peace News* attitude was hardening, and the begin-nings of 'Voters' Veto' were apparent. 'Compass' (the political columnist of *Peace News*) wrote that there should be 'no vote, except for the man [*sic*] who clearly promises that in Parliament he will speak *and vote against* anything to do with nuclear weapons. If no-one makes the promise, no-one gets the votes! They must be withheld'.[51]

This mood did not crystallize into positive proposals until the South-west Norfolk by-election was announced. The constituency provided a particularly appropriate venue for DAC political inter-vention as it included important US bases, and the DAC announced its intention of trying to persuade the electors 'to withhold their vote unless some candidate will take a real stand on atomic weapons'. Moreover, the project was envisaged 'as the prelude to a country-wide campaign along similar lines in connection with the

[47] April Carter, in conversation with the author, Jan. 1978. Michael Randle expressed similar views in conversation with the author, May 1978.

[48] Rev. (Guthrie) Michael Scott, an Anglican priest from the Community of the Resurrection, was active in DAC and CND from the outset. He always favoured civil disobedience and rejected working through the Labour Party. Active for many years in African politics, he took part in the Sahara protest (see below) and the World Peace Brigade initiative in East Africa. He was co-founder of the Committee of 100 with Bertrand Russell (see ch. 5).

[49] See e.g. his speech at Reading in 1958, at which he denounced all 'politicians and all parties. The real enemy was the "party line" ' (*Peace News*, editorial, 18 Apr. 1958).

[50] Ibid.   [51] *Peace News*, 6 June 1958.

General Election'.[52] This was to declare war on the Labour left: and the imminence of the general election made the issue of some real urgency and relevance to all concerned. Frank Allaun's response was typical: 'Voters' Veto' would, he argued, 'antagonise the rank and file of the Labour Party . . . in certain marginal constituencies [it would] lose the seat for Labour and thus possibly lead to the return of another Conservative Government; it would take votes away from the Labour candidates but hardly from the Tories.' The campaign could be valid, therefore, only if it was argued that there were no differences between the Conservative and Labour Parties. This, of course, Allaun rejected, on two main counts: 'out of two hundred and seventy MPs I could name roughly seventy who believe in total unilateral renunciation of the Bomb'; and that there were several aspects of Labour policy which were, if not unilateralist, conducive to disarmament (e.g. the commitment to the unilateral suspension of nuclear tests; a halt to the building of new missile bases until a new attempt had been made at summit negotiations; no flights of planes carrying H-bombs over British territory; no nuclear weapons for West Germany; a foreign policy aimed at disengagement in Europe and co-existence in the Middle East and elsewhere).[53] Both John Baird MP[54] and Frank Allaun withdrew their sponsorship of the DAC following a continued public debate between Allaun and *Peace News*, in which the tone of *Peace News*'s commitment to 'Voters' Veto' became more strident and its opposition to the Labour Party became more extreme.

For the DAC the 'Voters' Veto' campaign was a logical extension of its populist, Gandhian direct action politics. The key, in both principle and practice, for achieving radical political change lay not in the established, centralized, and bureaucratic institutions of the political system and their rigid and stratified organizations, but in the potential for action of the mass of ordinary people.

Just as the rights of the individual are basic to the idea of democracy, individual responsibility and action are the key to a vigorous democratic

---

[52] Ibid., 9 Jan. 1959.

[53] Letter from Frank Allaun, *Peace News*, 16 Jan. 1959.

[54] John Baird expressed his strong misgivings in a letter to Pat Arrowsmith on 2 Mar. 1959: 'I am astonished and disappointed that you should be considering a campaign in S. W. Norfolk which might lead to the defeat of Labour. . . . If your Committee continues in their present attitude, I will reluctantly have to withdraw my support' (DAC archive).

system. They are also, we believe, the key to getting rid of nuclear weapons. Conscientious and courageous individual action is needed at every level. Scientists must refuse to work on nuclear weapons; labourers refuse to build rocket bases; Trade Unions be prepared to strike; Constituency Parties elect nuclear disarmament candidates; MPs vote against the Bomb; and above all the ordinary electors and taxpayers must be prepared to undertake civil disobedience, to withhold revenue and withhold votes.[55]

From the DAC viewpoint, therefore, this was not merely a rejection of the Labour Party in order to attempt to coerce the Party into adopting a unilateralist policy: it was a further extension of politics away from the party machines and into the community. At this level too, therefore, it represented a threat to Labour and Labourism. As Alan Lovell has observed,

unlike the Labour left we were prepared to go all the way ... whereas when it came to the crunch all Gaitskell and the Labour Party machine cared about was whether Mikardo and co. *voted* for Labour, *voted* for the Party—and they did of course ... one of the distinctive things about the DAC was that we were willing to break from the Labour Party.[56]

The CND leadership was, of course, wholly opposed to 'Voters' Veto' and its implications. Note has already been taken of Frank Allaun's Labour left reaction, and Michael Foot was similarly critical (though he had never been a supporter of direct action in any form). The CND leadership's hostility to 'Voters' Veto' was not confined to those active and committed on the Labour left, however. 'Voters' Veto' posed a double threat to CND's leadership: if the Movement were to adopt 'Voters' Veto' policies the Labour Party would be sure to proscribe CND, thus 'compelling' most of the Labour left, rank and file as well as MPs, to cease support for CND; and secondly, support for 'Voters' Veto' would push the Movement decisively towards direct action politics. Moreover, these two tendencies would be mutually reinforcing: the more Labour people left CND the greater the influence and control of the DAC, and the more this occurred the greater the exodus of all 'moderates' from CND, thus posing a threat to the CND leadership itself. It was thus of the utmost importance for the CND leadership vigorously to oppose this initiative. These fears were not spelled out in all their stark political reality in CND's statements, but there was

[55] DAC leaflet, 'Political Implications of a "Voters' Veto" ', n.d.
[56] Alan Lovell, in conversation with the author, Sept. 1978.

no mistaking the seriousness of the threat which they believed 'Voters' Veto' represented.[57] At one level, therefore, Pat Arrowsmith was correct in saying 'Voters' Veto' 'really got CND by the short hairs'.[58]

In the event, however, the CND line triumphed. As has been observed, the fact that the 'argument raged back and forth' over the issue ensured that the campaign was doomed to failure. The majority of the Movement was

prepared to accept the Executive's opposition to 'Voters' Veto', and without the united backing of the whole Campaign it would have been impossible to undertake widespread action along the lines envisaged by the advocates of 'Voters' Veto'. Even if the Campaign had been united in its support of 'Voters' Veto' and its active workers had matched those of the political parties, their ability to seriously influence established voting patterns would have been a doubtful matter. In addition to this the Campaign was not strong enough financially to conduct a widespread election campaign.[59]

With the odds stacked against it, it is not surprising that the campaign in South-west Norfolk was, despite vigorous local activities, politically ineffectual. The election results showed that the campaign had had only a marginal effect: Dye's majority in 1955 had been only 193. In the by-election A. V. Hilton, the non-unilateralist Labour candidate, won by 1,354.[60] Although the Labour share of the poll rose by only 0.7 per cent, it was difficult to construe this as any sort of a victory for 'Voters' Veto'—particularly when the voting turn-out was a 'respectable' 74.08 per cent (cf. 82.6 per cent in the 1955 general election).

The effects of this whole episode were clear, and long-lasting. When it 'became evident that it had been so unsuccessful we [the DAC] lost a lot of credibility'.[61] The 'Voters' Veto' idea was thus effectively buried until the Independent Nuclear Disarmament

[57] CND produced two documents in particular that were concerned with 'Voters' Veto': 'General Election Campaign' and 'Voters' Veto' (the latter being a special supplement to the *CND Bulletin* of Feb. 1959).

[58] Arrowsmith, in conversation.

[59] R. A. Exley, *The CND: Its Organization, Personnel and Methods in its First Year*, MA (Econ.) thesis, University of Manchester, 1959, p. 305.

[60] The full election result was: A. V. Hilton (Lab.) 15,314; Mrs E. Kellett (Cons.), 13,960; A. Fountaine (Ind.), 785; Labour majority 1,354. This compared with the 1955 general election result of: S. Dye (Lab.), 16,781; D. G. Bullard (Cons.), 16,588; Labour majority 193. DAC archive.

[61] Arrowsmith, in conversation.

Election Committee (INDEC) came into existence (see Chapter 3). The hold of the Labour Party had been shown to be too strong to be broken, either in the Nuclear Disarmament Movement itself, or in the wider electorate. More than this, however, the episode indicated the marginality of NVDA politics in an uninformed and fundamentally conservative political culture. Such support as the Movement and its policies had amongst the general electorate was articulated through the conventional media of the Labour Movement, the Churches, and so on. The lesson of 'Voters' Veto' was not so much that the electorate *rejected* the DAC's politics but rather that it failed to understand the alien ideology which underpinned the DAC's specific political demands. Thus the DAC had failed signally to attract the popular upsurge of support for which it had been aiming: but it had permanently alienated such Labour left support as it had previously enjoyed. Initially, this was something of a blow to the DAC, but in the long term it can be argued that it helped to clarify and develop the DAC's NVDA politics, 'unhampered' by ties with Labourism and the inherent compromises which this entailed. Whatever the balance of gains and losses, however, there is no doubt that, from early 1959 onwards, both the DAC and *Peace News* were permanently distanced from the Labour Party and electoral politics.

The DAC and the pacifist movement

Not only did these events clarify, if not polarize, opinion within the DAC and the wider Movement: they also served to exacerbate the already existing tensions between the DAC and the 'traditional' pacifists of the PPU.

At one level the disagreement was over the nature and objectives of pacifism *per se*. The individualist and social action models of pacifism lay at the heart of these differences.[62]

Between the individualistic pacifism of the PPU, based upon Dick Sheppard's movement of the 1930s, and the 'non-violent social revolution' pacifism of the DAC there was an unbridgeable gulf. The former approach was Christian in inspiration, firmly moral in orientation, and largely apolitical. The latter, although numbering

[62] See e.g. articles by Esme Wynne Tyson and Gene Sharp in *Peace News*, 6 Jan. 1956.

among its supporters many active and committed Christians, was, as noted earlier, Gandhian in its approach—combining morality and political action for radical social change. In one sense, therefore, the DAC can be seen as a staging post along the road of radical pacifism within the anti-nuclear movement which begins, in the post-war context, with the PPU and ends with the mass civil disobedience and quasi-anarchistic orientation of the later Committee of 100.[63]

There were other areas of difference between the PPU and the DAC, however. Most obviously there was the PPU's deep suspicion of CND, the DAC *et al.* for their apparent willingness to differentiate qualitatively between nuclear war and 'conventional' war. For the PPU, the problem was war itself, and the task was to abolish war—not to be fooled into thinking that, if nuclear weapons could be abolished, the problem of war would be solved. This message was hammered home week after week in Sybil Morrison's regular *Peace News* column, which appeared throughout the heyday of the DAC and ended only after *Peace News* became an 'independent newspaper' and severed its institutional links with the PPU.[64]

There can be no doubt of the initial and persistent hostility of the PPU to the new Movement.[65] In a letter from the executive committee of the PPU to the *New Statesman* on 6 December 1957 (which the *New Statesman* did not publish) the full pacifist argument was put strongly.

It is interesting to see how the demand for the abolition of tests is passing into a demand for the abandonment of nuclear weapons by Britain, but why stop there? ... the only alternative to total war is total peace ... instead ... of thinking in terms of a new organization to deal with one aspect of war, it would surely be better if all those who are concerned will

[63] See ch. 5 *passim*. It is also the case, however, that the DAC remained quintessentially a radical *pacifist* movement, and its ideology was rooted in the individualistic pacifist perspective, albeit overlaid with both Gandhian and libertarian socialist conceptions and concerns.

[64] Both Sybil Morrison and Stuart Morris of the PPU had resigned from the board of *Peace News* in April 1960 (reported in *Peace News*, 29 Apr. 1960). On 5 May 1961 the separation of the PPU and *Peace News* was announced. It was stressed that the paper remained committed to 'the abolition of war and the promotion of international peace'. The reason for the separation was that *Peace News* had 'grown up' and that 'no one organization in any country should have an exclusive right to control the paper's policy in the interests of its own programme'.

[65] According to Brock (in conversation), 'it was from the general secretary and the campaign organizer [of PPU] that the difficulties arose.'

now help to create the public opinion which will demand not the abolition of this or that weapon, but the adoption by Great Britain of total disarmament.[66]

Following the inaugural meeting of CND in February, Stuart Morris called an emergency meeting of the PPU to 'launch a campaign not for nuclear disarmament but for the unconditional total disarmament of Britain as an example to the world'.[67] At the AGM of the PPU in April 1958, there was an inconclusive battle between Skinner, Sharp, and others, and the old guard of the PPU. In the end, the PPU emerged with its basic policies unchanged.[68]

The combined effects of the 'Voters' Veto' campaign and the North Pickenham demonstration brought the ethos, as well as the activities, of the DAC into focus. For many in the PPU this marked the turning-point, and some dissociated themselves from the DAC and the wider Movement. The 'debate' continued intermittently in the correspondence columns of *Peace News* but by 1959 the PPU was to all intents and purposes a spent force and the energies and dynamism of the pacifist movement were almost wholly directed towards the DAC.

The major significance of the DAC campaigns over 'Voters' Veto' and North Pickenham was thus that they gave practical political expression to what had previously been a somewhat abstract adherence to the Gandhian concept of non-violent revolution. Although there were subsequently some important developments in DAC action and strategy (such as the industrial campaign, the Sahara project, and the Holy Loch demonstrations, all of which are discussed below), the basic pattern, image, and political profile of the DAC was now formulated.

The rocket base demonstrations

Over the next two years the DAC organized a large number of rocket base demonstrations and other actions based on the North Pickenham 'model'. Immediately following North Pickenham it was agreed to stage a demonstration at Watton, Norfolk in the

---

[66] Reprinted in *Peace News*, 3 Jan. 1958.

[67] *Peace News*, 28 Feb. 1958. Morris also made the point, in the same issue, that 'you cannot destroy the knowledge which is in people's minds of how to make [nuclear weapons]. . . . It is war itself which must be eliminated'.

[68] See conference report, *Peace News*, 25 Apr. 1958.

form of a picket and demonstration in May 1959. A 'field-work' programme of activity similar to that which preceded North Pickenham was planned, but the response was not encouraging and it was decided not to organize a civil disobedience demonstration. However, a limited campaign was mounted in Suffolk to protest against the base at Rattlesden and the H-bomb storage site at Sutton Heath. This culminated in weekend vigils at both sites, ending on 27 July 1959. A major and co-ordinated campaign was mounted in the East Midlands to protest at the construction of the following rocket bases: North Luffenham (near Stamford), Polebrook (near Oundle), Harrington (near Rothwell), Folkingham (near Sleaford), Great Dalby (near Melton Mowbray), and Woolfox (near Stamford). Of these, the campaigns at Polebrook and Harrington were the only protests really to 'take off'. Although civil disobedience had been planned originally at Polebrook, it was decided that the prominence of the nuclear issue in the public mind as a result of the debates in the trade union movement through mid-1959 meant that such a demonstration 'would not be appropriate'.[69] Implicit in this decision was the desire not to alienate the trade union movement, and local workers generally: in the summer of 1959 the climate within the Labour Movement was changing rapidly towards support for the unilateralist policy, and the DAC rightly surmised that any advocacy of militant NVDA might well alienate such working-class support.[70]

In the event the demonstration, on 22 August 1959, was something of an anti-climax, with 200 demonstrators listening quietly to speeches denouncing the rocket bases and dispersing, with no apparent impact on the workers at the base. There was, however, reasonably good local press coverage[71] and, although it is

[69] DAC circular, 'Rocket Base Campaigns', 1 Aug. 1959, DAC archive.

[70] It was, however, a strangely pragmatic decision, verging perhaps on the unprincipled, to abandon temporarily the politics of non-violent direct action. It was also inconsistent, to say the least, to claim by implication that the DAC's *raison d'être* was to 'focus public attention' on the nuclear issue (DAC, 'Rocket Base Campaigns').

Two Polebrook workers, Herbert Ingall and Tom Godfrey, resigned from work on conscientious grounds; and the demonstration received support from local Labour Party and trade union groups (though, significantly, the DAC had no co-operation from the TGWU despite a direct approach to Frank Cousins by April Carter. See letter from Cousins to Carter, 13 July 1959, DAC archive.)

[71] This was in marked contrast to the patronizing and sexist report which appeared in the *Leicester Mercury* on 10 June 1959. Reporting Pat Arrowsmith's visit to a rocket site 'somewhere in Lincolnshire' the paper continued: '[it was] a nice

difficult to quantify, there can be no doubt that the whole campaign had made the nuclear issue a matter of some concern in the locality. The next major DAC demonstration, at Harrington on 2 January 1960, took a more militant form. It was preceded by a two-month field-work campaign in the area, but the demonstration itself was firmly in the North Pickenham tradition. However, before the demonstration took place, all six members of the DAC[72] were arrested and charged with 'being disturbers of the peace and with inciting people to break the law'.[73] All refused to be bound over when brought to court on 15 December and were sentenced to two months in prison. (An *ad hoc* committee took over responsibility for organizing the demonstration.) Eighty-two people were arrested at the demonstration, although all were conditionally discharged at the Northampton Court hearing on 6 January. Greville Janner, representing all the defendants, described the case as 'one of the most extraordinary ever to come before an English court', and the DAC leaders said that 'the magistrates took the only way out which we were able to accept'.[74] CND supporters, as before, found themselves in a rather difficult position: over 400 took part in a supporting demonstration, including Mrs Diana Collins. Canon Collins, in a letter to the *Sunday Times*, whilst disclaiming any CND support for illegal action, stressed the 'common aim' of the two movements.[75] A supporting CND rally was held in London (Marble Arch) on 3 January: the speakers included Rev. Donald Soper and Ian Mikardo.

The demonstration certainly achieved wide press coverage— although in the popular press there was the almost inevitable trivialization. Moreover, the use of the somewhat anachronistic 1361 Act to prosecute the DAC leaders led to a vociferous

happy quiet rural sort of atmosphere . . . then came t-r-o-u-b-l-e in the shape of attractive Miss Pat Arrowsmith. . . . Burly, bewhiskered Irish navvies were astonished . . . broad grins broke out and since it wasn't even opening time they knew it couldn't be the drink for sure. Miss Arrowsmith was asking them to stop work . . . as an Ulsterman grinningly told a reporter later "Sure and who the devil is going to give up twenty five pounds a week even for a lady". He winked enormously.'

[72] Pat Arrowsmith, Hugh Brock, April Carter, Frances Edwards, Allen Skinner, and Will Warren. (Inez Randall agreed to be bound over.) Michael Randle was in West Africa on the Sahara project (see below) with Rev. Michael Scott and others.
[73] DAC press release, 15 Dec. 1959, DAC archive. Imprisonment was under the 1361 Act.
[74] Cited in the *Daily Mail*, 7 Jan. 1960.
[75] *Sunday Times*, 10 Jan. 1960.

campaign of parliamentary support. Sydney Silverman and thirty-seven other MPs had written to the Home Secretary, R. A. Butler, asking the Queen to intervene and release the prisoners from jail, and although this request was refused the resultant publicity was most welcome to the DAC.

There were, though, considerable problems within the DAC as a result of the Harrington demonstration. Most immediately, the court's decision to release all eighty-two defendants posed the problem of a follow-up, given the expected failure of the demonstrators to immobilize the base. Pat Arrowsmith and April Carter, writing from prison, argued for a return to the base.[76] But the imprisonment of the DAC leaders, the difficulty of marshalling large enough numbers to make a return to Harrington viable, and, above all, doubts about the efficacy of what might be seen as merely a ritual reflex gesture by returning to the base, led to the DAC's decision not to return to Harrington.

These doubts about the established NVDA position were voiced by Alan Lovell in *Peace News*, where he called for a more condemnatory attitude to the police who, he claimed, were at best aiding and abetting mass murder. Pat Arrowsmith echoed this view and *Peace News* also advocated a more militant stance.[77] All this represented a significant change of policy: the change within the direct action movement which resulted eventually in the creation of the Committee of 100 can be discerned clearly in this hardening of attitude.[78] Despite the doubts and criticisms expressed by many in the pacifist movement,[79] the DAC and its activist leaders began, from this time, to concentrate more on *mass* civil disobedience as an objective. Similarly, the policies of total openness with the authorities, and the compliance with police arrest, came under heavier criticism—thus presaging the demonstration tactics of the later Committee of 100.

Why did this new mood come over the DAC after Harrington? In part it was because of frustration at the seemingly impenetrable hostility of the Government and the authorities; in part because of a

[76] Letter from Pat Arrowsmith and April Carter to DAC, from Holloway Prison, 11 Jan. 1960, DAC archive.
[77] See Pat Arrowsmith, letter; and editorial, *Peace News*, 29 Jan. 1960.
[78] As George Clark, in conversation with the author, Jan. 1978, has recalled.
[79] e.g. Katherine Duthie was 'seriously disturbed' by Lovell's arguments. 'It is in fact an essential part of the spirit of the British police', she argued, 'that they are neutral and do not let their own opinions interfere with the course of their duty' (letter in *Peace News*. 12 Feb. 1960).

sense of futility at the anticlimatic results of the North Pickenham/
Harrington-style demonstrations, preceded as they had been by so
much field-work in the locality; and in part because of the perceived
urgency of the nuclear threat and the consequent shortage of time
available to achieve policy objectives.

However, the most important factor was the ideological change
which came over the DAC following the heavy and dispiriting
electoral defeat of the Labour Party in 1959. As noted in Chapter 2,
Labour's almost total concern with material and economic issues in
the campaign had disillusioned very many peace activists. Following the 1959 election, *Peace News* called unequivocally for a 'new
politics', arguing that the defeat was the result of 'the socialist
betrayal of half a century ago. . . . What is needed is not a careful
steering between two parties but a completely fresh examination of
what are the major problems confronting man.'[80]

As if to emphasize the DAC's distance from Labourism, the
anarchists embraced the direction actionists, claiming that they
were 'pioneers in a struggle which, by its very nature, brings to the
fore at once the contemporary relevance of anarchist ideas: the
struggle between people and governments'.[81] The DAC had come a
long way—whether retrogressively or progressively is a matter of
opinion of course—since the days of Harold Steele and the early
Committee. The climate was now right for a more militant and
ambitious initiative—which was to come later in the year in the
form of the Committee of 100 (although, as George Clark and
others have recalled, the general idea was in the air from the time of
the 1960 Aldermaston March).[82]

This is to anticipate, however. Following Harrington, the DAC
organized demonstrations at Feltwell and Lakenheath, Foulness
and Finningley. The first of these, at Feltwell and Lakenheath, was
a relatively small-scale demonstration on 6 March 1960, involving
no civil disobedience. About 400 took part in a protest march
followed by a rally addressed by Canon Collins. The demonstration
at Finningley RAF V-bomber base in Yorkshire was an altogether
more impressive affair. It was organized jointly by Doncaster CND
and Northern DAC. There was considerable trade union and

[80] Editorial, p. 1 and headline, 'A Time for New Politics', *Peace News*, 16 Oct.
1960.
[81] *Freedom*, 9 Jan. 1960.
[82] George Clark, in conversation; confirmed also by Randle and Carter, in
conversation.

Labour Movement support for the demonstration and the Church
was also actively involved: of fifteen non-conformist ministers in
the area, thirteen supported the demonstration, and Rev. L.
Barnett and the Archdeacon of Doncaster both spoke at the rally following
the march. The Chaplain on the base, Rev. Raine of Thorne, was
dismissed because he too supported the demonstrators' objectives.
Over 100,000 leaflets were distributed and the membership of
Doncaster CND grew, over three months, from fifty to 200. The
demonstration itself, on 30 July 1960, attracted 2,000 people
to the ten-mile march from Finningley to Doncaster. The DAC
demonstration was preceded by a 100-hour vigil at the base:
twenty were arrested on the demonstration itself, eighteen of whom
were jailed for seven days.

The whole affair was an undoubted success, in terms both of its
publicity and propaganda achievement and of its raising of local
consciousness on the issue. It represented, however, a rather special
and atypical example of political activism: South Yorkshire has had
a reputation for many years as a strikingly militant socialist area,
with the trade unions and the Labour Movement generally very
much in the vanguard of political radicalism. Finningley must be
seen as very much a special case.

In a very different sense the long campaign of protest mounted at
Foulness was also atypical. 'Operation Foulness Committee' (OFC)
was formed after a meeting on Southend front on Hiroshima Day
1959 at which Will Warren had called for some radical action at
the AWRE at Foulness. The resulting local committee was inexperienced and almost completely Quaker in composition. Although the
demonstration was originally planned for Christmas 1959 it was
decided, on advice from the DAC, to postpone it until Easter 1960.
Through the winter an intensive campaign of leafleting was
organized, and a petition also circulated successfully. Money was
collected from local householders and used, in part, to employ
David Fairbanks to work with Southend CND and YCND on the
project.

The original plan for the final demonstration consisted of four
parts: a meeting and march from Southend to the Lardwich road-
block; a vigil from 2 p.m. Saturday to 7 a.m. on Monday; a 'rivercade' from Shoebury East beach to Foulness Island and an attempt
to land on the island; and a civil disobedience demonstration at
7 a.m. on Monday.

The meeting and march were carried out satisfactorily, if without any spectacular success (200 or so took part). The vigil was rather less successful, and the rivercade was cancelled as being too difficult and too hazardous. At the civil disobedience demonstration on 25 April, twenty-one people were arrested: all were fined 40s., and all refused to pay and were thus sentenced to seven days in jail (although both Cyril King and Will Warren had money confiscated to pay the fine and were thus released). Contrary to the developing mood in the DAC, and generally on the radical wing of the Nuclear Disarmament Movement, the demonstration was couched within a Quaker, 'public witness' framework.

Despite opposition from OFC, Will Warren decided to proceed with plans for a follow-up demonstration. On 2 May a further civil disobedience demonstration took place: fifteen were arrested, of whom thirteen were sent to prison for six months. This was a surprisingly heavy sentence and was indicative of the authorities' increasing determination to quell the rising tide of civil disobedience—even when it took such a passive and respectable form.

Foulness was atypical because it was basically a locally organized and inspired operation. Somewhat out of touch with the national 'mood' of the DAC *et al.*, OFC went ahead on a fundamentally Quaker basis. At one level, therefore, both Finningley and Foulness were isolated, albeit relatively successful, actions.

The key events, in terms of British demonstrations in 1959–60 which formulated DAC politics, were the North Pickenham demonstration, 'Voters' Veto', and, to a lesser extent, the Harrington demonstration. There were, of course, other influences and important events outside the immediate national demonstration context, and it is to these that attention must next be directed. However, in terms of the events analysed thus far, a clear progression within DAC politics is evident: from a variegated, but primarily Gandhian and Quaker, basis the DAC developed its own unique brand of direct action politics, brought to the public attention initially by the Aldermaston March and vigil (and later picket), and the North Pickenham action. Through the succeeding eighteen months further experience of missile base demonstrations was gained, and the movement had begun, by early 1960, to develop a more militant, mass civil disobedience orientation, moving away from the essentially individualistic and passive approach deriving from the Quaker tradition. Superimposed upon this process was the increasing disillusionment with parliamentary democracy, social democracy, the Labour Party, and Labourism. This found its first concrete expression in the eventually unsuccessful but significant 'Voters' Veto' campaign, but was to crystallize, following the 1959 election campaign and Labour's defeat, into a deep and lasting distrust and distaste for conventional party politics. An evaluation of this whole DAC development, in terms of its theoretical and practical viability, is attempted in the final section of this chapter.

By mid-1960 the various events and experiences described thus far in this chapter had produced a context in which some new initiative to create a mass civil disobedience movement was imperative. Before moving on to discuss the DAC's response to this development, and its eventual decision to disband and merge into the new Committee of 100 following the Holy Loch demonstration in 1961, we must first analyse several other important aspects of DAC activity which took place contemporaneously with the missile base demonstrations already discussed. These fall under three main headings: the industrial campaign; the Sahara protest mission; and other international collaborative activities.

The DAC industrial campaign

The DAC industrial campaign was one of the most important aspects of its politics: its significance went well beyond its specific achievements which were, generally, rather modest. The industrial campaign was central to the DAC's conception of taking politics to the people. Its intention was to arouse the consciences of those involved directly in the production of nuclear weapons and the preparations for nuclear war: a crucial part of this process was to try to activate those workers, both individually and collectively, into opposition to nuclear weapons through strike action.

Pat Arrowsmith was centrally concerned with this whole campaign, and the amount of work, energy, commitment, and enthusiasm she put into it was phenomenal. Without her driving force it is most unlikely that the industrial campaign would have ever got off the ground.

At a meeting on 26 February 1959 the DAC resolved to 'Carry out an intensive campaign at Stevenage . . . approaching Trade Unions and picketing the factory where the rockets were being made, in an attempt to rouse local opinion, get work on the rockets blacked and get individual workers to leave their jobs if they were working on making the Blue Streaks'.[83] In fact the DAC had been seeking for some time to make contact with the trade union movement. In a long exchange of letters with the DAC in 1958 and 1959, the TUC, in the person of Sir Vincent Tewson, refused to have anything to do with the DAC.[84] However, contacts at this level were anyway out of harmony with the whole ethos of the DAC approach. Direct contact with workers and a militant attempt to persuade them, as individuals, to cease work on nuclear armaments was much more congruent with the DAC's politics, and it was in a series of intensive, locally based actions that the industrial campaign was to evolve its style and make its impact.

The first of these, the campaign in Stevenage, began in April 1959. The DAC, having 'ascertained that fifty per cent or more of the industry of Stevenage was tied up with missile manufacture at De Havillands' Propellors (Blue Streak) and English Electric (Thunderbird)',[85] decided to organize a two-week campaign in the town immediately following the Aldermaston March. About ten DAC activists moved into the area, under the guidance of Pat Arrowsmith. A variety of action was undertaken: leafleting (the leaflets set out the general unilateralist case, and urged all the people of the town to 'refuse to make [nuclear weapons] or be a party to their manufacture'); door-to-door canvassing to obtain signatures to a letter to the development corporation asking for more alternative peaceful industry for Stevenage ('over one thousand people in the town signed. . . . In addition seventy five local people promised financial assistance to any rocket factory worker who decided to quit his job on conscientious grounds');[86] an exhibition in the town centre; and daily poster parades, both in the vicinity of the factories and in other parts of the town.

The main thrust of the campaign, however, was undoubtedly

[83] DAC minutes, 26 Feb. 1959, DAC archive.
[84] See letter from Sir Vincent Tewson to April Carter, 16 Dec. 1958, in which he stated that 'unilateral nuclear disarmament is contrary to the policy of the TUC . . . furthermore your organization has no connection with Congress and in these circumstances I am unable to accede to your request' [i.e. for a meeting], (DAC archive).
[85] 'Brief Summary of the Stevenage Campaign', unsigned (probably written by Pat Arrowsmith), n.d., DAC archive. Subsequent quotations relating to the Stevenage action are taken from this document unless otherwise stated.
[86] Pat Arrowsmith, April Carter, and Michael Randle, letter to the *Guardian*, 15 Apr. 1959.

aimed at the industrial workers—not only those engaged directly in armaments work, but the whole trade union community. A number of trade union contacts was made prior to the campaign, largely by two local CND members, one a *Peace News* reporter and the other an active Amalgamated Society of Woodworkers (ASW) member. As a result, the DAC received invitations to send speakers to local union meetings and to the trades council. 'At the latter there was lively discussion, leading to a decision to refer the whole matter back to the branches represented. The chairman of the trades council said in his opinion there should be a token strike.' An Amalgamated Engineering Union (AEU) shop steward from English Electric 'also said privately later to the Committee that he thought there should be a token strike, and did his best to get other shop stewards in the factory to agree. He was unsuccessful in this.'[87]

The most significant success, however, was with the Amalgamated Union of Building Trade Workers (AUBTW). At a branch meeting at which a DAC member spoke, a resolution was passed 'recommending workers not to work at English Electric or De Havillands, and that a fund be set up to help any who did quit, and that alternative work should be sought for them . . . it was also decided to call a one hour token strike at 4 p.m. [on 10 April 1959] to attend a rally in the town centre in support of the campaign.' The idea for this came *from* the AUBTW. Both the ASW and the National Union of Furniture Trade Operatives (NUFTO) also supported the strike, though with less enthusiasm. Four canteens on building sites were addressed by Committee and AUBTW representatives in order to urge the men to carry out the strike resolution. In each case there were majorities in favour of strike action (in two cases fairly narrow ones). In the event 'most of the thousand or so builders downed tools an hour earlier than usual'.

However, support for the strike was by no means total. A number of CND groups refused to give official backing to the Stevenage campaign (e.g. Letchworth, Welwyn Garden City, and Luton and South Bedfordshire), although their memberships were divided over the NVDA issue.[88] There was a division of opinion,

[87] However, he did give the campaign support, and 'reported to the Committee that we had stirred up a lot of feeling—quite a bit on our side—in the factory'.

[88] See e.g. DAC report, 'Discussion with Letchworth CND', unsigned, n.d., DAC archive. It was partly on the basis of these discussions that the DAC decided against any immediate follow-up of the Stevenage campaign. See DAC minutes, 7 June 1959, DAC archive.

too, in the Labour Party. The local Labour candidate was neither a DAC supporter nor a unilateralist, whereas the chairman of Hitchin Divisional Labour Party had marched in support of the DAC and gave his personal backing to the campaign.

The 'official' attitude of the trade unions to the strike was, predictably, one of cautious hostility. On the day of the strike, for example, an ASW official came to the site and emphasized to his members that, as the strike was not official, there was no need to support it. Very little, if any, progress was made with the AEU or the ETU (Electrical Trades Union), although after the campaign the De Havilland AEU branch passed a resolution in favour of the action.

The numbers coming out on strike were perhaps slightly disappointing for the DAC. (The local paper had predicted that 'as many as 1,200 men could be involved'.[89] In the event something in excess of 1,000 took part.[90]) Moreover, 'a disappointingly small number of workers [about 100] actually marched to the rally in the Centre.' On the following day a town centre rally (the third to be held during the campaign) was addressed by Rev. Donald Soper, Benn Levy, and Dr Alex Comfort. Again, the rally was 'not as well attended as we had hoped', although this was at least partly because of the rain.

The campaign had a considerable impact on the town. Among subsequent activities were CND film shows and discussion meetings, and a Labour Party management committee resolution supporting a town meeting on alternative industry. (The trades council also established a subcommittee to look 'into the balance of industry problem in Stevenage'.) In the long term, however, the campaign produced no constructive alternative proposals: the appeal remained at the absolute moral level.

This moral imperative was carried forward to the more generalized industrial campaign launched through the following summer. (The interim period was taken up with other campaigns: notably the rocket base actions). Encouraged by the relative success of the Stevenage campaign, and the associated actions at the East Anglian rocket bases, the DAC planned over the spring of 1960 an ambitious campaign centred on the following industrial armament locations: A. V. Roe's Vulcan 2 H-bomber plane production plants

[89] *Stevenage Pictorial*, 10 Apr. 1959.
[90] This was the estimate of the *Daily Herald*, 11 Apr. 1959.

at Woodford, Manchester, and Chertsey, Surrey; also in Surrey at Weybridge, where Vickers were engaged on developing the TSR2; at the Bristol Siddeley Engines plant in Bristol where the engines for both the Vulcan and the TSR2 were made; and finally, in Slough, where there were a number of firms making component parts for military aircraft. The Manchester campaign, under the direction of Douglas Brewood (senior), who gave up his job as a sheet-metalworker to take on this role, began on 8 August and lasted for three weeks. In Bristol, where the campaign had the official support of Bristol CND, the campaign organizer was Pat Arrowsmith: the campaign began on 11 July and ended on 3 September. The Surrey campaign, beginning on 30 June and lasting for a month, was under the direction of Ian Cooke (later replaced by Wendy Butlin). The Slough campaign began on 5 September, shortly after the Manchester action had been completed, and was under the direction of Douglas Brewood (senior).

The DAC's strategy, explained in a statement of May 1960, was to conduct 'a multi-pronged campaign, directed at a central company responsible for making actual H-bombers, at a company supplying some major component part, like the engine, and at one or more companies supplying small component parts'.[91] The aim was to halt production and to bring to public attention the extent to which the economy relied upon weapons manufacture.

These were ambitious objectives. How far were they achieved? Of all the actions planned only that at Bristol yielded any real success. The main focus of activity in Bristol, however, was within the trade union movement:

Thirty four meetings were addressed, including District meetings, branch meetings, Bristol Trades Council and BSE and BAL Shop Stewards' meetings.

Nine of the Trade Union meetings passed resolutions in support of the campaign. ... The AESD [Association of Engineers and Shipbuilding Draftsmen] District Council passed a resolution which included the following statement: 'It is desirable that trade unionists should recognise their direct responsibility when employed in armaments; and accordingly the District Council agrees that diversification of the aircraft industry is desirable with emphasis on production for peaceful purposes as opposed to production for military use.'

[91] DAC circular, 'Proposed Summer Industrial Campaign', 6 May 1960, DAC archive.

Factory gate meetings, sponsored and introduced by shop stewards in the firms concerned, were held at eight firms, including BSE and BAL. The Management of Bristol Commerical Vehicles agreed to the meeting being held on the works' premises. A resolution was passed by the meeting in favour of the Direct Action campaign. At a meeting outside another civil engineering works a resolution was passed advocating direct industrial action to get rid of the Bomb.[92]

Two lunch-hour factory gate meetings, sponsored and chaired by the shop stewards' committee, were held at Bristol Siddeley Engines. One hundred and fifty to 200 men attended the first, which was addressed by Pat Arrowsmith. The shop stewards' committee invited Donald Soper to address the second meeting on 1 August 1960. There was an audience of about 500, about 100 of whom decided to prolong their lunch hour unofficially for twenty minutes in order to extend the meeting, in response to a suggestion by the chairman. The meeting was also addressed by the local AESD official, and attended by three delegates from other engineering firms in Bristol who got time out from work for the purpose. 'At the end of the meeting Dr Soper, accompanied by these delegates, the Convenor of BSE Shop Stewards' Committee and one or two others tried in vain to have an interview with the Management in order to hand in the petition. Both these meetings had some local and national press publicity and were reported on radio and TV.'[93]

The Bristol campaign thus made some headway, and built a base from which, perhaps, further meaningful political progress within the organized working-class movement could have been achieved. But, despite a proposal from Pat Arrowsmith for a return to Bristol, nothing significant materialized, and, after the final rally on 3 September organized by the DAC in conjunction with the Bristol trades council and the British Peace Committee, the campaign effectively ended.

The DAC's own overall conclusion to the summer campaign was forthright and honest. 'The declared aims of these campaigns were direct industrial action against nuclear arms production. This aim was not achieved in any of the areas where projects were organized

[92] For details of these campaigns see Richard Taylor, *The British Nuclear Disarmament Movement of 1958 to 1965 and its Legacy to the Left*, Ph.D. thesis, University of Leeds, 1983, ch. 7.
This quotation is taken from DAC circular, 'Report on Recent Activities: The Summer Industrial Campaign', 17 Oct. 1960, DAC archive.
[93] Ibid.

... though in Bristol one event verged on being "industrial action".[94]

The industrial campaign was couched within the same broad ideological framework which characterized the DAC in general, the nature of which has been touched upon already and will be analysed in more detail below. There were, however, a number of distinctive features of this particular branch of DAC activism. It was within this context that the DAC's pervasive populism came closest to a socialist perspective. The DAC consistently believed in taking the issue of nuclear disarmament directly to the people, confronting them with the nuclear choice, and insisting upon their power to change policies, perspectives, and politics. Their populism thus took a dualistic but complementary form: real change could come about only through decentralized direct action, which avoided the compromises, the filtering and neutralizing processes of the established institutional political system; also, the very process of direct action, and hence real political involvement, would raise not only the level of political consciousness but the confidence of the participants in their own power. These two aspects were thus mutually reinforcing in building up a mass direct action politics. Translated into the industrial context, this approach led to a concentration on 'shop-floor', rank-and-file trade unionists and other workers, rather than the official trade union structure. The objective was to persuade the mass of workers, both those in the direct armaments industries and those in unrelated unionized occupations, to strike over the issue of nuclear weapons production and the related nuclear policies, testing, etc. Although in practice this was manifested only in token strikes (as at Stevenage and Bristol), the long-term objective was, quite explicitly, far more ambitious. As Pat Arrowsmith has recalled, 'we always felt that if you could get a massive General Strike in this country on an issue of this sort, it might really be a more effective way of changing the Labour Party than marching, even in your millions, quietly from Aldermaston to London.'[95]

The classic syndicalist strategy of 'propaganda by the deed', and of building from localized, small-scale but militant strike action, both leading eventually to social revolution via an industrial general strike, bore a close resemblance to the DAC's own strategic

[94] Ibid.
[95] Arrowsmith, in conversation.

position.[96] There were of course major differences. The DAC was
wholly and centrally committed to non-violence whilst the
syndicalist tradition had always recognized the need for militancy
(and at times for violence) and certainly did not have a pacifist
ethos as its central motivating force. Moreover, the DAC had
neither a class-based nor a formally anarchist ideological outlook,
as will be argued.

This modified syndicalism was complemented by the radical
moralism of the Independent Labour Party (ILP) tradition. This,
too, characterized the whole DAC perspective but was perhaps
particularly marked in the industrial campaign and in Pat
Arrowsmith's own politics. It was the moral imperative which lay
at the centre of the campaign: it was neither an economic nor a
political message which the DAC concentrated upon. As the Stevenage leaflet put it: 'if you believe it is wrong to threaten to kill
millions of people in another country, if you believe that nuclear
weapons are suicidal, if you believe that Britain must set an
example by the abolition of these weapons . . . then should you not
refuse to make them or be a party to their manufacture?'[97]

This ideological position thus presented a clear and reasonably
coherent basis for an industrial strategy, and nobody could have
worked harder to achieve the objectives than Pat Arrowsmith.
Moreover, in terms of tactics to achieve the long-term strategic
objective, a considerable realism characterized the campaign (e.g.
the attempt to begin with *token* strikes; the realization that militant
and well-organized trade unions which were not directly involved
in armaments production could be equally relevant to the
campaign's success). And yet the campaign, as Pat Arrowsmith has
since acknowledged, was not a success, and we may now return to
an analysis of the reasons for this failure.

The most obvious, and in some ways most important, reason is
the gross disparity between the ambitious objectives of the
campaign and the extremely limited resources, human and
financial, which the campaign could command. Part of this
problem related to the sociological and political fact, noted by
Parkin among others,[98] that the Movement was the latest in a series

[96] As Hugh Brock recalled, in conversation, 'Allen Skinner . . . called himself a
Guild Socialist'; and, later '[the DAC was] not really anarchist, no, more, perhaps,
syndicalist.'   [97] DAC Stevenage leaflet.
[98] Frank Parkin, *Middle Class Radicalism: The Social Bases of the British
Campaign for Nuclear Disarmament*, Manchester, 1968.

of *middle-class* protest movements which were 'expressive' rather than 'instrumental' in character. Whether or not the full implications of Parkin's thesis of CND as an essentially 'middle-class radical' movement are accepted, there is no doubt that the leadership and the large majority of the Movement generally, and perhaps the DAC in particular, was predominantly middle-class.[99] This applied to the social class backgrounds of the activists, but it also applied to the *culture* of the Movement. The assumptions, the language, the style, and the politics of both CND and the DAC were, in their different ways, almost exclusively middle-class.

To break through to the industrial working class, particularly to the non-activist, largely apolitical, rank and file, on an issue which was not seen as directly relevant to their immediate self-interest was an extremely difficult task.[100] It required some understanding of, and empathy with, the Labour Movement, its practices, decision-making processes, and language. The CND, at leadership level at least, was wholly unsuited and unsympathetic to this 'industrial militancy' approach, and much preferred to work through the official trade union and Labour machine to secure the somewhat hollow victory of 1960. But the DAC activists, who were so committed to the industrial campaign, were also, for very different reasons, out of touch with all but a small number of isolated activists in the Labour Movement and the working class. There were four particular aspects to this: first, the moral absolutism of the DAC; second, the individualism which characterized DAC activism; third, the lack of any economic dimension; and fourth, the political extremism implicit in DAC politics. The centrally moral tone of the DAC propaganda in its industrial campaign has already been noted. However, because DAC activists in general, and Pat Arrowsmith in particular, were so totally committed to the campaign, they were unable or unwilling to take any account of 'practical' reservations that ordinary people were likely to have about such extreme measures as closing down all armaments-related factories. Whilst such a position may have been morally correct, and even logically faultless given the DAC's assumptions, it

[99] This is confirmed by the detailed statistical survey of Movement activists which forms pt. ii of Richard Taylor and Colin Pritchard, *The Protest Makers: The British Nuclear Disarmament Movement of 1958–1965, Twenty Years On*, Oxford, 1980.
[100] Although it was not of course a wholly impossible one. The impact made on trade union opinion through the orthodox Labour Movement channels on the nuclear issue was considerable through 1959 and 1960. See ch. 6.

was hardly likely to appeal to the average worker with a family to support, rent to pay, etc. [101]

The individualistic basis of the DAC's politics was an integral constituent and was, it will be argued, one of the movement's fundamental weaknesses. In the industrial campaign this individualistic approach was at odds with the most basic of Labour Movement characteristics: group solidarity. The success of general DAC politics, such as it was, lay ultimately in its appeal to individuals to stand out explicitly against what they believed to be wrong. Through long years of experience and struggle, and indeed through the very formative experiences of the working class itself, the Labour Movement had come to realise that its strength lay in its collective power and that, if it were to achieve its objectives, it must *act* collectively. Although the DAC *did* call, generally, for 'collective action', in the sense of token strikes, its message was couched essentially in moral and individualist terms. It was the conscience of the individual worker in the armaments and defence industries to which the DAC's appeal was directed, and not the collective industrial action of the Labour Movement *per se*. The DAC's appeal was essentially for individual sacrifice on a moral issue and, as such, was doubly likely to fail. (Although the potential linkage with the ILP's moralistic tradition of socialism should not be ignored in this context.)

The failure to take adequate account of the 'collectivist' ideology of the Labour Movement was linked to the DAC's failure (and indeed the failure of the wider Movement) to appreciate the crucial *economic* dimension to the problem. It was, in part, this that first led those like Frank Allaun to distance themselves from the DAC. There were several reasons for emphasizing the importance of the economic dimension. There were wide social differences between DAC activists and the mass working class, and without a strong economic dimension the DAC was unlikely to make real contact with working-class consciousness. The overall life situation of the DAC activists was wholly different from that of the workers to whom they were appealing. Whilst there were significant *class*

[101] In fairness, it should be pointed out that the DAC initiated campaigns in all the locations to provide short-term financial support for any workers who were persuaded to leave armaments-related work in the period whilst they were seeking alternative employment. However, the sums raised were so small that had the campaign had any real success in this respect, such schemes would have been virtually useless.

differences (most of the DAC activists being middle-class), the fundamental factor was a *cultural* one: the DAC activists were arguing from within a perspective whose assumptions, objectives, and criteria were both distinctive and alien to all but a tiny minority of working-class people. The sacrifices demanded by the DAC, in material and personal terms, were of a high order, and, as has been argued earlier, the DAC's appeal was couched largely in moral terms. For good or ill, moral appeals alone have not generally been effective in arousing working-class opposition to the established order. The DAC was thus doubly disadvantaged, arguing from within a general perspective which had few links with the working-class culture, and on moral ground which were unlikely to win over substantial sections of working-class opinion.

The dominant issues in the trade union and Labour Movement since the nineteenth century have generally been material and/or economic. Dick Nettleton made the point very forcefully that the Movement failed to

grasp . . . that . . . the question of *jobs* was important. . . . You can carry lots of people a long way on that strongly moral position . . . but [you] have to face up to this issue and to battle on it in real hard terms. . . . it's OK for union annual conferences to be passing resolutions saying nuclear weapons are a bad thing, get rid of them; it's a different thing for Union conferences to be discussing in detail the actual future of their industry.[102]

Finally, it is important to note that the DAC was ill-equipped for the catalytic political role which it saw itself playing. The British Labour Movement has been characterized, as numerous analyses have argued at length,[103] above all by its constitutionalism and its parliamentarism. With a very few, though arguably important, exceptions, the history of industrial struggle conducted via British trade unionism in the twentieth century has been a history of constitutional, legal action over strictly industrial issues. Even in the brief 'revolutionary' periods, the amalgam of issues involved has been, without exception, centrally economic in nature even though the implications of industrial struggle may sometimes have been political and 'revolutionary'. Thus to campaign for unofficial trade union action on a political issue—although arguably desirable—

---

[102] Dick Nettleton, in conversation with the author, Jan. 1978.
[103] See e.g. Ralph Miliband, *Parliamentary Socialism*, 2nd edn., London, 1973; David Coates, *The Labour Party and the Struggle for Socialism*, Cambridge, 1974.

was to ask for a radical break with the whole Labourist tradition. What is beyond doubt is that it was a radical demand, and one which presented an enormous political and ideological task to which the DAC was unequal in every respect. This inadequacy was reinforced not only by the cultural gap between the DAC and the Labour Movement which has already been noted, but also by the stability and security of the capitalist economy of the period, and of the wider society and its institutions. Nowhere, therefore, was the disparity between the DAC's ambitious objectives and its political inadequacy so graphically illustrated as in its industrial campaign.[104]

Given all these problems, it is perhaps surprising that the industrial campaign had as much success and impact as it did. At all events, by the end of 1960 the DAC's campaign was virtually over,[105] and, as Pat Arrowsmith somewhat ruefully recalled, there could be no doubt that the DAC 'came unstuck [because] trade unions as a whole . . . didn't see this as a trade union issue. And in a strict sense I suppose it wasn't.'[106]

The Sahara project

More than any other part of the Movement, which tended on the whole to be characterized by an insular and at times chauvinistic attitude, as has been seen, the DAC had a real involvement with radical peace initiatives and organizations in Europe, America, and the Third World. It is thus not surprising that it was the DAC which

[104] This whole area related to the continuing problem of the relationship between the DAC and the Communist Party. Many of the most militant and experienced trade union activists were, of course, CP members or sympathizers. But the politics of the DAC was always in conflict with that of the CP, in both theory and practice. The CP was always suspicious of direct action politics and in fact never really understood the bases on which such actions were undertaken. Communism was viewed by the DAC with total political and ideological hostility, although attitudes to Marxism were more ambivalent, as will be argued below. In the specific context of the industrial campaign the role of the CP was certainly a problem. Any link with the CP would smear the DAC's campaign with Communist affiliation and thus put off large numbers of workers, and might also result in the CP controlling any major development of mass industrial action over the nuclear issue. All in all, therefore, the Communist embrace, tentative and ambivalent though it was for the Party's own good reasons, was seen as a distinct disadvantage for the DAC's campaign.

[105] Pat Arrowsmith continued with her industrial campaigning, however, and was later involved on Merseyside for six months organizing a CND/trade union liaison committee (Arrowsmith, in conversation; see ch. 5, pp. 256–7).

[106] Ibid.

took the initiative in organizing protests against the French declaration in the summer of 1959 that nuclear weapons tests were to be carried out in the Sahara. The DAC, in conjunction with the Committee of African Organizations, organized a demonstration in Trafalgar Square on Sunday 30 August 1959 (preceded by a poster parade at the French Embassy in London on 28 August). The message of the demonstration, attended by approximately 2,000 people, combined a denunciation of European colonialism with vociferous opposition to the proposed French tests.[107]

It was not a very big step from this explicit linking of NVDA for peace with anti-imperialist, liberation struggles, to the launching of the DAC project for a non-violent entry of the testing area. In fact, the DAC had already mooted such an idea early in 1959 and, at its committee meeting on 7 June 1959, had decided that it should make plans to enter the testing area (Reggan, an oasis south of Columb Bechar), and that contacts in France and elsewhere should be approached about the project. Contacts were made with the US group 'Committee for Non-Violent Action' (CNVA) and with the French organization 'Fédération Français contre l'Armament Atomique', neither of which was very keen initially to participate. Indeed, in the case of France, full support for the project was never forthcoming.[108] Although one of the eventual 'team' was French (Esther Peter), the hoped-for Anglo-French sponsorship for the project did not materialize, perhaps because, despite their genuine pacifism, the French were suspicious of the Anglo-US group's criticism of *French* nuclear weapons and testing. Chauvinism, and the suspicions of its existence even in the Peace Movement, was a deep and fundamental problem confronting all those who looked to a genuinely European and/or international unity over the nuclear issue.

In the case of the USA these problems did not exist. Although initially sceptical, and offering only 'moral support', the CNVA, following a meeting between A. J. Muste, Bayard Rustin, and Bill Sutherland, agreed 'to reconsider its earlier decision', for two reasons (according to George Willoughby, the chairman of CNVA): the clear involvement of Africans, and the 'commitment

---

[107] DAC leaflet for 30 Aug. 1959 demonstration, DAC archive.
[108] See correspondence between Pasteur André Trocmé and Michael Randle, 22 Aug. 1959, in which Trocmé argued that such protests would be seen as anti-French rather than as anti-nuclear demonstrations (DAC archive).

of Michael Scott to the project'.[109] It should be noted that both Sutherland and Scott, especially the latter, were key figures in the whole project. Sutherland, a longstanding peace and civil rights activist, provided the crucial link between Western, and particularly American, peace groups and the African political scene, having been personal assistant to Ghana's Finance Minister, K. A. Gbedemah. Scott was an internationally known campaigner for peace and, even more important in this context, famous throughout Africa 'for his work at the UN for the people of South West Africa'.[110] The impact of his arrival in Ghana was tremendous: *Peace News* reported that 'since his arrival the Sahara protest has become a national issue and is headline news in press and radio.'[111]

From the outset it was stressed that the project was intended to involve direct action and not merely a purely symbolic protest against the tests. There was concern, too, that the project should be seen as a linked protest against nuclear weapons and colonialism, rather than solely against French colonialism and its nuclear policies, and it was this concern which underlay the decision to base the project in Ghana rather than Morocco (which was considerably closer to the testing area). In addition to the DAC's desire to avoid entanglement with the anti-colonial movement in Morocco, there were positive aspects of Ghana's foreign policy and general ideological stance which also underlay the DAC's decision. In April Carter's view, there were elements in Ghana's policy

which encouraged a more comprehensive dislike of nuclear strategies, and which blended with the protest team's avowed opposition to *all* nuclear bombs and tests. Ghana had become independent in 1957 and was committed to support principles which were the antithesis of the imperialism and militarism associated with the colonial powers. Nkrumah had also avoided taking sides in the cold war and stood for nonalignment along the lines enunciated at the Bandung Conference in 1955.[112]

Even more important, in the DAC's eyes, was Kwame Nkrumah's commitment to 'positive action'—a concept not dissimilar to the DAC's own NVDA. Nkrumah's position was articulated clearly in

[109] Letter from George Willoughby to April Carter, 26 Sept. 1959, DAC archive.
[110] April Carter, 'The Sahara Protest Team', in Paul A. Hare and Herbert H. Blumberg (eds.), *Liberation Without Violence*, London, 1977. (April Carter's paper was written in 1972 but not published until 1977.)
[111] Cited in ibid., 131.
[112] Carter, op. cit., 128. This provided a strong link between the DAC's perspective and that of the New Left, at least in terms of 'practical politics'.

his leaflet 'What I Mean by Positive Action'. He referred to Gandhi's liberation of India through 'moral pressure', and declared that of the two means of achieving self-government—'by armed revolution and violent overthrow of the existing regime, or by constitutional and legitimate non-violent methods'—he much preferred the latter. The Convention People's Party (CPP) was pledged to a policy of positive action to achieve self-government and end colonial rule throughout Africa. Positive action was defined as follows:

by positive action we mean the adoption of all legitimate and constitutional means by which we can cripple the forces of imperialism in this country. The weapons of positive action are:
   1. Legitimate political agitation.
   2. Newspaper and educational campaigns and,
   3. As a last resort, the constitutional application of strikes, boycotts, and non-co-operation based on the principles of absolute non-violence.[113]

The DAC also believed, according to April Carter, that the CPP was committed to 'openness and fair play in dealings with the British government, the need for democratic endorsement of the leadership's policies, and the importance of mobilizing the masses through the power of suffering for a just cause'.[114] How well-founded this view was is another question, but there can be no doubt that, given the DAC's perceptions, Ghana's expressed ideals were in close harmony with those of the DAC team. Given this seemingly positive ideological climate there was some justification for the enthusiasm of Michael Randle and the DAC, and their belief that the project could mark a political turning-point, both in African politics and in the Peace Movement's campaign against nuclear weapons.

The nineteen-strong international team[115] left Accra on 6 December on the first attempt to reach the testing site. They were intercepted by officers at Bitton sixteen miles inside Upper Volta. The team refused to leave, and after some delay the French brought

[113] Dr Kwame Nkrumah, 'What I Mean by Positive Action', first published Jan. 1950, reprinted Apr. 1960 (DAC archive).
[114] Carter, op. cit., 156.
[115] The team included Michael Scott, Esther Peter, Bill Sutherland, Michael Randle, Francis Hoyland (Britain), Bayard Rustin and A. J. Muste (USA), and Pierre Martin (France). There were also several Africans, including Ntsu Mokhehle (president of the Basutoland National Congress Party), Hilary Arinze (Nigeria), and a number of Ghanaians.

in troops and sealed off the town from the locals to prevent the distribution of propaganda. After five days the team returned to Bolgatanga to reconsider the position. The team had abided, of course, by the DAC practice of informing the authorities of their intentions; indeed, they had officially applied for visas to enter French West Africa, which had been refused, so it was almost certain that they would be stopped. Not surprisingly the African members of the team, not well versed in the quasi-Jesuitical intricacies of DAC ideology, found this approach somewhat self-defeating and frustrating. The resulting tensions were exacerbated by the fact that, although Africans predominated in the team, the policy planning committee was composed of two Americans, two Britons, and only two Africans.

Following this first failure it was agreed to make a second attempt, but with only seven in the team this time: Michael Scott, Michael Randle, Bill Sutherland, and four Ghanaians, Benjamin N. Akita (a book-keeper), R. Orleans-Lindsay (a science teacher), K. Frimpug-Manso (a businessman), and K. M. Arkhurst (a driver).[116] The team crossed the Upper Volta on 17 December, but was stopped eleven miles inside French territory at the military post of Po. A sit-down was staged at the barrier and leaflets were distributed, along with local recordings in the native language. This continued for two weeks. The French officers agreed to transmit the team's protest, and request for permission to travel across the territory towards the testing area, to the president of the Upper Volta parliament. However, the team was informed that this was a matter for Paris rather than the Upper Volta authorities, and no progress could therefore be made. The team announced plans for further protest action—at which point the vehicles were impounded and they were compelled to return to Accra. The public support for the team's mission grew to new heights, however, during this second attempt. Pierre Martin fasted for twelve days outside the French Embassy in Accra. This culminated in a public meeting addressed by the Ghanaian Finance Minister Mr Gbedemah, the mayor of Accra, Mr Quaye (also chairman of the Ghana council for nuclear disarmament), and the Minister of State, N. A. Welbeck. Nkrumah sent a message of thanks and support to Pierre Martin. There were

---

[116] Again, although Africans predominated, it was the experienced DAC/CNVA activists who tended to dominate the decision-making.

also demonstrations at the French Embassies in London and Lagos, demanding that the team should be allowed access to the test area.

A third, and as it transpired final, attempt was made by the team to reach the test area in January 1960. Enough money was collected to buy another Landrover and the team set out on 17 January. The border was crossed on foot but, as before, the team was apprehended by police—this time sixty-six miles inside Upper Volta. The team was returned to Ghanaian territory and all border routes were put under twenty-four-hour guard to prevent further attempts.

There was considerable coverage of the team's protest in the French press, in large part due to the efforts of Esther Peter who formed an *ad hoc* committee for NVDA in Paris, which organized demonstrations at a nuclear centre near the city in early 1960. There were also very large demonstrations opposing the tests in a number of North African countries.

On 13 February 1960 at 6 a.m. the French carried out the test at El Hammoudia, near Reggan. There were continent-wide protests: Nasser, the Arab League Council, Nyerere, and most North and West African States issued statements deploring the test and its effects. Ghana froze all French assets. Michael Scott had been touring African states addressing public meetings and talking with leading politicians about the French test and the team's protest mission.[117] As a result of these discussions and subsequent talks with Nkrumah, it was agreed to call a special 'All African Congress' with the dual purpose of co-ordinating protest and action against further French tests and implementing the ideas contained in Nkrumah's 'positive action' proposals.

For the Sahara protest team the proposal to establish a 'positive action centre' was of central importance. As Randle said in a confidential memorandum to Muste, Rustin, and Hugh Brock, the possibilities of such a centre, combining the study of non-violent positive action and the planning of opposition to further French tests, were 'staggering'.[118] Indeed, at the outset Randle, who had

---

[117] Scott's absence from Ghana for prolonged periods in early 1960 caused Michael Randle considerable anxiety, as it left the team directionless. Moreover, Scott did not inform other members of the team of his whereabouts or his objectives. See various cables and letters from Michael Randle to DAC in early 1960, DAC archive.

[118] Memorandum from Randle to Muste *et al.*, 20 Mar. 1960, DAC archive.

been on the point of leaving Ghana for England and was then called in to a meeting between Scott and Nkrumah to be told of the conference plan, was extremely enthusiastic.[119]

And yet there were grievous problems from the beginning. It was obviously essential that the positive action centre should be, and be seen as, an *African* initiative. 'Nothing could be better calculated to bring about the downfall of the project than the suggestion that it is an attempt by Westerners to import and impose their own ideas.'[120] At the same time, Nkrumah was concerned above all to use both the conference and the centre to promote the Pan-Africanist movement against colonialism and in support of the Algerian and South African liberation struggles. The ideology of the DAC, inherently differing in both theoretical and cultural fundamentals from the Pan-Africanism and anti-colonialism of Nkrumah, was thus pushed further into the background by these two factors: the concern of the team members themselves not to engage in cultural and ideological imperialism, and the Africans' overriding concern with issues other than nuclear weapons and NVDA. For the DAC, and the others in the team, the nuclear weapons issue and the NVDA method were central, and colonialism and the African liberation struggles, whilst not exactly secondary, were seen as complementary and ancillary to these central concerns.

The conference took place on 7–10 April 1960, was sponsored by a number of independent African states, and was thus a major and representative gathering of African opinion. The tone was undoubtedly militant and angry—and the central concern was the liberation struggle against colonialism. Few of the African delegates espoused the cause of NVDA; indeed, most of them gave explicit backing to violent liberation movements, especially the FLN's (Front Libération National) war in Algeria. Nevertheless, the conference did pass several resolutions directly relating to the French nuclear tests and the positive action centre.

Also, at the conference Nkrumah had proposed a mass crossing into French Africa with the object of proceeding to the testing area. This could be, claimed Nkrumah, 'as dramatic and successful as the

[119] In a letter from Randle to April Carter and Pat Arrowsmith, 5 Mar. 1960 (DAC archive), ambitious plans for the Centre, put by Randle to Nkrumah, were outlined. These involved three main areas of activity: the study of non-violent positive action; consideration of action by independent African states against France's policy in Algeria and against the Sahara tests; and the neo-imperialist threat to Africa and ways of achieving economic and political integration amongst African countries.   [120] Memorandum from Randle.

famous Gandhi Salt March in India'. Although envisaged initially as concerned with this particular project, Nkrumah argued that 'much needed research into non-violent positive action could also be undertaken there'.[121]

Thus the results of the conference appeared initially to the team activists to be most encouraging. After the conference, Scott, Randle and Sutherland met with Nkrumah to discuss the implementation of the conference proposals. Nkrumah agreed to give £30,000 for the establishment of the centre in Ghana in the hope that other African states would be encouraged to create similar centres. This funding was intended to finance capital outlay and the running costs for one year. A site for the centre—a disused school at Winneba, thirty miles from Accra—was agreed. At this meeting the 'non-violent assumptions' underlying the centre's existence were also agreed in general terms, although it was noted by Scott that

non-violence is far less important to Nkrumah and the other African leaders than finding efficient and if possible humane ways of freeing Africa. The interest in non-violent action is largely tactical. [The centre may thus become] a resistance headquarters where any methods of liberation are advocated.[122]

Nevertheless, agreement on the main aims of the centre was reached, according to Randle, at this meeting. The centre was to be centrally involved in

(a) . . . practical and action training for volunteers to enable them to carry out more efficiently the task of liberating Africa from foreign imperialism, and the dissemination of suitable literature (to all parts of the continent).

(b) . . . action research into methods of liberation, and study of factors, internal and external, affecting the liberation movements.

(c) . . . development [of the Centre] internally as a community . . . [similar to those] developed by Gandhi in India and South Africa.[123]

These high hopes were quickly dashed, however. Little happened for three months:[124] Randle became involved in the Bureau of

---

[121] Randle's report of Accra conference, 10 June 1960, DAC archive.
[122] Ibid.
[123] Ibid.
[124] Attributed by Randle to two factors: 'the Congo had made non-violent action in the African situation look like an interesting sideline . . . and other elements have been at work behind the scenes' (letter from Randle to Chris Farley, 16 Aug. 1960, DAC archive).

African Affairs publication *Voice of Africa*, and by August he could report that, despite having fallen out with Welbeck, he was continuing 'to virtually edit, and produce ninety per cent of the articles'[125] for the *Voice of Africa*. However, this was incidental to the team's main concern. After three months of virtual inaction the centre was established at Winneba, as had been promised. It was on a very different basis to that which had been envisaged by the team, however. Significantly, it was entitled the Kwame Nkrumah Institute, one of many indications of the growing personality cult in Ghana, which was to reach more and more obsessive heights as Nkrumah's political and economic policies disintegrated. The change of title reflected a major change of emphasis in the institute's role. The functions envisaged were twofold: one 'dealing with the training of Party Members and Trade Union people, the other dealing with training for positive action'. Moreover, wrote Randle at the time, the institute would be under direct CPP control, and neither he nor Sutherland was to be a member of the committee directing the institute.[126] In Randle's view there were fundamental problems with the proposed institute. Given the necessity of largely African staffing, there were very few people available who were committed to non-violence. Moreover, as the institute was under direct governmental control there were certain to be conflicts over issues such as civil rights.

As Randle himself noted, the choice was 'between presenting non-violent action as a completely amoral tactic designed to harass and embarrass authority but without any ethical basis or force, or frankly stating its opposition to totalitarian acts by whomsoever committed'.[127] There could be little doubt which alternative the CPP forces in Ghana opted for. The representative of the Pan-Africanist Congress put the general perspective honestly, if starkly, to Randle: non-violence was, he said, a tactic and only 'a prelude to the revolution: whites in alliance with blacks must be prepared to shoot other whites'.[128]

This was indeed a far cry from the role and perspective that had originally been envisaged. Although Randle and Sutherland were eventually included on the staff of the institute, their influence

[125] Ibid.
[126] See ibid.
[127] See Carter, op. cit., 142.
[128] Mr Bloke Modisane, representative of the Pan-Africanist Congress. Conversation with Randle, in his report of Accra conference.

was minimal. When France announced further tests Randle and
Sutherland proposed that a protest team should attempt to reach
the site through French-controlled Niger.[129] There was no response
from either the embryonic institute or the Ghanaian Government.
This finally convinced the remnants of the team that there was no
realistic possibility of the positive action centre being established
along the lines originally envisaged. Randle returned to England in
October to become secretary of the newly formed Committee of
100: he had been in Ghana for one year and, despite the final dis-
appointments, had experienced a 'most wonderful project [which]
. . . will have a lasting value. It has been a tremendous and most
useful experience for me personally.'[130] Thus 'the Sahara protest
team had, after more than fifteen months of planning and activity,
finally come to an end.'[131]

What lessons can be drawn from the whole experience? Of
course, the objectives were not achieved: 'there was almost no
response to the venture in France',[132] and, eventually, the initial
enthusiasm for both the project and the general aims of NVDA, in
Ghana itself, became submerged, if not obliterated, in the overall
anti-colonial ethos of Pan-Africanist politics. The crucial breakthrough for which Gandhian direct actionists had been searching
ever since Gandhi's successes in India was not to be found in
Ghana—nor indeed in Africa as a whole. At this level, then, the
DAC's 'failure' in Britain was mirrored in the failure to create a
symbiosis between Nkrumah's direct action-tinged nationalism and
anti-colonialism, and the Gandhian direct action politics of the
DAC (and the CNVA). As in other contexts, the magnitude of the
task that the DAC set itself contrasted with the paucity of its
resources.

Yet, on another level, the project achieved considerable success.
It 'did have a major impact on Ghana, and served as a focus for
opposition in other parts of Africa'.[133] A. J. Muste ajudged that 'an

[129] A detailed paper from Randle and Sutherland entitled 'More Sahara Tests:
The Need for Effective Protest' was submitted in Oct. 1960 (DAC archive).
[130] Letter from Randle to Pat Arrowsmith and April Carter, 26 Feb. 1960, DAC
archive.
[131] Carter, op. cit., 143.
[132] Ibid.
[133] Ibid., 144. It should be noted here that the experiences in Ghana were very
influential in the World Peace Brigade activities in East Africa from 1962 to 1964. It
is not relevant in this study to enter into an analysis of the WPB, as its activities and

immense propaganda job for the idea of non-violence has been done among the masses'.[134] There can be no doubt that, principally because of Nkrumah's support, the protest against the French tests and, to a lesser extent, the NVDA principles underlying the action, gained real mass public support in Ghana. This exceeded the popular support for such actions or ideas in either Britain or the USA at any time during the movement's history.

However, important though this was, the extent to which public support depended upon Nkrumah's personal following (and hence media coverage, etc.) and the generalized anti-colonialist ethos of Africa, can be judged by the short-lived enthusiasm of Ghana's Government and people for NVDA against nuclear weapons and their testing. Public support for the project, which had erupted so quickly, subsided even more rapidly. As April Carter has concluded, 'the enthusiasm generated for non-violence and disarmament was temporary and superficial.' Her further conclusion— that 'when the team moved away from the realm of Direct Action where it did have the initiative, to the realm of Conference politics and of bidding for long-term official support, it was likely to lose out to the rivalries governing that level of political activity. The team could no longer inject their own moral and political concepts into the situation'[135]—is less tenable. Such a view was to hold, optimistically, to the DAC strategy. But the success in Ghana, such as it was, depended on factors fundamentally *unrelated* to DAC politics and ideology. If it had not been for Nkrumah's support, for the generalized anti-colonial ethos, the personal appeal of Michael Scott, and the fortuitous linkage of the French nuclear test and the anti-colonial struggle, the project would, presumably, have been very small-scale and would have had very little impact. It was thus not the direct action project *per se* which constituted the success. On the contrary, as Randle implied at the time, if this success were to be capitalized upon and secured on a more permanent basis, it was essential to ensure that Ghana's positive action centre be established, roughly on the lines that the DAC envisaged. The fact that

politics had no direct links with DAC or the wider British Disarmament Movement. (Full details are given in Charles Walker, 'Non-violence in Eastern Africa 1962–4: The World Peace Brigade and Zambian Independence', in Hare and Blumberg, op. cit.)

[134] A. J. Muste, writing in the US journal *Liberation*, Jan. 1960. Cited in Carter, op. cit., 146.					[135] Ibid., 147–8.

this did not materialize constituted the real and fundamental failure of the project. This failure related ultimately, not to the specific context of the Sahara protest project, but to the gulf that existed, in Africa as in Europe and America, between the ideology and politics of the DAC and the established political cultures and power relationships of all contemporary societies—East, West, and (as in this case) Third World.

Other international links

The Sahara protest was, however, only one, albeit the most dramatic and arguably the most important, manifestation of the DAC's internationalism. From the outset the DAC was internationalist in outlook, and had well-developed international contacts. The centrally important Gandhian influence has already been noted. In addition there was contact, in the late 1940s and early 1950s, with the American 'Peacemaker' radical pacifist group, which was closely involved with the Congress of Racial Equality (CORE), the precursor of the American civil rights movement. It was from this early date that DAC/US civil rights involvement stemmed. Thus, by the time of the Sahara protest, there were firm ideological and personal links between American pacifists (and civil rights activists such as Bayard Rustin) and their pacifist counterparts in Britain.

The DAC's adherence to the politics of non-violence and the creation of a non-violent society provided a natural point of contact with American political culture, and this contrasted with the politics of the Labour left and other socialist groupings in relation to peace issues. Moreover, just as the US peace groups were heavily involved in the civil rights movement from the outset, so the DAC activists always had a central concern with civil rights and liberation struggles in Africa and elsewhere. (This was another source of conflict between the DAC and *Peace News,* and the traditionalist leadership of the PPU, which regarded such issues as a somewhat dubious diversion from the central pacifist orientation.[136])

There were contacts with European pacifist groups too, but the central link was with the USA. This was not entirely due to the cultural factors discussed above: the DAC's leading activists were, on the whole, young and/or inexperienced, and tended to look to

[136] Brock, in conversation.

the US movement for guidance, inspiration and advice. Such men as
A. J. Muste and Bayard Rustin exercised such influence from the
outset, and as mentors were second only in importance to Gandhi.

The DAC's policy objectives followed logically from its non-
violent politics and its internationalist perspective. Thus, unlike
CND, which rejected (at least at leadership level) unilateralism by
the USA and the USSR as well as Britain, the DAC demanded
nuclear disarmament by all countries, and repeatedly declared its
support for unilateral nuclear disarmament campaigns in the USA
and the USSR. Similarly, the 'pre-DAC' movements—the Third
Camp *et al.*, mentioned earlier—were solidly internationalist in
orientation.

This commitment to international militant pacifist activity did
not remain at the merely rhetorical level. From the outset the DAC
participated in a variety of imaginative projects across national
frontiers. Some of these were individual protests, such as Michael
Randle's attempt to enter Hungary in the winter of 1956-7 and
Harold Steele's attempt to sail into the testing area in 1957. It was
in fact Steele's project which led to an attempt by a group of four
Americans to enter the US nuclear testing area in early 1958.

Although unsuccessful,[137] this US/British liaison led eventually to
a significant project which depended crucially on international co-
ordination and understanding amongst the peace groups: the San
Francisco to Moscow March of 1961. (This was sometimes referred
to as a 'walk' rather than a 'march' in CNVA propaganda.) This
major peace initiative was sponsored by the CNVA, whose president, A. J. Muste, and secretary Bradford Lyttle, took leading roles
in the organization of the march. April Carter became the European
phase organizer for the march. Thus she, and the DAC, became the
central link between the CNVA and the European project—which
involved crossing through both Western and Communist countries
en route for Moscow.

The march began in San Francisco on 1 December 1960, and
reached Moscow on 2 October 1961. It took six months for the
thirteen marchers (plus two photographers) to cross the USA. The
thirteen then flew to London where a rally was held in Trafalgar
Square on 4 June 1961. The team was joined by two Britons, two
Swedes, one Norwegian, one Finn, and one West German. The

[137] For detailed reports of this and a subsequent attempt, see *Peace News*, 17 Jan.
1958, 28 Mar. 1958, 9 May 1958, 27 June 1958.

group marched to Southampton, via Aldermaston, and attempted to land at Le Havre in France. They were refused entry, and eventually decided to march via Belgium into West Germany. Further changes to the European composition of the team were made as the march passed, not without incident, through West Germany, East Germany, Poland, and finally into Russia.

The ideology of the CNVA was very similar to that of the DAC.[138] The commitment was to an eclectic, non-aligned, and non-socialist politics, whose internationalism was demonstrated in the wide range of nationalities represented amongst the protesters, and indeed in the nature of the project itself. This explicit internationalist perspective was well expressed by Muste:

These walkers are not 'Americans' cast in the conventional image of Americans *versus* Europeans, Americans *versus* Russians. These are people who have worked and suffered for peace, who have been beaten up and jailed, who boarded Polaris submarines in the struggle against militarism and the abomination of nuclear war at *home*. . . . They feel themselves to be *human* beings, part of the family of mankind, not 'Americans'. [139]

There is much you can do to prevent war, to establish peace. The individual is never helpless. When enough people begin to think and act, every government must take heed.[140]

It was this emotive, deeply felt ethos—inspired often but not always by a Christian commitment—which fired the enthusiasm of the DAC as well as the CNVA. And it was a belief in the *ideology* of the CNVA, as much as support for the project *per se*, which led the DAC in general, and April Carter in particular, to become so heavily involved.[141]

The DAC's internationalism was a key component of its make-up, and both the Sahara project and the San Francisco–Moscow March were important events and had a considerable impact. The fact remained, however, that in the international, as in the national, context the NVDA movement, which had such ambitious objectives, was confronted by overwhelmingly strong opposition.

[138] Considerable detail of the policies and organization of the march and its organizers can be found in the DAC archive. A fuller account of the march is contained in Taylor, op. cit., 580–588.

[139] CNVA leaflet, n.d. (?1960), DAC archive.

[140] A. J. Muste in letter to Dr Heinz Kloppenburg, 18 May 1961, DAC archive.

[141] And it was the DAC that organized the march's British programme, including a rally in Trafalgar Square on 4 June. The CND leadership was reluctant to become too closely involved.

Before proceeding to a final consideration of the DAC's ideological and political stance and an assessment of the overall context in which it operated, two further aspects of the DAC's activities and attitudes must be examined: the Holy Loch demonstration of 1961, and the relationship with the Committee of 100.

The Holy Loch demonstration of 1961

The Holy Loch action was the last and, in some ways, the most successful of the DAC's demonstrations. Proposals for the action stemmed in part from the DAC's American connections. The CNVA had held a prolonged campaign at the boat-yards in Groton, Connecticut, where the Polaris submarines were being built. Their campaign included picketing the workers, and frequent civil disobedience demonstrations. At the launching of the second submarine, the 'Ethan Allen', one demonstrator managed to climb onto the fin of the submarine at it was moving. Nine demonstrators were arrested on 22 November. The 'Proteus' submarine was moored in Holy Loch in March 1961 along with the 'Patrick Henry' and, later, the 'George Washington'. The DAC planned to mount a major demonstration whose 'aim . . . is nothing less than the removal of the Holy Loch base'. Moreover, the same DAC leaflet went on to say, 'this goal is attainable, more attainable than any other yet attempted in the campaign.'[142] For the first time the DAC felt that it might achieve its campaign objective: if this were to happen, the political credibility barrier would be broken and (the DAC thought) mass popular support for NVDA might be forthcoming.[143]

The stakes for the DAC were thus pitched high, and all available resources were thrown into the campaign. The local community had already begun a campaign to prevent the construction of the base and the DAC planned to mount a series of concerted actions in support. The central action was a march from London to Holy Loch beginning immediately after the finish of the Aldermaston March on Easter Monday, 3 April and reaching Holy Loch on Whitsun weekend, 20–1 May. Supporting action would take place through the spring at Holy Loch, and the march was planned to

[142] DAC leaflet, 'Non-violent Direct Action Against Polaris', Jan. 1961, DAC archive. [143] See, April Carter, *Peace News*, 31 Mar. 1961.

include as many large cities as possible, with supporting rallies being organized *en route.*

On the final weekend there was to be a series of demonstrations: and this ambitious programme was fulfilled with a reasonable degree of success—although, of course, the major objective of closing down the base was not attained. Twenty-five people planned to march all the way from London to Holy Loch, the march leader being Mrs Pat O'Connell, and the march organizer, Pat Arrowsmith. In the event sixteen people managed the whole distance (and a total of thirty-five spent several weeks on the march), being joined by supporters from the various regions and localities for different stages. There were thus, at different stages, anything from a few score to several hundred marchers. They were a varied group: the oldest, Miss Evelyn Poppleton, was seventy, and the youngest eighteen. Pat O'Connell was a forty-one year old teacher of backward children, mother of five, and previously 'apolitical', who typified the rise of the mass, apolitical protest against 'an evil and an abomination'.[144] Moreover, 1960–1 marked the high point of public concern and public protest on the nuclear issue, and hundreds of thousands of previously inactive supporters of the Movement were stimulated to make some positive protest for much the same reasons as Pat O'Connell.

The marchers attracted considerable attention in both the national and local press. (Among the local papers giving the march extensive coverage were those in Nottingham, Luton, Northampton, Loughborough, Hinckley, Coventry, Rotherham, Chesterfield, Wakefield, Leeds, Newcastle, and Edinburgh.)[145] The meetings and demonstrations held *en route* generally attracted considerable local support and public attention, although of course response varied from place to place.[146] In terms of contact with the ordinary people at local level, and the transmission of the unilateralist case,

[144] See 'Profile' by George Clark, *Peace News,* 7 Apr. 1961. Pat O'Connell was also the subject of a chapter ('The Protester: The Conscience of Pat O'Connell') in Norman Moss, *Men Who Play God: The Story of the H-bomb,* London, 1958.
[145] The DAC archive contains a comprehensive press cuttings file for the Holy Loch demonstration.
[146] e.g. meetings of 1,500 in Nottingham and 600 in Ripley were followed by an almost total lack of interest in Barnsley and Rotherham but a meeting of several hundred in Harrogate, addressed by John Braine. See 'Polaris Protest' press release 3, 29 Mar. 1961, and Pat Arrowsmith's report, 'Marching Through England', 9 May 1961, DAC archive.

the march was undoubtedly the most successful and worthwhile exercise ever undertaken by the DAC in Britain.

There were, however, major problems. 'A declared aim of the march was to create a focus for direct industrial action in the main cities *en route*.'[147] Some considerable preliminary work had been undertaken prior to the march to build up both trade union and CND contacts and support. Michael Randle and Ralph Schoenman visited Glasgow between 4 and 6 November 1960, and had several meetings with CND and trade union activists. Although Glasgow trades council had passed a strong anti-Polaris motion, and some guarded support was given by the Scottish National Union of Mineworkers (NUM), overall the trade unions were unwilling to become involved.[148]

In England there was also some trade union support, although the response was on the whole rather disappointing for the DAC. (Among those backing the march were the Derbyshire area miners' council and executive committee, which decided unanimously to join the march as it entered Chesterfield, and the Tyne and Blythe confederation of shipbuilding and engineering unions.[149]

Despite various manifestations of local trade union support, Pat Arrowsmith noted that, as many activists had suspected, the 1960 Labour conference victory had been won because trade union leaders and Labour Party activists, rather than the rank-and-file trade unions members, were committed to the policies of the Disarmament Movement: 'The very liveliness of discussion at factory-gate meetings on Tyneside, in Darlington, Leeds and Luton has demonstrated how many members of unilateralist Unions are still convinced that "so long as they've got the Bomb we must have it too".'[150] The response of CND to the march was also ambiguous and ambivalent. Eventually, Scottish CND agreed to organize a supporting march from Dunoon to Sandbank on the weekend of the DAC's action, but only one member of the Scottish executive was in full support of the project.[151] The national CND leadership

[147] Arrowsmith, report.
[148] See report from Randle and Schoenman on Glasgow visit, 10 Nov. 1960, DAC archive.
[149] For full details of trade union support, largely at local branch level, see Pat Arrowsmith, London to Holy Loch march report, and appendix, 1 May 1961, DAC archive.
[150] Arrowsmith, Holy Loch report, 9 May 1961.
[151] See report from Colin Smart, n.d., DAC archive.

had by this time hardened its attitude against civil disobedience actions, following the development of the Committee of 100 and its mass sit-down protests, and its reaction to the DAC's Holy Loch march and demonstrations was thus considerably cooler than had been the case with previous DAC actions.

Given all these difficulties the march progressed remarkably successfully and harmoniously. And the supporting action carried out in Scotland by a DAC team using canoes to impede the Polaris programme,[152] and a supporting march by 1,000 Scots at Dunoon on 4 March 1961, kept the campaign at a high point in the lead-up to the march and demonstration in May. Almost at the end of the march, however, an incident took place in Edinburgh which threatened to ruin the whole project. The police and Pat Arrowsmith clashed over whether or not the march should be allowed to proceed via Princes Street. For Pat Arrowsmith this was a matter of principle, 'a question of civil rights'.[153] Some of the marchers agreed, others did not. The march thus split and, to the accompaniment of major media coverage in Scotland, fourteen were arrested following a sit-down in Princes Street.

After this fracas, which caused considerable dissension amongst the marchers, the march proceeded to Holy Loch. A supporting demonstration took place at Dunoon on 14 May. Approximately 2,000 took part, and the rally was addressed by Michael Foot. Terry Chandler, in attempting further disruption of the 'Polaris' submarine and supply ship, was arrested and jailed for sixty days.

On the Whit weekend, 20–1 May, the DAC organized the following 'package' of demonstrations: two marches, one on the north and one on the south bank, beginning on the Saturday and the Friday respectively; a 'sea action', with the aim of making 'a non-violent attempt ... to board the "Proteus" and any submarines in the Loch at the time'; a 'land action', 'to occupy non-violently the two piers used by the crews of the Proteus and submarines—the Ardnadam Pier at Sandbank and the Cardwell Bay Pier near Gourock' (this latter action was planned to follow the rally at 4.30 p.m. at the end of the march on Sunday, and continue until twelve noon on Monday 22 May). The DAC was, as

---

[152] Including Laurens Otter and Terry Chandler. This group was 'unofficial': indeed, as Pat Arrowsmith has recalled, 'there was some friction about this, we were getting rather bureaucratic and we frowned on this: [but] in fact it was a very good thing they did this I think' (Pat Arrowsmith, in conversation).

[153] Pat Arrowsmith, cited in the *Scotsman*, 13 May 1961.

always, at pains to emphasize the non-violent nature of the demonstration.[154]

Several thousand took part in the marches, and, although no demonstrators were successful in their attempts to board the submarines, the twelve canoes made repeated and daring attempts (and achieved very wide Scottish and national press coverage). The sit-down at the Ardnadam Pier involved hundreds of demonstrators, of whom forty-three were arrested. Twenty-six were brought to court and fined a total of £249.

However, despite the 'success' of the demonstrations, and despite the very wide and generally favourable press coverage,[155] there were serious criticisms and misgivings following the demonmonstration. There was, from the press and from some of the demonstrators, considerable criticism of police behaviour at the demonstration. 'Reporters from most of Britain's major newspapers made formal statements of complaint against the police.'[156] 'I had not thought I would ever see British police using unnecessary violence in public. But I saw it yesterday at Holy Loch . . . twice I saw a police sergeant grab a demonstrator by the hair and hurl him several yards on to gravel. I saw a woman of seventy-one thrown bodily at a heap of other people.'[157] This marked a sharp break with the previously cordial, and mutually respectful, relations between the DAC and the police, and was due in part to the persistent canoe obstruction campaign at Holy Loch, and in general to the considerably more lengthy, well-organized, and well-supported Holy Loch project.

Above all, however, this deterioration in relationships arose from the changed climate between police and Movement activists which had rapidly followed the creation of the Committee of 100 at the end of 1960, and its subsequent mass demonstrations. No longer could the police treat the DAC protesters as a small, well-behaved, peaceful, and co-operative group of 'typically English cranks'. The Committee of 100 had shown the possibilities of mass direct action and the Holy Loch campaign was viewed in this new tradition, not only by the police but *by some of the demonstrators too*. It was this

---

[154] DAC leaflet, 'Polaris Protest', Whitsun 1961, May 1961, DAC archive.

[155] e.g. Laurence Turner, *Daily Mail*, 22 May 1961: '[the demonstrators] are largely serious-minded, intelligent people who mean business . . . their motives are humanitarian . . . their Executive Committee is non-Communist.'

[156] *Newcastle Evening Gazette*, 22 May 1961.

[157] Laurence Turner, *Scottish Daily Mail*, 22 May 1961.

latter aspect which particularly worried some of the DAC's leaders. Michael Randle, whilst fully supporting the march project itself, was very worried by the absence of non-violence, as he saw it, at the final demonstration. There had been 'little attempt to use non-violence as a positive weapon to deal with an ugly situation and break through police hostility'.[158] It was, he went on, quite contrary to the principles of non-violence to take legal action against police 'brutality'. The DAC, in other words, was worried that the direct action movement was moving away from its central Gandhian commitment, towards a more politically militant campaign, motivated by revolutionary activism rather than non-violence. Not all those in the Movement agreed, however. George Clark, replying to Randle, argued that 'if the forces representing law and order are inherently violent, the only way to prevent them getting out of hand is to ensure that control of these forces remains in our hands and that they are compelled to account for their actions to the whole community'.[159] Chris Farley took the argument an important stage further:

I believe that certain things can be done about brutality by police or opponents. . . .

Too many campaigners still look on [the police] in old-fashioned liberal terms. The police are not neutral in this struggle. They are the instruments which protect the machinery of mass violence, which ensure that it is not immobilised. If ever we become too much for the police to counter, we shall be confronted with the armed forces.

Those working in the agencies of social control must therefore be encouraged in every possible way to disobey orders and come over to support the protesters. 'There is little doubt that this will happen eventually, but it will be as difficult as getting workers out of armament factories—and for the same reason, because livelihoods are at stake.'[160] Although there is no advocacy here of violent resistance, there is a marked increase in the militant, oppositional tone of the argument and, ideologically, Farley's argument represented a move towards a quasi-Marxist position, thus presaging the general drift of a section of those in the vanguard of the Committee of 100 and related organizations in the 1960s.

[158] Michael Randle, writing in *Peace News*, 26 May 1961.
[159] Clark, letter, *Peace News*, 2 June 1961. Clark was less committed to the DAC tradition, and had from the first been an enthusiastic supporter of the Committee of 100.   [160] Chris Farley, *Peace News*, 2 June 1961.

Ultimately, then, Holy Loch must be seen as a bridge between the DAC's style of politics and that of the Committee of 100. In some ways Holy Loch marked the DAC's greatest impact on the public consciousness—and its greatest, most sustained, and widespread project in Britain. However, the crucial breakthrough which the DAC leadership had foreseen did not occur. April Carter had argued prior to the demonstration that the Swaffham demonstration had shown that people were prepared to put their lives at risk, and the Committee of 100 had demonstrated the potentialities of mass, disciplined, non-violent action. The qualities of these previous demonstrations could, she argued, be combined at the Holy Loch. When thousands of people were prepared to take NVDA and accept fully the risks and sacrifices inevitably involved in a serious struggle, then nuclear disarmament itself would become an attainable goal. This was not to be, and although Holy Loch was a creditable achievement for the DAC, its success was limited, and that very success derived in large part from the fusion in the public mind, and to some extent in the Movement, between the DAC and the Committee of 100. The future of direct action politics in the Movement lay with the Committee of 100. The time had come for the DAC to disband and merge itself into the Committee.

Indeed, the DAC had decided some time before the Holy Loch March, to disband.[161] By early 1961 Michael Randle was already working full-time for the Committee of 100, and there was in fact 'a certain amount of vituperation . . . and ill-feeling [because] the Committee of 100 people thought we should pack up and stop'[162] before the Holy Loch demonstration. However, given the amount of planning and preparation that the DAC had already put into the project, it was natural that the dissolution of the DAC should be postponed until after the Holy Loch demonstrations had taken place. Following Holy Loch, however, there was no delay.

To our [DAC's] eternal credit, after that Holy Loch demonstration we went into voluntary liquidation . . . some of our supporters were quite dewy-eyed but April and I were quite cold-blooded . . . although there was

[161] According to Pat Arrowsmith, the idea of the Committee of 100 was first mooted 'while we were having our direct action campaign in Bristol and I got the word that somebody I had only met at conferences had decided that after our Harrington demonstration and more particularly the ones at Foulness and Finningley . . . something new was needed' (Arrowsmith, in conversation).

[162] Ibid. George Clark was especially outspoken on this issue: see his letter to Wendy Butlin on 28 May 1961, DAC archive.

a certain difference in philosophy we were sensible enough to see that it drew on the same forces as the Committee of 100, and it was effectively the same sort of thing. We didn't have a vested interest in going on with a Committee that had ceased to be useful.[163]

However, the two organizations *were* very different and, with the closure of the DAC, the direct action section of the Movement moved into a new, different, and dramatic phase.

CONCLUSION

It remains to analyse the ideological nature of the DAC, and to evaluate its impact both upon the Movement as a whole and upon the wider general public. The DAC arose in response to the heightened public and political consciousness over the nuclear threat, as did the other Movement organizations. And, as with other organizations, its activities were in part cause and in part effect of this general mood. Its *ideology* was, however, far more specific and far more homogeneous than was the case with either CND or the Committee of 100. Despite differences over tactics and priorities, there was a remarkable consensus in the DAC over ideology, strategy, and objectives. The central tenets of this ideology were however rather diffuse, and were, with only rare exceptions, kept at the implicit rather than the explicit level. This was in part because of the inherent pragmatism and empiricism which characterized, and still characterizes, most British political movements and organizations. It was also due, as April Carter has pointed out, to the sense of extreme urgency that characterized the Movement as a whole, and the DAC in particular—the notion that time was of the essence because the world was on the brink of nuclear holocaust.

Nevertheless, the ideological basis *was* strong and did unite those in the DAC—especially those in and around the leadership. As was noted earlier, the basis of this ideology resulted from a merger of the British pacifist tradition, in particular the Quaker strand, with the non-violent social revolution politics of Gandhi. It was this latter philosophy which sparked the initial attempt to develop a new pacifist politics in Britain in the late 1940s and early 1950s. And for men like Hugh Brock, Allen Skinner, and Reg Reynolds, who were the 'elder statesmen' of the DAC, the Gandhian message

[163] Arrowsmith, in conversation.

provided the coherent articulation of the militant and more socially orientated and socially responsive pacifism in which they had believed for some years.

Partly because of this Gandhian basis, and partly because of the DAC's involvement with American and other international movements and campaigns, the Movement had a deep-seated concern with anti-colonialism and with the liberation movements of the Third World. However, as has been seen in relation to the Sahara project, this internationalism was construed by the DAC (and the US CNVA group) very much in terms of an international movement to achieve the non-violent society. Whilst the concept of the non-violent society stressed social justice, its central thrust and defining characteristic remained its non-violent nature and ethos. Other attributes of the non-violent society were thus seen, implicitly, as ancillary if not actually secondary. This perspective was of course at variance with those of the indigenous movements of the USA, and Africa, which tended to emphasize the primacy, respectively, of civil rights and anti-colonialism. It was thus not surprising that difficulties and conflicts over priorities arose.

This was indicative of one of the most important aspects of the DAC's ideology: its underlying belief that the creation of the non-violent society, and the use of NVDA means to achieve this society, were the central objectives to which all else must be subordinated. (Indeed, reflecting the Gandhian view, the DAC held that the means and ends relating to non-violence were closely interrelated and in fact merged into one another, an important legacy of the Movement as a whole to the radical politics of Britain in subsequent decades.) Non-violence was thus much more than a 'method' for the DAC, it was a central tenet of ideology. Of course, the immediate and overwhelming task of the DAC was seen to be the campaign against nuclear weapons, but this was a part of the macrocosm of a more generalized non-violent politics. Whereas the socialist left argued, in various forms and contexts, that it was a *capitalist* society that had produced nuclear weapons and therefore it was *capitalism* that must be replaced by socialism to achieve the desired objective of a nuclear free world, the DAC argued that the bomb was 'the product of assumptions and attitudes that are by no means confined to capitalists or capitalist societies. It is firstly fear, in this country fear of Russian domination, and secondly the reliance on traditional methods of meeting any real or supposed threat that leads people of all classes, bricklayers as well as bank managers, to support the manufacture of the Bomb.'[164]

It was the centrality afforded to the concept of NVDA that underlay both the DAC's hostility to the Labour Party and Labourism and its enthusiasm for schema, such as Sir Stephen King-Hall's advocacy of non-violent resistance,[165] which attempted to advance the cause of non-violence and the theoretical formulation of how to put these principles into action. For the DAC, radically different though its policies were from those of the traditional pacifists of the PPU *et al.*, was still primarily a *pacifist* organization. Many of its supporters and leaders might, like Hugh Brock, have been 'keen supporters of the Labour Party when it came to local politics, social politics, local government',[166] but the record of the Labour Party on the issues of *supreme* importance, war and peace, foreign policy and 'defence', was such that all but a few in the pacifist movement were deeply sceptical about the Labour Party as a vehicle for the implementation of pacifist politics.

The DAC thus rejected the Labour Party and Labourism on two grounds: first, that Labourist socialism was operating with a set of ideological assumptions and criteria that were at least partially at odds with those of the DAC; and second, that the actual record of Labour in the twentieth century was open to considerable criticism on the crucial issues of war and peace. The DAC traced the downfall of Labourism to its failure to surmount the moral and political crisis of 1914, and its general incorporation into the State and the 'war machine'. There was thus a wholesale revulsion with the perceived *immorality* of Labourism's political stance.[167] For the DAC, the Labour Party had long since surrendered its commitment to idealism, and there was a common recognition 'that the way forward was not through the Labour Party: we didn't want to get stuck in party politics—what we were trying to do was mobilise a much wider movement.'[168] Different activists saw different modes

---

[164] Michael Randle, 'Direct Action—The Way Forward', n.d., DAC archive. This was written, on behalf of the DAC, in reply to Peter Fryer of the Socialist Labour League.

[165] As exemplified in Sir Stephen King-Hall, *Defence in the Nuclear Age*, London, 1958, and *Power Politics in the Nuclear Age*, London, 1962.

[166] Brock, in conversation.

[167] Thus a *Peace News* editorial on 10 Oct. 1958 claimed that: 'both the Trade Union and Labour Movement are rotting for the lack of [a moral basis for politics]. ... The question of man's willingness to use the H-Bomb cannot be realistically considered apart from morals.'   [168] Carter, in conversation.

of advance: for example, Pat Arrowsmith's perspective was populist, almost syndicalist, whereas Alan Lovell advocated a fusion between DAC's politics and the New Left. But there was no disagreement over the rejection of Labourism, and both were influenced, in broad terms, by anarcho-syndicalist ideas.

It was an espousal of a radical moralism that underlay the DAC's justification of NVDA. This position was combined with an insistence upon extra-parliamentary, *populist* activism. This was an extra-parliamentary strategy founded not upon a revolutionary socialist perspective (whether Marxist or otherwise) but upon the moral imperative of the nuclear issue which every individual must ultimately be made to confront. It would thus be misleading to think of this extra-parliamentary stance as in any fundamental sense deriving from a political, principled rejection of parliamentarism, and the institutions and practices of the contemporary social system. (Though it is true that the dominant DAC view was that NVDA was justified because, over the supremely important nuclear issue, the public had no freedom of choice, both major parties adopting very similar pro-bomb stances, and the media power residing in the hands of a biased minority.) Whilst there were some within the DAC who inclined towards a New Left analysis, the majority espoused a broadly *liberal* interpretation of contemporary British (and Western) society. It was not until the Committee of 100 that the direct actionists generally began to move towards a more generalized libertarian socialist critique of the 'Warfare State', and the need for a confrontation with the power of the State in order to instigate a wholesale social change.

Fundamentally, the DAC's criticism was a moral one. The nuclear issue was a moral issue, and unless politicians were prepared to 'stand up and be counted' in an unambiguous way the DAC wanted nothing to do with them. The DAC's ties were to the Peace Movement and its politics and traditions: the Labour Party was thus regarded as at best a potentially useful ally and at worst a dangerous enemy. The solution to the nuclear problem, and indeed to the world's problems as a whole, lay in the substitution of the peaceful for the violent society. If this were to be achieved it was to the moral conscience of the mass of ordinary people that attention must primarily be paid. The DAC must appeal over the heads of the established parties (and trade union leaderships, etc.) and make contact with the people to get across its fundamental, stark message which was couched in the most urgent of moral terms. Before turning to discuss this populism, mention must be made here of the DAC's attitude to Communism and Marxism.

The DAC was most emphatically opposed to Communism.[169] This was due in part, of course, to the prevailing 'Cold War' mentality of the time, and to the then much more significantly pro-Soviet stance of the British CP, in terms not only of policy but of propaganda and public image. This opposition to the CP related also to the DAC's perceptions of the CP's authoritarian, hierarchical, and underhand methods. Over and above this, however, the DAC's politics were completely divergent from Communism. Most important of all was the moral, idealist basis of the DAC's perspective compared to the dialectical materialist basis of the CP. This basic divergence also manifested itself in 'practical' policy differences: for example, whereas the CP was committed to democratic centralism, working through the official trade union and Labour Movement structure, and pressurizing, sometimes covertly, through the parliamentary system, the DAC operated through grass-roots contacts and a more direct democracy, believed in decentralization, total openness, and NVDA, and rejected much of the practice (if not the theory) of representative democracy.

The position in relation to Marxism as a system of analysis was more ambivalent. Michael Randle has recalled that the DAC 'did turn away from Marxism to some extent, partly because of its association with pro-Soviet peace groups. But it wasn't a *complete* break . . . there was a *strong* Marxist influence there, even if it was a *critical* Marxist influence!'[170] The appeal of Marxism, such as it was for the DAC, lay in its emotive pull towards a revolutionized socialist society: it was the inspiration of the 'early Marx' decrying exploitation, alienation, and human degradation under capitalism, and arguing for the full realization of human potential within an egalitarian, decentralized, and genuinely Communist society, that touched a chord with the DAC activists. The more developed economic analysis of the 'later Marx' and the subsequent formation of Communist theoretical (as well as Leninist organizational) orthodoxy held no appeal for the DAC.

[169] This was reiterated repeatedly, explicitly and forcefully, by the leading DAC activists, Carter, Lovell, Randle, Brock, and Arrowsmith (in conversation with the author).
[170] Randle, in conversation. As Randle also pointed out, the influential A. J. Muste of the CNVA had his political origins in the American Trotskyist movement.

Even this degree of 'embryonic' empathy with Marxism may be overstating the case, however, as far as the majority of DAC activists were concerned. Apart from their absolute rejection of the contemporary Communist system and the politics of the British CP, there was a fundamental rejection by the DAC of the most basic tenet of Marxian socialism. The DAC did not accept that politics was at base a process of struggle between social classes whose economic and social interests were inherently different under capitalism; and it thus rejected the notion that *conflict* was an inherent part of the political process. Indeed, as has been argued, the whole DAC strategy was geared to attaining a consensus across as broad a front as possible over the nuclear issue.[171]

Whilst there was thus a major gulf between the ideology of the DAC and those of both orthodox social democracy and orthodox Communism, there is no doubt that the DAC 'was in the broad socialist/anarchist tradition'.[172] In part this was, as noted at the beginning of this chapter, found in the affinity, on the moral, idealistic plane, between the motivations of the DAC and those of the pacifist Labour left—as exemplified by organizations such as the 'No Conscription Fellowship' and the PPU, and individuals like George Lansbury and Donald Soper.

This applied, however, to the *general* pacifist ideological position rather than to the DAC specifically. There was also a range of ideological positions which linked the specific politics of the DAC into at least one strand of the socialist tradition. Whilst the overriding objective of the DAC was the abolition of nuclear weapons, and whilst the dominant motivation was a pacifism based upon morality, there was a consistent though generalized concern with what might be termed libertarian socialism, and at this level the DAC was linked to the political position of the New Left. The commitment was not to traditional anarchism[173] but rather to a decentralized, non-bureaucratic, people-centred socialism concerned in part with workers' control but, centrally, 'very keen on the notion of people controlling their own lives'.[174] As part and parcel

[171] It is interesting to note, however, that with the passage of time and the renewed interest in 'non-Muscovite' Marxism since the late 1960s, some at least of the DAC activists have become more sympathetic towards Marxism. See e.g. April Carter's and Michael Randle's own descriptions of their (1978) political views, Taylor and Pritchard, op.cit., appendix III.   [172] Randle, in conversation.
[173] As Brock, Carter, and Randle all testified in conversation.
[174] Carter, in conversation.

of the non-violent society, an egalitarian and decentralized framework was envisaged. It was, therefore, a *socialist* society that was the objective—in the sense of an equality of wealth and power, an absence of State (or indeed any other) coercion, and an insistence upon the 'socialist values' of co-operation, fraternity, mutual aid, and so on. And yet, despite this genuine commitment to socialism, it was a commitment that was in some senses superficial. The reference point for the DAC remained the individual, not the class. Despite its rhetoric, its fundamental belief was in the *moral* conversion of as many individuals as possible to the cause of nuclear disarmament (and ultimately the wider cause of non-violent politics). The DAC's socialism was thus almost entirely at the level of an emotive commitment to socialist values, and it had little if any comprehension of socialist analysis, of either Marxian or other varieties.

This is not in any way to cast doubt upon either the sincerity or the militancy of the DAC: what it did indicate, however, was not only that the DAC was operating against hopeless odds (in that the whole weight of the establishment of the Labour Movement, and indeed of British political culture generally, was opposed to its politics) but also that its frame of reference and its ideology were based on different fundamental premises from those of the Labour Movement. Added to this was the DAC's 'exclusivity': there was an undeniable self-righteousness and élitism about the DAC leadership. Repeated references were made in DAC memoranda and minutes to the need for all demonstrators to be well-versed in the theory and practice of non-violence, and there were instances of 'unsuitable' individuals being dissuaded from participating in DAC demonstrations. This was not of course an élitism based upon class, status, or organizational principle. But the DAC did operate on the *de facto* assumption that only a relatively few, reliable, non-violent *cognoscenti* were capable of mounting legitimate direct action demonstrations (much though, in theory, it would have liked to see a mass NVDA movement developing). Control was always in the hands of the (activist) leaders at the centre—and the coherent and complex DAC perspective was thus maintained consistently throughout (which would have been impossible had the movement grown, and embraced those who had no such full commitment to and understanding of the DAC's politics). The price that was paid, however, was to restrict the numbers involved, and thus to

undermine the potential of the DAC as a *mass* direct action movement. (It was this disparity in size and support, which amongst other
factors, differentiated the DAC sharply from the Committee of 100).

Despite claims to the contrary there can be no doubt that the
DAC's tactics and 'style' ensured that it would remain a small,
cohesive, but somewhat esoteric organization. As Stuart Hall has
said, the DAC was 'no more involved in a mass movement, nor
prepared for a mass campaign, than the CND leadership were!'[175]

Both the DAC's individualism and its militancy found their most
'pure' and dramatic expression in the attempt by Pat Arrowsmith to
mount the industrial campaign. This was linked directly into the
socialist populism analysed above, and was aimed directly at
appealing to the moral sensibility of individual workers. Moreover,
as with all DAC projects, the dramatic impact of direct action
played a central role:

> it is a way of making the H-Bomb something real and personal. When the
> general public reads in the papers that fifty of their fellow citizens have
> risked injury, death and imprisonment by non-violently resisting the
> construction and operation of a missile site they can scarcely avoid some
> speculation about the matter. If they recognise that most of the resisters
> are ordinary members of the community with families and careers to think
> about—people just like themselves with whom they can identify—they are
> bound to start wondering what it was that led them to take such extra-
> ordinary action. They may start thinking about the nuclear disarmament
> issue seriously for the first time.[176]

The motivation behind the industrial campaign was partially of this
type: to bring home the individual responsibility to each worker.
Also, of course, the DAC emphasized the potential power of 'ordinary people' to change the course of events. Repeatedly, this
populist message characterized their campaigns—both at the
missile bases and at industrial locations. And this militancy was
certainly extreme, having implicit syndicalist orientations.[177]

At first sight this determinedly militant attitude would appear to

---

[175] Stuart Hall, in conversation with the author, Mar. 1978.
[176] Pat Arrowsmith, 'Direct Action and Nuclear War', *Flame* (with *Slant*), 1. 6,
June 1960.
[177] However, DAC activists appeared unwilling to be 'labelled' syndicalist: e.g.
Pat Arrowsmith ('I don't think anyone consciously thought of it in these terms in the
DAC') and April Carter ('some people ... were concerned not exactly with
syndicalism—that's not quite right—but certainly with workers' control')
(Arrowsmith and Carter, in conversation).

have been in sharp contrast to the DAC's almost obsessive concern with 'openness' with the authorities, and with its determination to avoid any suggestion of 'unacceptable' behaviour on demonstrations. For the DAC 'the readiness to go to prison was an important factor. . . . We felt that planning in secrecy was violent—secrecy was a military tool—and you'd come into a head-on clash with other people.'[178] This absolute commitment to non-violence was even more central to the DAC than was the commitment to revolution (though they were seen as inextricably linked). Moreover, non-violence was defined in very rigorous terms—so that at various times wire-cutting, obstruction at the bases, etc., were all questioned by DAC activists as being either violent or coercive. 'Secrecy' was defined in similar terms: the purpose of demonstrations was for everybody the DAC was 'brought in touch with, to understand exactly what we were doing and why we were doing it . . . in the, perhaps rather naive, hope that they would, as it were, down tools, on the Gandhian pattern'.[179]

In a full exploration of this view April Carter argued that there was a fundamental difference between 'non-violence' and 'direct action'. The non-violent perspective was basically constitutional, in that it accepted the legitimacy of the State and its laws and institutions; but it hoped to persuade people to change their attitudes 'through voluntary witness and suffering and [it] does not lay sole stress on reasoned discussion as Liberal theories of democracy tend to do'. On the other hand, 'the pure Direct Action approach is basically anarchist and anti-authoritarian—the Direct Action approach to a rocket base is "let's demolish the damned thing".'

If the non-violent approach were adopted, then openness with the authorities would be essential. On the whole, the Movement, as a minority in a liberal democratic society,

should probably stress non-violence in order to make clear its members are essentially peaceful and law-abiding citizens. . . . Openness with the authorities is not compatible with excessive emphasis on Direct Action aims; nor is non-violence strictly compatible with a full-blooded Direct Action programme. Therefore any genuine synthesis of Direct Action and non-violence must allow for some modification of the Direct Action approach and some respect for a more 'constitutional' position; it must also accept that the basic principles of non-violent openness with the

---

[178] Brock, in conversation.
[179] Ibid.

authorities appears to be sufficiently intrinsic to non-violence to be a *sine qua non* of truly non-violent action in a liberal democracy.[180]

The DAC's ideology was thus, more than that of any other single constituent organization in the Movement, an original, cohesive, and coherent amalgam of a number of hitherto disparate traditions. At its core was the traditional positive pacifism based upon an individualistic moralism, and concerned above all with the abolition of war and violence by means of a moral appeal to as many individuals as possible. The originality, the spark which provided the jumping-off point for the Movement in the late 1940s and early 1950s, was the philosophy of Gandhian non-violent social revolution. This amalgam was then translated into the specific political culture of twentieth-century Britain with its strong liberal democratic traditions and the specific political climate of the 'nuclear debate' in the late 1950s and early 1960s. It was, of course, this latter condition which gave the sense of urgency, and enabled the NVDA movement to attract not merely the 'public witness' of pacifists, but the resolute determination of a significant number of people to achieve their objectives by more militant non-violent action than had been seen in Britain for many decades.

To achieve such an ideological amalgamation was no mean feat and says a lot for the intellectual ability, as well as the organizational energy and commitment, of leading DAC activists.[181] If the varied assumptions of the DAC's ideology were accepted, its intellectual framework hung together—and the strategy followed from the assumptions. Yet it was this rather inflexible and introverted ideological stance which ensured that the DAC remained a relatively small, and (despite its propaganda impact via the media) ultimately unsuccessful movement. As has been noted earlier, there was a marked disparity between the objectives the DAC set itself and the means it had at its disposal. The objectives were no less

---

[180] April Carter, 'Secrecy and Non-violence', *Peace News*, 21 Oct. 1960.

[181] Brock claimed (in conversation) that he was 'hopelessly "green"—and wasn't really a political animal. I'd become interested in pacifism and non-violence and I was utterly absorbed in that. So, when it came to working out political thinking and political ideas I tried to gather around me people like Gene Sharp . . . and then, later, April [Carter] and Adam Roberts, Christopher Farley and Michael Randle. . . . I was incredibly lucky in having them around me to work out these things.'

Brock was being over-modest here, however. The influence of Skinner, Brock, and other 'elder statesmen' was very great indeed—as was that of Muste, Rustin, and others from the USA.

than the wholesale transformation, not 'merely' of the socio-political structure, but also of the total culture of both Britain and subsequently the international community. Moreover, virtually ignoring the vast cultural gulfs between East, West, and Third World, the DAC attempted to transplant intact its ideology and strategy to vastly different environments. The resources at its disposal were, of course, wholly inadequate. The point need not be laboured; but, given the paucity of its resources, the degree of its achievement was remarkably high.

In reality, however, the DAC was 'never able to work out'[182] the politics of the non-violent society for which it was striving. Indeed, relatively little attention was devoted by DAC activists and theorists to analysing or even defining the nature of that society. And the demonstrable gulf between the objectives, and the wholly inadequate means at its disposal, was never seriously confronted by the DAC—in either theoretical or practical terms. However, DAC's recognition of the *need* for a greater degree of mass involvement was demonstrated in its organizationally selfless acceptance of the Committee of 100, and the strategically hard-headed decision of the leading DAC activists to disband and merge into the Committee of 100 following the Holy Loch demonstration.

The DAC was, in fact, much more concerned in practice with developing a range of protest activities on the issue of unilateral disarmament than it was with the wider task of transforming society. (And it did develop a remarkable variety of imaginative, provocative and relatively effective methods of protest, across the whole range of political action.[183])

Thus, despite its superficially coherent ideology the DAC's theoretical position was fatally flawed at its core because it had no adequate conception of the non-violent politics and the non-violent society it was trying to achieve. Moreover, the attempt to carve out for itself a distinctive ideology based upon assumptions and criteria outside the mainstream of the British socialist tradition, although vigorous, interesting, and courageous, made its failure almost certain from the outset. If nuclear disarmers were serious about achieving their objectives, as indeed they were, it was essential for

---

[182] Ibid.

[183] Among DAC protest activities not analysed in this chapter is the revenue refusal campaign of 1960–61. See final statement by the DAC, 22 June 1961. DAC archive.

them to have moved outside the narrow confines of the orthodox pacifist movement, which had always been tangential within modern Britain. Activists as diverse as Canon Collins, Donald Soper, Stuart Hall, and E. P. Thompson (the first two themselves pacifists, the latter two, not), realized that the Movement would succeed only if it mobilized a considerably larger constituency than the pacifists.

In the final analysis the DAC was a single-issue pacifist campaign concerned in the first instance with unilateral nuclear disarmament, and seeing itself as a ginger group to spur on the more timid and diluted CND.[184] It also saw the unilateral issue as 'the thin end of the wedge towards a wholesale rethinking of defence policy'.[185] The central focus was thus the traditional pacifist concern with conflict and war. Thus paradoxically the DAC, innovative and radical though it was, remained at base a relatively traditional pacifist body, not of course in terms of its methods and its Gandhian influences, but rather in the sense of both its central policy concerns and the moral and individualistic kernel of its ideology. Having established a new and important variant of British pacifism, the DAC failed to develop theoretically and thus, ultimately, failed to develop the practice which might have had some chance, not only of achieving the immediate objectives of the unilateralist movement, but also of securing a permanent shift in the balance of British politics. Both the New Left and the Committee of 100, for all their diverse and deep-seated ideological and political weaknesses, had a partially worked-out strategy of how the objectives of the Movement, and the wider radicalization of society, might take place. The DAC did not. Despite its conviction and enthusiasm, its innovative ideas for protest, and its absolute commitment to the cause, it was destined to remain a small, somewhat élitist, radical pacifist grouping within the wider Peace Movement.

The DAC's history was thus one of contrasts: it was supremely successful in developing a dramatic, relevant, and imaginative style of protest in response to a new situation. Moreover, its ideological development was ingenious, and united diverse traditions. On the

---

[184] 'We saw ourselves very much as trying to influence from within—we saw ourselves as part of the Movement of which CND was the main organizing body: we weren't ever going to challenge that. . . . What we wanted to do was to argue about the policy that the whole campaign should adopt and to influence that policy by our own campaign' (Carter, in conversation).

[185] Ibid.

other hand, it was a failure—in all its major individual actions, and in its collective performance from 1957 to 1961. It did not achieve any of its major objectives—but then neither did the Movement as a whole. More significantly, it did not achieve that breakthrough in credibility which would have enabled it to attract a mass following, and given it some chance of seeing its goals attained. The odds against its success were, of course, enormous. But these odds were lengthened considerably by the DAC's refusal to come to terms, in both ideology and practice, with the issues it faced.

As it was, the development of a mass radical consciousness was left, in some senses by default, to the Committee of 100 and, in a rather different context, to the subsequent socialist groupings of the later 1960s and beyond.

5

THE COMMITTEE OF 100
Mass Civil Disobedience, Radical Politics, and the Peace Movement

THE inaugural meeting of the Committee of 100 was held on 22 October 1960, but the idea of creating such a body had been under active consideration since the spring of 1960. The initial idea came from Ralph Schoenman, a young American postgraduate student at the London School of Economics. In July 1960 he approached Russell with his proposals and found Russell 'eager . . . to start a movement quickly which would be more in keeping with the needs of the situation'.[1] Russell has confirmed this in his autobiography, noting that

> it seemed more than ever as if new methods must be sought to impress upon the public the increasingly precarious state of international affairs. . . . [Ralph Schoenman] acted as a catalyst for my gropings as to what could be done to give our work in the CND a new life. He was very keen to start a movement of civil disobedience that might grow into a mass movement of general opposition to governmental nuclear policies so strong as to force its opinions upon the Government directly. It was to be a *mass* movement, no matter from how small beginnings.[2]

International and domestic events had combined to create a situation in which such a dramatic initiative seemed, to many Movement activists, not only plausible and defensible but essential. On the international scene the U2 crisis and the shooting down over the USSR of the RB47 reconnaissance aeroplane had increased tremendously the tension and mutual distrust between the two

[1] Ralph Schoenman, preface to Schoenman (ed.), *Bertrand Russell: Philospher of the Century*, New York, 1967. Although Schoenman claims that the visit took place in Apr. 1960, both Russell and his biographer claim that Schoenman's visit took place in July 1960. See Bertrand Russell, *Autobiography*, vol. 3, appendix, 'Private Memorandum concerning Ralph Schoenman', London, 1969, pp. 640–51; and Ronald Clark, *The Life of Bertrand Russell*, London, 1975, p. 573.

[2] Russell, op. cit., vol. 3, 104–10. (All subsequent references to Russell's autobiography are to vol. 3.)

super-powers. The collapse of the ill-fated Paris summit in June 1960, and the subsequent Soviet denunciation of American actions and policies, further heightened the Cold War climate. In Britain there was a growing sense of urgency, almost of desperation, within the Nuclear Disarmament Movement. And to many activists it seemed as though the orthodox methods of CND 'had reached the limit of their effectiveness':[3] the ambitious ideas of Schoenman gained ground quickly in the Movement.

There were also other, more specifically political factors on the domestic scene that gave impetus to the mass civil disobedience idea. The defeat of the Labour Party at the 1959 general election had been a major set-back for those in the Movement who had argued that unilateralist policies could and would be implemented via the election of a Labour Government. In the deteriorating international situation the prospect of a long period of Conservative, nuclear-orientated Government was not merely distasteful to Movement activists: it necessitated, in their eyes, dramatic action to awaken the general public to the imminent dangers of nuclear war and the need to adopt unilateralist policies if there were to be any chance of avoiding the holocaust. Moreover, for many in the Movement, as has been noted, the 1959 Labour election campaign gave irrevocable evidence of the amorality and inadequacy of Labourism. For many, then, political alternatives had to be found. For some this meant the New Left and INDEC, but for many it led to the exploration of extra-parliamentary, direct action politics. The success of the 1960 Aldermaston March, where for the first time the Movement became aware of its power as a *mass* movement and where the numbers involved had at least doubled from the previous year, combined with this disillusion with Labourism to create a political vacuum which the Committee of 100 was to fill. Finally, there was a realization that the DAC, valuable though its work had been, was unable to meet the task of building a mass civil disobedience movement. Nicolas Walter may have been a little over-harsh in his criticism of the DAC as 'puritanical' and in his contention, echoed by Russell,[4] that its demonstrations were 'really propaganda by deed, but they weren't very effective deeds, nor were they very effective propaganda either'.[5] But, as was argued in

[3] Ibid., 109.　　　　　　　　　　　　　　　　　　　　[4] Ibid., 110.
[5] Nicolas Walter, 'Non-violent Resistance: Men Against War' (reprint of *Anarchy*, 13 and 14), *Non Violence*, 63, 1963, p. 31.

the last chapter, there can be no doubt that the DAC was an inadequate formation for broadening out extra-parliamentary protest on to a mass scale.

Although the DAC activists had reservations about the Committee of 100 in terms of both objectives and methods they were heavily involved in the setting up and running of the Committee. In fact it was a virtual condition for their support that 'their people' should have a decisive hand in organizing the new Committee.[6] The DAC activists—in particular Carter and Randle—were astute enough politically to realize the potential of a prestigious movement committed to mass civil disobedience. Randle's reaction to Carter's invitation to return to London, from Ghana, to head up the new Committee as secretary, was that the proposed Committee 'was fantastic—really what we wanted'.[7] Randle's support was crucial in bringing in a number of other leading activists, notably George Clark, who had been involved in both CND and DAC, and who was to become a key figure in the Committee of 100.[8]

Meanwhile, Russell, encouraged and assisted by Schoenman, had begun to gather together a prestigious group of supporters for the proposed Committee, among them John Osborne, Arnold Wesker, Herbert Read, Ethel Mannin, John Braine, Compton Mackenzie, and Miles Malleson.[9] Schoenman, Rev. Michael Scott, and Russell held a number of meetings in London during August to plan the new initiative. The idea for the title of the new organization came from 'Schoenman and a colleague' (Gustav Metzger, according to Christopher Driver) and was based upon the historical precedent of 'the Guelphs and the Ghibellines with their Council of 100'.[10]

The two processes, of convincing the Movement activists and of recruiting sufficient 'big names', were thus both well under way by August 1960. Indeed, the idea of the Committee had already been publicly launched in the spring by Schoenman, at the celebratory gathering following the 1960 Aldermaston March.

[6] Hugh Brock perhaps felt this unease more than most: 'I was very uneasy about the Committee of 100, and the only reason we agreed to wind up the DAC and support the setting up of the Committee of 100 was that Michael Randle be brought home from Ghana to head it up as secretary. If they did that—OK, we went along . . . and I think while Michael was maintaining the leadership of the Committee of 100 we thought it was OK' (Hugh Brock, in conversation with the author, Mar. 1978).
[7] Michael Randle, in conversation with the author, May 1978.
[8] This was confirmed by George Clark, in conversation with the author, Jan. 1978.   [9] According to R. Clark, op. cit., 578.   [10] Ibid., 576.

Thus, by the time the news of the Russell/Scott initiative became public knowledge in late September, sufficient groundwork had been undertaken to ensure that the new venture would have a major impact on both the Movement and the general political life of Britain.

THE COMMITTEE FROM OCTOBER 1960 TO MAY 1961

The public birth of the Committee was appropriately sensational and dramatic. Throughout August and September 1960 letters had been going from Russell, Scott, and Schoenman to eminent people who were thought likely to support the Committee of 100 proposal. That this was done behind the backs of the CND leadership, and that it caused great consternation when it came to light, are matters that have been discussed in Chapter 3 in the context of the general development of CND, and the specific nature of the personal and political clash between Bertrand Russell and Canon Collins. Here we need reiterate only that all the complicated to-ings and fro-ings between Russell and Collins, concerning the advisability of withholding any announcement until after the crucial Labour conference vote on unilateralism, came to nothing because of the inadvertent 'leak' to the press of the plan to create the new Committee. The letters inviting participation in the new Committee were quite explicit. Recipients were invited to join a Committee of 100, to express through non-violent civil disobedience their opposition to the 'ever-growing menace of nuclear war'. The letter continued:

a group of people from within the CND is concerned to find ways of carrying these proposals into practical action. They have conceived the idea of forming this Committee in the belief that this will spread the responsibility for the proposed action. It is felt that if there are no office holders the danger of the work being paralysed by action against key individuals will be minimised.

It is proposed that no demonstration or other action will be undertaken without a minimum number of two thousand volunteers.[11]

Although Russell repeated his assurance to Canon Collins (who knew nothing of these letters until telephoned by Victor Gollancz,

[11] Letter cited in Christopher Driver, *The Disarmers: A Study in Protest*, London, 1964, p. 106.

one of the recipients) that nothing would be made public until after the Labour conference, the plans were in fact leaked.

One of the letters, intended for John Connell, a friend of Compton Mackenzie,[12] was sent to John Connell the military historian[13] and a firmly establishment figure. Connell replied to Scott in strong terms[14] and also passed on the information about the invitation to George Hutchinson of the London *Evening Standard*. The story was given headline treatment on Wednesday 28 September. Not surprisingly the reactions of the CND leadership were extremely hostile, as was discussed in Chapter 3. Equally predictably, the press commentaries were widespread and highly critical. The *Daily Herald* commented that 'the strongest argument against this course is not, simply, that it is illegal, but that it is anti-democratic'. The *News Chronicle* linked the proposal to the political tradition of civil disobedience:

Gandhi, in the context of the India of his day and as spokesman for millions of illiterates, resorted to methods which are wholly out of place in an adult democracy. Persuasion is open to Lord Russell without a call to self-martyrdom. We think that the plan for the Committee for 100 and two thousand volunteers for defiance of the law, is both wrong and unjustified. The nuclear disarmers have every right to demonstrate. There is no need to start a conspiracy.[15]

The reaction of the more Conservative press was even more critical—and even *Peace News*, whilst giving full coverage to the formation of the Committee, held back from declaring its full support until after the turn of the year.[16]

[12] This is the version given by Herb Greer, *Mud Pie: The CND Story*, London, 1964, p. 48. Greer attributed the information to Ralph Schoenman. This version is corroborated by Nicolas Walter, in a review of Driver, op. cit., in *Solidarity*, 3.7, p. 11.

[13] It has also been suggested that the sending of this letter was no mistake and that Russell and Schoenman used this as a device to thwart the 'Labourist' leadership of CND and steal its thunder prior to the Labour conference vote. As Clark has observed, this 'Byzantine operation' does seem a rather far-fetched scenario, but it 'would not have been untypical of the events which coloured Russell's last decade' (R. Clark, op. cit., 578).

[14] Letter from Connell to Scott, 28 Sept. 1960, cited in Frank E. Myers, *British Peace Politics: The CND and the Committee of 100, 1957–1962*, Ph.D. thesis, Columbia University, 1965, p. 162.

[15] The *Daily Herald* and the *News Chronicle*, both on 29 Sept. 1960, cited in David Van Deusen Edwards, *The Movement for Unilateral Nuclear Disarmament in Britain*, BA thesis, Swarthmore College, Mar. 1962.

[16] Although it is interesting to note that as far back as Jan. 1960 *Peace News* had advocated an initiative very similar to the subsequent Committee of 100.

The continuing and developing 'crisis' in the Movement between
the CND leadership and the Committee of 100, all of which took
place against the equally dramatic debates over unilateralism and
the Gaitskellite leadership of the Labour Party following the
Scarborough conference, ensured the Committee of 100 maximum
publicity during its formative weeks. Scarcely a day passed without
some further newspaper 'story' on the Movement and its 'personality clashes'. This was indeed a situation tailor-made for the
personality-orientated British press, and although the Committee
received very full coverage, it was both predominantly negative
and almost exclusively concerned with the personalities rather than
the politics and policies of the Movement.

It was thus in the full glare of publicity, and in the atmosphere of
tension created by the Russell/Collins split, that the Committee held
its inaugural meeting on 22 October 1960, at the Friend's Meeting
House in Euston Road, London. Russell, who only the previous day
had formally resigned as president of CND, became president of the
Committee, Scott, chairman, and Michael Randle, secretary. The
central orientation of the new Committee, at this early stage, was
clear. The urgency of the nuclear situation made dramatic action
essential. Only extra-parliamentary civil disobedience on a mass
scale would bring home to people the need to pressurize the
Government into unilateralist policies. There was general endorsement of the sentiments contained in the Committee of 100
'manifesto', 'Act or Perish', issued by Russell and Michael Scott, in
which it was stated that the purpose of the new grouping was to
'form a body of such irresistible persuasive force that the present
madness of East and West may give way to a new hope. . . . Our
immediate purpose, in so far as it is political, is only to persuade
Britain to abandon reliance upon the illusory protection of nuclear
weapons.'

The main thrust of 'Act or Perish', however, was moral and
humanistic rather than political:

We shall continue, while life permits, to pursue the goal of world peace and
universal human fellowship. We appeal, as human beings to human beings:
remember your humanity, and forget the rest. If you can do so, the way lies
open to a new Paradise; if you cannot, nothing lies before you but universal
death.

The emphasis upon awakening the public to the dangers was
exemplified even more clearly by Russell in an interview published

in *Encounter* shortly afterwards, in which he argued that civil disobedience was the only means of 'breaking through the barrier of silence and deceit by means of which populations are being lured to their doom'.[17] There were, however, portents of the ideological divisions to come: Alan Lovell, for example, questioned whether the new Committee was to be merely a publicity stunt or 'more than that'.[18] But, generally, the participants were willing to come together on Russell's terms in the new organization.

The intention was not to look upon civil disobedience as a form of direct action against the civil and military authorities, but to mobilize large numbers of people into dramatic action against nuclear weapons. As with the early CND leadership, Russell's emphasis was thus upon attracting 'VIPs'. If sufficient eminent people could be brought together to support the new Committee, it was argued, its programme of action would snowball and become irresistible.[19]

The original Committee of 100 was certainly an impressive list.[20]

[17] Russell, in *Encounter*, Feb. 1961, p. 93, quoted in Myers, op. cit., 163.

[18] Committee of 100 minutes, 22 Oct. 1960, Committee of 100 papers, deposited at South Place Ethical Society, London.

[19] There were, however, inconsistencies even here, as Myers has noted. In press release 3, 13 Feb. 1961, Russell claimed that civil disobedience was essential because 'even the government is ignorant of things which it ought to know'. Michael Scott, however, emphasized that 'all are living in fear and dread . . . and this is undermining society'. Thus on the one hand it was being claimed that people were too ignorant to be afraid, and on the other that they were paralysed into inaction because of fear. (Myers, op. cit., 164.)

[20] Lindsay Anderson, John Arden, Mrs M. Arden, Miss Pat Arrowsmith, Ernest Bader, Robert Bolt, E. J. Boothby, Jack Bowles, Margaret Bowles, John Braine, Douglas Brewood, Douglas Brewood Jnr., Wendy Butlin, April Carter, George Clark, Major C. V. Clarke, Norman Coe, Peter Collingwood, U. C. Collins, Alex Comfort, John F. Crallan, Mrs Liesl Dales, J. Alun David, Shelagh Delaney, Francis Deutsch, Ian Dixon, Robin Flor [sic], Hilda E. Fitter, John Fletcher, Harold Foster, William Gaskill, Dorothy Glaister, Michael Gotch, David Graham, Bob Gregory, Janet Goodricke, Brian Harrison, Trevor Hatton, Laurie Hislam, John Hoyland, Alex Jacobs, Sally Jacobs, August John, Nicholas Johnson, Ida Kar, B. M. Kaye, Mrs Anne Kerr, Dr Fergus King, Father Kirby, Ed Lewis, Christopher Logue, K. Alan Longman, Alan Lovell, David Lumsdaine, Hugh MacDiarmid, J. N. McNamee, George Melly, Gustav Metzger, Bernard R. Miles, Dr Jack Mongar, John Nicolls, Mrs Margaret O'Connell, John Osborne, Colin Painter, Helen Pallegranza [sic], Adam Parker Rhodes, Malcolm Pittock, Joan Pittock, Michael Randle, Sir Herbert Read, Diana Readhead, Heather Richardson, Victor Richardson, Mary Ringsleben, E. G. P. Rowe, Bertrand Russell, Ralph Schoenman, Rev. Michael Scott, Ivan Seruya, Teddy Seruya, Colin Shaw, Colin Smart, Peter Digby Smith, R. D. Smith, Tony Smythe, Robin E. Swingler, Nicolas Walter, Will Warren, Sarah Watson, Barbara Webb, Dr W. Weinberg, Arnold Wesker, Alan White, Shirley Wood, Norman Wormleighton, Biddy Youngday, Alastair Yule. This information is taken from *Peace News*, 16 Dec. 1960. Membership of the

However, the somewhat ephemeral nature of much of this support was evident from the fact that ten of those attending the first meeting never attended another,[21] and a further thirteen attended only two or three further meetings. Fifty-three people attended the inaugural meeting and, of these,

> only eighteen ... attended any meetings after the demonstration on 17 September 1961. Some of the Committee's most distinguished members—such as Augustus John, Sir Herbert Read, John Braine, Lord Boyd Orr and John Berger—never attended any meetings at all. By the end of 1961, no less than fifty-one members had joined since the September sit-down. With the exception of the regulars it amounted to a brand new Committee.[22]

This is to anticipate later problems, however. In October 1960 the Committee, by Russell and Scott's criteria, could be judged to have made a promising start in terms of 'big name' supporters. Less satisfactory, perhaps, was the diversity of proposals for initiating action (for example, NVDA at military installations or the Houses of Parliament; disruption of official functions, such as Trooping the Colour; jamming the BBC). The Committee reached no firm decisions about its protest activity, perhaps inevitably. It did, however, entrust its affairs to a working group which was, in the early months of the Committee, the decision-making body and the effective controlling agency of the Committee. Of this working group of thirteen, four were DAC members: in subsequent re-shuffles of the working group the DAC members, or ex-members, involved were seven of twenty-one (March 1961), and six of sixteen (May 1961). Thus, although DAC activists were only one component of several in the new Committee, they had a disproportionate influence on the new Committee. This was especially so in view of the considerable experience and commitment of DAC activists—in

Committee changed continually and, if this list is accurate, there were in mid-Dec. only 97 members. In fact, the membership fluctuated around the 100 mark. Several members who had attended the inaugural meeting had, by mid-Dec., resigned from the Committee: e.g. Doris Lessing, Bernard Kops, James Corbett, and Reg Butler.

According to Myers, op. cit., the total membership of the Committee through late 1960 and early 1961 was as follows: 26 Nov. 1960, 102; 21 Jan. 1961, 103; 12 Mar. 1961, 106; 7 May 1961, 109; 27 May 1961, 106. For fuller information of subsequent membership changes, see 'From Protest to Resistance', *Peace News* pamphlet 2, 1981, p. 62.

[21] And, according to the *Guardian*, some members criticized the composition of the Committee, even at this first meeting. 'Alex Comfort objected that there were not enough scientists; Michael Scott was sorry there were no other clergymen, and Reg Butler thought that the list lacked very important people in general' (*Guardian*, 25 Oct. 1960).   [22] Myers, op. cit., 173.

particular Michael Randle and April Carter, who became perhaps
the key figures on the Committee's working group.

The organizational structure of the Committee of 100 reflected
its genesis, and the purpose of its creators. The publicity and
propaganda impact would be ensured by the presence of prestigious
figures, but the *work* of the Committee could be undertaken by a
much smaller group, subject only to the most basic of safeguards.[23]
In this sense it was an unashamedly élitist body concerned, not with
popular involvement in a democratic mass movement, but rather
with the creation of the necessary mechanism for triggering off
mass protests. The distinction is a crucial one: Russell, and the
inaugural Committee generally, saw the Committee's task essentially in this ginger group, catalyst role. Its function was, precisely,
to arouse unmanageable public protest, in the form of civil
disobedience, on the nuclear issue. It was emphatically not to be the
embryo of a more generally extra-parliamentary, libertarian
movement of protest. At one level, the history of the Committee of
100 is the story of the transition from this initial model to the quasi-
anarchist organization which, from late 1962 onwards, the
Committee became.

At all events, the working group structure began to operate most
effectively following the 22 October meeting. The Committee's first
demonstration, announced by Russell at a press conference on 14
December 1960, was to be a four-hour sit-down outside the Ministry of Defence in Whitehall on 18 February 1961, timed to coincide
with, or immediately precede, the arrival of the 'Proteus' in the
Clyde. It had been a cardinal strategic principle of the Committee of
100 as its inception that it would proceed with demonstrations only
if *mass* support could be guaranteed: 'a minimum of two thousand'
pledged volunteers, according to the original Russell/Scott letter of
invitation. Michael Randle has recalled the difficulties this
presented: 'We'd never had a DAC demonstration with more than
one hundred people! . . . I was very sceptical as to whether we'd get
over two thousand'[24] Despite sending out 34,000 leaflets, only 500
pledges had been received by 21 January, and several people,
including Doris Lessing, had resigned from the Committee. At the

[23] See 'Interim Constitution of the Committee of 100', drafted by Francis Deutsch
and others. Cited in Myers, op. cit., 226, and in minutes of Committee meeting,
22 Oct. 1960.
[24] Randle, in conversation.

January meeting there was 'a long discussion on whether to proceed with the demonstration at all if fewer than twelve hundred pledges came in'. But the Committee kept its collective nerve and, by 11 February, the two thousand pledges had been received.[25]

The event itself was, in most respects, a notable success for the Committee. Estimates of the numbers involved varied, but there were probably around 2,000 sitting down, with a further 3,000–4,000 supporting.[26] The demonstrators marched in silence down Whitehall, after a march from Marble Arch to Trafalgar Square, and speeches in the Square. The sit-down then took place, for two and a half hours, outside the Ministry of Defence. Russell attached a declaration to the front door of the Ministry of Defence, demanding unilateral action by Britain and calling on 'people everywhere to rise up against the monstrous tyranny . . . of the nuclear tyrants of East and West'.[27]

There was a rather low-key and somewhat patronizing view on the part of the authorities, at this early stage of the Committee's activities. It can be argued that this was representative of the much-vaunted tolerance and 'Englishness' of the powers that be in Britain. The fact that no arrests were made, and that the police displayed 'gentle, almost Gandhian characteristics', according to one press report, further reinforced such a view. Again, senior police officers thought it was 'the quietest, most orderly, most impressive mass demonstration [they] could recall'.[28] The reaction of the national press was generally sympathetic. *The People* referred to Russell as 'a twentieth century saint', and he was compared both here and in *The Sunday Dispatch* to Gandhi. *The Sunday Telegraph,* estimating the crowd as 'at least three thousand', likened Russell to King Lear and the crowd to 'a gallery queue outside Covent Garden'.[29]

However, this mood of tolerant acceptance (although of firm disagreement on policy, of course) had changed markedly by the autumn of 1961. Both the governmental and police authorities had

[25] According to Myers, op. cit., 164–6.
[26] A supporting demonstration, protesting against the Polaris missile base, was held in Scotland on 18 Feb. There was a brief report in the *Observer*, 19 Feb. 1961.
[27] Committee of 100 declaration, as reported in the *Observer*, 19 Feb. 1961.
[28] Ibid.
[29] All quotations taken from press review collection of 18 Feb. demonstration, Committee of 100 papers, London. The international coverage was also very widespread. Among countries whose leading newspapers carried details of the demonstration were the USA, Italy, France, and New Zealand.

by then decided upon a very aggressive opposition to the Committee, its leaders, and its activists. The most likely explanation is that the rather patronizing and sentimental tone of the press coverage, and the tolerance of the authorities, resulted quite simply from the fact that the Committee was not yet taken to be a serious political force. It was seen rather as a somewhat eccentric, if not crackpot, organization whose idealism could be admired but whose policies were so obviously hare-brained that very few would be seriously attracted by them. The events of the spring and summer, and the build-up of support for the Committee, were to alter this view radically and convince the authorities that some firm action needed to be taken to counteract the civil disobedience movement.

The leaders of the Committee of 100, whilst expressing general satisfaction with the demonstration, were somewhat frustrated by the patronizing tolerance of officialdom. 'We do not want forever to be tolerated by the police', said Russell at a press conference on 20 February. 'Our movement depends for its success on an immense public opinion and we cannot create that unless we rouse the authorities to more action than they took yesterday.' Schoenman added, with a characteristic ideological gloss of his own, 'we want to put the Government in the position of either jailing thousands of people or abdicating.'[30]

It was as a result of this combination of reactions to the 18 February demonstration—principally of the urgency, the need to build upon an initial success, and the frustrations of not having been taken seriously—that the Committee decided to organize its next demonstration in three months' time rather than wait and plan a further demonstration that might have had more political relevance.

Before this demonstration, however, the 1961 Aldermaston March (in fact a two-pronged march, one section marching from Wethersfield) took place at the beginning of April. The Committee had no plans for a demonstration during the Aldermaston March, however, and its working groups had more than enough to do planning the next Committee demonstration for later in April, in Parliament Square. But for Ralph Schoenman the huge gathering in Trafalgar Square was too good an opportunity to miss and, 'without the knowledge of the Campaign officials and against the counsel of many of his fellow members of the Committee of 100',[31]

[30] *Guardian*, 20 Feb. 1961.   [31] According to Edwards, op. cit.

Schoenman led a group of about 500 or 600 with 'a Highland piper in full regalia and two large banners bearing the words "US Embassy sit down Protest. Polaris Must Go" ',[32] from Trafalgar Square to the US Embassy in Grosvenor Square. The demonstration was not only unplanned and officially unsanctioned, it was also conducted in a very different spirit from the 18 February sit-down. Four people were arrested in Trafalgar Square and charged with threatening behaviour, obstructing the police, and obstructing the passageway.

Two more were arrested in Grosvenor Square in a demonstration characterized by its tension and barely concealed hostility between police and marchers.[33] But the real trouble occurred when demonstrators followed the police vans back to West End Central police station, where something approaching a brief pitched battle took place. Twenty-five people were arrested and charged with a range of offences (mostly assault). All this was a long way from the 'responsible', non-violent action practised by the DAC, and urged upon the Committee of 100 by both DAC activists and others. Later, a group of demonstrators marched to the Soviet Embassy and staged a sit-down on finding that they could get no nearer than the gateway to Kensington Palace Gardens. Despite the fact that the Aldermaston March had been a four-day protest, culminating in a rally, according to some estimates attended by 150,000 people, it was the maverick protest by a few hundred that took the attention of the media to the virtual exclusion of CND's march. Understandably, the CND leaders were furious. What seemed to them to be such completely irresponsible action was precisely what they had feared when the Committee was originally founded.[34]

The tensions created in the Movement generally by this occurrence made it essential that the Committee's next demonstration, scheduled for 29 April in Parliament Square, should be well organized and successful. The demonstration was timed to take place shortly after the Budget proposals were to be announced in Parliament, thus confirming the Government's defence expenditure plans. The Committee committed itself quite explicitly to the objective of attracting twice as many to its April as it had to its February demonstration: i.e. 10,000 compared to 5,000.

---

[32] *Guardian*, 4 Apr. 1961.   [33] See report in ibid.
[34] Canon Collins issued a statement, cited in ibid., condemning the demonstration and dissociating CND from it.

It proved extremely difficult to gather enough pre-demonstration pledges, but there could be no turning back. In the event a far smaller number (2,500) than had been hoped for took part.[35] However, as the Committee had hoped, the police were put in a position where their previous policy of non-arrest was no longer tenable: 826 arrests were made, although many were not arrested and moved onto the pavements.[36] Although there was some disquiet over the tactics and organization of the demonstration,[37] there was no doubt that overall it could be regarded as a success for the Committee. Had outside events not had a major impact on the Committee through the summer of 1961 it is more than likely, however, that the Committee would have changed course—certainly in terms of its short-term tactical decisions on demonstration organization.[38]

There was, as Myers has noted, a move 'organizationally towards a more elaborate apparatus' on a decentralized, group basis following the 29 April demonstration.[39] But, although such proposals were first discussed in May 1961 their implementation did not take place until October (although an area convenor system was introduced), largely because of the impact of external crises upon the Committee and its perspectives in the summer of 1961. It was only in the aftermath of the September 1961 demonstration that these organizational matters, and the ideological pre-occupations which underlay them, came to the fore again. Discussion and analysis of the organizational changes in the Committee thus belong properly to the 'post 17 September' Committee of 100 debate, which in turn leads into the demonstrations at Wethersfield and elsewhere in December 1961, and the events of 1962.

This, then, is an appropriate point to pause in the historical narrative of the Committee's development and discuss its ideological complexion immediately prior to its climactic period, in late August to mid-September 1961.

[35] This was the figure given by *Peace News*, but according to Myers (op. cit.) it was only 1,200.
[36] Russell was ill and unable to take part. Among those arrested were Vanessa Redgrave, Arnold Wesker, and John Neville.
[37] See George Clark, *Second Wind*, London 1963, p. 11.
[38] See George Clark, quoted in the *Sunday Telegraph*, 30 Apr. 1961, where he argued that other forms of demonstration should be devised 'which will provide a lot of trouble for the government while not inconveniencing the police so much'.
[39] Myers, op. cit., 288 ff.

IDEOLOGICAL PROFILE OF THE COMMITTEE
IN THE LATE SUMMER OF 1961

The summer of 1961 was a period of acute international tension. In July the Berlin crisis broke and, by August, tensions had reached boiling point and the world was on the brink of nuclear war, as was later admitted by Lord Home in his first speech as Prime Minister.[40] The crisis did much to give credibility to the Committee of 100's message of urgency, and the tension produced an increasing tide of activity through the summer.[41] It was thus in an atmosphere of some tension, with the 17 September Committee of 100 demonstrations in Trafalgar Square and at Holy Loch only a few days away, that the authorities decided to take action against the Committee and its leaders. What was the ideological complex of the Committee, on the eve of its greatest success and public impact?

The original Committee of 100 was a diffuse ideological coalition. The DAC may have contained disparate ideological stances, but there was a core of ideological as well as personal unity around certain very specific and fundamental values and theories. This legacy of Gandhian, non-violent civil disobedience was carried on through into the Committee of 100 and certainly formed one centrally important strand. There were, however, other important dimensions to the Committee of 100 in both organizational and ideological terms.

Over and above the DAC framework it is possible to distinguish the following major ideological positions in the Committee (although it should be borne in mind that these perspectives overlapped): the Schoenman position, populist/libertarian; the anarchist; the libertarian socialist, quasi-syndicalist, as exemplified by the journal *Solidarity for Workers' Power;* and the morally committed, non-Gandhian pacifist. In relation to the last group, some consideration of the pacifist position has already been undertaken in Chapter 2. With the preceding two, discussion is most appropriately left until the analysis of the Committee in the period from 1962 onwards, when these ideas began to develop more fully

[40] See Driver, op. cit., 127.
[41] e.g. on Hiroshima Day over 2,000 attended a vigil at the Cenotaph and, in the afternoon, there were 5,000 at a Hyde Park rally; at the end of August, when the USSR resumed nuclear testing, the Committee held a sit-down demonstration outside the Embassy and 116 were arrested, and, when the USA resumed testing shortly afterwards, a similar demonstration was held and 150 arrested.

and dominate the Committee. We are thus left with two dominant strands—the DAC influence and the Schoenman influence.

In Stuart Hall's view,

the new element was less a kind of pacifist philosophical rationale for direct action and more a *political* one; people who may not have been committed philosophically to that way [i.e. the DAC way] of going about it, nevertheless saw the *political* significance of stepping beyond the confines of traditional politics, parliamentary-oriented politics.[42]

This distinction may serve as a useful starting-point for the discussion of the two positions, which will focus, although not exclusively, on Schoenman himself and on Michael Randle.

Bertrand Russell

What is omitted from this framework, however, is the unique and central role played by Russell. Any account of the ideology and practice of the Committee must begin with an attempt to analyse Russell's highly individual perspective and motivation: the subsequent analyses of Schoenman, Randle *et al.* are, at one level, defined by their relationships to Russell's own position. To identify this position in relation to the Committee of 100, it is necessary to begin with a discussion of the genesis of Russell's views on the 'nuclear question' generally.[43]

Inevitably, given his immense personal magnetism, fame, intellect, past involvement with all manner of radical campaigns, and great age, Russell is not readily classifiable. His perspective was initially very similar in orientation to the scientist/environmentalist group (i.e. scientists in and around the Pugwash conference group). His primary motivation from 1945 and the Hiroshima and Nagasaki bombings was to save the world from nuclear destruction. 'The salvation of the human race from a nuclear holocaust was the last great attachment of Russell's life.'[44] Far from viewing the development of nuclear weapons as indicative of a general *malaise* in society or the end-product of an unworkable and/or

---

[42] Stuart Hall, in conversation with the author, Mar. 1978.
[43] The section concerning Russell draws heavily on Richard Taylor and Colin Pritchard, *The Protest Makers: The British Nuclear Disarmament Movement 1958–1965, Twenty Years On,* Oxford, 1980, pp. 85–92.
[44] R. Clark, op. cit., 517.

immoral system, Russell, in the 1940s, was urging the West to coerce the USSR into agreeing to a system of world government by using the threat of nuclear weapons. (The USSR did not explode her first A-bomb until 1949.) Russell's advocacy of 'preventive war' with the USSR when the USA had the monopoly of nuclear weapons, has often been held to be an aberration, incompatible with his later stance.[45] In reality the opposite was the case: not only was it quite in character for Russell to make shocking and outrageous statements, on political as on other matters; the fundamentals of the position he adopted in the 1940s were also consistent with his continued insistence in the 1950s and 1960s that nuclear weapons and the probability of the imminent destruction of mankind *must* be seen as the paramount issue overriding all other political questions. Once it is acknowledged that the prevention of nuclear war, and hence mankind's destruction, was the guiding aim of Russell's life and politics post-1945, then his advocacy of the need for world peace and disarmament via world government, to be achieved, if necessary, through coercion, became not only rational but necessary.

Russell's attitudes were, of course, founded on the liberal assumptions of his own, lifelong ideological framework: much else may have changed during Russell's life but he was consistent in his political philosophy. As one commentator has put it, 'he was individualistic rather than state-centred, democratic rather than authoritarian, pragmatic rather than ideological, empirical rather than theoretical, rational rather than emotional, international rather than parochial'.[46] Despite Schoenman's attempt to persuade us otherwise, it is clear that Russell was, and to a greater or lesser extent remained, a non-Marxist in ideological/theoretical terms.[47]

---

[45] Not surprisingly, the Communist Party never really forgave Russell for this period of his political life. George Matthews, for example, commented that 'we used not to take it up very often but we did remember that Bertrand Russell himself advocated the dropping of the A-bomb on Moscow in the late '40s' (in conversation with the author, Jan. 1978).

[46] Edward F. Sherman, 'Bertrand Russell and the Peace Movement: Liberal Consistency or Radical Change?', in G. Nakhnikian (ed.), *Bertrand Russell's Philosophy*, London, 1974, p. 255.

[47] Schoenman argues forcefully that, during his last years 'his attitude towards Capitalism and American imperialism ... bears a decidely Marxist character' (Ralph Schoenman, 'Bertrand Russell and the Peace Movement', in Nakhnikian, op. cit., 227–8). But Schoenman's argument here is not convincing. Russell undoubtedly came to see American aggression, in Vietnam and elsewhere, as a greater threat to

Russell's stance, however, was not merely non-socialist: in true nineteenth-century style he viewed politics as a process of imposing a set of clearly formulated utilitarian ideals emphasizing the benefits of world order, rationality, and international co-operation through a formal diplomatic and pragmatic political process.

His implicit acceptance of the efficacy and desirability of the élite and formal processes of world politics and diplomacy were indicative of his own superlative aristocratic pedigree. Moreover, he had the intellectual and aristocratic self-confidence to believe that he could use, and even transcend, these processes. There was, as Schoenman noted, an ambivalence between Russell's support for democratic movements and his élitist belief that

cultural excellence and unique achievement were the product of favoured circumstances. . . . He felt that excellence came from the special nurturing of individual talent and that meritocracy or cultural decline would follow the overthrow of privilege. He desired its overthrow but he mourned in advance some of the consequences as he saw them.[48]

Having been the moving force in establishing the Pugwash conference and the subsequent pressure group, Russell was content to leave it to others to administer and develop,[49] and was concerned to open up other avenues for publicizing the nuclear issue. As early as 1954 Russell, in a memorable radio broadcast,[50] had set the tone for his later passionate, all-or-nothing advocacy of the nuclear disarmament cause. Although Russell had relatively little contact with either the NCANWT or the DAC,[51] there is no doubt that he was from the outset of the Movement concerned to involve himself and lend his weight to the creation of a national organization. Russell was, of course, one of the original small group which gave

world peace than Soviet expansionism, following the Cuba crisis. He also came to be far more sympathetic to some aspects of Communism as a social and governmental system than he had been previously, but he did not change his long-standing individualist liberal stance on ideological questions—and never became even remotely convinced of Marxism as an ideological, let alone philosophical, framework of analysis.

[48] Schoenman, 'Bertrand Russell and the Peace Movement', 233.

[49] See R. Clark, op. cit., ch. 20, for details of the Pugwash conference development and Russell's and Rotblat's involvement.

[50] Russell's 'Man's Peril', broadcast on BBC radio, 23 Dec. 1954. Extracts from this were used in the launch statement of the Committee, 'Act or Perish'.

[51] Although Russell was a sponsor of both the NCANWT and the DAC, and gave frequent verbal and financial support.

birth to CND, and from the very beginning he favoured more militant measures to achieve the aims of CND than others in the leader-
ship were prepared to countenance. But Russell was not in the same ideological camp as the DAC.
Although a pacifist in the First World War, his pacifism had been of
a very different tradition from that of the non-violent Gandhians of
the DAC, and had been based more on the immediate, *ad hoc* issues
at the time than on a political philosophy centring on non-violence.
His concerns in this field had been civil liberties, anti-conscrip-
tionism, and individual anti-militarism.

Russell rejected the DAC's militant objectives of a 'non-violent
society', and their specific policy commitment to *American* (and
Russian) unilateral disarmament as well as British. In this very
important sense Russell was arguing on the same ideological
assumptions as the CND leadership of Collins *et al:* that is, he
accepted that nuclear weapons were an isolated evil of contemporary society, albeit an evil of unprecedented and hitherto
unimaginable magnitude. The problem was thus to rid the world of
these weapons, which could be achieved quite independently of
other social and political structural change. Unlike the DAC (and
for that matter the socialist left), Russell saw no connection
between the form of society and the development of nuclear
weapons. For him, nuclear disarmament was a genuinely 'single-
issue campaign'. The reasons for Russell adopting this perspective
are numerous, but it was the philosophical and ideological tradition
to which he belonged that led him to reject[52] the specifically socialist
perspectives of the New Left and other Marxist groupings. But
more importantly, in the Disarmament Movement context, it also
led Russell to reject—or perhaps ignore or pass over—the
Gandhian-inspired politics of non-violence advocated by the DAC.
Moreover, for all his immense erudition and intellectual ability,
Russell had always tended to see politics in very black and white
terms. His humanist radicalism was outraged by the existence of
nuclear weapons, and he threw his immense influence and political
tenacity and ingenuity behind the Movement for disarmament. But
he was always distanced to some extent from his radical supporters

[52] It might be more accurate to say that Russell ignored and failed to comprehend
the analysis of the left (both 'Marxist' and 'libertarian') which linked the bomb to
wider social and political questions. It is certainly true that Russell never wrote or
spoke publicly, at any length, about his reasons for rejecting these views.

and their organizations, partly because of this ideological gulf—
and partly, of course, because of the very great differences in age,
social milieu, and intellectual interests and abilities that existed
between himself and the Movement's rank and file.

As we have seen, Russell's relationship, as president of CND,
with the rest of the CND leadership, and in particular with Canon
Collins, the chairman, was somewhat strained from the beginning.
It is less often acknowledged that Russell was also out of touch, and
to some degree out of sympathy, with many of the Committee of
100 activists.

What then was Russell's perspective on the Committee of 100,
and how far was his stance consistent with his earlier activities?
Russell's interest in and advocacy of civil disobedience was wholly
consistent with his radical individualism. (As Clark has noted, the
espousal of civil disobedience was 'easy enough for those born into
the aristocratic tradition but slightly shocking to the respectable
middle classes who supplied the cannon-fodder of the movement'.[53]) As early as 1936 Russell had made his position on civil
disobedience quite clear:

> I know well that this [civil disobedience] is a dangerous doctrine and that
> the claim to set up one's own individual judgement in defiance of legally
> constituted authority leads logically to anarchy. At the same time almost all
> great advances have involved illegality. The early Christians broke the law;
> Galileo broke the law, the French revolutionaries broke the law; early
> trade unionists broke the law. The instances are so numerous and so
> important that no one can maintain as an absolute principle obedience to
> constituted authority.[54]

Civil disobedience was thus seen as a necessary means of achieving 'progressive' ends at certain critical times in man's history.
Given this perspective it is not surprising that Russell advocated
civil disobedience to further the nuclear disarmament cause. By the
summer of 1960 he had become disillusioned both with CND as a
vehicle for achieving the goal of unilateralism and, more specifically, with Canon Collins's over-cautious leadership. He thus gave
enthusiastic backing to Schoenman's proposals: but there was a
very wide division between them from the outset about the purpose

[53] R. Clark, op. cit., 560.

[54] Russell, 'Which Way to Peace?', 1936, quoted in R. Clark, op. cit., 573–4. And
of course, Russell had broken the law much earlier, in 1915–16, in the No Conscription Fellowship movement.

of and justification for civil disobedience. Russell's viewpoint was characteristically pragmatic. Asked in an interview in 1963 why he had backed civil disobedience, Russell replied: 'Purely to get attention. All the major organs of publicity are against us. . . . I have no views in principle either for or against civil disobedience . . . with me, it is purely a practical question of whether to do it or not, a method of propaganda.'[55]

Russell's much-publicized dispute with Collins was thus personal and tactical rather than ideological. To be sure, there were those within the CND leadership for whom the question of civil disobedience *per se* was a major ideological division (Jacquetta Hawkes, for example). But in reality it was a division over tactics—over the best way to secure the agreed objective of British unilateral nuclear disarmament—although of course deeper divisions were linked to the conflict. Russell was no more in favour of 'Movement power' than was Canon Collins—save in so far as the pressure of a mass civil disobedience movement would lead in a tactical sense, in Russell's view, to the attainment of unilateral nuclear disarmament. Paradoxically, therefore, there was perhaps more in common between Russell and the CND leadership in ultimate ideological terms than there was between Russell and the militant young activists of the Committee of 100 of which he was president.

Thus, although Russell remained the undisputed 'leader' of the Committee, and although the Committee was associated overwhelmingly in the public mind with his name, he was at odds ideologically with both the DAC position, and the stance taken by Schoenman and other 'militants' within the Committee. There was in many respects a parallel with CND here. As long as the Committee remained successful and united on the one common objective, the fragile unity could be maintained. But, once that momentum was broken and that overriding unity on the single issue questioned, the fundamental incompatibility of the Committee's coalition became apparent, and the constituent parts began to pull in their own directions. Just as, in CND, the tension grew between the Labourist/political wing and the moral/individualist wing, following the realization that the Scarborough victory could not be consolidated, so the tension and divisions grew in the Committee following the Wethersfield *et al.* demonstrations. Russell's function in the Committee, from its inception until late 1961 at least, was

[55] Russell, interview with *Playboy*, Mar. 1963, quoted in R. Clark, op. cit., 574.

thus to provide inspiration and leadership, and to unify the Committee around his commitment to the single-issue objectives. Once the conditions which enabled these roles to be fulfilled had altered, Russell's position *vis-à-vis* the Committee became untenable. Thus, although Russell appeared to command an invincible position in the Committee, and although the Committee, at least initially, was united under him, he was in reality very dependent upon favourable circumstances to maintain that dominance and was, in fact, to a very large extent an *isolated* figure within the leadership. Moreover, his fundamental ideological position was at variance on so many crucial points with the other major components of the Committee that, even at the height of its success, the Committee was never fully at one with Russell's perspectives.

Ralph Schoenman

What then were the alternative positions taken by Schoenman and Randle, which distinguished their perceptions, ideologically, so markedly from those of Russell? Schoenman's was certainly an extreme political position. In many ways he foreshadowed the anarchist developments of the Committee of 100 in 1962 and beyond. Yet he was not advocating orthodox, traditional anarchism of any variety, and he had few of the anarchistic or libertarian preoccupations with decentralized, community-style campaigns which were to emerge after 1962 in the Committee. Similarly, although there was much in common between Schoenman's militancy and that of the *Solidarity* group there was little of orthodox socialism (of any variety) in his ideological stance. Most notably of all, there was no indication of any concern with either the working class or the Labour Movement as the agency of revolutionary change; nor was there support for any type of socialist political party (quite the opposite, in fact). Finally, although there was obviously much in common between Schoenman and the DAC activists, not least in the total commitment of both to the nuclear issue, there was a divergence over the concept of non-violence. As many of the DAC activists have commented,[56] Schoenman's commitment to non-violence in general was thought to be at best ambivalent, and on the specifics of demonstration

---

[56] i.e. Hugh Brock, April Carter, Pat Arrowsmith, and, to a lesser extent, Michael Randle, all in conversation with the author, 1978.

tactics and organization, his views were sharply divergent from those of the DAC activists. His whole approach was pragmatic rather than principled. It is thus clear that Schoenman was a difficult person to place ideologically.

Moreover, the spectrum of Committee of 100 opinion which he articulated so forcefully did not fall into any of the conventional political categories, though there were, as Stuart Hall has commented, aspects of his position which were anarchist and others which were Trotskyist.[57]

Schoenman's political preoccupations during 1961–2[58] are best illustrated in two articles in *Peace News:* 'Civil Disobedience to Halt Polaris' in February 1961; and 'Resistance in Mass Society' in August 1961.[59] In the first of these articles, which is focused on an appeal for Movement supporters and others to join the first of the Committee of 100 demonstrations on 18 February, Schoenman stressed the need for the individual to take a principled stand against the technological society which had produced nuclear weapons, and which had generally repressed and alienated humanity.

Despite Schoenman's natural desire to dovetail his arguments and perspective with those of Russell and Scott, something of his own radically distinct position comes through clearly in this article. First, there is his identification of modern mass societies generally as being the adversary against which radicalism must struggle. Within these mass and totalitarian societies, the determining factor was neither capital nor ideology (the former is not mentioned by Schoenman, and the latter is dismissed as 'almost an irrelevance'), but rather technology. It is therefore strongly implicit that it is advanced industrialism, which necessarily creates centralized autocratic political structures, which is, of itself, the fundamental enemy. Schoenman thus belongs to the anti-industrial strand of Anglo-American, romantic, utopian populists. Closely related to this stance was Schoenman's populist, quasi-anarchistic rejection of *all* political parties, *all* leadership, and *all* bureaucratic structures. If

[57] Hall, in conversation.

[58] His later move towards a more Trotskyist ideological position, which falls outside our concerns here, is best illustrated in his critique of Russell's politics, and defence of his own, in Schoenman (ed.), op. cit. For hostile accounts of Schoenman's influence on Russell, and analyses of his political actions and motivation, see Russell, *Autobiography*, and R. Clark, op. cit.

[59] *Peace News*, 17 Feb. 1961 and 25 Aug. 1961, respectively.

alienated man was to overcome the mass society and the obscenities it produced—principally nuclear weapons and the resultant imminent holocaust—it must be through the example of a large number of individuals taking direct, non-violent action to assert the rejection of the dominant society and the affirmation of human values. There is here a spontaneist, situationist ideological stance (with parallels perhaps with the more libertarian elements of the May 1968 revolt in Paris). This entailed, of course, a complete rejection of all socialist orthodoxies—whether social democracy and Labourism, or Communism, or Trotskyism, or the New Left. It is hardly necessary to add that Schoenman's position was as hostile to the USSR as it was to the USA, at least in ideological as opposed to political policy terms. Arguably this changed, for Schoenman and for Russell, in the years immediately following their involvement in the Committee of 100, as their attentions turned increasingly to opposing the US involvement in the Vietnam War.[60]

It should however be noted that Schoenman's position, although somewhat esoteric in any context, had strong links with the ideological framework of the *American* New Left between approximately 1964 and 1968. In its anti-industrial, anti-technological emphasis, and its populist and wholly anti-Marxian analysis, Schoenman's ideological perspective had affinities with a number of influential figures within the American context (Roszak and Marcuse, for example).

Schoenman elaborated on his quasi-insurrectionary and certainly highly militant policy objectives in the *Peace News* article 'Resistance in Mass Society', and explained in more detail the basis of his political stance. Schoenman took for his starting-point a 1954 essay by Professor H. H. Wilson, 'The Dilemma of the Obsolete Man', in which it was argued 'that the values derived from liberal democratic and socialist traditions were no longer operative'[61] because contemporary society was *mass* society. In Western societies, Schoenman argued, 'power is concentrated and is private'. Economically, power lay increasingly with the multinational industrial sector; ideologically, control was exercised through the centralized media. Not only were Western societies therefore organized on a centralized basis in all respects, but the

---

[60] See R. Clark, op. cit., 615–28, and appendix, 'Private Memorandum concerning Ralph Schoenman', 640–51.

[61] This and the quotations that follow are from 'Resistance in Mass Society'.

control was becoming increasingly international in character. American society was geared totally to war and was in fact a 'warfare state': a concept that was to become central to the Committee's analysis in 1962 and beyond. For Schoenman it was 'patently clear that the nature of the conflict with the Soviet Union has nothing to do with an ideological preference for liberal values or civil liberties. The United States is as monolithic and autocratic a society as is likely to be produced.'

Reverting back to the argument of the previous article, Schoenman claimed that the totalitarian nature of both Western and Eastern societies related far more to the 'nature of vast industrial technology than it [did to] ideology'. Contemporary society was characterized by its apolitical character. 'We are inhabiting societies where decisions are administrative and are not seriously political because the areas of choice are peripheral.' The Committee of 100 was the 'first serious effort in Western society' to encounter the total alienation that had resulted from this situation. This revolt was possible only because of the perceived imminence of annihilation.

The critical point that I wish to make is that the covering of the planet with a fantastic network of rocket bases, the full direction of the technology of industrial societies for murderous production, make explicit the active values—the unvarnished character of our present social arrangement. . . . [The Movement must] never forget that we must expose the fraud of these institutions, never forget that we cannot rely on them for communication with masses of men.

Schoenman made the policy objectives, which stemmed from this set of arguments, quite explicit:

We must learn to use our vast numbers in waves so that a base like Polaris will suffer one thousand demonstrators every fortnight. Above all, we must be clear that we are arguing by example, that we are displaying a method which enables people to affect and to effect events. If this is to be done we must realise that we are conducting a resistance movement. We are seeking to obstruct systematically to the point where the authorities have to give way. . . . Demonstrations must not end with the 'sit-down. We must begin to pledge people in their thousands to carry the challenge further. The model of our objective should be the General Strike. We are not a political party. We have no intention of providing a civil service as an alternative body of administrators. We have precise demands which must be pressed on authority. They will acquiesce or face national disruption.

There shall undoubtedly be a host of political consequences of our resistance. We must not be deluded by them. If we hand over our consciences to
any political party we will be betrayed ... the heart of our movement is
resistance. We must constitute the articulate expression of an active
populace, alive to human rights and to human responsibility.
    Short of this Eichmann stands for Everyman.

    It is notable that, although at the outset of the piece Schoenman
adopts virtually a Marxist view of capitalist control in contemporary Western society, there is an ultimate insistence upon the *moral*
basis for radical political action. Again, the problem is emphatically
not seen as one of 'capitalism versus socialism': modern totalitarian societies are explicitly characterized as apolitical. What is
required is a reassertion of humanistic, moral values against this
onslaught. The parallel with the later Orwell is, as Schoenman
claimed, very close. For Schoenman, as for Orwell, the solution, the
salvation, of humanity lay not within the parameters of socialist
analysis, Marxist or otherwise, but in the reaffirmation of human
values and the right of the individual to protest and to resist vigorously the attempted imposition of morally obscene developments—
in particular the extreme aberration of nuclear weapons.[62]
    In some senses, then, Schoenman's was a less revolutionary
position than it at first appeared. Despite all the blood-curdling
rhetoric, his framework rested essentially on the moral humanism
that had characterized the Western liberal tradition from the time
of the Enlightenment. Added to this was the genuinely populist
perspective which, it is not unreasonable to surmise, was a product
of his American cultural experience, where populist democratic
ideas are a more important element in the political culture than they
have been in Northern and Western Europe. Finally, there was a
difficult to define, but pervasive and very effective demagogic,
millenarian, almost apocalyptic style to his writing, which gave the
whole an urgency and punch which was compelling and, for many,
convincing.
    Although the elements of the analysis were neither unique nor
especially original, there is no doubt that Schoenman was a very
effective popularizer of ideas. But the real and potent militancy of

---

[62] For a discussion of the moral commitment politics of Orwell see Richard
Taylor, 'George Orwell and the Politics of Decency', in J. A. Jowitt and R. K. S.
Taylor (eds.), *George Orwell*, Bradford Centre Occasional Paper 3, Leeds, 1981. In
this respect Schoenman's position is close to Russell's.

his ideology lay in the specific tactical and strategic policies he advocated for the Committee. Stuart Hall has explained a crucial difference between Schoenman and other militant Committee of 100 members in the differing views over the objectives to be attained by 'filling the jails'.

I think a lot of people did think that there would be serious problems posed for the State if a large number of very respectable people were turning out time and time again willing to go to jail. They were clearly not criminal subversives etc. etc. and, although this *might* produce logistic problems— where to put them and so on, it *would* produce an *ideological* problem for the State, in the sense of explaining *why* this was happening. . . . But I think behind that there is a more consistent political position of that kind: namely, throw yourself time and again against the walls of the State and ultimately they will crumble—which very few people believed in that full sense. And in some ways Schoenman did: and in that sense his was a very extreme position.[63]

Thus, whilst his ideology may have been relatively moderate, even though unorthodox in an English context, Schoenman's political programme was certainly extreme. The influence which such ideas exercised over the Committee was very strong up to and including the September 1961 demonstration, though there remain mystery and enigma over his motivations and personality.[64]

Whatever the truth about Ralph Schoenman, 'there is no question that he was *very* important in bringing the elements together'.[65] Moreoever, his political strategy of combining a Kropotkin-type anarchism—'the capacity of the single individual will and the individual action to spark something off'—with a quasi-Trotskyist 'kind of vanguardism among revolutionary forces'[66]—had a profound impact on the Committee of 100 and its development.

[63] Hall, in conversation.
[64] Russell's disavowal of Schoenman is reprinted as an appendix to R. Clark, op. cit. Others in the Movement were far more critical. Jacquetta Hawkes described him as 'an evil person . . . there was something extraordinarily unpleasant about him'. Arthur Goss pronounced him 'evil', and Canon Collins accused him of working consciously *against* the Peace Movement, possibly as a CIA agent (Hawkes, Goss, and Collins, all in conversation with the author.) Despite repeated attempts, the author has been unable to make direct contact with Ralph Schoenman to discuss these issues in detail. No final opinion on his role and motivations can therefore be expressed here.
[65] Hall in conversation; and as Randle, in conversation, has observed, 'he was the person who had the dynamism'. [66] Hall, in conversation.

However, his specific proposals for action were open to quite legitimate and practical objections. Was it really realistic, April Carter asked, to believe that 100,000 committed civil disobedience demonstrators could ever be mustered? Moreover, would the State's institutions *really* crumble under such a non-violent onslaught?[67] His actual proposals for political action by the Committee, from the spring of 1961 onwards, were undoubtedly both impractical and unreaslistic. Such a suggested scenario would have been problematic in even the most favourable conditions: that is, when the wider society was in crisis, politically and economically, and was culturally in turmoil. And, of course, the 1950s and early 1960s in Britain were relatively *stable* years: there was no 'crisis of confidence in the system', and no economic or political upheavals fundamentally to challenge the status quo. Over and above these important, contextual points however, it is necessary to note again the disparity between the direct action, quasi-anarchistic politics advocated by Schoenman and others, and the mainstream radical and socialist traditions of the British Labour Movement. For good or ill, radicalism in Britain, certainly since the Industrial Revolution, has generally found expression, not in anarchic, insurrectionary movements, but within the broad parameters of Labour Movement politics, both social democratic/parliamentarist and extra-parliamentary. Without linking into these strata of radicalism the direct action movement had little chance of achieving its objectives, as was argued in Chapter 4.

Michael Randle

Randle's was a more orthodox DAC perspective and was more representative of the general orientation of the Committee of 100. It would be mistaken to assume, however, that there was a clear division between the radical newcomers into the Committee of 100 and the cautious 'old-timers' of the DAC attempting to hold back militancy.[68] Randle was certainly correct when he argued that the

[67] Carter, *Peace News*, 18 Aug. 1961.
[68] Myers, op. cit., claims the exact opposite: that is, that it was the build-up of the DAC predominance in the Committee from late 1961 onwards, combined with a dropping-off of support from the original Russell-orientated Committee members, that resulted in the Committee's move towards a more anarchistic policy position in 1962 and beyond. This argument is the core of the subsequent article by Myers, 'Civil Disobedience and Organizational Change: The British Committee of 100', *Political Science Quarterly*, 86.1, Mar. 1971.

whole experience of the Committee of 100 was an experience of radicalization for all those who took a central, activist part. Thus the DAC activists were themselves radicalized by their Committee of 100 experience, as were many others.

The ideological picture is thus considerably less clear-cut and more complex than it would at first appear. Randle was a key figure in this whole process. In part, of course, this was because of his organizational and leadership roles as chairman of DAC and secretary of the Committee of 100. But, even more than this, Randle developed his ideological position in relation to the new context, and redefined his political objectives according to the possibilities opened up by Schoenman's and Russell's initiative, though always within DAC parameters.

The objective of non-violent social revolution as a legitimate, indeed necessary long-term objective was part of Randle's ideological position in the DAC as well as the Committee of 100.

Mass civil disobedience means revolution. . . . [But this] is only part of a much larger question: does unilateral nuclear disarmament imply revolution? I believe that it does, or at least that it implies a profound political and social upheaval that will not be achieved within the framework of existing parties or existing politics.[69]

Given the success of the Movement, in terms both of the CND victory at the Scarborough Conference of the Labour Party and the initial sit-down demonstration of the Committee of 100 on 18 February 1961, the initial educative stage had been completed: it was now the time to move forward via civil disobedience.

Unilateralism was a revolutionary demand because it involved 'a complete break with the military and political tradition of the country, including, alas, the tradition built up in the Labour Party over the last fifty years. Only a profound political and social upheaval can upset this tradition.' Moreover, there were powerful vested interests in the multi-million-pound armaments industry. Finally, in terms of foreign policy, unilateral nuclear disarmament would involve 'not only a complete readjustment of foreign policy but a new concept of defence, based on non-violent action'.[70] It was

[69] Michael Randle, 'Is it Revolution We're After?', *Peace News*, 10 Mar. 1961.
[70] Non-violent alternatives to orthodox defence policy was to be a developing field of enquiry for many peace activists and theorists in the decade following the 1960s. In 1979 Randle became full time co-ordinator of the Alternative Defence Commission, a body of notable experts from a wide range of backgrounds and

thus unrealistic to place reliance on a Labour Government. Unilateralism was a revolutionary policy: the Labour Party was a constitutionalist party. 'If the unilateralists [in the Labour Party] really stuck to their guns, the Party would split. They are unlikely to do so.'[71]

Randle saw the Committee very much as an extension of the DAC. There were notable differences, as well as obvious similarities, between Randle's ideological position and that of Schoenman. Randle held unequivocally to the centrality of non-violence, and his advocacy of civil disobedience was couched very much in the context of the radical pacifist perspective. The purpose of the desired revolution was to create the non-violent society within which their ideals could be realized. For the Schoenman militants (as, in this respect, for the *Solidarity* supporters who came to the fore later[72]), resistance to authority through the collective, spontaneous revolt of the mass of people was itself the objective: there was scant attention paid to the ideology of non-violence.

The centrality of this concept for Randle *et al.*, however, raised a number of crucial political problems. The first of these related to the justifications for 'coercive' civil disobedience. Closely linked to this was the seemingly tactical question of whether the Committee was right to concentrate its activities in central London—or whether it should follow the DAC's policy of making protest at the bases and other military installations.

On the first point Randle was taken to task in the columns of *Peace News*. It was argued that for the Committee of 100 to break the law to draw attention to a minority viewpoint, within a democratic society, was both morally dubious and tactically mistaken.[73] Randle's response encapsulated the basic DAC/Committee of 100 case, justifying civil disobedience: 'I am only prepared to accept

occupations, engaged on research into alternative defence and foreign policies. (Its books *Defence Without the Bomb*, London, 1983, and *The Politics of Alternative Defence*, London, 1987 have had a considerable impact on defence thinking, especially in the Labour Party in the 1980s).

[71] Randle also had reservations about the specific policy proposals of the New Left, over and above their ultimate commitment to the Labour Party and constitutionalism. In particular he was critical of what he regarded as the New Left's somewhat facile view of positive neutralism. See Randle, *Peace News*, Mar. 1961.

[72] Supporters of the journal *Solidarity for Workers' Power,* whose role and ideology is discussed below.

[73] Alan Litherland, *Peace News*, 21 Apr. 1961, echoing Allen Skinner's earlier argument on similar lines. See ch. 4.

[majority rule] in so far as it respects certain basic human rights, my own and other people's ... human rights are the first priority, majority rule the second.'[74]

The second, tactical issue was more problematic. It was necessary for the Committee to organize mass sit-downs in central London at the outset of its campaign to attract large numbers and to ensure media coverage. To have followed the DAC pattern of demonstrations at the bases would have guaranteed failure as far as building a mass following was concerned. On the other hand, it was more difficult, from the DAC perspective, to develop a rationale for blocking the streets of central London than it had been to justify the earlier attempts at disrupting the bases.

For neither Russell nor Schoenman did such problems exist. The *publicity* value of sit-downs in Trafalgar Square was undeniable. And, from the point of view of creating a mass movement of resistance in order eventually to paralyse the State machine, mass sit-downs in central London were obviously the best way forward, at least at the beginning of the Committee's life. For Randle and the DAC activists, however, there were political principles involved. If the objectives were not to strike at the politicians and the bureaucracy, but rather to appeal directly on moral grounds to the people who were responsible for carrying out the nuclear weapons policies, then demonstrations must be focused primarily on the bases. This had always been the DAC's view, and it remained central to the ex-DAC activists on the Committee of 100. For Randle there was a legitimate connection between the DAC's approach of moral, direct contact with the workers and the more explicitly politically militant campaign of the Committee. As he has said, 'a lot of us favoured doing some of each!'[75]

Randle was instrumental in the Committee's decision to move away from the central London demonstration format and out to the bases. This was the decision taken immediately after the 17 September 1961 Trafalgar Square demonstration (see below). Although in the event unsuccessful, such a move was in some senses inevitable. The Committee had at some stage to move outside London: otherwise it was trapped into a meaningless, and ultimately self-destructive, pattern of geometric progression in terms of numbers involved in demonstrations. In the euphoria of the Committee following the 'triumph' of 17 September, it was

[74] Randle, *Peace News*, 21 Apr. 1961.   [75] Randle, in conversation.

assumed that amassing a total of 50,000 for the various demonstrations planned for the bases would present few problems,[76]
particularly in the light of the insistence of the local and regional
supporters of the Committee that demonstrations be organized in
their localities.

Thus, whilst Randle's ideological position and political acumen
may have moulded the DAC and Committee of 100 perspectives
into a passable unity, there remained potentially fundamental
divisions of perspective, and insoluble strategic problems. On this
latter point it is worth noting that whereas Schoenman's position
allowed for an uncomplicated avowal of militant civil disobedience
leading to insurrection of some (undefined) type, Randle's strategy,
although more realistic, was fraught with problems. The Committee was trapped in a strategic and ideological dilemma which,
unless Schoenman's grandiose objectives could be realized, was
insoluble. For all his political skill in bridging the two organizations, Randle could not solve this central problem: the Committee
had embarked, consciously or unconsciously, on the path of revolution, and its resources were wholly unequal to this task.

There was another seemingly tactical problem which in reality
represented a major issue of principle for the ex-DAC activists
within the Committee. Reference has been made in the previous
chapter to the DAC's insistence upon 'openness' concerning
demonstration plans, and to the concentration upon persuading the
police and military personnel, as individuals, of the rectitude of the
DAC view. Some elements in the Committee, however, took a very
different view from the DAC over such matters. The whole thrust
of Schoenman's position, particularly, was that the Committee
should see itself as the spearhead of a movement of resistance
against the forces of the state. The police and the public bureaucracy, as the front-line defenders of that State, were thus the natural
and immediate enemies of the Movement. To inform them in
advance of demonstration plans—still less to regard them individually as potential allies—would thus have been irrational.

Whilst the Committee as a whole did not accept Schoenman's
perspective in 1961—and adopted a rather different form of libertarian militancy in its post-1962 period—it was predominantly
Schoenman's view of the role of the police and public authorities,
and his view too of the need for less openness and more secrecy

[76] This was Randle's recollection (in conversation).

concerning the Committee's plans, which characterized the Committee's thinking. There were four principal reasons for this. First, many DAC activists, like Randle himself, were rather less sure of their 'line' in the new context than they had been in the past, and were prepared to compromise in order to preserve the unity of the Committee. Secondly, a large number of Committee supporters were not subscribers to the DAC's ideology and could not therefore appreciate the significance of 'openness' and 'non-coercion'. Thirdly, a number of key people in the Committee of 100, who shared the broad perspective of Randle and other DAC activists, were not committed to these 'pure' articles of faith in the DAC ideology. Fourthly, and most importantly of all, external circumstances generally, and the attitude of the police in particular, changed markedly through 1961. By September the Movement had become more militant, and more powerful and popular, and the authorities had decided to crack down hard. The fact that they made a grave miscalculation tactically in the arrests prior to 17 September is a matter to be discussed below. The relevant point here is that, rude awakening though it was for many Committee of 100 supporters, the police could be hard, authoritarian, and formidable opponents when the occasion demanded.

On the eve of the Committee's greatest triumph, then, in September 1961, its ideological, political, and strategic profile was markedly different from that of the DAC. The decisions had been taken to adopt an aggressive, coercive policy of mounting civil disorder to force the Government to change its defence and foreign policies. Moreover, most Committee leaders had explicitly committed themselves to a revolutionary perspective—an ideology and a programme that saw unilateralism as both entailing and being part of a revolutionary change in social structures, social values, and political ideology, as well as demanding specific defence and foreign policy changes.

Randle's synthesis of the DAC and the Committee thus led, logically, to the attempt to move on from the initial successes in London to begin the serious business of immobilizing the bases, or some of them, prior to the attempt to immobilize the Government and the State machine itself. The failure to achieve these objectives, and the results of that failure, are the prelude to the final phase of the Committee's existence. However, before moving on to discuss the Committee and its years of problems and decline, attention

must be turned to the events of September 1961, which marked the
height of the Committee's popular influence, and the organizational
changes which occurred in the Committee as a result.

THE HIGH POINT OF THE COMMITTEE: SEPTEMBER 1961

The lead-up to 17 September

Tension between the Committee and the authorities built up
through the summer of 1961 as the international crisis deepened
and support for the Committee grew. Russell and three other
members of the Committee—Schoenman, Randle, and Clark—
were summonsed following the Hyde Park demonstration on
Hiroshima Day and were fined at Marlborough Street Court on
Wednesday 13 September 1961. By this time, however, all four
defendants were already in prison. The authorities, having experienced the commitment and increasing militancy of the Committee's
supporters through the summer, decided to take legal action to
forestall the mass demonstrations in London and at Holy Loch on
17 September. In all, thirty-two[77] members of the Committee were
sentenced for inciting a breach of the peace. (Thirty-seven had
originally been charged under the Justices of the Peace Act of 1361,
but of these, five agreed to be bound over to keep the peace.)
Russell was sentenced to two months' imprisonment, and there
were cries of 'shame', 'fascists', and 'poor old man', in court.
However, following the submission of medical certificates, the
sentences for both Russell (who was eighty-nine years old) and his
wife, were reduced to seven days. Clark and Schoenman were
sentenced to two months, and the remainder to one month.

This was a major boost to the Committee's campaign and was an
inept blunder on the part of the authorities: a blunder from which
the authorities, rather than the Committee, drew the correct
lessons. No such mistakes were to be made in future, as was to be
seen in the Official Secrets trial in 1962. At this stage, however, it
did seem that 'someone in Whitehall had decided to give Russell a
martyr's crown'.[78] Russell was not slow to take advantage of the

[77] According to Myers, op. cit., the number was 31. All press reports, however,
confirm that 32 were sentenced. See e.g. *The Times, Guardian, Birmingham Post,* 13
Sept. 1961 (source: Committee of 100 papers, London). This was increased to 33
when Bernard R. Miles, who had overslept and missed the hearing, was sentenced.

[78] R. Clark, op. cit., 590.

situation: 'we were not so innocent as to fail to see that our imprisonment would cause a certain stir,' he wrote later.[79] In the dock, Russell 'made one of the best short speeches of his life'.[80] He emphasized his own long involvement with the nuclear issue, the seriousness of the immediate situation, and the probable imminence of nuclear war, and contrasted this with the governmental and media indifference and blindness to the dangers. In this situation, he argued, it was

a profound and inescapable duty to make the facts known and thereby save at least a thousand million human lives. We cannot escape this duty by submitting to orders which, we are convinced, would not be issued if the likelihood and the horror of nuclear war were more generally understood.

Non-violent civil disobedience was forced upon us by the fact that it was more fully reported than other methods of making the facts known, and that caused people to ask what had induced us to adopt such a course of action.[81]

Immediately Russell ended, 'applause broke out in the court and continued for half a minute before the ushers got silence again'.[82]

In propaganda terms the whole affair was a triumph for the Committee, and a disaster for the authorities. Press coverage was enormous, not only in Britain, but across the world. 'Abroad, the fact that the British appeared to regard as dangerous a member of their own Order of Merit now in his ninetieth year proved the well-known point that they were an eccentric race. But the pictures of Russell's arrest, and the news of his sentence, drew massive attention to the nuclear-disarmament movement.'[83]

From prison, through the Committee, Russell issued a highly charged, emotive statement, the final section of which read:

You, your families, your friends and your countries are to be exterminated by the common decision of a few brutal but powerful men. To please these men all the private affections, all the public hopes, all that has been achieved in art and knowledge and thought and all that might be achieved thereafter is to be wiped out for ever.

Our ruined, lifeless planet will continue for countless ages to circle aimlessly around the sun, unredeemed by the joys and loves, the occasional wisdom and the power to create beauty which have given value to human life. It is for seeking to prevent this that we are in prison.[84]

---

[79] Russell, *Autobiography*, 115.   [80] R. Clark, op. cit., 590.
[81] Reproduced in Russell, *Autobiography*, 145.
[82] *Guardian*, 13 Sept. 1961.   [83] R. Clark, op. cit., 591.
[84] *Guardian*. 14 Sept. 1961.

Apart from the Russells, and the three who had been sentenced to two months, a number of other leading activists had also been sentenced.[85] A new shadow Committee of 100 immediately came into existence, however, and declared, through its acting secretary Pat Pottle, that it intended to go ahead with the sit-down demonstration as planned.[86] The reaction of the press, which gave very full coverage to the unfolding story of the demonstration, was generally sympathetic to the Committee although, not surprisingly, with virtual unanimity, it opposed the Committee's policies. Moreover, it was generally thought that the Home Secretary had made a mistake in escalating the tension between the demonstrators and the authorities, by prohibiting demonstrations under the Public Order Act.[87]

Support for the Committee grew rapidly. Financial contributions and messages of support for the demonstration came from all over the world.[88] Both the CND leadership and some Labour MPs, in addition to the National Council for Civil Liberties, expressed their opposition to the Government and police ban on the demonstration. The stage was thus set for a major and public confrontation between the authorities and the Committee and its supporters, including a wide range of individuals and organizations opposed to the policies and methods of the Committee, but concerned about the draconian measures taken by the Government and police, and the consequent threat to civil liberties.

17 September demonstrations

Both the London and the Scottish (Holy Loch) demonstrations were major successes for the Committee. Twelve thousand took part in the sit-down demonstration[89] and many more attended as

[85] These included Michael Scott, Robert Bolt, Arnold Wesker, Margaret O'Connell, Ian Dixon, Trevor Hatton, Anne Kerr, Michael Lesser, Douglas Brewood (senior), Gustav Metzger, Tony Smythe, Wendy Butlin, and Christopher Logue.

[86] The start of the demonstration was put back to 5 p.m., in order to avoid any clash with a Battle of Britain Sunday parade and procession.

[87] See e.g. the leader in the *Guardian*, 14 Sept. 1961.

[88] Including a message of warm support from Dr Albert Schweitzer.

[89] For once this estimate was generally agreed by all sides. Thus, both *The Times*, 18 Sept. 1961 and *Peace News*, 22 Sept. 1961 gave this same figure. (Dennis Gould, however, in 'From Protest to Resistance' (op. cit., 30), estimated the crowd at 'some fifteen thousand').

onlookers and supporters. More importantly, 1,314 were arrested, and the demonstration received very widespread national and international coverage. The mood of the demonstration was quite different from the earlier DAC demonstrations.

> Every few minutes the crowd tried to break through the cordon around it ... there was isolated fighting and constant jostlings as swaying, jeering crowds shouted insults at the police as they placed demonstrators in the waiting vehicles. Those driven away waved to the crowds and the crowds waved back and cheered.[90]

Police tactics were to prevent the demonstrators using the centre of Trafalgar Square as a rallying point for assembly, after they had been prevented from carrying out their original objective of marching to Parliament Square. In this the police were only partially successful. They cordoned off parts of the square and although 'small groups escaped through the police cordons ... to sit on the road ... only once did they succeed in blocking a way to traffic'.[91] By allowing spectators into the square in the afternoon the police effectively split the demonstrators into small groups, and the job of rounding them up was made easier. Arrests began shortly after 5 p.m. and continued through the evening and into the early hours of the following morning. However, only a relatively small proportion of those sitting were arrested.

The demonstration marked a new stage in the Committee's development. It was, seemingly, on the verge of creating the *mass* civil disobedience movement through which its objectives could be achieved. Of course, these expectations were not fulfilled, and in fact the 17 September demonstration marked the high point of the Committee's activism. But at the time, the Committee was jubilant, and the optimism created by the demonstration's success was a major factor in the decision to mount the over-ambitious series of demonstrations in December 1961.

The Scottish demonstration at Holy Loch over 16 and 17 September had also been dramatic and successful. Because of bad weather only 500 demonstrators took part. However, as the *Guardian* noted, 'had it not been for the storm the number would have been more than two thousand'.[92] Three hundred and fifty-one arrests were made but, in contrast with the London demonstration, relations between police and protesters were very good.

---

[90] *The Times.*   [91] Ibid.   [92] *Guardian*, 18 Sept. 1961.

Whilst the magistrates in both London and Scotland dealt very leniently with the demonstrators,[93] there were serious allegations made against the police in connection with the Trafalgar Square demonstration. Adam Roberts, writing in the *New Statesman*,[94] catalogued a series of assaults both at the time of the arrest and later at the Bow Street police station. Nor was this the only evidence. The National Council for Civil Liberties issued a report, 'Public Order and the Police', which contained thirty-one allegations of police violence during and after the Trafalgar Square demonstration. The NCCL demanded a judicial inquiry into the events surrounding the demonstration, and an investigation in particular of six important issues on which, stated the report, the public was entitled to clarification:

> The almost unprecedented refusal by the Ministry of Works of permission to book the square on September 17; the invoking of the Public Order Act 1936; the announcement to the public of an extension of orders prohibiting processions and assemblies when the police had no such powers; allegations of violence and misconduct against the police; remarkable statements by police officers on oath when stating that they had advised arrested persons of the Commissioner's directions under the Public Order Act when this appeared to onlookers to be almost impossible; and the refusal to permit contact with legal advisers or family to those under arrest.[95]

In the Commons debate, on 17 October, despite a long and detailed speech from Anthony Greenwood, with supporting arguments from Joyce Butler and Sydney Silverman, the Minister of State from the Home Office, David Renton, refused on behalf of the Government, to instigate an inquiry.

This whole episode marked the final break between the Gandhian pacifist practice of the DAC *vis-à-vis* the police, and the

---

[93] Fines imposed on the London demonstrators were generally £1 or £2. For those who refused to pay, the sentence was, generally, 28 days. In Scotland, demonstrators were fined between £3 and £15. Pat Arrowsmith was sentenced to three months' imprisonment, but this was exceptional. Characteristically, 'as she was led away to the cells she shouted (to friends in the public gallery) "Cheerio chums". There was a burst of applause, and the sheriff ordered the court to be cleared' (*Guardian*, 19 Sept. 1961).

It was significant, given the Committee's strategic objective of 'filling the jails', that relatively few of the demonstrators opted for prison sentences as opposed to paying the minimal fines imposed. 658 took immediate bail. In that sense, the creation of even an embryonic mass movement of resistance was a long way off.

[94] *New Statesman*, 22 Sept. 1961.

[95] NCCL report, cited in *The Times*, 18 Oct. 1961. 45 letters containing allegations of police violence were received by the NCCL.

new militancy of the Committee of 100 with its mass resistance perspective. Pat Arrowsmith's Holy Loch demonstration was the last major occasion at which the police and demonstrators indulged in mutual congratulations and cordiality. In part this was due to the different ideological influences at work: the strongly DAC style of the Holy Loch demonstration contrasted with the more 'resistance-orientated' mood of the London protest. More important, however, was the disparity in numbers. Low-key, low-profile police tactics could cope quite easily with 500 demonstrators; moreover individual police officers did not feel threatened, either physically or psychologically, in such circumstances. With more than 12,000 demonstrators—and over 1,300 arrests—the situation was transformed. Both the Committee and the police realized that the Movement was now perhaps on the verge of achieving a mass presence. As has been noted, from 17 September onwards the attitudes of the police, and the State authorities in general, hardened considerably. Where there was a real threat to the maintenance of law and order the State was, as always, prepared to act with whatever measure of force was necessary to counter and ultimately to destroy the movement of resistance. And, when it came to the test, the Movement was in no sense strong enough to counter such power. Before moving on to analyse this process, however, we should return to the immediate aftermath of the September demonstrations and the events leading up to the demonstrations at Wethersfield and elsewhere in December.

Aftermath of 17 September

For Russell, as, for perhaps rather different reasons, for Schoenman, Randle and other Committee leaders, the demonstration had achieved its objectives. Press reaction to the demonstration was, predictably, generally both hostile and trivializing. There were notable exceptions. Both *The Times* and the *Guardian* carried full and fair news coverage of the events. And the *Daily Worker,* although always uncomprehending of the Committee and its ideological complexion, contributed a somewhat vague but undoubtedly supportive editorial, in addition to full news coverage.[96] In terms of serious editorial comment, however, *The Times* was probably representative of the views of the establishment

[96] See 'Next Steps to Peace', *Daily Worker*, 18 Sept. 1961.

(although the more emotional and jingoistic outburst of René MacColl in the *Daily Express* articulated a more populist, reactionary view of the Committee).[97] Under the editorial heading 'Muddled Emotions', *The Times* argued first that the breaking of trivial and irrelevant laws was an inappropriate method of protest on the nuclear issue, particularly in a democratic society where all the protesters had a wide and permissive range of civil and political freedoms through which to express their point of view. Secondly, it argued that whereas the emotive, moralistic assertions of the protesters were 'understandable . . . a movement which has the adherence of so many intellectuals should exhibit a rational purpose'. The immorality of nuclear war was incontestable. But the specific, detailed demands of the Committee (and CND) *were* contestable precisely because they entailed political and diplomatic, rather than moral, judgements.[98] There was thus a *political* rejection of the Committee's case in two respects: in terms of method (the Committee being characterized as anti-democratic), and in terms of substantive policy proposals.

None of this deterred the Committee, jubilant following its success. Financially, too, the Committee was prospering. According to Driver, £6,726 was received in September 1961 alone, and income for 1961 as a whole was over £14,000.[99] Circumstances seemed propitious for the Committee to move forward to become a major national political force.

THE DECEMBER DEMONSTRATIONS AND THE BEGINNING OF THE COMMITTEE'S DECLINE

The decision to embark upon the ambitious series of demonstrations at Wethersfield, Ruislip, Brize Norton, York, Bristol, Cardiff, and Manchester, was taken in this euphoric atmosphere. But the Committee's position was, in reality, weak. A number of the Committee's most experienced and politically mature leaders were in prison and thus unable to participate in the crucial post-September discussions, and Russell himself was both tired and preoccupied with matters arising from his imprisonment.[100] And

[97] 'After Trafalgar: My Verdict', by René MacColl, *Daily Express*, 18 Sept. 1961.
[98] *The Times*, 20 Sept. 1961.
[99] Driver, op. cit., 123. As Driver went on to note, this was approximately £2,000 more than CND had received during its first year of operation.
[100] See Russell, *Autobiography*, 120.

Schoenman's visa was renewed only on the understandintg that he took no further part in political activities.

Important though such factors were, however, the main problem lay in the logic of the Committee's strategy *per se*. Michael Randle has described this clearly. Given that the long-term aim of the Committee was to create a mass movement to immobilize the State's war machine—an assumption shared by the radical leaders of the Committee, if not by Russell and many of the Committee's supporters—it was obvious that, despite the huge successes of the London demonstration, 'the insurrectionary stage [was] a very long way' off.[101] Nevertheless, the Committee had to begin this process of immobilization by rendering one or more of the bases inoperable through mass, non-violent direct action. It was thus essential for the Committee's strategy to attempt a 'move out to the bases'.[102]

This pressure resulted not only in the decision to go ahead with the dispersed demonstrations of 9 December, but also brought about a fundamental reorganization of the Committee's structure. In October 1961 the proposal to implement a subgroup structure, which had first been mooted in May, was put into operation. Eleven groups were established: provincial and convenors, welfare, international, publicity, schools, treasury, speakers, present action, future action, trade unions, and the working group (i.e. management or executive committee). At least one person from each group was to be on the working group. The establishment of this structure was the first stage of the Committee's response to the pressure from its grass-roots activists, with their libertarian, decentralist ethos, to reform its undemocratic and élitist organizational structure. However, 'most of the sub-groups did not function well. Most of their meetings degenerated into fruitless debates and proposals.'[103]

The reorganization also saw the creation of a decentralized, provincial committee structure. In much the same way as CND's success in 1958–9 had created a host of problems, the Committee realized that the original élitist structure through which the demonstrations had been organized with a discipline and an organizational simplicity, had to give way to a decentralized structure, given the successful growth of 'miniature' and autonomous

[101] Randle, in conversation.
[102] And there was mounting pressure from local and regional groups for action outside London, as Randle (in conversation) has testified.
[103] Myers, op. cit., 229.

committees outside London. All that the original Committee could
do was to offer 'help and guidance'.[104] The working group recommended 'fully autonomous free-standing Committees of 100',
partly for legal reasons and partly to encourage provincial support.
This recommendation was confirmed at the meeting of the
Committee held on 17 December 1961. At this meeting it was also
agreed that decentralization should be taken to have three major
facets: more representation of provincial committees on the
national committee; more representation for supporters who were
members of the Committee; and the development of the main
national committee in London into a strictly co-ordinating body,
with the specific projects and activities being planned and executed
by autonomous regional committees. Finally, the Committee
passed a resolution, by forty-three votes to ten, to form a separate
London Committee of 100 which would have sole responsibility for
London area demonstrations.

These proposals were the subject of further negotiation and
discussion through 1962, and will be discussed in that context
below. The important point to note here is that the decision to go to
Wethersfield and the other bases was a function of this decentraliz-
ing tendency within the Committee.

The December 1961 demonstrations

The decision to go to Wethersfield (and to hold simultaneous
demonstrations elsewhere) marked the decisive shift towards a
programme of action which was to lead to a more anarchistic view
of the Committee's role and function, and the adoption of a
perspective which was no longer concerned exclusively with the
issue of nuclear weapons. For Russell, and for many others, such a
move was disastrous.

The Committee had already begun to weaken itself . . . long discussions
were beginning to be held amongst its members as to whether the Committee should devote itself only to nuclear and disarmament matters or should
begin to oppose all domestic, social and governmental injustice. This was a
waste of time and a dispersal of energies. . . . Such widespread opposition,
if to be indulged in at all, was obviously a matter for the far future when
the Committee's power and capabilities were consolidated.[105]

[104] Committee of 100 notes on future organization, 29 Sept. 1961, quoted in
Myers, op. cit., 231.   [105] Russell, *Autobiography*, 120.

From this time onwards, as it became more anarchistic in its outlook through 1962, Russell began to lose interest in the Committee and its policies.

There is no doubt that the Committee overreached itself in attempting the 9 December demonstrations. It was over-optimistic to call for 50,000 demonstrators at seven dispersed locations and in mid-winter. The prospects for a successful demonstration were considerably decreased by two further factors: the administrative problems encountered by the Committee, and the effective action of the authorities in arresting the leading Committee activists immediately prior to the demonstrations.

There were inherent administrative difficulties in arranging transport to a relatively remote base (Wethersfield) in mid-winter. The Committee had booked a fleet of twenty coaches to take demonstrators from London to Wethersfield but, after a series of problems, these arrangements were cancelled. (As Michael Randle subsequently surmised, this 'was almost certainly a deliberate ploy to cause the maximum disruption to our transport arrangements at the last moment'.[106]) Nevertheless, the Committee managed to make arrangements for transport, by rail or private car, for all those intending to demonstrate at Wethersfield.

Many supporters, however, may have been frightened off by the authorities' action—both by the arrests on 8 December, and by the extraordinary precautions being taken at Wethersfield, a previously accessible base. A twelve foot wire fence was erected round the perimeter, all leave for the Essex police was stopped, and in all about 3000 civil and military police were mobilised. A large secondary school at Braintree was taken over as a courthouse. At Wethersfield, 180 specially erected boards read: 'Official Secrets Act. Prohibited Entry. Penalty of two years imprisonment'. Tents were pitched at fifty-yard intervals inside the wire.[107]

It was, however, the arrest of the six Committee of 100 workers on 8 December that dealt the final blow to the Wethersfield demonstrations and, in the longer term, to the Committee itself. On 6 December the Committee of 100 offices at 13 Goodwin Street, Finsbury Park were raided by Special Branch officers with search warrants issued under the Official Secrets Act. Visits were also made to the homes of leading Committee members. Files,

---

[106] Letter from Randle to the author, 16 Oct. 1986.
[107] Driver, op. cit., 124.

documents, and maps were removed. On 8 December, Ian Dixon, Terry Chandler, Trevor Hatton, Michael Randle, Pat Pottle, and Helen Allegranza[108] were arrested, and remanded on bail under charges alleging conspiracy under the Official Secrets Act. Thus began the chain of events which led to the Official Secrets trial of 1962. The authorities had learned from their earlier mistakes prior to the September demonstration. As Nicolas Walter has written, 'in September they arrested the wrong people, but in December they arrested the right people. Before Wethersfield the initiative was in our hands, after Wethersfield it was in theirs.'[109]

Given the adverse circumstances, it was perhaps surprising that the 9 December demonstrations proved to be so relatively successful. There were approximately 600 at Wethersfield ('less than half the 1,500 ... the Committee had regarded as a desirable minimum'[110]); 1,000 at Bristol; 2,600 at Ruislip; 800 at Brize Norton; 1,250 at York; and 1,300 at Manchester. There was a total of 848 arrests, only seventy of which were made at Wethersfield.[111] In their own terms, 'the demonstrations had failed'.[112] Objectively the demonstrations 'made a good showing', as Russell later claimed,[113] and, as Driver has pointed out, 'it was, after all, about fifty times the numbers that the DAC was able to mobilise for similar operations in equally inaccessible spots two years previously'.[114] But the declared objective had been to immobilize, temporarily, one or more of the bases: and this had not been achieved. And the numbers involved had fallen far short of the Committee's target. 'The important thing would have been to have had people feel that there was a definite purpose, that there was a progression, that we were still getting somewhere.'[115]

This did *not* happen and the demonstrations were agreed by all

[108] The first five were the key Committee of 100 workers. Helen Allegranza, the Committee's welfare officer, was minding the Committee headquarters when the Special Branch called.
[109] Walter, op. cit., 32.
[110] *Peace News,* 15 Dec. 1961.
[111] All information taken from ibid., except the figure of arrests at Wethersfield which is taken from *Peace News,* special issue, 2054, 7 Oct. 1977, p. 13.
[112] Ibid., editorial.
[113] Russell, *Autobiography,* 120.   [114] Driver, op. cit., 124.
[115] Randle, in conversation. Randle also pointed out that the arrests could have backfired on the authorities: 'It's *so* hard to say at the time which way the thing is going to go: I thought, when they arrested us before the demonstration, that it could be another big boost for us: that it would have the same effect as arresting half the Committee before the September demonstration.'

to have been a failure. As Randle said subsequently: 'however much we denied that the demonstrations had been a flop, it was true, in terms of what we'd said we were going to do.'[116]

There now began the wholesale discussion in the Committee over its role, political functions, and organizational structure which resulted in a rapid and fundamental change in the nature of the Committee and its policies. The inquest on Wethersfield, and the Offical Secrets trial, marked the real beginning of this process.

Other Committee activities in late 1961

First, though, brief note must be taken of other Committee of 100 activities in late 1961. Although 9 December had been the focus of attention for the Committee since September, there were other issues of immediate concern and importance. Perhaps the most important was the Committee's vigorous demonstration at the end of August against the USSR's decision to resume nuclear testing. One hundred and thirty-six people sat down in the road near the Russian Embassy, and subsequently 116 appeared in court charged with obstruction. A further Embassy protest was carried out when four members of a five-strong delegation to the Russian Embassy staged a sit-down on 17 October and had to be removed by police. This was followed by a mass rally, march, and sit-down on Saturday 21 October. More than 500 were arrested (of whom 480 adults were charged), and a protest letter signed by a number of doctors and scientists was handed in.

Further demonstrations were organized as the USSR proceeded with massive nuclear testing. More than twenty were arrested following a sit-down demonstration outside the Russian Embassy on 30 October 1961. On 5 November 1961, in the words of the following day's *Daily Mail*, 'Pram pushing mothers led four hundred Ban the Bomb marchers' to deliver a protest letter to the Embassy. Similar letters were sent to President Kennedy and Prime Minister Macmillan, and the marchers delivered them to the US Embassy and to Admiralty House, and demonstrations were held elsewhere including a 1,000-strong torchlit march in Glasgow on 18 November 1961. Related to this was the 'Voice of Women' movement begun in November by Judith Cook, a writer and mother of young children, in response to the Berlin crisis. She wrote

[116] Ibid.

to the *Guardian* to ask what, if anything, women could do. Her answer was 1,000 letters in four days—almost 1 per cent of the paper's entire female readership. These two women's organizations—'Women Against the Bomb' and 'Voice of Women'—articulated a growing resurgence of concern as the nuclear situation deteriorated. For the most part these activists were so convinced of the urgency of the situation that they were willing to support and participate in civil disobedience actions.[117]

Finally, there was a rash of what might charitably be described as idiosyncratic manifestations of the Committee of 100 sit-down idea. A few examples from the many will suffice to give a flavour of the atmosphere. Mrs Taya Zinkin suggested that 'a chosen demonstrator . . . should take a purificatory bath and starve to death, hugging a hot-water bottle, by the side of a large portrait of Lord Russell'.[118] The Committee of 100 distributed labels marked 'radioactive', which were attached to milk bottles and left outside the Russian and American Embassies. And, to the delight of the media, in November 1961, CND supporters staged a sit-down in Russell's Chelsea home to try to bring about a reconciliation between Russell and Collins.

At one level, of course, all these and many more unconventional protests were part of a 'silly season'. However, they did articulate a growing concern on the part of the Movement's activists who believed sincerely that, with a rapidly worsening international situation, the urgency of the issue demanded dramatic and eye-catching methods of protest. They were, too, indicative of the degree to which the Committee's civil disobedience methods had come to dominate the Movement by late 1961. This domination was shortlived, however. After Wethersfield the Committee entered a period of crisis and decline. It is to an analysis of the events of 1962 and their impact upon the Committee that attention must now be turned. We will then be in a position to examine the ideological complexion of the Committee after 1962.

THE COMMITTEE IN CRISIS: 1962

Whatever the objective reality concerning the 9 December demon-

---

[117] Among other, small-scale Committee activities were attempts to involve dock-workers in the blacking of nuclear-related 'cargoes'; and the pirate broadcasting of anti-nuclear propaganda on television.

[118] Driver, op. cit., 125. Information taken from the *Guardian*, 9 Oct. 1961.

strations, the psychological, subjective reaction to the disappointing turn-out was one of pessimism. The bubble of infectious enthusiasm which had underlain the Committee's remarkable growth through 1961 had burst. The reaction was as exaggerated as had been the previous over-optimism. Gloom and despondency pervaded the Committee. The mood was one of introversion and recrimination, and there was an almost obsessive concern with an analysis of 'what went wrong'.

In terms of future activity, the Committee was again dispirited and unsure about which direction it should take. There was pressure from some of the more militant members of the Committee for a return to Wethersfield in February to demonstrate solidarity with the arrested six.[119] In Nicolas Walter's view this would have been the correct decision. 'I still think we were wrong not to go back to Wethersfield in February,' he wrote in 1963. 'This was our greatest test, and we failed.'[120] This was the view of *Peace News* too. In an editorial, the Committee was urged to obtain 1,000 pledges for a return to Wethersfield.[121] However, the Committee, which was in debt to the tune of £1,700, was understandably fearful of repeating its earlier failure at Wethersfield. At a meeting on 28 January 1962, a motion advocating a return to Wethersfield, proposed by Pat Arrowsmith, was defeated thirty-two to twelve with two abstentions. The degree of demoralization in the Committee would have ensured that any return to Wethersfield would have backfired. Moreover, the Committee's energies and resources were at a low ebb following the December effort, and, with the leaders due to stand trial, Schoenman and Russell effectively out of action, and 'public opinion' committed to the view that 9 December had been a 'flop', the Committee was in no position to confront a confident and successful civil and military State.

In fact, as is often the case in such movements when things begin to go wrong, the Committee devoted its efforts largely to two areas: the prolonged 'inquest', already referred to, and the organizational changes which were held to be necessary if the Committee were to reflect genuinely the libertarian spirit which had developed through 1961. Both were related, of course, to the conflict in the Committee about priorities and objectives. The whole debate was carried on

---

[119] There is good reason to believe that some of the imprisoned Committee leaders would have welcomed such a move too. See e.g. Arrowsmith, in conversation.

[120] Walter, op. cit., 32.

[121] *Peace News*, 19 Jan. 1962.

under the shadow of the Official Secrets trial of the six. The trial had considerable significance for the Committee and for the Movement as a whole. It was the combination of the effects of this trial, the demoralization after Wethersfield, and the Committee's reorganization which produced the new-style Committee of late 1962.

The 1962 reorganization of the Committee

The reorganization proved to be considerably more complicated than might have been envisaged. Indeed, as Randle has recalled, even after the new arrangements had been finally agreed 'there was uncertainty and disagreement about the authority and responsibilities of the National Committee'.[122]

In January 1962 the organizational subgroup submitted a memorandum, written by David Hougham, and proposing the creation of a co-ordinating Council of Committees of 100, representing regions covering England, Scotland, and Wales.

A series of discussions at Committee of 100 meetings then took place. There was some dispute over the title (Committee of 100, Committee of 1000, Co-ordinating Council, etc.) and, more importantly, over the method of representation. If the same regional representatives always attended the Committee there would be a danger of élitism, argued the libertarians on the Committee. On the other hand, there were obvious dangers of inefficiency and confusion if there were a continually changing national membership. The Committee agreed to call a meeting for 17 February, as a 'one-off' arrangement, at which there would be a Committee of seventy-five representatives from the various regional Committees of 100 (over half the representatives were to come from the London, central, Committee).

However, many Committee members were unhappy with these proposals, and an emergency meeting was called for Sunday 4 February 1962, to discuss the motion 'that this Committee rejects the proposed dissolution of the [national] Committee'. The meeting, held at Student Movement House, Gower Street, London, was attended by only twenty-nine people.[123] There were, it was argued, several reasons why the resolution should be adopted. The

---

[122] Randle, *Peace News,* special issue, 2054, 7 Oct. 1977, p. 13.
[123] Committee of 100 minutes, 4 Feb. 1962, quoted in ibid.

dissolution of the Committee would be premature and untidy—and would appear to be a victory for the State. To lose 'big name' membership would seriously undermine the popular appeal of the Committee. Moreover, the successes of 1961 had come about 'as a result of a small working group of about a dozen people only, who were virtually self-appointed', and a strong core of people was needed to resist police action. These were powerful arguments, and, when the vote was taken, the resolution was carried by twenty-one votes to six, with one abstention. Further confusion resulted because the meeting was by now inquorate, one person having left before the vote was taken! Five people were however delegated to represent the views of the meeting at a special Committee meeting on 17 February.

At the meeting on 17 February (where there was again an ominously low attendance, only forty-five of the expected seventy-five attending), a statement from Russell supporting the emergency resolution was read out. However, although this viewpoint was supported by Schoenman, the strength of feeling in favour of a decentralized structure which allowed a provincial voice in central decision-making, and the generally libertarian tenor of the majority of the Committee's activists, ensured that this policy was defeated.

The meeting decided unanimously that a new body should be created and should be entitled the National Committee of 100. The functions of the National Committee were to be 'in general that of co-ordination, and that as national need requires it, the National Committee of 100 shall take the national initiative'. (This was agreed by twenty-four votes to sixteen. It was opposed by George Clark who wanted the organization of demonstrations to take priority over the co-ordinating of regional Committees.) In relation to the constitution it was agreed without dissent that

membership of the National Committee of 100 be restricted to representatives from each of the regional Committees of 100; that five members from each regional committee be allowed, except upon the formation of the London Committee of 100, it being entitled to ten. A fewer number of representatives would be allowed from local and embryo Committees. Any permanent officers would also be members of the National Committee of 100.

Up to twenty co-options were to be allowed. Further constitutional decisions were deferred until the 17–18 March meeting of the Committee, scheduled to take place in Leeds.[124]

At the Leeds meeting the Committee agreed that, rather than a formal constitution, there should be a set of working rules, that could be amended without entailing major constitutional and procedural discussions. Four ground rules were agreed: the National Committee was to meet 'as often as the situation requires'; 'major policy and action decisions shall only be taken if two-thirds of those present vote in favour'; one-third of the membership attendance should be the quorum; and details of meetings should be sent to regional Committees at least fourteen days in advance. Membership of the National Committee, which was to be decided according to the previously agreed system, was subject to confirmation by all the regional Committees. The establishment of thirteen such regional committees was ratified.

Two working groups were established as subcommittees of the National Committee: a demonstration working group and an administrative working group. The former was to be a changing, *ad hoc* group, based upon the region where the demonstration in question was to take place. It was to have the power to take decisions 'within the framework of National Committee policy', subject to the two-thirds majority rule where major policy decisions were involved. The administrative group was to be selected every six months from the National Committee and had as its main 'function day-to-day policy and planning'. Again, it was empowered to take decisions, under similar conditions to the other group.

This body, which was given power to co-opt and to establish subcommittees, was thus in effect the executive or management committee for the restructured Committee of 100 organization. This *de facto* executive committee was required to submit regular reports to the National Committee, and any member of the National Committee was entitled to attend if he or she thought the committee was acting improperly.

This final agreement on reorganization was undoubtedly complex and, equally undoubtedly, was the result of a compromise

---

[124] There were some who felt so strongly against these decisions that they resigned from the Committee. On 4 Mar. seven members of the Committee resigned: David Hougham, John Morris, Pat Arrowsmith, Wendy Butlin, Mary Clark, Anthony Southall, and Mary Ringsleben. They objected particularly to the dissolution of the original Committee and the tactic of calling an emergency meeting. However, they later rejoined the Committee.

between those who would have preferred a simple, single, central Committee with the emphasis on quick and decisive action, and those more libertarian Committee activists who wanted a fully decentralized, quasi-anarchistic system. The final agreement clearly favoured this latter group. Instead of one central Committee of 100 there were thirteen regional Committees (including a newly formed London Committee). Although the National Committee was intended to operate, through its subcommittees, as a co-ordinative agency, it never had any real presence or power as a national body. The London Committee continued, *de facto,* to be the most powerful and well-supported wing of the Committee, and was the focal point of activity through most of the remainder of the Committee's existence.[125] Thus there persisted an organizational confusion as the theoretical structure, where the National Committee was the leading body, was at odds with the situation in practice, with the London Committee predominating. The net result was, as noted above, confusion and disagreement about the general decision-making structure of the Committee, and in particular about the role of the National Committee.

The new system failed to operate effectively. Attendance at National Committee meetings steadily declined. There were no regular regional delegates. Most important of all, the National Committee found that it had little real work to do. By the end of 1962 Morris reported that the supposedly central functions of the National Committee—to co-ordinate local groups, facilitate internal communications, and generally act as the central Committee body—were either being carried out by three individuals (Pat Arrowsmith, Wendy Butlin, and Stan Allegranza) or by the London Committee of 100, or more often than not were not being executed at all.

By any reckoning the reorganization was thus a failure. The objective of achieving a decentralized and revitalized Committee was manifestly not achieved. The effect, rather, was further to weaken and demoralize the Committee, already in steep decline. Moreover, the protracted discussions not only produced confusion, complexity, and inefficiency but diverted attention from the urgent business of picking up the pieces after Wethersfield and organizing effective civil disobedience actions. The reorganization was thus

---

[125] By the mid-1960s the whole structure had really become moribund, and the only real activity outside London was undertaken by virtually *ad hoc* groups.

intimately related to both the increasingly anarchistic ethos and perspective of the Committee through 1962, and to the declining influence of and support for the Committee.

Committee demonstrations in 1962

In the circumstances it was perhaps hardly surprising that the Committee's demonstrations in 1962 (leaving aside 'Cuba week', which was a somewhat special case), were rather insignificant and uninspired, at least in relation to those of 1961. In January fifteen people staged a sit-in in Parliament to demand 'unequivocal assurances' that there would be no more British nuclear tests.[126] But the first major Committee event of 1962 was the sit-down in Parliament Square on 24 March. Having rejected the proposal to return to Wethersfield, the Committee, understandably if somewhat unimaginatively, decided to try to repeat the previously successful formula of a mass sit-down in central London. For the first time police arrested all those who committed civil disobedience. A total of 1,172 arrests was made: this was a 'respectable number' and indicated that support for the Committee had by no means disappeared. 'Nobody could call the demonstration a failure,' as a *Peace News* editorial remarked. 'Yet there was something missing in the atmosphere . . . a certain coldness, a lack of creative feeling.' Suddenly, the whole exercise seemed rather pointless: any realistic hope of building the mass, non-violent revolutionary movement had disappeared, and everyone realized that this was the case. The quasi-Sorelian myth of the mass civil disobedience movement had been destroyed. To add to the feeling of pointlessness, demonstrators could not help noting that Parliament was not sitting, and that there were virtually no people in Parliament Square (apart from the police) upon whom their protest might exert some influence. The Committee appeared to have lost any clear conception of its *raison d'être*. In some ways civil disobedience had become a ritualized process akin to the later Aldermaston marches (although in this latter case the process perhaps took longer to develop).

Through the middle months of 1962 the Committee was

---

[126] *Peace News*, 26 Jan. 1962. Also in January, a Committee of 100 demonstration, in which 1,200 took part, took place in Glasgow (see *Peace News*, 19 Jan. 1962).

involved in various Movement events, initiatives, and conflicts (INDEC, the Glasgow May Day 'Peanuts' affair, etc), many of which were discussed in Chapter 3. There were also numerous other demonstrations organized by the Committee. On 9 and 10 June, the Whit weekend, the Committee organized a demonstration at Holy Loch: a disappointingly small number of demonstrators took part, and only 142 arrests were made. On 23 and 24 June a march to Greenham Common base was organized and the base was immobilized for twenty-three hours: there was a total of 323 arrests. These were 'by now routine demonstrations which attracted relatively little public attention and progressively fewer participants'.[127]

The next major Committee demonstration was planned for 9 September 1962: a mass sit-down in central London. Again, this was an attempt to recapture the initiative and the dynamism created by the Trafalgar Square sit-down of almost exactly a year earlier. With hindsight, it is not difficult to understand the almost inevitable failure of such an attempt. History cannot be recreated in precise replicas: the idea of the demonstration failed to capture the imagination of either the public or the media. The Committee, sensibly, had stipulated that the demonstration would go ahead only if a minimum of 7,000 pledges were obtained in advance. By August less than 2,600 had been obtained. There was confusion as to whether the demonstration should proceed. Russell issued a press statement saying that, as the specified number of pledges had not been obtained, the demonstration would probably not be held. Jon Tinker, of the Committee, however, was keen to proceed, and criticized Russell, who then apologized. On 2 September the London Committee met and formally cancelled the demonstration: only 3,900 pledges had by this time been received. It was decided instead to hold a 'public assembly' at the Air Ministry on 23 September which would involve no illegal activity. Two thousand took part, including Vanessa Redgrave and Earle Reynolds, the captain of the American 'peace boats', 'Everyman III' and 'Phoenix'. (The autumn was, however, overshadowed by the Cuban missile crisis and the Committee's major activity was as a part of the whole Movement's response to this immediate threat of nuclear holocaust.)

It was the confusion over this demonstration that convinced Russell that he should resign from the Committee, though he had been increasingly unhappy with the Committee and its overall direction throughout 1962.[128] However, Russell still had 'great sympathy with the early aims and actions of the Committee',[129] and did not wish publicly to denigrate the Committee and its work. He therefore gave 'two plausible and innocuous reasons'[130] for his resignation: his involvement in work 'which was slightly different though having the same ends';[131] and his geographical remoteness from the centre of the Committee's activities, as he now lived almost exclusively in north Wales.[132]

Russell's departure was a grievous blow. As long as Russell was active in the Committee, the media, international as well as domestic, were guaranteed to pay at least some attention to the activities and pronouncements of the Committee. With Russell's departure, and the general demoralization and ineffectiveness of the Committee through 1962, its public image, which had been riding so high in the autumn of 1961, deteriorated rapidly. By early 1963 the Committee had become 'a small, crankish group of young extremists who were hardly taken seriously even by many who were sympathetic to unilateralism'.[133]

Before retracing the narrative to February 1962 to analyse the decisive Official Secrets trial, two other aspects of activity should be noted: the Honington base demonstration of 20 October 1962, and the 'Troops Against the Bomb' group of the Committee.[134] The Honington demonstration was in many ways a throw-back to the

[128] The National Committee of 100 minutes for 17 and 18 Nov. 1962 recorded Russell's resignation from the London Committee of 100 and his transfer to the Welsh Committee of 100.
[129] Russell, *Autobiography*, 125.
[130] R. Clark, op. cit., 603.
[131] Ibid., 604.
[132] However, as Russell's biographer has argued, these were not the only reasons for Russell's resignation. He sensed that the Committee's peak had passed and, as with other political commitments (e.g. Pugwash, CND) he decided that the time had come to move on. There was a strand of egotistical ruthlessness in Russell's treatment of political allies and organizations, and a restlessness which made him desire constant political change. Having resigned from the Committee he went on, with Schoenman's assistance, to found the Bertrand Russell Peace Foundation and the Atlantic Peace Foundation—and, of course, became subsequently very influential in the international movement of opposition to the American involvement in Vietnam.
[133] Myers, op. cit., 199.
[134] There was also some activity on the industrial front which is discussed below in the context of Committee ideology in 1962–3.

old DAC style of protest. One hundred and seventy-two demonstrators sat down and there were forty-four arrests. The intention had been to reclaim the RAF base (at Angel Hill, near Bury St Edmunds) for peaceful purposes, and demonstrators attempted to scatter seeds, symbolically, onto the base. There was also a small supporting CND march. The demonstration was a low-key, poorly supported, poorly reported, seemingly rather pointless, even faintly ludicrous spectacle. Honington did nothing to revive the flagging spirits of the Committee—if anything, the reverse.

The 'Troops Against the Bomb' campaign was of a different order. The concentration on this campaign was indicative of the new priorities of the Committee, and was an issue that was to continue to dominate Peace Movement circles, in different forms, for several years. The campaign was linked closely to the industrial action urged by the Committee. Pat Arrowsmith argued that 'if industrial action is achieved the troops may be called out to deal with civil disobedience. We must therefore think about aiming propaganda directly at the armed forces. We should think about providing leaflets inciting troops to sedition.'[135] The campaign was launched in October/November 1962 with the aim of persuading servicemen to side with the Movement at a time of nuclear crisis and to refuse to obey orders in the event of a nuclear war, and to refuse to strike-break over nuclear issues.

On 11 March 1963 the *Guardian* reported that two RAF techni-cians were being sentenced to jail for attempting to form an anti-bomb group. Disciplinary action was taken against several other men over the next few years. For many in the Committee these few servicemen who courageously rejected military mores and dis-cipline represented an important advance for the Committee and its values and objectives.[136]

However much the militants may have backed such campaigns, they created yet further divisions in the Committee. The Welsh Committee of 100 felt that the campaign was an 'irresponsible idea and out of touch with reality'. The Welsh resigned from the national structure, but rejoined in February 1963. By the beginning of 1963 only approximately forty of the original Committee remained, and hitherto enthusiastic activists, such as Vanessa

---

[135] Committee of 100 minutes, 29 and 30 Sept. 1962, quoted in Myers, op. cit., 195.
[136] See e.g. Walter, op. cit., 33.

Redgrave, had become disillusioned. 'I don't believe', said
Redgrave in a newspaper interview in January 1963, 'that what I
should be doing is preparing for "demo" after "demo" . . . I do in
fact think the Committee of 100 should dissolve itself.'[137]

Thus, by the beginning of 1963, the Committee of 100 was in
serious decline. 1963 was to bring a temporary resurgence of activity, but 1962 had been a very bad year. There were many aspects to
this decline, but the year was dominated, and all other events
overshadowed, by the Official Secrets trial of February 1962.

The Official Secrets trial of February 1962

The trial, which began at the Old Bailey on 12 February 1962,
arose from the arrest of the six Committee of 100 activists prior to
the demonstrations at Wethersfield and elsewhere in December
1961. All had been remanded on bail following their arrest on 8
December under the Official Secrets Act.[138]

The trial was remarkable for a number of reasons. Despite the
Attorney-General's assertion at the outset that it was not a 'political
prosecution. . . . They are being prosecuted . . . on account of their
conduct which . . . amounted to the commission of a criminal
offence',[139] the trial was above all else a highly charged confrontation between the ideology of the Committee of 100 and the ideology of the State. The contrast between the refusal of the judge to
allow evidence relating to the beliefs and motivations of the
Committee and the overtly political nature of the prosecution's case
brought into sharp relief the nature of the State, and did much to
reinforce the already extant move of Committee activists towards
an anarchist or libertarian socialist analysis.

It is not necessary here to go into detail over the lengthy proceed-
ings of the trial,[140] but it is instructive to note some of the key

[137] Redgrave, reported in the *Sunday Telegraph*, 13 Jan. 1963.

[138] Pat Pottle, however, went into hiding, evaded the police and gave occasional
interviews to the press at anonymous locations. Eventually, at a press conference on
9 Feb., he gave himself up to the police, and all six defendants were duly in the dock
when the trial began.

[139] Sir Reginald Manningham-Buller, the Attorney-General of the Conservative
Government, in his opening statement of the trial. The quotation is taken from
'Official versus Radical England', in David Boulton (ed.), *Voices from the Crowd*,
London, 1964. The account of the trial was compiled from the various reports which
appeared originally in *Peace News* in early 1962.

[140] A good, full, though naturally biased account is given in ibid. See also Driver,
op. cit., 162–70.

aspects. Early in the trial the judge ruled that, whilst the *purpose* of the accused in going to the base was relevant, their motives or beliefs were not. In his opening statement the Attorney-General had outlined three questions for the jury to decide, the last of which was to decide whether the protesters' purposes were prejudicial to the safety and interest of the State. In his submission, he had added, any interference with the defence system of the country must obviously be so. Mr Jeremy Hutchinson, who acted for all the defendants save Pottle, based his defence on three basic points: that the defendants did not intend to prejudice the safety and interest of the State by their actions; that their beliefs were reasonable and well supported by the evidence; and that their actions were not *in fact* prejudicial to the safety and interest of the State.

By his ruling that evidence relating to motives and beliefs was inadmissible, and his further statements that any evidence which sought to challenge the defence system of the country, and any evidence about the effects of nuclear explosions, dangers of war, etc. were also to be disallowed, the judge effectively ruled out of order the whole defence case.

The defence case rested ultimately on the moral duty of using non-violent resistance to oppose genocide through nuclear war. Parallels were drawn with Nazism and the Nuremberg judgments. (In the circumstances, Pat Pottle's achievement in establishing that the prosecution witness, Air Commodore Magill would, if ordered, 'press the nuclear button', was nevertheless a telling point in the defendants' case.) In an exchange with the judge, for example, Randle argued:

> Every individual must finally decide whether millions of lives are threatened by a particular act, and in that situation I think they have the right to make that decision. . . . There were people in Germany during the Nazi regime who were ordered to commit what have since been defined as crimes against humanity. They would have been going against the law of their country by disobeying their order. I feel they have a moral duty to disobey that order in that situation.
>
> J: As far as I can see it means this, doesn't it, if you disagree with the law you break it?
> R: Not in general, only in particular situations. . . . Where I think it is flouting basic human rights I will certainly disobey it, and I feel it would be a moral obligation to disobey. . . . I feel that the use of nuclear weapons is always contrary to basic human rights. I cannot see any situation in which they would be justified against human beings.

e

Randle went on to put forward the Committee's objective of filling the jails so that the Government 'would have to face up to the logic of being prepared to commit genocide. If they are prepared to do it against people they must be prepared to do it against us. That is the position we want to put them in.'[141]

There was a conceptual, ideological, and cultural gulf between the Attorney-General and the defendants that was unbridgeable. Sir Reginald appeared genuinely baffled: 'What he [Randle] said amounted, did it not, to this: "we have decided what laws we broke, after very careful consideration. . . . And where we think fit we break the law." It is really an admission of rather an astonishing character.'[142] Ultimately the case turned on these rival conceptions —which were fundamental, moral, and political—and not upon legal niceties. The legal smokescreen merely disguised, somewhat ineffectively, the clash of ideologies and cultures. There was never any doubt that the judge would virtually direct the jury to find the defendants guilty. In his summing-up the judge made his view quite clear. Even so, the jury was out for four hours before entering a 'guilty' verdict, and even then recommended leniency. The sentences were harsh (the judge, incidentally, ignoring the plea for leniency). All five men were sentenced to eighteen months in prison and Helen Allegranza to one year.

However well the defendants acquitted themselves, the net effect on the Movement was disastrous. Not only was the Movement deprived of its most able and experienced leaders for a long period, but the deterrent effect of the sentences was certainly a major contributory factor in the Committee's decline during 1962. The trial brought home to the Committee its inadequacy when faced by the might of the State. It was probably this more than anything else which brought about the demoralization which, as we have seen, affected the Committee increasingly through 1962 and into early 1963. The trial indicated that the use of NVDA alone, on the lines advocated and practised by the Committee of 100, was neither powerful nor sophisticated enough to challenge seriously and in the long term the power of the State.

THE IDEOLOGY OF THE COMMITTEE IN 1962 AND 1963

Despite Nicolas and Ruth Walter's claim that most supporters of

[141] Taken from the transcript of the trial, pp. 149–50, quoted in Driver, op. cit., 167–8.   [142] Ibid.

the Committee of 100 'didn't really care whether they were anarchists or not . . . [it] was a time for action, not argument: for
movement, not *a* movement: for propaganda by deed, not word',[143]
there can be no doubt that the programme, the policy, the assumptions, and the priorities of the Committee became more and more
closely attuned to anarchism through 1962 and 1963, although the
influence of 'formal Anarchism' remained small. The ' "emotional
anarchists" . . . [who] were a permanent section of the rank and
file of the Committee'[144] had little knowledge of the anarchist
tradition, and had little interest in whether they followed a more
Bakuninite as opposed to Marxist view of social revolution.
Nevertheless, both the practice and ideology of the Committee
in 1962–3 were strongly anarchist in flavour, and in underlying
ideological assumptions.

Anarchism and the Committee

On the theoretical level, 'Nicolas Walter's articles on Direct
Action and Disobedience probably had', according to one authority, 'a more widespread and immediate influence than anything else
written at the time.'[145] Certainly, Walter's articles[146] provide a lucid
and wide-ranging analysis of the links between the anarchist tradition and the Committee of 100.

For Walter there was a sharp and crucial distinction to be drawn
between *socialist* (whether Marxist or otherwise) revolution and
libertarian revolution: 'The revolutionary goal is liberty, equality,
and fraternity, but the revolutionary way leads straight to slavery,
inequality and misery. The idea of libertarian revolution—of rebellion or insurrection—is that there is no distinction between ends
and means, because *means are ends*.'[147] Personal responsibility,
individual actions, and the direct action of the individual in rebellion against the authority of the State, lie at the heart of Walter's
anarchism.

The struggle then was seen to be, not between socialism and

[143] Nicolas and Ruth Walter, 'The Committee of 100 and Anarchism', *Anarchy*,
52, June 1965, p. 177.
[144] Ibid., 176.
[145] Diana Shelley, 'Influx or Exodus? Anarchists and the Committee of 100',
Anarchy, 50, Apr. 1965, p. 104.
[146] i.e. 'Direct Action and the New Pacifism', and 'Civil Disobedience and the
New Pacifism', subsequently brought together in Walter, 'Non-violent Resistance'.
[147] Walter, 'Non-violent Resistance', 7.

248 *The Radicals*

capitalism (or fascism), but 'between life and obedience',[148] that is
between the assertion of individual, human freedom on the one
hand, and the repressive, authoritarian 'warfare state' on the other.
It was authority, and obedience to it, that must be opposed: and
that opposition began, not in the 'class' or the (Labour) Movement,
but in the immediate social environment of the individual in the
practice of his or her everyday life. There is thus no sharp distinction to be made between means and ends. 'We do not know our
goal,' said Gandhi. 'It will be determined not by our definitions but
by our acts.'[149]

   This then was the framework; the focus of this generalized view
of social and political struggle was the anti-militarist, anti-nuclear
weapons Movement. For anarchists, 'war is the health of the State':
never are nations more united, conforming, organized, and
obedient to authority than at time of war; never are people so
willing to be coerced, so willing to see minorities and ideological
'deviants' subdued and silenced. Yet, when it has to come to the
crisis point, not only socialists (for example, the Second International in 1914), but also anarchists (for example, Kropotkin in
1914 and Rudolph Rocker in 1939) have failed to oppose war, and
have actually advocated that to which they should have been totally
opposed. In the nuclear age, however, it is not a question of opposing war once it has started—it is rather a question of becoming
'peace criminals' before war begins.

   There is thus much in common between the anarchists of the
Committee and the pacifist movement.[150] But the real problem with
pacifism, it is claimed, has lain in its naïvety and sentimentality—in
its hoping to get rid of war without changing anything else. In
reality, anarchists in the Peace Movement believed, 'pacifism is
ultimately anarchism, just as anarchism is ultimately pacifism.'[151]

   From the fusion of these two traditions—anarchism and
pacifism—there emerged, in the West, the concept of non-violent
resistance, or active, non-violent, non-co-operation. The Committee of 100 thus focused upon mass NVDA not merely for tactical
and strategic reasons but for coherent political reasons. It drew

[148] Alex Comfort, *The End of a War,* cited in Walter, op. cit., 10.
[149] Cited in Walter, op. cit., 24.
[150] Ibid. Walter detailed the history of the pacifist tradition in the Christian
Church, arguing that the 'story of pacifism is in fact the story of the way saints and
heretics defended the doctrine of Christ against the Church' (15).
[151] Ibid.

selectively upon pacifism, anti-militarism, socialism, liberal individualism, and not least Gandhianism.

A rather different but none the less important and authentic anarcho-pacifism also exerted an influence within the Committee, as it had in various forms in a variety of pacifist movements. Moral rather than ideological in tone, this tradition stemmed more directly from *Christian* radical pacifism, and was characterized by a spiritual rather than an intellectual intensity. At the heart of this creed lie two *a priori* assumptions: that because 'God is Love', 'the purpose of life is to exemplify goodness at the expense of badness, and thus to strengthen the force of goodness in the world'.[152] From this must follow a total rejection of the most evil of all acts— killing. The second assumption is that it is from the organized and institutionalized power of the State, as manifested especially through government, that the violence and evil in the world stems. The creation of such institutions in turn 'results from the all-consuming, devouring determination of some individuals to obtain, consolidate, and if possible expand their power over their fellows'.[153] Upon this foundation is built an anarcho-pacifist ideology which emphasizes both the centrality of individual action for change and the primacy of *spiritual* change.

This latter position has been a long and tenacious, if minority, strand within the British Peace Movement: and it continued to exercise an influence in the period of the Committee of 100 under discussion. But it was the former theoretical framework, linking anarchism, pacifism, and militant NVDA resistance to the 'warfare state', which predominated in the 1962–3 Committee of 100, and which characterized the Committee's 'anarchism'.[154]

The ideology and practice of Solidarity supporters in the Committee

One of the most important influences in 1962, 1963, and beyond in the Committee of 100 was the *Solidarity* group (i.e. the group in and around the journal *Solidarity for Workers' Power*). It was in

---

[152] Ronald Sampson, 'Society Without the State', Housmans (pamphlet), 2nd edn., London, June 1980, p. 17.

[153] Ibid., 5.

[154] The 'official' anarchist movement, whilst supporting the Committee of 100 and NVDA, was somewhat distanced from it. Like Marxists, in this sense, anarchists

practice a combination of *Solidarity* and anarchistic activists who constituted the militant hard core of the Committee in this period. Whilst the DAC inheritance was still important, the most effective and authoritative of its leaders were in jail, and its politics, anyway, had been somewhat discredited by the events of 1962. From Wethersfield onwards the initiative lay predominantly with this new group: the peak of its activity in the Committee lay in the 'Spies for Peace' operation in 1963.

Solidarity emerged first in 1961 under the title of 'Socialism Reaffirmed'. Among its first members were some who had been expelled from the Socialist Labour League, including Dr Christopher Pallis, alias Martin Grainger, who became the most dominant individual within the group. *Solidarity* was loosely organized and never had more than a few hundred members, but its activists were dynamic and enthusiastic. Its ideological stance was based largely on the work of Paul Cardan.[155] Although *Solidarity* rejected labels—arguing that 'we are ourselves and nothing more. We live here and now, not in Petrograd in 1917, not in Barcelona in 1936. We have no gods, not even revolutionary ones'[156]—it was clearly anarcho-Marxist (or libertarian socialist) in orientation, thus drawing hostility from almost every conceivable ideological quarter.

At the core of its ideology lay its affirmation that only spontaneous proletarian revolutionary action would bring about the socialist society. It was thoroughly Marxist in its analysis of the

were unwilling to give either the conceptual or political primacy to nuclear weapons that was accorded by the Peace Movement. As early as 15 Feb. 1958, *Freedom* laid down the objectives, as it saw them, for the Peace Movement:

'The following, in order of importance, are the only positive steps which can lead to the abolition of war:

1. reorganization of production and distribution on a world scale and based on human needs and not profits.
2. refusal by workers to be employed in industries engaged on war production.
3. mass resistance to conscription, military or industrial, as well as refusal to join Forces on a voluntary basis in spite of financial or other inducements.

This was to remain the anarchist position. But their demands and their rhetoric, as with their Trotskyist counterparts, had little practical political effect. It was the 'emotional anarchists' of the Committee of 100 who were influential in the Movement.

[155] Among Cardan's works are *Socialism or Barbarism, Modern Capitalism and Revolution,* and *The Meaning of Socialism,* all of which were published, in translation, by *Solidarity.*

[156] Introduction to Cardan, *Modern Capitalism and Revolution,* London, 1965, p. iii.

genesis of capitalist political economy, but it insisted that, first and foremost, 'socialism is about freedom',[157] and that the central contradiction in capitalism lay in the *necessary alienation* of the worker under the capitalist productive system. This is mirrored by the political alienation in modern society in which formally participatory structures in reality preclude, *necessarily*, real democratic involvement. Hence the political apathy and cynicism which characterize all contemporary industrial capitalist societies.

In an attempt to resolve these developing contradictions within the capitalist system, it was argued, the ruling class has tended to utilize State control, thus rendering societies dramatically more totalitarian. The root *cause* of this process lies in the productive sphere, but its *effects* permeate all aspects of life. The authoritarian, and eventually totalitarian, State comes to dominate everything; and it is the process of *bureaucratization* through which this process is accomplished. This was the focus of 'Solidarity's' attack:

> bureaucratization implies the 'organization' and 'rationalization' of all collective activity *from the outside.* . . . The inherent objective, the 'ideal tendency' of bureaucratic capitalism is the construction of a totally hierarchic society in constant expansion, a sort of monstrous bureaucratic pyramid where the increasing alienation of men in labour will be 'compensated' by a steady rise in the standard of living, all initiative remaining in the hands of the organizers.[158]

> The result, socially, has been to make the revolt of the exploited fail by directing it into a personal pursuit of the standard of living, by breaking up working class solidarity through hierarchy and differentials, and by preventing all attempts at collective action from below.[159]

This process cannot, however, succeed: it cannot make capitalism work. 'The bureaucratic drive must fail. It cannot overcome the fundamental contradiction of capitalism.' Thus the only solution is in the collective revolt of the working class. Bureaucratic capitalism 'can only be eliminated by establishing collective management of production and society by the collective producers, the working class'. There is a sharp contrast between the class struggle *'in production* . . . [where there is] an intensity formerly unknown . . . [and] *outside of production* [where] the

[157] Cardan, *The Meaning of Socialism*, Solidarity pamphlet 6, London, 1965, p. 19.
[158] Cardan, *Modern Capitalism and Revolution*, 3.
[159] Ibid.

class struggle hardly shows itself at all, or only distorted by bureaucratic organizations'.[160]

The revolutionary movement *must* therefore focus on the struggle for control at the point of production. The working class must itself take power: there can be no transitional period other than that which 'starts with the proletarian revolution and ends with communism'. *Solidarity* was thus bitterly opposed to Trotskyism: to interpose a vanguard organization between the class and its struggle at the point of production was to ensure that socialism's basic objectives would not be achieved. Class consciousness and revolutionary activity could only grow from the direct, everyday experience of the working class inside the production process. *Solidarity* thus did 'not offer . . . leadership, but solidarity'.[161] This was the essential political message of *Solidarity* to which the foregoing ideology led. 'Socialism means workers' management.'[162]

Given this analysis, it is not surprising to find that *Solidarity* was also highly critical of the USSR. In their leaflet 'Against All Bombs', which was distributed in Moscow in July 1962, the *Solidarity* supporters of the Committee of 100 argued that, although the means of production in Russia had been nationalized following the Bolshevik revolution of 1917, 'the relations of production . . . which determine the class nature of society' remained unchanged. It was within this context, then, that *Solidarity* viewed the Committee of 100. The Committee had created an alternative political framework, outside the orthodox, organized political system: the majority of the Committee

clearly recognizes that the fight against the Bomb is a fight against the Government . . . many members of the Committee, moreover, sense that in the conditions of today the working class and the working class alone has the concentration, the cohesiveness and the power fundamentally to challenge the Establishment and its preparations for war.[163]

In addition the Committee, by being unequivocally against all nuclear weapons and by asking people to act themselves, rather than through 'bureaucratic, self-seeking cliques', had created a

[160] Ibid.
[161] John Chappell, in *Solidarity*, 3.12, p. 14.
[162] Cardan, *The Meaning of Socialism*, 11 (heading of sect. 4).
[163] 'The 100 vs. The State', a joint Independent Labour Party/*Solidarity* pamphlet, n.d. (1962), p. 5.

genuine, populist, and non-manipulative movement. And the emphasis upon 'militant mass consciousness and an autonomous mass action' had developed the radical potential of the Movement in directions long urged by libertarian socialists. The success of the Committee's actions had compelled the Government 'gradually to withdraw the iron fist from the velvet glove',[164] thus in turn radicalizing further sections of the Committee's support and bringing home to previously apolitical or non-socialist activists the truth of Marx's dictum that the State is but the executive committee of the ruling class.

What then were the lessons that *Solidarity* drew from the experience of late 1962 in the Committee of 100? In terms of the Nuclear Disarmament Movement itself, *Solidarity* argued that 'the traditional channels of protest have themselves become built-in stabilisers of the whole society . . . although many CND groups remain active and in many cases extremely radical, CND has degenerated as an organization beyond the point where it is worth trying to reform it.'[165] The Committee was seriously weakened by four particular failings, in *Solidarity's* view: its tendency to revert to traditional methods of demonstration; the 'lack of common ground among its members and supporters'; 'the absurd extremes' to which libertarian principles had been taken, which resulted 'in a determined minority' being able to prevent any decisions being reached; and the reliance of the Committee on ' "Big Names" rather than carefully formulating . . . collective ideas'. The future success of the Movement lay, for *Solidarity*, in building upon these experiences to create a Movement which was not restricted to opposition to nuclear weapons, and which had illusions neither about 'liberal democracy' nor about 'non-violence'.[166] The Movement must therefore 'realize that the struggle against the Bomb is a struggle against a whole hierarchical organization of society'.[167] The key to advance was to achieve unity between the militants of the Nuclear Disarmament Movement and the militants of the unofficial, rank-and-file trade union movement.

[164] Ibid., 6.
[165] 'Beyond Counting Arses', a paper submitted to a Committee of 100 conference by eight Committee activists, all sympathetic to *Solidarity's* viewpoint. This was reprinted in *Solidarity*, 2.2, pp. 7–14. Quotations that follow are taken from this reprint, this first being p. 8.
[166] Ibid., 9–10.
[167] 'The 100 vs. the State', 11.

By early 1963 the means proposed for initiating this process had become not only more specific but more militant, aggressive, and anarchistic. In a paper submitted to the Committee discussion conference in February 1963,[168] a range of subversive acts of sabotage and direct action, of a very different type from those advocated and practised by the DAC, was proposed. The immediate forms of do-it-yourself action advocated, which caught the attention of the national press,[169] were certainly attuned to this perspective. In what can be seen with hindsight as a direct reference to the 'Spies for Peace' project, it was argued that

the Committee of 100 should announce that it intends to unmask and publicise the most secret preparations of the Warfare State . . . we should undertake to publish the location of rocket bases and what goes on in germ warfare centres. We must give details about the secret hide-outs of 'civil' defence—and the secretly kept lists of those who will be catered for in the event of nuclear war. We should publish the names of the emergency government 'Gauleiters' and details of phone-tapping and of the activities of the Special Branch.

Other proposals were no less subversive: they included acts of resistance in the armed forces; mass disruption of civil defence; linking in to militant campaigns over rents, housing, etc.; the disruption of the Fylingdales early warning station; and the revival of illegal broadcasting.

The overall objectives of *Solidarity* have not of course been achieved, either through the Committee of 100 or through subsequent radical formations and initiatives. But the point here is to note the considerable influence which this perspective exerted in the Committee from 1963. Whilst many of the Committee's militants did not subscribe explicitly to the fairly specific ideological position of *Solidarity,* the policy objectives and strategies in which *Solidarity's* perspectives resulted gained considerable support within the Committee.[170]

An overview of Committee ideology in 1962–1963

The overall conclusion to be drawn concerning the ideological profile of the Committee of 1963 is thus that, compared to 1960–1,

[168] 'Beyond Counting Arses'.   [169] e.g. *Sunday Telegraph*, 28 Apr. 1963.
[170] Other ideological influences on the Committee of 100 in 1962–3 included Peter Cadogan, later to become secretary of the National Committee of 100 in 1965, and a prominent and persistent radical activist from the 1950s through to the

the parameters of ideological belief had shifted decisively to the left. Russell, and the 'big names' drawn in largely under his influence, those attracted by the subsequent excitement of involvement in the Movement in the glare of media publicity, and, to an extent, those who had come in from the pacifist movement had all withdrawn or lost their influence. Schoenman's somewhat idiosyncratic revolutionary stance had much in common with the libertarian socialist position, but with his enforced exclusion from the Committee of 100, his considerable influence evaporated. Randle, and the other DAC leaders, had either been effectively silenced by the State or had undergone a diminution in ideological credibility because of the *experience* of the escalating conflict between the Committee and the State. The position of the radical pacifist group had thus declined in the Committee and, although activists like George Clark and Peter Cadogan remained a considerable force, the initiative remained predominantly on the libertarian socialist axes analysed above, through 1963 and beyond.

We are now in a position to make an analysis of the sometimes dramatic attempts by the Committee during 1963 to articulate this new militancy into effective action.

THE COMMITTEE AND THE EVENTS OF 1963

Industrial activity

For the Committee, 1963 was dominated by two events: the 'Spies for Peace' episode, and the programme of action surrounding the Greek Royal visit in the summer. One other aspect of Committee activity, which related closely to the ideological change of direction analysed above, was also of some importance, however: the attempt to mount a meaningful industrial campaign. *Solidarity* had high hopes of the industrial subcommittee of the Committee of 100 (formed as early as October 1961).[171]

1980s. Though close to the anarchist position discussed earlier, Cadogan espoused a tradition attuned to the indigenous libertarian radicalism of the British Labour Movement (as delineated by E. P. Thompson, in many works but pre-eminently in *The Making of The English Working Class*, London, 1963). For a full account of Cadogan's politics in relation to the Peace Movement at this period, see Peter Cadogan, 'The Politics of Direct Action', *Anarchy*, 13.2, Mar. 1962, and Cadogan, 'Non-violence as a Reading of History', *Anarchy*, 20.2, 1962.

[171] By late 1961 several successful meetings had been held at the Royal and West India Docks in conjunction with the Portworkers' Liason Committee. There was

Such hopes remained largely unfulfilled, however. Ironically, it was only Pat Arrowsmith who made any real impact on the seemingly intractable problem of linking working-class, militant industrial action to the radical non-violent resistance of the Committee. As with her DAC industrial campaigns, Pat Arrowsmith operated very much as an individual, working in conjunction with local CND groups and militant trade unionists, rather than through any centralized Committee of 100 structure. In that sense her campaign was in keeping with the new, decentralized and libertarian ethos of the post-1962 Committee. However, her ideological position had not changed appreciably since her DAC involvement. Her commitment remained to the DAC's radical pacifism, and she was always less happy with the Committee of 100, ideologically as well as personally, than she had been with the DAC. She was, therefore, not a part of the movement towards a more 'Solidarity' view of the Committee's role, nor did she subscribe to *Solidarity's* conception of the key role of the industrial working class in creating a libertarian socialist revolution. The role of the industrial working class was indeed crucial for Arrowsmith––but for DAC, radical pacifist reasons, which were very different from those of *Solidarity* and the post-1962 Committee of 100.

Be this as it may, Arrowsmith certainly achieved some success in the field through 1962 when she worked full-time for Merseyside CND. Her brief was to

set up a Trades Unionists Committee with a mandate to work for direct industrial action against nuclear weapons. ... It was my task to get together a committee with workers on it, and I don't mean people in left groups posing as workers! We had a docker, George Green, who (I can safely say it now because he has since died) sabotaged Fylingdales equipment as it came into Merseyside docks. I had to go around making contacts, lobbying and setting up factory-gate meetings. I got lifted for speaking at a dockside meeting [on 13 April 1962] and charged with obstruction, despite nothing being obstructed. The dockers came up to court and paid my fine.

Perhaps the most significant events of that campaign were the shop stewards committees and the on-site meetings. There was a stoppage of 800–1000 workers at the Carrington petro-chemicals site,[172] between Manchester and Liverpool, which was then under construction. They

considerable optimism about the potential indicated by such contacts, within *Solidarity* circles. 'Civil Disobedience and the Working Class', *Solidarity*, 1.9, 1961.

[172] On 14 May 1962. See Tony Southall and Julian Atkinson, 'CND 1958–65, Lessons of the First Wave', *Socialist Challenge* pamphlet, n.d. (1981), p. 30.

stopped because of the resumption of atmospheric tests by the USA. None of these things [i.e. these events or the earlier DAC campaigns] got any publicity.[173]

The achievement was considerable: but it was shortlived and isolated, and did not in the event prove to be the beginning of any more substantial workers' involvement industrially (or, for that matter, politically).

For all its rhetoric, however, *Solidarity* was ineffective in creating the industrial/political link between the Committee of 100 and the trade union rank and file.[174] There were no significant examples of *industrial* action through 1963 and beyond. One of the single greatest weaknesses of the Movement—its lack of working-class involvement—thus permeated the Committee of 100 just as, in a very different ideological and political context, it permeated CND.[175]

'Spies for Peace'

However, by far the most important development resulting from the *Solidarity*/anarchist grouping in the Committee of 100 were the 'Spies for Peace' revelations at Easter 1963 on the Aldermaston March. Despite the very detailed accounts[176] of the whole episode which have subsequently been written, the precise identity of those involved remains undisclosed, and, despite police investigations, no arrests were ever made. And despite the almost universal condemnation of their actions—'Canons have deprecated, columnists

[173] Pat Arrowsmith, 'What About the Workers?', in 'From Protest to Resistance, 12. See also 'Threat to Rights of Assembly', *Solidarity*, 2.3, pp. 19–21.

[174] For a detailed account of the industrial subcommittee of the Committee of 100, see *Solidarity*, 2.2, pp. 19–21.

[175] Other areas of Committee of 100 activity in 1963 included a relatively successful campaign to encourage and support servicemen who protested against the nuclear and defence policies of the Government. Some half-dozen servicemen were involved in separate incidents of this type and considerable press coverage was given to the resultant Peace Movement campaigns. Demonstrations also took place in Scotland (at the Holy Loch base) and in England (at Marham RAF base, and at Porton). There were also Committee of 100 links and supporting action in France and Sicily. Finally, a Committee of 100 campaign in solidarity with London's homeless was begun, and from this and the activism of Committee of 100 members such as George Clark and Jim Radford sprang the Committee of 100's links with the developing community activism of the 1960s and 1970s.

[176] i.e. *Guardian*, 9 Apr. 1966; 'The Spies for Peace Story', *Anarchy*, 29.3, 1963, pp. 197–229, *Inside Story*, 8, 9, Mar.–Apr. and May–June 1973.

deplored, cabinet ministers dithered, communists denigrated, constitutionalists dissociated themselves . . .'[177]—the combined power of the establishment has remained unable to identify the perpetrators. Thus was the final link between the DAC tradition of 'openness with the authorities' and the militancy of the new Committee of 100 dramatically severed.

The 'Spies for Peace' document was entitled 'Danger! Official Secret', and 'gave in considerable detail what it claimed were the Government's plans for Regional Seats of Government (RSGs) from which the country would be administered in the event of nuclear attack'.[178] The motivation behind the 'Spies for Peace'—a title, incidentally, which, according to the *Guardian,* was chosen in part 'as a joke at the expense of the Communist Front organizations—doctors, teachers, scientists, artists, musicians and so on—for "Peace" '[179]—was fully in accordance with the libertarian socialist ideology of a substantial section of the Committee of 100. The 'Spies' were 'dangerous because they question the basic assumption of all bureaucracies: that the State knows best. Such thinking threatens the Russian rulers as much as it does our own.'[180] 'The moral of the discovery was that the plans, which were undoubtedly known to the governments of foreign countries, were being kept secret from the people of this country—and that they would not work.'[181]

Planning for the operation had been in progress since early in 1963. The group which was to form into the 'Spies' emerged from the London Committee of 100 during the winter of 1962–3, and the basic idea for the initiative had been mooted semi-publicly in the 'Beyond Counting Arses' discussion document submitted to the 'Way Ahead' conference in February 1963.

The decision to make RSG6 at Warren Row, near Reading, the focal point for the action was taken at a meeting of the group on 15 February following discussion of several other options. On the following day, four members of the group drove down to Reading to investigate further. After obtaining more detailed information from a contact, they found the RSG at the east end of the village of Warren Row, eight miles out of Reading. Finding the premises

[177] 'The Spies for Peace Story', 197.
[178] *Guardian*, 1966.
[179] Ibid.
[180] 'The Spies for Peace Story', 197.
[181] *Inside Story,* 8.

unlocked, they gathered what papers they could and left. They met again on 20 February to discuss what had happened. 'The overwhelming majority of those present agreed that they should independently produce a pamphlet about RSG6 on the basis of the material discovered in Warren Row, and secretly distribute it to the Movement in time for the Aldermaston March.'[182] There was dissent from a minority, which argued that a secret cell operation would wreck the Committee of 100, and that the group should rather argue its case openly. This group then left the meeting and took no further part in the 'Spies' organization. The group also decided to exclude the 'more prominent and vulnerable members' of the Committee of 100. Those that remained formed the 'Spies for Peace'.[183]

On 23 February, four members of the group returned to Warren Row and, having picked the doorlock, spent several hours in the bunker, where they went meticulously through all the papers, maps, charts, and directories. After the necessary information had been extracted everything was put back exactly as it had been found. Gloves were used throughout. A suitcase of material and a camera full of pictures gave them more than enough detailed information to produce the leaflet. The efficiency of this operation, which was to characterize the whole episode, was demonstrated by the fact that, after the leaflet had been distributed, both the media and the authorities assumed that there must have been a 'leak' from within the national security system.

The group took exceptionally careful precautions to prevent their plans being exposed. The Warren Row material was looked after for a few days by a contact in a bookshop, just in case the police noticed anything. Then the group met every Monday night, at the same time as the London Committee of 100 on the assumption that this would disperse any surveillance. Meetings took place in one of three flats in Hampstead, where six of the group lived within walking distance of one another. Other informal contacts were maintained between individuals.

Every single action involved in the operation must have a complete cover story which sounded convincing and could be checked ... the absolute

[182] Ibid.
[183] According to ibid., they were mainly male (two women only in the group), and mainly of middle-class origin. They had all been active in the Committee of 100, and had had a variety of involvements with radical and left-wing organizations. They were now all committed to libertarian socialism.

minimum of material was to be kept in writing or said on the telephone. Everything was decided at the meetings, and nothing was recorded.[184]

Between 15 and 23 March three drafts of the document were prepared by different members of the group, and the final version agreed by the whole group on 25 March. Other members prepared the maps and photographs, and all the material taken or copied from Warren Row was then burnt, apart from the photographs.

The document was duplicated, having been typed on stencil. Again, all material was handled only with gloves. About 2,000 copies were sent out to those likely to be on the March, Committee of 100 contacts, CND and YCND contacts, the New Left, and left-wing magazines. A further 1,000 was sent to national newspapers, a list from *Who's Who*, Conservative and Labour ministers and MPs, etc. By the weekend of 6-7 April the document was ready. The necessary £100 needed to pay the costs of the operation was collected from previously sympathetic donors to the Committee. The copies were posted at various locations in London, and all the incriminating material that could be, was burnt. 'The typewriter was thrown into a river outside London, and—as a last touch of political malice—the cardboard boxes were left in dustbins outside the *Daily Worker* office in Farringdon Street.'[185]

The 'Spies' themselves had no part in organizing the demonstration which took place at Warren Row on the Saturday of the Aldermaston March, nor with the duplications and summaries of the document that were distributed by the thousand during and after the March. The demonstration on Easter Saturday at Warren Row ensured, finally, that the authorities would be unable to keep the revelations out of the newspapers. Much to the annoyance of the CND leadership, hundreds of marchers diverted to go to Warren Row. There was no mistaking the turning:

on the one hand stood the red and black flag of the old London Anarchist Group and a silent Committee of 100 supporter holding up a placard pointing the way. On the other hand stood the vociferous Duff bawling into the microphone of a CND van. The gist of her patter was on the lines

---

[184] Ibid. The authors add, rather acidly, that 'as is so often the case, those who did the most talking tended to do the least work'.

[185] Ibid. Also, 'the photographs were posted to Bertrand Russell to provide him with any evidence he might need if he were approached by the press—and he was; it was later discovered that when the police hunt began they were buried in his garden, where they may be to this day.'

of 'Keep moving, marchers . . . on to your lunch break . . . no diversions marchers. . . . Keep moving'. . . . However, to her horror, the militant section of marchers were more interested in unilateralism than in being fed and watered. . . . We should remember this when Peggy Duff says that 'the Executive Committee of CND had welcomed the revelations of the "Spies for Peace" '.[186]

The demonstrators surrounded the RSG, after a token attempt by the police to restrain them. A two-minute silence was held, and the demonstrators then rejoined the March.[187] Press coverage was enormous: virtually every national newspaper carried major accounts of the demonstration and the nature of the revelations. For a while the press was restrained from giving full details, including the location and nature of RSG6, by the D-notices issued by the authorities prohibiting the publication of RSG details (though *Peace News* ignored this instruction). Ironically, it was the *Daily Telegraph* which, on 19 April,

broke ranks . . . by printing what was alleged to be the transcript of a Radio Prague broadcast quoting extensively from the 'Spies for Peace' pamphlet. On the same day *Private Eye* published a full-page parody of the pamphlet, and on the next day it was shown on *That Was The Week That Was.*[188]

In the meantime the authorities had made themselves appear somewhat ridiculous. Whilst hundreds of marchers chanted the location of Warren Row through the centre of London on the final day of the March, and Vanessa Redgrave gave the exact location to 80,000 people from the platform at the final rally, the police arrested a man for 'singing the secret', and another man 'who had walked fourteen miles carrying a placard naming the Centre'.[189]

The 'Spies for Peace', as far as their initial objective was concerned, had succeeded beyond their expectations. As *Anarchy* put it: 'total damage to the State resulting from this demonstration: Damage to State property two pounds; Damage to State's image (already pretty fly-blown): immeasurable'.[190] The impact on the

[186] 'The Spies for Peace Story', 201. The quotation from Duff is taken from the *Guardian*, 16 May 1963.
[187] According to ibid., 202, 'a handful of anarchists and Committee of 100 supporters remained behind until about 7 p.m., when they were thrown right off the site by the police'.
[188] *Inside Story*, 9.
[189] Press accounts quoted in 'The Spies for Peace Story', 203.   [190] Ibid., 202.

Nuclear Disarmament Movement as a whole may have been debatable; but the effect on the Committee of 100 was undoubtedly beneficial: 'the whole Committee of 100 movement took on a new lease of life'.[191]

For some time the ripples of the RSG6 revelations continued to spread. Other, related information soon began to be circulated. Details about RSG4, which had been sent to Cambridge contacts, were published in a similar, though shorter, pamphlet on 25 April. On 2 May a typed leaflet appeared, stating that the communications system connecting the RSGs and the central Government was located in underground bunkers near Chancery Lane underground station in London. Secret telephone numbers were passed around, by word of mouth, in the Movement, and were used by activists to harass the authorities. At Dover Castle on 5 May there was a demonstration, followed by a break-in, by local activists. In September, Nicolas Walter, following the reprinting of 'Beyond Counting Arses' by *Solidarity*, and the pamphlet 'Resistance Shall Grow' by a coalition of the libertarian left, published a *Solidarity* pamphlet, 'The RSGs 1919–1963', giving the full historical background of the RSG system.[192] According to the *Inside Story* account, the effect of this on the authorities' attitude was dramatic: 'over the next few years the Civil Defence organization was completely dismantled, though no doubt a skeleton system survived.'[193]

After these successes, the 'Spies' resumed their work in the autumn of 1963. Through the summer, members of the group had participated in various Committee of 100 events,[194] but when, in the opinion of the 'Spies', 'the Committee once more relapsed into the same paralysis as had afflicted it before Easter, the group was reformed'.[195]

The objectives of the group were now to expose the emergency government system that lay behind the RSG structure. They were not, on the whole, successful. Having discovered only a derelict

[191] *Inside Story*, 9.
[192] 'Resistance Shall Grow' (an acronym for RSG) was reprinted in *Anarchy*, 29 as 'The Spies for Peace Story'; the *Solidarity* publication was Nicolas Walter, 'The RSGs 1919–1963', *Solidarity* pamphlet 15, 1963.
[193] *Inside Story*, 9.
[194] e.g. Marham, Porton, 'Greek week', the Cuban Embassy demonstration, and the Notting Hill anti-eviction struggles. See ibid.
[195] Ibid.

deep shelter at Belsize Park, the group moved on to explore an 'enormous military complex'[196] at Corsham: but the group found it impossible to get far enough into the complex to gather sufficient evidence to confirm its suspicions. Throughout January 1964 the group attempted to break into various places, without success. From February to May there were largely abortive visits to the West country, and to the Ilford civil defence headquarters (the latter by a separate group). Here, references were found to a site near Kelvedon Hatch in Essex: this was raided on 29 March but, although a mass of information was uncovered, it related largely to the Royal Observer Corps structure and its exercises. It emerged from these papers, however, that London had apparently been eliminated from the RSG system altogether: 'the implication was that in the event of nuclear war London would be virtually abandoned to its fate.'[197] In May the Wanstead civil defence headquarters was broken into and three people were arrested and charged with both this and the Ilford break-in: a total fine of £350 was imposed. In October 1964 a further, unsuccessful raid was made on the Corsham complex.

Given this general lack of success, the group disbanded at the end of 1964, though individuals remained active (at the 23 May Committee of 100 Bentwater demonstration, and the Warren Row 'picnic' on 16 August 1964, for example).[198] They also participated in the attempt to revive the 'Voice of Nuclear Disarmament' in 1964–5; although they left the group before its first and last broadcast at Easter 1965, they did take part in the demonstration, publicized by the broadcast, at the Rotundas in Monck Street at the end of the 1965 Aldermaston March.[199] Members of the group were later involved in the production of fake American dollars bearing slogans against the Vietnam War in 1966 and 1967, and several of them took part in the Brighton Church demonstration of October

[196] Ibid.

[197] Ibid.

[198] Another, separate response to the situation took place in Scotland where the Scots Against War group distributed a leaflet ('How to Disrupt, Obstruct and Subvert the Warfare State') at the Holy Loch demonstration on 25 May 1963. Sporadic sabotage was undertaken by the group from 1963 to 1966. 'The Group was never broken, but in the end it faded away.' The publication in June 1966, by the Scottish *Solidarity* group, of the pamphlet 'The Way Ahead', in reality marked the end of activism on this front in Scotland.

[199] This was suspected of being 'the site of the London RSG (if any) or even of the emergency seat of government' (*Inside Story* 9).

1966. There was also some involvement in the Greek Embassy demonstration in April 1967, and in the Committee of 100 demonstration at Corsham in May 1967.[200]

In 1968 some of the 'Spies' joined the Aldermaston March on Easter Saturday to take part in a YCND demonstration at Warren Row (where Julie Felix gave an impromptu concert).

This commemorated their success five years earlier; but it also marked their failure to achieve any further success, and indeed the final failure of the movement as a whole—for that was the last Aldermaston march, and 1968 also saw the disbandment of the Committee of 100 and its replacement as the vanguard of the radical left by the new student movement.[201]

Committee of 100 activists subsequently became involved in a wide range of disparate political activities. As is claimed in *Inside Story* there are connections, albeit tenuous, between the anarchistic wing of the Committee and the quasi-terroristic 'Angry Brigade' politics.[202] Less tenuously, and perhaps more constructively, some of the Committee's activists became prominent in the ' "squatters movements", the campaigns to urge disaffection among US servicemen during the Vietnam war, the anti-racist campaigns, [and] the campaigns against the South African [sports] tours in the early 1970s'.[203]

Nevertheless, the central objective of the radical Committee activists—of stimulating and taking part in a workers' revolution, created by an alliance of Nuclear Disarmament Movement militants and industrial militants—never even began to materialize. In a sense, therefore, the creative and determined Committee militants

[200] According to ibid. Also, 'A few were involved in the springing of George Blake from Wormwood Scrubs in October 1966', according to ibid. (But no evidence is produced to substantiate this claim.) However, allegations that Michael Randle and Pat Pottle of the Committee of 100 were involved have persisted. In 1970 Sean Bourke, a fellow prisoner of Blake's in Wormwood Scrubs, published a book (*The Springing of George Blake*) in which he claimed that he had organized Blake's escape but with some outside assistance. In a recent book (*George Blake: Superspy*, 1987) M. Montgomery Hyde has claimed that Michael Randle and Pat Pottle (under the aliases Michael Reynolds and Pat Porter) were involved with Bourke in Blake's escape. Randle and Pottle neither confirm nor deny this claim. In a statement reported in the *Guardian*, 9 Oct. 1987, they say: 'If we were involved in Blake's escape we clearly could not say so publicly without pointlessly inviting prosecution. But we would have no apologies or regrets for an act of human solidarity that cut across political disagreements and across the lies, and murderous obsessions of superpower politics and the Cold War.'

[201] Ibid.
[202] See ibid.   [203] Letter from Randle to the author, Oct. 1986.

were *forced*—partly through frustration—into these other, more attainable forms of opposition to the 'warfare state'.

At all events, the whole episode was of considerable importance for the Movement. It revived (only temporarily, as it proved) the Committee of 100, and again ensured that the initiative remained with the Committee rather than CND throughout 1963. More importantly, though, it accomplished the transition of the Committee of 100 from its former perspective (that of Russell *et al.*) to the libertarian socialist position, advocated with increasing force through late 1962 and early 1963. And it was this perspective which was to dominate the Committee for the remainder of its existence.

Within its own terms of reference, tactical and ideological, the 'Spies' operation could be counted a satisfying success. But the notion, banded about by some Committee of 100 militants, that it heralded the coming together of a mass revolutionary movement, was absurd. The Committee was smaller, weaker, and less effective than it had been in 1961—and the Nuclear Disarmament Movement generally was undeniably in the process of steep decline.

Moreover, there was an absence—total and persistent—of the one crucial factor upon which the whole libertarian socialist strategy depended: working class industrial militancy on a significant scale in support of the Committee. But nothing was more guaranteed to alienate the Labour Movement activists (let alone the working class *en masse*) than clandestine sabotage activity. This may, or may not, have shown a deplorably underdeveloped sense of revolutionary consciousness on the part of the British working class. But whilst the morally inspired activites of the DAC struck some sort of chord with at least the ILP/pacifist left tradition within the Labour Movement, the quasi-anarchistic, insurrectionary ideology and activities of the 'Spies for Peace', and the Committee of 100 generally by 1963, were far removed from any of the significant Labour Movement perspectives, minority left as well as mainstream Labourist.

The net results, then, of the episode were to strengthen, temporarily, the libertarian socialist wing of the Committee, but at the expense of any possibility of long-term success; to strengthen the Committee's position in the short term but to weaken it in the long term; and to divide further an already gravely weakened and divided Movement. Even with this rather negative crop of outcomes, however, it must finally be emphasized that within its own terms of reference, the 'Spies for Peace' organized an audacious, efficient, and original operation. At one level it remained, therefore, an autonomous political act, perfect and complete in itself.

The 'Greek dimension'

Just as the 'Spies for Peace' dominated the Nuclear Disarmament Movement and captured public and media interest in the spring of 1963, so the involvement of the Movement with Greek politics through 1963 and into 1964 became the focus of attention.[204]

The murder of Grigoris Lambrakis, an independent socialist MP and prominent peace activist, in which there was evidence of government connivance if not instigation, brought to a head an already tense conflict between left and right. Lambrakis's funeral turned into a huge peace demonstration. On 28 May at least half a million people took part in what David Boulton, editor of *Sanity*, described as the greatest march he ever saw. The whole episode made a great emotional and political impact on CND and the Committee of 100 in Britain. The linking of the cause of peace with the cause of liberty, all in the context of opposition to a demonstrably authoritarian and repressive regime, attuned well to the prevailing mood of the British Movement, not least in terms of its desire to broaden out from the central issue of nuclear weapons.

However, it appeared at first as though there was little directly that could be done in Britain. Then, fortuitously, a State visit by King Paul and Queen Frederica[205] to London was announced.

CND was somewhat reluctant to become involved in protests over the State visit, though it organized a silent march on 7 July from the Byron statue at Hyde Park Corner in tribute to Lambrakis. But the Committee (through the *ad hoc* 'Save Greece Now Committee') not surprisingly took a more militant line. A march from Trafalgar Square to Buckingham Palace was organized for the evening of 9 July when King Paul and Queen Frederica were due to arrive at the Palace. This was, of course, illegal, and, on the night of

---

[204] A clear though brief account of the Greek political context is given in Peggy Duff, *Left, Left, Left,* London, 1971, pp. 245–57.

[205] Queen Frederica was unpopular in her own right, being associated with Prussian monarchism and its values, in part because she was a German princess of the Kaiser's family.

the demonstration, the demonstrators clashed with police in Trafal-gar Square and Whitehall.

On 11 July the Royal party, which included Queen Elizabeth II, visited the Aldwych Theatre. In a jostling crowd of demonstrators the Greek royal couple were booed vigorously. 'The ever hostile press reported that the dear queen was booed, but they got the wrong queen.'[206] The Home Secretary, Henry Brooke, was quick to seize on this incident. 'Red faced and trembling', according to the *Daily Express*, Brooke condemned the demonstration: 'The Queen of England was booed tonight and I am furious.'[207] The following evening, when the Queen drove to Claridges for a banquet, there were again noisy demonstrations.

Out of this chaotic series of demonstrations, in the course of which the Movement had at least the satisfaction of seeing the royal tour wrecked, arose a number of arrests. Whilst the Movement undoubtedly suffered as a result of these events, it was, equally undoubtedly, the already tarnished images of the police and the judiciary which were most severely harmed. First, there were the cases of George Clark, Peter Moule, and Terry Chandler. Clark was sentenced to eighteen months' imprisonment on an 'incitement' charge. The Establishment, enraged no doubt by the attack on royalty, had overreached itself. There were protests in the national press, and the *Daily Herald* pointed out that Clark had received a longer sentence for a non-violent crime than some crimes of savage violence at about the same time. CND leaders wrote to the press on 24 September complaining of the injustice of the sentence. On 18 November Clark won his appeal: the Appeal Court ruled that the jury which convicted him had been improperly directed. (Moule and Chandler were less fortunate and were jailed for four and nine months respectively.)

The other arrests were to lead to much greater exposure of the State's malpractices, however. Eight others had been arrested during the demonstrations. In all cases the only witnesses were policemen. The first three defendants were found guilty and fined £5: they were advised against appeal by counsel as there were three police witnesses.

Donald Rooum, however, produced an expert witness to prove that, although the brick alleged to have been found in his pocket was in a highly crumbling condition, there was no trace of brick

---

[206] Duff, op. cit., 249.
[207] *Daily Express*, 11 July 1963.

dust in his pocket. He was thus acquitted.[208] *Peace News* accused the police of planting the brick on Rooum and thereby trying to frame him: Rooum decided to take legal action against the police officer concerned. Eventually, 'On 13 November the State dropped its last defences. Rooum, Hill, Ede and Apostolou [other defendants involved] were offered nearly £1,600 in compensation and the Home Secretary announced an internal, private, investigation into the arrests.'[209] Despite widespread demands for a public inquiry (from MPs, the press, etc.), the Home Secretary refused.

It then became known that Detective Sergeant Challenor, the senior officer responsible for the arrests, was a patient at Netherne Hospital. As a result of the police inquiry, Challenor, with three other policemen (David Oakley, Frank Battes, and Keith Goldsmith), was charged at Marlborough Street Magistrates' Court with conspiracy to pervert the course of justice. All were committed for trial at the Old Bailey. When the trial began the principal medical officer at Brixton jail stated that Challenor was suffering from paranoid schizophrenia. (Subsequent internal police inquiries revealed further miscarriages of justice and other prisoners were released.)

The police thus emerged from this whole episode with little credit. Nevertheless, the net effect of the 'Greek Week' demonstrations undoubtedly harmed the Movement, in the long term, far more than it did the authorities and the Establishment. The Movement was, of course, already in decline; and the 'Spies for Peace' and other activites had disturbed both the radical pacifist and the 'moral protester' constituencies within CND and the Committee of 100. The Greek demonstrations were, for some, the final proof that the Movement had changed, and changed in an unacceptable way. No longer was the central focus the bomb, or so it appeared: the Campaign had become more broadly and aggressively concerned with left-wing political issues. In particular, in the 'Greek Week' context, the Movement appeared to have associated itself with opposition to both the Queen (of England) and the institution of the monarchy. According to Peggy Duff, this had a disastrous effect on the level of support for the Movement.

This was not the end of the story, however. In Greece, following a Hiroshima Day March in 1964, Marathon marches in 1965 and

---

[208] Rooum's detailed account is given in 'Arms of the Law', *Anarchy*, 36.4, 1964. A Penguin Special, Mary Grigg, *The Challenor Case*, was published in 1965.

[209] Duff, op. cit., 251.

1966, and a prolonged political crisis, the right-wing junta took power in 1967. There was a continuous, but insignificant, involvment by CND and Committee of 100 activists in Greek events— marches, demonstrations, etc.—prior to the *coup d'état*. On 2 April 1967, a group of fifty (sixty according to *Solidarity*) from the 'Save Greece Now' *ad hoc* committee staged a 'non-violent invasion' of the Greek Embassy in Upper Brook Street, Mayfair at 8 p.m., to protest against Britain's prompt recognition of the new, 'fascist' regime. The demonstrators were treated roughly by the police and sentences were heavy. Terry Chandler was given fifteen months' imprisonment, Michael Randle twelve months, and Des Foley six months.

Others in the Nuclear Disarmament Movement indicated their revulsion at the British Labour Government's acceptance of the junta by resigning from the Labour Party. (It was over this, combined with Labour's support for American action in Vietnam, that Peggy Duff resigned.[210])

The connection between the British Nuclear Disarmament Movement and the Greek left thus persisted beyond the immediate events of July 1963. For Movement activists on the political left, whether libertarian socialists, Marxists, or Labour left, there was a clear connection between the British Nuclear Disarmament Movement and the Greeks' struggle for peace, liberty, and socialism. For many others in the Movement, the connection was anything but clear, and the Greek demonstrations were seen as offering conclusive proof that the original 'Ban the Bomb' Movement had been subverted, and was no longer worthy of support. Such reactions were indicative of the Movement's ultimate failure to 'internationalize' itself, despite Peggy Duff's involvement in the International Confederation for Disarmament and Peace.

The Committee was to continue in existence until 1968, but its days as a mass movement, as an important force in the Nuclear Disarmament Movement, and as a potentially significant organization in the wider context of British political life, were over.

POSTSCRIPT: THE COMMITTEE 1964–1968

Although the Committee was, formally, a long time a-dying, its effective political life ended in 1963. Committee of 100 campaigns

---

[210] Bertrand Russell had also resigned, in Oct. 1966, over the Vietnam issue, and had publicly torn up his Labour party membership card.

to involve service personnel in the Peace Movement continued throughout the mid-1960s, but, although achieving some individual 'successes', they made no major breakthroughs.

There were also Committee demonstrations at bases throughout the mid- to late 1960s, but these were increasingly overshadowed by the larger protests against the American involvement in the Vietnam War (in which CND participated, but which were dominated by other organizations).

The Committee was out of ideological and political line with the rest of the socialist-dominated British left. Whereas the British left was to a greater or lesser extent increasingly supportive of the National Liberation Front (NLF), as well as being opposed to American policy and military intervention, the Committee had no sympathy with either side in the war—as befitted a libertarian socialist organization.

The only libertarian attitude to the Vietnam war is summed up in Mercutio's dying words: 'A plague on both your houses'. The only libertarian action against the Vietnam war is that which rejects power politics and works for the Vietnamese people against all governments and armies.[211]

Resistance, in the same article, urged the libertarian left to recapture the initiative from the Marxists and redirect protest against both Western capitalist *and* Chinese and Russian Communist intervention. 'It is time the libertarian left got going again. Let us act or perish.'[212] In the event there was precious little action—and, for a time at least, it did seem as though the libertarian left had been extinguished, as the wave of the second, quasi-Trotskyist New Left grew through the late 1960s, at first in organizations related directly to either the Anti-Vietnam War movement (the Vietnam Solidarity Campaign), or the radical student movement (the Radical Student Alliance, the Revolutionary Socialist Students' Federation). In the years following 1968, these fed into the more generalized Trotskyist and quasi-Trotskyist movements, which all grew rapidly in the 1969–73 period (International Socialism, the International Marxist Group, *et al.*).

[211] *Resistance*, July 1965, pp. 3–4. The Committee's attitude was similarly emphasized in its poster slogan, 'Who Loses in Vietnam? The People.'
[212] Ibid., 4. Vietnam Peace Action *was* formed as a non-aligned, pacifist alternative to the Vietnam Solidarity Campaign (VSC), but it had little lasting influence.

An exception to the ineffectiveness of the Committee's activities, however, was the Brighton Church demonstration held on 2 October 1966. During the Labour Party conference a number of activists decided to interrupt Harold Wilson as he read the second lesson at Dorset Gardens Methodist Church during the dedication service. This was a well-organized and well-publicized demonstration, and was taken seriously by the authorities. Nicolas Walter and Jim Radford were both sentenced to two months in prison in November, following their conviction. (About twenty people took part and nine were arrested.) Considerable press coverage and discussion, almost all of it hostile of course, was generated by this affair and gave the Committee's perspective perhaps its final major public expression.

By late 1967 the Committee of 100 (in a statement from the London Committee) had widened its policy aims to include the 'small is beautiful' concept, and the 'alternative life-style' message of the embryonic 'hippie' movement. The 'activist' orientation also continued to characterize the Committee. Peter Cadogan, for example, took issue with Theodore Roszak (the editor of *Peace News*, following Hugh Brock's retirement in 1964) over the non-activist direction that the paper had taken. The paper, Cadogan claimed, was concerned with academic and peace research, rather than with the Peace Movement and ordinary people. There was some truth in this, but this process was itself indicative of the *de facto* collapse of the Movement. From the mid-1960s there *was* no mass activist Movement, although a far more dispersed and less influential movement for decentralized social change persisted (through such activites as squatting and community politics).

As Cadogan, Secretary of the National Committee of 100 from 1965 to its dissolution in 1968, has subsequently noted:

after 1963 CND and the Committee of 100 nose-dived to near nothingness because supporters switched to the petty politics of Harold Wilson and failed to face the challenge of the real world. Soon the movement was upstaged by the Vietnam Solidarity Campaign and 'Save Biafra'.[213]

Thus on the one hand CND was overwhelmed by the orthodox socialist left with its new hopes of a 'socialist' Labour Government and its struggle within Labourism against the Government's

---

[213] Peter Cadogan, Statement on Poland, 22 Jan. 1982.

support of America's policy in Vietnam, and on the other hand the Committee was overtaken by the neo-Marxist revolutionary left, again grouping around the Vietnam issue.

By the late 1960s the Committee structure of regional committees and a national co-ordinating committee was demonstrably failing to operate effectively, and both morale and support had disintegrated. Despite organizational restructuring the decline continued apace. By the autumn of 1967 the Committee, by common consent, had outlived its usefulness. By this stage almost everyone agreed with the advice given some years earlier by *Freedom*:

However successful it might have been it could not have continued indefinitely, and in our opinion, those who now seek to revive the Committee are doomed to failure because such movements, by their very nature, must have a limited existence, as well as limited scope.[214]

Peter Cadogan called a meeting of interested peace activists on 10 February 1968, entitled 'The State of London: The Condition of the Anti-war Movement in London and What to Do About It'. The national committee staggered on for a few months more under Cadogan's guidance but, by September, financial difficulties and yet further decline persuaded even the indefatigable Cadogan that the time had come to disband. At the meeting of the Committee on 14–15 September 1968, the decision was taken to disband. By the time of the massive October 1968 anti-Vietnam War demonstration in London, the Committee of 100, which had been dead in all but name for some time, had been finally buried.

[214] *Freedom*, 22 Aug. 1964. The London Committee dissolved on 14 Jan. 1968.

PART III

THE SOCIALIST DIMENSION

6

THE LABOUR MOVEMENT AND THE
PEACE ISSUE
1957–1964

THE CND leadership always regarded the Labour Party as the natural vehicle for bringing CND policy into effect. There was at first an antipathy towards politics as such; and the early CND leadership policy was to debar MPs of any political party from membership of the executive or other committees.[1] This view soon changed, however; indeed the genuineness of this apolitical stance was always questionable. Even those members of the early leadership who were not 'political' had, as Jacquetta Hawkes recalled,

all been 'leftish', 'pinko', or whatever kind of term you like to use. I suppose we had all been Labour Party voters, though most, not, I think, actual Party members. There was a very strong tradition on the professional left, middle-class left, at that time. It meant we had a great deal in common, it was just assumed one had grown up with it.[2]

The leadership was committed, as discussed in Chapter 2, to working within the parliamentary democratic framework as a legal, 'respectable' pressure group: the question of extra-parliamentary action, in the sense of rejecting conventional political channels, did not therefore receive serious consideration from the CND executive. There was thus an early and clear commitment to political action through the Labour Party:

if CND were going to be at all successful, it would need to take into consideration political expediences, and to gear itself to the realities of Britain's

[1] Canon L. John Collins, *Faith Under Fire*, London, 1966, p. 295. See also CND executive committee minutes, 28 Jan. 1958, where it was agreed that 'at present, no MPs should be included' on the committee (executive committee minutes, Modern Records Centre, University of Warwick Library).

[2] Jacquetta Hawkes, in conversation with the author, Jan. 1978. Although the moral, and apolitical, non-Labour Party presence on the early executive was very strong, as A. J. P. Taylor has recalled: 'Priestley wasn't interested in capturing the Labour Party, nor was James Cameron. Arthur Goss . . . wasn't interested in the Labour Party either: he was interested in the Campaign' (A. J. P. Taylor, in conversation with the author, Apr. 1978).

parliamentary democracy . . . one of our first aims should be to win a
majority for CND policy within the Labour Party, and a second, so to put
the case for British nuclear disarmament to the British public as a whole
that, at a general election, a Labour Party committed to our policy would
be returned to power.[3]

Although there were thus 'strategic' reasons for the CND leadership's adherence to the Labour Party, it reflected also a deeper, and
prior, predisposition, socially and culturally as well as politically,
towards Labourism. Most of CND's leaders had been involved
previously in Labour Party pressure groups of varying types—
usually in the peace or social fields—and they regarded the Disarmament Movement as being of the same genre. After the triumph at
the Labour Conference of 1960 had been reversed in 1961 with
such devastating effect, the CND leaders had no alternative
strategy: indeed, there *was* no alternative—for them.[4] After 1961
the history of CND, as far as the leadership was concerned, was, as
was seen in Chapter 3, a story of slow but sure disintegration and
decline as the frustration of the Labour Party failure exacerbated
the tendency, already inherent, for the Movement to fragment into
its incompatible and often mutually hostile component ideological
parts.

If the Labour Party was crucial for CND's strategy, the CND
campaign was also important for the Labour Party—both left and
right. The left had been campaigning on the issue of nuclear
weapons and defence expenditure from the time of the first atom
bomb and before; and *Tribune* had been conducting a campaign for
unilateral nuclear disarmament from 1957 onwards. The issue was
in the tradition of moral protest on defence and foreign policy
which had been strong in the Labour Party, on the left, since its
inception. Moreover, the whole issue was a part of the dispute in
the Party between the right wing under Gaitskell and the left wing
which opposed his 'revisionism' root and branch. By 1959–60 the
defence issue, apart from its intrinsic importance, had become the

---

[3] Collins, op. cit., 326.
[4] As A. J. P. Taylor observed: '[By 1962 the Committee of 100] could say we
hadn't achieved results either, which is perfectly true. And in this sense, one of my
reasons for withdrawal in 1962, when the Campaign became democratic, was the
feeling that the Committee of 100 should be allowed to go ahead and try—they
wouldn't succeed, but I couldn't use the argument that we were on the point of a
breakthrough, or that we had just about succeeded . . . so we should step down' (in
conversation).

focal point in the struggle between right and left for control of the Party.

The CND/Labour Party/Labour Movement relationship was therefore of central significance for all those concerned. The debate not only decided the future of CND but had an important effect on the future shape of Britain's defence and foreign policies, and on the nature of the Labour Party itself.

ANEURIN BEVAN AND THE H-BOMB

Any consideration of the Labour Movement's[5] attitude to nuclear weapons and to CND and the Disarmament Movement in the post-war period should take as a starting-point the position of Aneurin Bevan. From the time of the 1945–51 Governments Bevan had been far and away the dominating figure on Labour's left; and, since his resignation from the Labour Government (with Harold Wilson and John Freeman) in 1951 there had been a deep division within the Party between left and right. Throughout the first half of the decade the intensity and scale of the division grew,[6] and was exacerbated both by the clash of personalities between Bevan and Gaitskell and by the successive general election defeats of 1951 and 1955. The conflict over defence and foreign policy issues was an important aspect of this general, and fundamental, ideological division. Bevan, Wilson, and Freeman resigned in 1951 because of the insistence of the Labour Cabinet on imposing welfare cuts (prescription charges in particular), in order to finance defence expenditure. And, throughout the period, the question of the H-bomb itself, and the related issues of German rearmament and the Atlantic alliance, provoked sharp differences of opinion in the Parliamentary Labour Party (hereafter PLP). As early as 1946, a group of fifteen young back-bench MPs developed the demand for a 'third way' between the USA and the USSR in the 'Keep Left' pamphlet. After Bevan's

[5] In this chapter, 'Labour Movement' signifies the Labour Party and affiliated organizations and the trade unions, and does not refer to those socialist groups and organizations outside the orthodox framework, the Communist Party, and the various Marxist groupings. These are discussed, in their relationship to the Nuclear Disarmament Movement, in ch. 7.

[6] For full accounts of this period and its political implications see Ralph Miliband, *Parliamentary Socialism*, 2nd edn., London, 1973; David Coates, *The Labour Party and the Struggle for Socialism*, Cambridge, 1975, ch. 4; and Michael Foot, *Aneurin Bevan* (2 vols.), vol. 1, London, 1962, and vol. 2, London, 1973.

resignation in 1951, the policy of this group, although still a minority in the PLP, gained strength and influence rapidly, and by 1952 six of the seven Constituency Labour Party (CLP) seats on the national executive committee were held by Bevanites. Throughout 1953 and 1954 the Bevanites attacked the foreign policy of the PLP leadership—on German rearmament and on the Atlantic alliance— and Bevan eventually resigned from the shadow cabinet in 1954 over Attlee's handling of the SEATO (South East Asia Treaty Organization) policy.

Through 1956 and 1957 Bevan's attitudes and behaviour underwent a major change, culminating in his 1957 conference speech where he opposed strongly the motion calling for unilateral nuclear disarmament. It is this event which, as we have seen, prompted the article by J. B. Priestley in the *New Statesman*,[7] which in turn played a major role in the creation of CND.

What had been Bevan's views on the bomb before the 1957 speech? Bevan had been a member of the Labour Government of 1945–50 and he therefore, presumably, accepted the decision of that Government to manufacture atom bombs. In 1955, when the Conservative Government announed its intention to go ahead with the manufacture of thermonuclear weapons, the Labour opposition accepted the decision. It is true that Bevan, having failed to get an assurance from Attlee that the PLP would oppose in all circumstances the first use by Britain of nuclear weapons, abstained, with sixty other MPs, from voting for the amendment. But at no stage in the debate did he question the necessity for Britain manufacturing the bomb. It has been claimed by Peggy Duff and Michael Foot, for example,[8] that this shows that Bevan was never a unilateralist and that consequently his 1957 speech was quite consistent with his earlier pronouncements.

This does not tally with the facts, however. Throughout early 1957, as concern over the H-bomb and the dangers of nuclear tests was mounting, Bevan came out more and more strongly for unilateral action by Britain: 'I wish to heaven that Britain would rise to her moral stature by surrendering the H-Bomb experiment. I can see no good purpose at all in Britain arming herself with that useless weapon.' And again: 'If Britain had the moral stature she could say:

---

[7] J. B. Priestley, 'Britain and the Nuclear Bombs', *New Statesman*, 2 Nov. 1957.
[8] Peggy Duff, *Left, Left, Left*, London, 1971, and in conversation with the author, Jan. 1978; and Foot, op. cit.

"we can make the H-Bomb, but we are not going to make it, we believe that what the human race needs is leadership in the opposite direction, and we are going to give it." [9]

At the NEC meetings immediately preceding the 1957 conference Bevan was, at the *first* meeting, clearly in favour of the unilateralist resolution and opposed to the draft declaration on defence put forward by Gaitskell. In fact, an amendment to the resolution was proposed in the following terms by Sydney Silverman, Barbara Castle, *and Bevan*: 'there should be an addendum to the resolution stating the Party's case for stopping unilaterally the manufacture of nuclear weapons.' [10] No progress was made at this meeting and the decision on the NEC resolution to be put to conference was deferred. (It is interesting to note, however, that Ian Mikardo has recalled that Bevan took full part in his discussion and held to a firmly unilateralist line. [11])

By the second (Friday) meeting of the NEC Bevan had reversed his position. In response to the Mikardo/Silverman resolution urging the Labour Party to 'renounce the testing or manufacture of nuclear weapons in any form whatsoever', Bevan argued that to accept the resolution 'would mean the dismantling of international alliances and commitments, dismaying the Commonwealth and reducing Britain to complete negation in the councils of the world'. [12]

What happened to change his mind between the two meetings? Ian Mikardo is certain that it was a discussion with Sam Watson, the miners' leader, that finally convinced Bevan to change tack. 'I had a very long talk with Nye,' recalled Mikardo;

on the Saturday we met for a drink, . . . and he'd talked with Sam Watson the miners' leader who'd said to him that only through Nye's becoming Foreign Secretary could détente be brought about, and there was no way he could become Foreign Secretary if he stuck to the unilateralist line. And that's what I think caused the change. [13]

It seems clear, then, that Bevan decided that 'some influence within the party was better than none'. [14] He realized that if he had

[9] Bevan, cited in Foot, op. cit., vol. 2, 552.
[10] NEC minutes, cited in ibid., 568.
[11] Ian Mikardo, in conversation with the author, Apr. 1978.
[12] Cited in Foot, op. cit.
[13] Mikardo, in conversation.
[14] Foot, op. cit., 581.

continued the divisive movement in the Party the prospects of Labour forming the next Government and of his having a major role (hopefully as Foreign Secretary) would be virtually nil. And, as well as being a romantic and a traditionalist, Bevan was a political realist and a committed parliamentary socialist who desired, passionately, political power for himself and for the democratic socialist party. Bevan realized also that some *modus vivendi* must be reached with the leadership, and he thus adopted an increasingly conciliatory attitude in 1955, 1956, and 1957. Moreover, the Suez débâcle achieved for the Labour Party the unity that had been eluding it since the late 1940s. For a short period the Party was united on a political campaign appealing at both the moral and the political level to the whole Labour Movement. The effect of this was to secure for the Party a positive dynamism which Bevan was reluctant to relinquish once the Suez crisis had passed. Also, by 1957 there had been a shift away from Cold War politics as a result of Khrushchev's revelations about Stalin at the twentieth congress of the CPSU, and Bevan, as the probable future Foreign Secretary of a Labour Government, was keen to exert his influence on the world stage to secure détente, and to ensure that disarmament and co-existence could be brought to reality as soon as possible.

There was thus a rationale more complex (and arguably more worthy) behind Bevan's volte-face than the traditional, hostile, left-wing criticism that he 'sold out' his principles in order to advance his own career. There was, undoubtedly, an element in his reasoning that related to his self-advancement—but it seems fair to conclude that to his mind at least this was connected inextricably to the wider objective of achieving a Labour Government committed to democratic socialist principles and, through those principles, to world peace.

The central resolution at the 1957 conference was proposed by Vivienne Mendelson of Lambeth, Norwood CLP (seconded by Harold Davies MP, Leek CLP) and was comprehensively and unambiguously unilateralist. The NEC opposed the resolution, of course, and Bevan, winding up the debate for the NEC, was unequivocal in his opposition. Bevan stressed that he had probably 'made more speeches to more people condemning the Hydrogen Bomb than anybody in this Conference'. He went on to emphasize the positive aspects of the Vienna declaration, and laid great stress on his interpretation of the NEC policy that a commitment to the suspension of tests entailed a *de facto* suspension of manufacture. Heralding larger disputes to come, Bevan insisted that if the resolution were accepted 'you have to say at once . . . that all the international commitments, all the international facilities afforded to your friends and allies must be immediately destroyed.' The crux of Bevan's argument was that if Britain surrendered the bomb, and thus severed her international connections and influence, she would lose the chance that Bevan believed she had of acting as the major bridge between East and West. 'We want to have the opportunity of interposing between those two giants modifying, moderating, and mitigating influences.' And in his most notorious and emotive asides Bevan claimed that to surrender, unilaterally, the British nuclear deterrent would 'drive Great Britain into a diplomatic purdah', and 'send a British Foreign Secretary . . . naked into the conference chamber'. The resolution was rejected by 5,836,000 to 781,000, a resounding victory for the platform and the trade union leadership.

It was not only the *content* of the speech that dismayed Bevan's erstwhile colleagues, although this was shocking enough; even more galling and surprising was the vicious tone of the denunciation.

Bevan must have known that his denunciation of unilateralism would provoke fierce opposition from the Labour left. But he could not have foreseen the eruption of popular feeling—both inside and outside the Labour Party, and inside and outside 'politics'— of which his speech was at least a partial cause. Priestley's *New Statesman* article and the subsequent growth of the Nuclear Disarmament Movement, sparked off by Bevan's speech, have been discussed earlier, and of course had repercussions wider than the confines of the Labour Movement. But the immediate reactions of the Labour Movement, and the subsequent events caused by Bevan's 'defection' were widespread.

Michael Foot wrote a reply to Bevan in *Tribune*,[15] despite the latter's strongly expressed opinion that there should be no comment made following the Brighton conference.[16] Foot concluded that nothing had convinced him that

the possession of a few bombs which can never be used except as an act of national suicide and which as long as we produce them will impose enor-

[15] Michael Foot, 'Bevan and the H-bomb', *Tribune*, 11 Oct. 1957.
[16] Foot, 'Bevan', 580.

mous burdens on our economy will assist in making Britain's voice more
powerful in the world. . . . Britain's readiness to renounce the weapon . . .
could capture the imagination of millions of people in many lands.

Tribune thus maintained its anti-bomb stance—which it had
formulated in 1955 and had been developing strongly ever since—
despite Bevan's change of direction. The anguish and sorrow of
those on the left close to Bevan, in both political and personal
terms, was extreme: 'Why has he done it? Why, why, why, why?'
asked Michael Foot in the biography written more than ten years
after the event.

Others on the Labour left had more bitter views on Bevan's
'defection'. Olive Gibbs was 'upset by Nye Bevan, horribly upset.
And I haven't a good word to say for him now: all this veneration
quite honestly makes me *sick*! How any man who had held the
views he had could make a statement of that sort. . . . Everything
was finished for me.'[17] Frank Allaun recalled a similarly shattering
experience: 'I was absolutely downhearted—absolutely heart-
broken. And there were many others who lost their faith in Aneurin
Bevan from that time onwards. It didn't cause a split in the Labour
Movement because those who were against the Bomb still went on
being against the Bomb.'[18]

The only justification for Bevan's action—and it was a strong
justification given the parameters available within the assumptions
of the parliamentary, Labourist position—was *political*. Bevan's
position demonstrated in microcosm, as Coates has pointed out,
'the perennial dilemma of the Labour Left MP, of needing a Labour
Government and a position within it if he was not to be totally
impotent, but having to pay a high price . . . for his position of
influence.'[19]

The unfolding scenario was cut short—by the general election
defeat of 1959 and then, of course, by Bevan's untimely death in
early 1960. But even had these events not occurred, it seems reasonable to assume that the whole operation had badly misfired for
Bevan: not only had he 'made [his] peace with Gaitskell, and on
Gaitskell's terms',[20] thereby renouncing unilateralism and sacrific-
ing, effectively, his freedom to make any radical criticism of domes-

[17] Olive Gibbs, in conversation with the author, Jan. 1978.
[18] Frank Allaun, in conversation with the author, Jan. 1978.
[19] Coates, op. cit., 193.
[20] Ibid., 193.

tic policy, he had also 'profoundly altered'[21] his relationship with the left of the Party. No longer did he have the undivided loyalty of the left rank and file, and 'for the first time, the left in the Labour Party moved beyond him, leaving him behind'.[22] Bevan was thus left without an effective power base, without a clear or coherent policy, and without the freedom of manoeuvre to present a challenge to the 'leadership of the man he disliked so bitterly'.[23] Ironically, the major effect of Bevan's speech was to bring into being the mass movement—CND—that had been promising to break through for some time. The fact that the Labour left was from the start well represented in CND and influential within it, testified to the ability of the Labour left to break with even such a powerful and magnetic leader as Bevan when it judged him to be clearly in the wrong. Had Bevan chosen to lend his enormous prestige and weight to the Movement, and had he lived to exercise his powers at the height of the Campaign's influence, it is conceivable that the course of politics might have run very differently indeed.

THE LABOUR LEFT AND CND: 1958

The Movement against nuclear weapons gathered momentum rapidly, following the 1957 Brighton conference. The NCANWT and the DAC were growing, and *Tribune* intensified its already vigorous campaign for unilateralism in late 1957. Interestingly, the *New Statesman* did not initially recognize the significance of the Brighton conference and its attitude was at best lukewarm.[24] Even when Priestley's article appeared, on 2 November 1957, the *New Statesman* was not convinced of the unilateralist case. In an editorial it followed Bevan in arguing that unilateral nuclear disarmament entailed leaving NATO and thereby lessening Britain's ability to influence matters.[25]

At this stage then, only *Tribune* and the left group associated with it in the political Labour Movement was backing the

---

[21] Foot, 'Bevan', 584.

[22] Duff, op. cit., 71.

[23] Ibid., 74.

[24] In an editorial it claimed that the conference resolution was 'basically pacifist and the party has never regarded pacifism as an effective means towards world disarmament, nor has this journal' (*New Statesman*, 12 Oct 1957).

[25] *New Statesman*, 2 Nov. 1957.

unilateralist campaign. Following Priestley's article, however, events moved swiftly, and the *New Statesman* carried supporting letters from Russell, Trevor Huddleston, Stephen King-Hall, Frank Beswick, and others, including a suggestion that Russell, Priestley, and the others should 'form an organization whose principal object is for Britain to abandon the H-Bomb'.[26] It had by now become apparent that a major new movement was developing. By the end of December, Kingsley Martin was expressing the hope that the NCANWT might be the 'embryo of a national movement',[27] and the *New Statesman* had come out four-square behind a commitment to a fully unilateralist policy. Martin himself was of course instrumental, with J. B. Priestley, in bringing together the informal group which eventually gave birth to CND itself. Thus, by the time of the inaugural meeting of CND at the Central Hall on 17 February 1958, the Labour left was fully involved in the Campaign. *Tribune* in particular gave major publicity and argued: 'the Labour Party should have put itself at the head of this campaign, one of our tasks is to ensure that it is persuaded to do so'.[28] In 1958, as the Campaign gathered strength, the Labour involvement grew, steadily rather than spectacularly. Occasional misgivings, often presaging problems to come, were voiced. Frank Allaun, for example, complained in a letter to the *New Statesman*[29] that there was 'an almost complete absence from [CND's] platforms of any spokesman of the organized working-class movement. . . . [CND] will only achieve its object if it harnesses that section of the people with power.'

Labour CND activists were more concerned, though, about the existence and growth of an anti-Labour Party, 'anti-politics' element in the Movement, centred in the DAC but also finding some response in the ranks of CND. Two distinct, indeed opposed, views must be distinguished. There were those, like Jacquetta Hawkes, Arthur Goss, and to some extent Collins himself, who saw the Campaign as essentially a moral crusade and rejected and resented the intrusion of politics. And, at the other end of the spectrum, there were the 'militants' of the DAC who rejected conventional parliamentary politics, and saw working through the

[26] Letter from J. G. James and others, *New Statesman*, 7 Dec. 1957.
[27] Kingsley Martin, London Diary, *New Statesman*, 21 Dec. 1957.
[28] *Tribune*, 21 Feb. 1958.
[29] *New Statesman*, 26 Apr. 1958.

Labour Party as, at best, of secondary importance. The 'moral crusade' arguments were easier for Labour activists in CND to counter, not least because in their wider ideological assumptions people such as Collins and Jacquetta Hawkes were firmly in the Labourist tradition. As far as the CND leadership was concerned, the issue thus tended to be one of emphasis and degree rather than a substantive difference of principle.

In practice, the CND leadership followed Collins's lead and realized that, even if the Campaign were to remain a 'moral crusade', the need to work with and through the Labour Party was of paramount importance if any progress were to be made. Most of the CND leadership would have accepted Mikardo's view that 'the only political force capable of effecting such a change was the Labour Party . . . the battleground *was the Labour Party*. It was the only arena in which the Campaign could ride.'[30]

The same cannot be said of the DAC opponents of Labourism: both Hugh Brock and Pat Arrowsmith have confirmed that, although they were not 'absolutely opposed to that idea',[31] they regarded 'constitutional action' as being secondary—the prime objective being to mobilize the people through direct action, 'to work from the bottom up more'.[32] A central part of this DAC philosophy was the 'Voters' Veto' campaign, as discussed in Chapter 4, and it was here that the DAC in the 1958–9 period ran up against the bitter hostility of the Labour left and the CND leadership. The campaign was vigorously conducted and, although unsuccessful, was widely publicized in the Movement, and to some extent in the national press. The whole notion of the Movement encouraging voters to abstain from voting for non-unilateralist Labour candidates struck at the heart of the Labour Party activists' view of politics and the purpose of CND. Apart from the risk of proscription, the very notion of attempting action outside the Labour Movement framework was, to Labour left-wingers, completely unacceptable. Mikardo put this view succinctly: 'It's what issues in action that counts. Another 10,000 or 20,000 or 50,000 non-political people don't compensate for the loss of those who can exert political pressure at the point of *action*.'[33]

[30] Mikardo, in conversation.
[31] Hugh Brock, in conversation with the author, Apr. 1978.
[32] Pat Arrowsmith, in conversation with the author, Apr. 1978.
[33] Mikardo, in conversation.

Thus, by the time of the 1958 Labour Party conference, the CND/Labour left relationship had grown firmer and stronger. At meetings held during the conference it was agreed that a Labour advisory committee should be established to replace the H-bomb national campaign. It was hoped that this would further strengthen CND/Labour Party links, and discourage initiatives such as 'Voters' Veto'.

The 1958 Labour Party conference was not as great a success for CND as might have been expected. In a major and lengthy debate on foreign affairs and disarmament, Bevan hedged on the issue of the bomb: 'We are not pledging ourselves to make it. We are not pledging ourselves not to make it, because we do not know what kind of weapon it will be. We must really leave ourselves some room for manoeuvre.'[34] But the opposition to Bevan and the NEC was evident from the support received for the straightforward unilateralist resolution proposed by John Horner of the Fire Brigades Union. The emotional and deeply held unilateralism of speaker after speaker showed a marked increase in 'unilateralist consciousness' since the 1957 conference. The key speech, though, was that of Hugh Gaitskell, who argued forcefully against unilateral nuclear disarmament on the grounds that there was no evidence that it would lead to multilateral nuclear disarmament, and that the consequences of British withdrawal from NATO would be disastrous for world peace. Despite the commitment of those opposed to the NEC policy, the FBU resolution, and a resolution condemning missile bases 'under any circumstances', were both defeated, by margins of approximately five to one and five to two respectively.

The crucial element missing in 1958 was, of course, the backing of the large trade union bloc votes. CND had made considerable inroads into public opinion, and had won considerable support from the Labour left. But the real power at Labour conferences lay, as it always has done potentially, with the large trade unions. By 1959–60 the six largest trade unions between them controlled a majority of the total vote at the Labour Party conference. Without gaining majority support within the trade unions, CND would not 'capture' the Labour Party.

[34] Bevan, Labour Party annual conference report (LPACR), 1958, p. 189.

THE TRADE UNIONS, CND, AND THE LEAD-UP TO THE 1960 DECISION

Through the early summer of 1959 trade union support for CND policy grew rapidly. The first major breakthrough was the adoption by the General and Municipal Workers' Union (GMWU) of a unilateralist resolution at its conference in June. (This was carried by 150 votes to 126, with 75 abstentions or absentees.) As Peggy Duff has remarked, this was rather 'like the Daughters of the Revolution tearing up their draft cards'.[35] The GMWU had been the most reactionary of the major trade unions, and this 'beautiful bombshell', as *Tribune* described the vote,[36] was a significant and unexpected boost to the Movement.

As a recent analyst has observed, 'It was in character with the union that the most outspoken critic of the union's policy during this period should be not a representative of one of the Marxist sects but a devout radical Catholic from Lancashire, Len McNamee.'[37] McNamee, moving the resolution, argued in strongly moral tones for unilateral renunciation, basing his appeal on the dual grounds of the horrors of nuclear war and the influence and moral example of a disarmed Britain, and the vote appears to have been influenced more by moral and emotional arguments than by political considerations. This reflected the trend of public opinion as shown in the polls, in the growing concern in the media with the dangers of nuclear tests, radiation, etc., and, of course, in the rapid growth of support for CND.

However, conference was recalled on 24 August, on the pretext that the original conference had not had the chance of discussing the Labour/TUC joint policy statement, 'The Next Step' (discussed below). The union's decision was duly reversed[38] (by 194 votes to 139) but the psychological damage had been done, and more trade unions were to adopt unilateralist policies during the summer.

The major blow to the leadership of the Party came when the

[35] Duff, op. cit., 186.
[36] *Tribune*, 12 June 1959.
[37] Lewis Minkin, *The Labour Party Conference: A Study in the Politics of Intra-Party Democracy*, London, 1978, p. 99.
[38] As noted in ibid., 100, the debate was weighted heavily in the GMWU leadership's favour. 'Only one motion, that of the union's NEC was allowed to be debated, and amendments were ruled out of order.' After this, the GMWU 'proved to be amongst Gaitskell's staunchest allies'.

TGWU rejected the 'official' policy of the Labour/TUC document and adopted instead a complicated seven-point statement which represented, in effect, a unilateralist declaration. The motion did not go the whole way to a straightforward CND policy, but, as *Tribune* pointed out, by proposing the simultaneous and permanent cessation of tests, the suspension of manufacture, and the adoption of a commitment never to use nuclear weapons first, the motion would have had the effect of a unilateral nuclear disarmament statement.[39]

At the TUC conference of 1959 the TGWU motion was defeated by 5,133,000 to 2,795,000 votes, but a further motion protesting against the installation of missile bases was narrowly carried. Because of the general election there was no Labour Party conference in the autumn of 1959 (although a special post-electoral conference was held in December)—but at the end of July it had been reported that over one-third of the resolutions submitted for the conference advocated unilateral nuclear disarmament (and of the 141 resolutions on disarmament 117 called for unilateral nuclear disarmament and only one supported the TUC/Labour proposals).[40] The conference which was to take place in 1960 had thus already taken shape in 1959.

Why did the tide of trade union opinion begin to swing behind the unilateralist policy during 1959? With the *Tribune* left the explanation is straightforward: the tradition of 'peace movement' politics on the left, the concern of the left with moral issues and moral crusades, and the high degree of ideological rapport between the CND leadership and the Labour left all contributed to the growing support for CND.[41]

Only a minority of trade union members were, of course, Labour left supporters. The rank-and-file pressure towards unilateralism resulted rather from other factors. First, the rise in public awareness and concern over the dangers inherent in nuclear weapons had its effect in trade union circles as elsewhere. Secondly, the coincidental rise of more radically minded trade union leaders, in particular

[39] *Tribune*, editorial, 17 July 1959.
[40] *Tribune*, 31 July 1959.
[41] It should, however, be noted that by no means all CLP delegates supported the unilateralist case at the Labour conference in any of the key years (i.e. 1957–61). In fact it has been calculated that the 50% of CLP delegates which supported unilateralism in 1957 and 1958 actually declined in 1960 and 1961. See Minkin, op. cit., 89. (However, there was some *increase* in Constituency Labour Party support for unilateralism between the 1960 and the 1961 Labour Party conferences.)

Frank Cousins, gave a considerable impetus to the Movement. It is important to note, too, that the trade union support for unilateralism did not, on the whole, indicate support for CND *per se*.[42] Following the 1959 election the pressure for unilateralism mounted, and in 1960 the trade union commitment to unilateralism increased rapidly: of the 'big six' trade unions the TGWU, the AEU, the Union of Shop, Distributive and Allied Workers (USDAW), and the National Union of Railwaymen (NUR) all came out in support of unilateralist policies, leaving only the GMWU and the NUM backing the NEC/TUC policy. (In the case of the NUR the vote was extremely close—the 1959 decision against unilateralism being reversed at the AGM in July 1960 by only one vote. However, the NUR delegates, although voting for the AEU resolution at the conference, voted against the TGWU resolution on the grounds that it did not correspond so nearly to NUR agreed policy as did the resolution of the AEU.)[43]

Thus, by the time the conference came, the bulk of trade union votes was mandated in favour of both the TGWU and the AEU resolutions. The total voting of the 'big six' for the Scarborough debated was mandated as follows: for the AEU resolution, 2,298,000; against, 1,292,000; for the TGWU resolution, 2,026,000; against, 1,546,000. If the mandated votes of several of the smaller trade unions are added to this, it becomes clear that before the conference took place at Scarborough, the NEC/TUC policy was virtually certain to be defeated.

LABOUR DEFENCE POLICY 1958–1960

The context of the 1960 conference debate was provided by the development of the Labour leadership's defence policy, culminating in the NEC/TUC policy statement which was presented (and defeated) at the 1960 conference.

[42] There were of course several exceptions, most notably John Horner of the FBU, amongst trade union leaders, but generally Frank Cousins's rather distanced attitude to CND was more typical. Cousins did in fact march from Aldermaston in 1959 and 1960 but, as A. J. P. Taylor has recalled, 'Cousins never worked with us in any way: he simply took his own line and expected us to follow him' (in conversation). Cousins himself has commented that he did not think 'there was ever a clearly fixed and defined attitude on the subject of unilateralism and/or the CND within either the political or Trade Union movements. Therefore opinions become simply personal' (letter from Frank Cousins to the author, 7 Nov. 1977). This would again lend weight to the argument that the bulk of trade union support resulted from 'moral' rather than 'political' motivations.   [43] Minkin, op. cit., 172.

The key figure in this whole area was Hugh Gaitskell. Duncan (later Lord) Sandys in 1958 described the official Labour defence policy as '99.5% sound'[44] and, indeed, Gaitskell was just as committed, emotionally and politically, to the maintenance of the British independent nuclear deterrent as was the Conservative Government. All the shifts and compromises of the Labour leadership have to be seen against this commitment: Gaitskell regarded any compromise on the independent deterrent principle as, at best, a regrettable political necessity.

The Labour Party policy document 'Disarmament and Nuclear War' was issued on 6 March 1958, following the leadership's decisive victory at the 1957 conference where Bevan had taken such a strongly anti-unilateralist line. The statement adhered strongly to the principle of deterrence, to the maintenance of the British deterrent, and to the importance of maintaining the NATO alliance; and, as noted earlier, the leadership's policy was accepted by a large majority at the 1958 conference. The policy emphasized the importance of summit negotiations leading to disarmament, and argued for the suspension of nuclear tests with Britain taking the lead, and the restriction of H-bomb flights over British territory.

In response to the mounting pressure throughout late 1958 and early 1959 (particularly in the trade unions), the Labour Party published a new declaration on 24 June 1959: 'Disarmament and Nuclear War: The Next Step'. This was a complex and comprehensive document which laid out a rather grandiose list of objectives 'as laudable as they were impracticable'.[45] These included the withdrawal of foreign forces from Europe and the subsequent reunification of Germany, the withdrawal of Germany from NATO, and of Poland, Czechoslovakia, and Hungary from the Warsaw Pact. On nuclear weapons the document urged a complete and permanent ban of nuclear tests, and a general and wholesale de-escalation to take place multilaterally. No suggestion was made as to how these major policy proposals might be effected. It does not seem unduly cynical to dismiss these proposals as 'window-dressing': at all events this was the reaction from CND and the Labour left.

The central proposal of the document, aimed at stealing CND's

[44] Cited in Christopher Driver, *The Disarmers*, London, 1964, p. 67.
[45] A. J. R. Groom, *British Thinking About Nuclear Weapons*, London, 1974, p. 314.

thunder, was for the formation of a 'non-nuclear club', with Britain agreeing to abandon her nuclear weapons unilaterally *provided* that all other nations except the two nuclear powers, USA and USSR, agreed to a document banning nuclear weapons. The intention, and the immediate impression, of this proposal was that Britain would take the lead in a great and dramatic moral movement to rid the world of nuclear weapons. But there was no chance whatsoever that other nations, France and China most obviously, would be parties to such an agreement.

Nevertheless, had the 'non-nuclear club' idea been a serious proposal there might have been some merit in it, as far as the Disarmament Movement was concerned. The basic problem was that the proposal was demonstrably the result of the realization by Gaitskell that some action would have to be taken to stem the tide of unilateralism following the success of the Aldermaston March of 1959 and the unilateralist vote of the GMWU. The proposal was thus in reality a straightforward tactical attempt by the leadership to head off the challenge of unilateralism. Having put up the 'camouflage' of the 'non-nuclear club', the document rejected unilateralism on the grounds that there was no evidence that such action by Britain would have any effect on either the USA or the USSR, but that it *would* lead to the break-up of NATO, and the possibility of US isolationism, and thus be a threat to world peace.

In this way the document sought to drive a wedge between the 'moral unilateralists' and 'those who supported NATO, but who disapproved of the British deterrent on strategic or economic grounds, by proposing a policy which was as appealing as it was unlikely to be accepted'.[46]

The combination of the leadership's approach and the imminence of the general election saved the day for the NEC/TUC policy at the TUC (where the AEU, the NUM, and the NUR supported the leadership). But the reasoning behind the policy statement was transparent, and seen to be transparent: in the aftermath of the election defeat, Gaitskell could not stem the tide of revolt.

The existing trend towards unilateralism in the Labour Movement was considerably reinforced by the final collapse of the last remnants of Britain's nuclear credibility when, in April 1960, the Government was compelled to announce the abandonment of

[46] Ibid., 317.

the Blue Streak project, and thus, *de facto*, the independent deterrent. Before this announcement the Co-operative Party, USDAW,
and the AEU had all passed unilateralist resolutions, and by June
the NUR, the TGWU, and the NUM had passed similar resolutions.
Gaitskell was forced to abandon his rigid stance, and the Labour
Party adopted a new policy. The new document, 'Foreign Policy
and Defence', was published on 1 July 1960. The new policy had to
cope with a chaotic defence situation: the Blue Streak decision had
rendered Gaitskell's central adherence to the British independent
deterrent redundant—although he himself had reiterated it, forcefully, only weeks before the announcement. Moreover, the non-
nuclear club proposals had proved to be manifestly unworkable by
1960 and had to be discarded. In the event the new policy provided
little fresh hope of compromise: it argued clearly for Britain
remaining in NATO, although it stated that Britain should press for
revisions of NATO policy (including an undertaking that the West
should never be the first to use the H-bomb, and urging a move
away from the 'present perilous dependence' on nuclear weapons).
It acknowledged that the 'Blue Streak fiasco has shown that Britain
cannot maintain herself as an independent nuclear power. In future
the provision of the thermonuclear deterrent must be left to the
USA.' (And this finally and explicitly differentiated the Labour
Party policy from that of the Conservatives, who were attempting
to negotiate for Skybolt to replace Blue Streak and thus preserve the
independent deterrent.) The document reiterated Labour Party
opposition to nuclear tests and to Thor missile bases, but introduced no new formulations which might have won over the
unilateralists.

The independent deterrent had been abandoned by circumstance
rather than by design: thus a part of the CND case had been gained
by default.

The basis and the nature of the argument changed radically after
the Blue Streak announcement: no longer could a 'simple' demand
to 'ban the bomb' be countered by an equally 'simple' reiteration of
Britain's need to be 'independent', to maintain the nuclear where-
withal for her own defence. After 1960 the argument on both sides
became more complex and, necessarily, more political. As far as the
Labour leadership was concerned the new situation enabled
Gaitskell to interpret the NEC's policy as belligerently anti-
unilateralist and to concentrate the attack even more than he had in

1959 on the extent to which support for the *moral* cause of unilateral nuclear disarmament would entail the *political* consequence of withdrawal from NATO.

THE 1960 LABOUR PARTY CONFERENCE

Given the various underlying issues and conflicting objectives, how did the set-piece debate, whose result was anyway predetermined by mandated trade union votes, proceed?[47] The debate opened with an acknowledgement by Sam Watson, the miners' leader, that the issue was already decided by mandated votes. In his speech he laid great stress on the need to preserve and strengthen NATO until such time as multilateral disarmament could be achieved.

In his speech proposing the AEU resolution[48] (William Carron, president of the union, had refused to move the resolution), Len Miseldine made a straightforward plea for international tolerance and coexistence, and added that in his view the only way to reach international disarmament was through the unilateral renunciation of nuclear weapons by Britain.

Cousins was considerably more obscure in his presentation of the TGWU resolution.[49] Having pointed out some of the areas where the TGWU resolution corresponded with existing Labour policy, Cousins moved on to consider the major area of dispute:

the disagreement is about Britain's right, by some means or other, to possess nuclear weapons . . . if we have the right to possess the nuclear weapons, then every other country in the world has that same right. And if they have the right, how do we ever get into that atmosphere of avoiding the accidental drift into war?

In a convoluted reference to NATO with which he closed his speech, Cousins said:

When I am asked if it means getting out of NATO, if the question is posed to me as simply saying, am I prepared to go on remaining in an

[47] Although as Peggy Duff, op. cit., 189–90, has pointed out, the outcome was not finally clear until the AEU executive, which had voted for both the NEC and the TGWU and AEU resolutions at the TUC conference, finally decided, on the night before the debate, to vote for the AEU and TGWU resolutions, and against the NEC resolution. For a full account of the discussion in the AEU, see Minkin, op. cit., 189–90.

[48] Voting figures for the AEU resolution were: for, 3,303,000; against, 2,896,000.

[49] Voting figures for the TGWU resolution were: for, 3,282,000; against, 3,239,000.

organization over which I have no control, but which can destroy us instantly, my answer is Yes, if the choice is that. But it is not that.

Seconding the resolution, John Horner of the FBU gave a clear, brief exposition of the case for unilateralism and against US bases, and ended with a plea to link defence policy with a commitment to democratic socialism and a socialist foreign policy.

However, by far the most significant contribution to the debate was the concluding speech by Gaitskell. It was an outstandingly important speech: 'one of the boldest and most forthright in the whole history of British party leadership'.[50] Having outlined the considerable areas of agreement over defence policy (including support for the UN, reform of NATO policy on nuclear weapons, opposition to German rearmament with nuclear weapons, opposition to the independent British deterrent and to the Thor missile bases, and support for the test ban negotiations), Gaitskell moved on to the nub of the disagreement: unilateral nuclear disarmament. On the issue of the independent deterrent Gaitskell reaffirmed two points: first, that he had supported the independent nuclear deterrent because it 'gave us . . . a certain degree of independence—additional independence—from the USA'; and secondly, that the possession of nuclear weapons by Britain was 'not, in my opinion, a matter of principle but a matter of the balance of arguments'. Gaitskell then moved to the heart of his argument: that the policy of unilateralism logically and morally entailed withdrawal from the NATO alliance, because it was a *nuclear* alliance. CND, he pointed out, had adopted this commitment to withdrawal from NATO in their programme of aims earlier in 1960—yet neither Cousins nor Foot had recommended this line of action in the debate.

Gaitskell then went on to defend the theory of deterrence, and make the case against neutralism and for NATO (arguing as he had before that British withdrawal would lead either to the break-up of NATO and American isolationism, or to the dominance within NATO of Germany).

In the closing stages of his speech Gaitskell moved on to consider the view that 'the issue here is not really defence at all but the leadership of the Party . . . [but] The place to decide the leadership of this party is not here but in the PLP.' Finally, Gaitskell made the

[50] Robert T. McKenzie, *British Political Parties*, London, 1963, 615. (The extracts from Gaitskell's speech which follow are taken from LPACR 1960.)

point that even if the NEC policy were defeated, the PLP itself would have to decide its future policy. Conference could not be allowed to dictate policy to the PLP, whose primary loyalty must be to the election pledges on which MPs had been returned to Parliament, and to the electorate which had voted them into Parliament. Dismissing his opponents as 'pacifists, unilateralists and fellow travellers', Gaitskell declared that '[we] will fight and fight and fight again to save the Party we love. We will fight and fight and fight again and bring back sanity and honesty and dignity, so that our Party with its great past may retain its glory and its greatness.'

The AEU and TGWU resolutions were duly carried, and the NEC/TUC defence policy statement duly lost. However, as was stated earlier, it is important to note that CLP delegate opinion at the 1960 conference gave substantial support to the leadership's policy. Approximately two-thirds of CLP delegates in fact backed the party leadership and rejected unilateralism. It is significant, too, that despite Gaitskell's triumphant reversal of the unilateralist decision at the 1961 conference (see below), CLP delegate support for unilateralism *increased,* albeit marginally, in 1961. CLP delegate opinion is a much more accurate representation of party activists' views than is the voting pattern of the large trade union bloc votes. Thus, even at the height of unilateralist/CND success in the Labour Party, there was evidence that Gaitskell's views commanded a lot of activist support (although this support *diminished* slightly during 1960–1). Moreover, these figures demonstrate just how dependent upon trade union bloc voting were both the leadership and the unilateralists throughout the whole debate in the Party. Thus the fact that 1961 could be presented as (and indeed in many ways *was*) a major reversal of the unilateralist decision of 1960, despite there having been an *increase* in party activist support for the unilateralist case, was indicative of the key role played by the trade unions as a whole, and the handful of leaders of the biggest half-dozen in particular.

This debate, and particularly Gaitskell's speech, marked a turning-point—some would say *the* turning-point—for CND. And it certainly had a profound effect on CND's relationship with the Labour Movement.

The victory at Scarborough certainly came as a surprise to many of those in the CND leadership: 'we were absolutely astonished . . .

we didn't realize what was happening in the Labour Party.'[51] In a sense the victory had come too early for CND: now that the whole machine was ranged against them, how were they to defend and secure their victory? This led into the problem, inherent in the debate, of the ambiguity of Cousins's commitment to CND in terms of both policy and organization; and the lack of any firm links between the organized trade union movement and CND in general terms. The crucial question was thus how the trade unions were to be held to the unilateralist line.

In terms of policy the CND and the Labour left were faced with a difficulty of both principle and tactics. Almost everyone on the Labour left supported the general case for withdrawal from NATO (given the reasonable assumption that the organization's policies were unlikely to prove flexible enough to embrace Labour's central demands). Most people in the CND leadership (but by no means all—Jacquetta Hawkes, Arthur Goss, and others disagreed[52]) also supported this view, although there was a considerable section of supporters which did not. The problem was, however, that neither the majority of the Labour Movement nor the majority of the electorate would support such a policy (to say nothing of the divisions that would be caused in the Disarmament Movement). Gaitskell was astutely emphasizing this aspect of CND policy to drive a wedge between what he saw as the 'soft' moral centre of CND support, and the 'harder' left elements: take away the simple emotive appeal of 'ban the bomb' and replace it with the more political, more complex, and more left-wing notion of 'neutralism' —and, Gaitskell and his allies argued, the mass support for CND would fade away, not least in the trade union movement, which, as far as the Labour Movement was concerned, was where the power lay.

There are two further central questions arising from Gaitskell's speech. First, he raised the issue of the leadership, his leadership. It was possible, he said, that some people were using the issue of unilateral nuclear disarmament in order to challenge his leadership.[53] This was certainly an astute move. The trade union

---

[51] Hawkes, in conversation. Although Collins, Duff, and Clark (in conversation) recalled that they had been in discussion with Labour Party and trade union people immediately prior to the conference.

[52] Hawkes, in conversation; and Arthur Goss, in conversation with the author, Jan. 1978.

[53] The *Tribune* and the *New Statesman* both took this line through 1960 with increasing force. See e.g. editorial, *New Statesman*, 24 Sept. 1960, and Michael

movement is characterized by a strong collective loyalty to the Labour Movement organization, to the duly constituted bureaucracy, and thus, in most circumstances, to the leadership. Furthermore, the left had nobody of sufficient political weight to challenge Gaitskell for the leadership, as he well realized.

Secondly, Gaitskell raised the whole issue of the relationship between conference and the PLP. Since the constitution of the Party had been agreed in 1918 there had been a more or less permanent alliance between the right-wing PLP leadership and the right-wing trade union leadership. Thus disputes over major items of policy had very rarely reached the level of open confrontation between conference and PLP. It had therefore been quite safe for the parliamentary leadership to pay lip-service to the idea that conference determined Party policy, because, in reality, the parliamentary leadership had put policy to conference which had been massively endorsed thanks to the bloc votes of the trade unions. In this instance, however, Gaitskell realized that the issue had to be brought into the open,[54] and he therefore put it as forcefully as he could in terms of the responsibilities of MPs to Parliament and, by extension, to their electors and to the parliamentary democratic system itself. For CND to insist on conference decisions being upheld could and would be construed by Gaitskell (and the media)

Foot's article, *Tribune*, 30 Sept. 1960. And Parkin has argued that the whole story of Labour's involvement in the unilateralist issue is understandable only in terms of a struggle for the leadership. Frank Parkin, *Middle Class Radicalism: The Social Bases of the British Campaign for Nuclear Disarmament*, Manchester, 1968.

[54] Although as Minkin (op. cit.) has argued, Gaitskell did in fact have a number of options open to him. He could have 'sought some accommodation' with his trade union opponents; he could have accepted the 1960 decision as an expression of the opinion of the Party's supreme authority, and then delayed a major policy pronouncement 'until he had quietly mobilised support behind a new expression of policy which nullified or circumvented the decision'; he could have accepted the decision, but resigned because he disagreed with it; or, finally, he could have behaved according to 'the pure theory of intra-party democracy' and accepted that he was 'tied and fettered' and must carry out the policy.

In fact, of course, Gaitskell chose a characteristically conflict-oriented stance, and took up 'a position unique in Party history—open defiance of the authority of the Conference, refusal to advocate its decisions and the open mobilisation of an intra-party campaign to secure that reversal' (Lewis Minkin, *The Labour Party Conference and Intra-Party Democracy*, Ph.D. thesis, University of York, 1975, pp. 753-4).

In this context Lord Stockton's [Harold MacMillan's] dismissive comment on Gaitskell is apposite: 'Whenever a big wound developed in the Labour Party, Gaitskell—most obligingly—would go and put a tourniquet below it' (cited by Alistair Horne, *Sunday Times*, 4 Jan. 1987).

as an attempt to bypass or even subvert the parliamentary democratic system, and thus the constitution.

THE AFTERMATH OF THE 1960 CONFERENCE
AND THE CAMPAIGN TO REVERSE THE DECISION

CND and the Labour left were thus faced with a problematic situation. It was not only that CND was not 'strategically prepared'[55] for the victory: more importantly, CND was not an organization capable of mounting the hard internal battle at trade union and constituency party level. To have achieved success CND would have to have been wholly committed to working through the political and industrial Labour Movement to ensure that that support was maintained and strengthened; and, moreover, there needed to be strong links between CND and the Labour Movement (political and industrial) at all levels. As we have seen, CND was by no means exclusively or even primarily a pressure group operating within the context and parameters of the Labour Movement.

Many CND supporters were not 'political' at all; and, of those who were, many were hostile, from different perspectives, to the Labour left. The CND effort was therefore muted through 1960–1: there was in reality no way in which the whole campaign could have been swung into action within the Labour Movement.

With regard to the second requirement the situation was, if anything, even less hopeful from CND's point of view. As the two major empirical studies of CND supporters have demonstrated,[56] the Movement was predominantly *middle-class*. There were, of course, working-class activists in CND, particularly amongst young people, but, as a proportion of the total support, working class involvement remained low throughout. Even more important than this was the low level of trade union involvement. There were a great many trade union branches, and even trade union national executives, which supported CND but, on the whole, the major national trade unions did not support CND. And where trade union leaders backed unilateralism and related policies there was little *organizational* contact with CND. Moreover, as was noted

---

[55] Stuart Hall, in conversation with the author, Apr. 1978.
[56] Parkin, op. cit.; and Richard Taylor and Colin Pritchard, *The Protest Makers: The British Nuclear Disarmament Movement of 1958–1965, Twenty Years On*, Oxford, 1980, esp. pt. ii.

earlier, trade union support for unilateralism at the rank-and-file level stemmed much more from moral and emotive impulses than from political commitment. And this was more amenable to pressure from the campaign instigated by Gaitskell in the 1960 debate to turn attention towards the political consequences of unilateralism, as he saw them: a commitment to withdrawal from NATO and to neutralism; and, in the context of the structure and ideology of the Labour Party, a sharp swing to the left involving a deep division in both the PLP and the Movement as a whole.

The vehicle for the promulgation of the leadership's policy was the Campaign for Democratic Socialism (CDS). It had three main sources of support: 'a group of back bench Labour MPs personally close to Gaitskell, academics and party workers in the Oxford area, and a group of Parliamentary candidates based mainly in London'.[57] The resultant organization, within which later prominent Social Democratic Party members, including William Rodgers, were central figures, was a 'highly centralised professional organization compared with its adversary VFS [Victory for Socialism]'.[58] The CDS—which took shape in late 1959 and became fully operational by the autumn of 1960—received full and favourable press coverage. From January 1961 a monthly bulletin, 'Campaign', was circulated to as wide a range of Labour Movement activists as possible. By early 1961, CDS had 'received 2113 separate offers of support from key party workers . . . by May 1961 . . . the total of individual supporters had increased to 3011, many of them local opinion leaders.'[59]

The CDS campaign had three principal objectives: to influence the trade unions to reverse their support for unilateralism; to increase the volume of media pressure in support of Gaitskell and against the policy of unilateralism and the implied political extremism of those supporting the unilateralist position; and to encourage the 'silent majority' in constituency parties and trade unions to involve themselves in the issue and defeat the left. In the first two of these objectives they were certainly successful. The central task of converting the major trade unions' leaderships was accomplished, as is discussed below. And the barrage of

[57] Minkin, op. cit. (Ph.D.), 114–15.
[58] Ibid.
[59] Lord Windlesham, *Communication and Political Power*, London, 1966, pp. 116–17.

pro-Gaitskell, pro-NATO propaganda in the press was widespread and effective through late 1960 and 1961. This campaign had the effect of bringing out 'from the backwoods many right-wingers who were normally rarely seen at party meetings. The backwoodsmen swung the balance.'[60] Thus the third objective too, was attained, at least partially.

It is hard to quantify the influence and importance of a group such as the CDS, which by its very nature worked informally. Yet it seems reasonable to suppose that its role *was* significant. It provided Gaitskell with visible, professional, and organized support, and avoided any danger that he might appear isolated and out of touch with his party and movement. Moreover, the CDS did mobilize numbers of hitherto inactive right-wingers, as Peggy Duff claimed, and succeeded in identifying the unilateralist campaign, at least in the eyes of the Labour Movement, as essentially a political *leftist* campaign. In that sense the CDS played a key role in enabling Gaitskell to outflank the unilateralists. By 1961 the CLP delegates may have moved marginally towards support for unilateralism, but their cause had become identified exclusively with the left. And this enabled Gaitskell to win over the really important section of Labour Movement opinion: the major trade unions which commanded the bloc votes at the Labour conference. And Gaitskell's trade union campaign was, of course, highly successful: of the 'big six', the NUR, the AEU, and the USDAW (as well as the GMWU and the NUM) all swung behind the leadership's multilateralist policy in 1961. 'Unquestionably, the greatest asset which Gaitskell possessed in the long run struggle to assert himself over Conference was the political commitment of senior Trade Union leaders.' Working in a loose alliance with the CDS, the trade union leaders Greene (NUR), Carron (AEU), and Padley (USDAW) 'bore most of the responsibility for Gaitskell's survival . . . in the end the victory over the unilateralists was theirs.'[61]

How did this 'conversion' come about? According to Parkin, the unions' *support* for unilateralism had been largely the result of their dislike of Gaitskell's leadership (in part because of his clumsy attempt to 'revise' Clause IV of the Constitution).[62] And, as they had little commitment on the unilateralist issue *per se*, it is argued

---

[60] Duff, op. cit., 192.
[61] Minkin, op. cit. (Ph.D.), 117–18.
[62] See Parkin, op. cit., 124 ff.

that they were persuaded with relative ease to change their opinions in 1961 in order to preserve party unity. But it is an exaggeration and an oversimplification to claim that this was the only, or even the major, cause of trade union support for unilateralism. The commitment of the trade unions to the moral, rather than to any political, issues is immediately apparent from the debates of individual trade unions and of the TUC in 1960. Moreover, there is no evidence whatever of an alternative leadership emerging to which the trade unions were prepared to give their backing. Cousins was often held to have had a personal vendetta against Gaitskell—but even the protagonists of this view did not argue that he had political ambitions for himself, or that he was 'manoeuvring' in order to replace the existing leadership with another group. Moreover, Cousins's behaviour following the 1960 conference decision suggests very much that it was he who was seeking a compromise, looking for a means of unifying the Party, and Gaitskell who was determined at all costs to have a confrontation. Cousins was prepared to compromise: during 1961 Cousins accepted 'both NATO and the American nuclear deterrent',[63] thereby clarifying (or perhaps modifying) his 1960 position to approach more closely to the leadership's view.

What changed the trade unions' views in 1961 was a complex of factors in which the concern for party unity constituted one important dimension, and the campaign for the leadership's policies by the CDS another. More important than either of these factors, however, was the changed nature of the context of the debate. No longer could the issue be presented as a clear-cut, emotive appeal to 'ban the bomb'. Through force of circumstance Britain's independent deterrent had been abolished with the cancellation of Blue Streak—and Labour's defence policy had had to be re-formed to take this into account.

In 1960, as has been noted above, Gaitskell had resisted firmly the compromise proposals on defence which would have committed the Party to the abolition of the independent deterrent whilst maintaining a strong commitment to NATO. Such policies, though

[63] *New Statesman*, 24 Feb. 1961. This referred to Cousins's acceptance of Crossman's compromise proposals (which Gaitskell rejected) put to the Labour Party's twelve-man subcommittee established to draft new foreign policy and defence proposals. Crossman's resolution stated that Britain should remain in NATO until her security could be guaranteed by a world authority; and also argued that the USA must retain her nuclear weapons whilst the USSR retained hers.

advocated by a wide range of Labour Party leaders—including Harold Wilson, Richard Crossman, and George Brown—had been rejected, and the official policy of the Party, in 1960, remained firmly anti-unilateralist. By 1961 both the external political and defence situation and the internal political complexion of the Labour Movement made a change of policy essential. The 'Policy for Peace' which emerged as the Labour Party's new defence statement embodied a commitment that Britain 'should cease the attempt to remain an independent nuclear power'—an unambiguous commitment that Gaitskell had been wholly unwilling to give in 1960. Major concessions *were* thus made to the unilateralists. The resulting policy document assured the Gaitskellites of victory in 1961.

> The concession was necessary if those who were united in support of membership of a nuclear NATO were to secure victory in the trade union conferences which mandated delegates for the 1961 Party Conference. Once the question of Britain's own deterrent was out of the way the issue could be focused clearly on the question of neutralism and NATO bases.[64]

Thus, whilst it was true to claim that the primary motivation of the trade unions in 1961 was to find a policy which would guarantee party unity, this was not because of a change of heart in the trade unions over the question of the leadership, nor was it *solely* because the trade unions realized that 'a similar vote in 1961 would have entailed the complete disruption of the Labour Party'.[65] It was also because the issue itself had become diffused, had lost its emotive appeal. The trade unions' espousal of unilateralism had been based on the fundamental moral appeal: that the H-bomb was morally wrong; that Britain, which was in an extremely exposed and dangerous position as an American base, could set the world an example by abandoning the weapon, unilaterally, and thus regain moral leadership and halt proliferation.

This is perhaps to oversimplify, but these were the bare bones of the motivation. After 1960 this was no longer feasible—the abandonment of our nuclear weapons, through economic and technological inadequacy rather than principle, had altered the context of the debate. Gaitskell's 1960 speech became more relev-

[64] Minkin, op. cit. (book), 58–9.
[65] Parkin, op. cit., 127.

ant whether the unilateralists liked it or not: *either* the questions became 'second-order' (for example, disengagement in Europe, withdrawal of nuclear bases from Britain, opposition to first strike by NATO and USA H-bombs); *or* unilateralism had to be taken, as both CND and Gaitskell agreed, to entail British withdrawal from NATO and the adoption of a thoroughgoing neutralist foreign policy. The unilateralists in the Party were placed in a very awkward position: those on the left of the Labour Movement were undoubtedly in favour of withdrawal from NATO. But they realized, as did Gaitskell, that to advocate this policy as the natural corollary to unilateralism was to ensure defeat: a good proportion, if not the majority, of those trade unionists who supported unilateralist policy on moral grounds would most likely not have been prepared to give backing to these sorts of political policy. Thus, whereas in 1960 it was the official NEC policy which appeared to be hedging, and fudging the issues, throughout late 1960 and 1961 it was the unilateralists who were, paradoxically, on the retreat and suing for compromise. Gaitskell's strategy on the issue had worked, and the unilateralists had been forced onto the defensive.[66]

Eventually the NEC approved the official 'Policy for Peace' proposals by sixteen votes to ten, and rejected both Cousins's and the 'compromise' Crossman–Padley proposals by eighteen to seven and fifteen to thirteen respectively. The TUC general council, similarly, ratified the official policy by twenty-six votes to six.

The unilateralists were, tactically, in disarray. CND itself *rejected* all compromise. But many of the powerful unilateralist figures in the Labour Movement *supported* compromise: thus Michael Foot backed the Crossman–Padley compromise proposals, and even Cousins came out in his initial policy more clearly and more nearly in favour of central aspects of the official policy than had been the case in 1960—and then proceeded to give his backing to the further compromise of the Crossman–Padley proposals. In the end

[66] The situation had been further complicated by the proposal from the centre–left (Crossman and Padley) for a compromise defence policy which in reality differed very little from the official multilateralist policy ('Policy for Peace') of the leadership. There was much debate and heart-searching in CND and on the Labour left over whether or not this was an acceptable compromise. In the end, such debate proved to be irrelevant. Despite, or more likely because of, Cousins's agreement to support the Crossman–Padley compromise, Gaitskell refused to compromise over the official document at all.

Gaitskell succeeded in virtually isolating the TGWU at the 1961 Conference, and the margin of his victory was substantial.

THE 1961 LABOUR PARTY CONFERENCE

As in 1960, the 1961 conference was something of an anticlimax because the result of the debate was known well in advance. The debate had a rather tired, ritualistic appearance. George Brown, in an opening speech of considerable length and little originality or fire, proposing the NEC resolution, reiterated familiar arguments, and made the expected plea for unity. Cousins urged unilateralists not to be 'dispirited by any vote that is taken here today. It will mean as much, or as little, as apparently, in some circles, the vote did that was taken last year.' He emphasized again his contention that 'nuclear weapons are not a deterrent', and concluded by stressing that the TGWU 'is proud to say it is multilateralist; but it thinks unilateralism by Britain helps to achieve that'.[67] Gaitskell's was a similarly downbeat performance—but for different reasons: he had known for sometime that the motion was won, and he therefore had no need to produce anything other than a statesmanlike reiteration of his previous position.

There was one set-back to Gaitskell's triumphant conference: a resolution, proposed by Clive Jenkins of the Association of Supervisory Staffs, Executives, and Technicians (ASSET), calling for the conference to 'condemn the establishment of Polaris bases in Great Britain' was carried by a comfortable majority. And a further resolution condemning the decision 'to allow the use of territory of Great Britain for the training of German military personnel', was also passed, against NEC advice, by a similarly comfortable margin.[68]

In defence policy terms this anti-Polaris commitment (and the anti-NATO commitment on the specific issue of German troops) could be seen as equally crucial as the unilateralist issue to the leadership's defence policy—if not more so. But it was the issue of the bomb itself that had been acknowledged, by both sides, as the

[67] LPACR, 1961.

[68] Voting on the resolutions was as follows: NEC 'Policy for Peace' statement: for, 4,526,000; against, 1,756,000. TGWU motion: for, 1,891,000; against, 4,309,000. NUTGW motion (on German troops): for, 3,519,000; against, 2,733,000. Resolution 297 (on neutralism): for, 846,000; against, 5,476,000. ASSET motion (on Polaris): for, 3,611,000; against, 2,739,000.

'test case', and, although the opposition to Polaris was 'a source of annoyance to the Party leader',[69] it was regarded as little more than a minor irritant.

LABOUR'S 'MORAL IMPERIALISM'

As a postscript to this analysis, a further sub-theme underlying the Labour left's view of nuclear weapons should be noted. From the very outset of the debate the Labour left, in common with a good many others in CND, had stressed the potential 'moral leadership' which Britain could exercise if she were to renounce nuclear weapons unilaterally. Bevan's whole approach to foreign affairs in the 1950s was predicated on the assumption that Britain had, potentially, a unique role as a bridge between East and West.

This Labour left belief in Britain's 'moral lead' stemmed in part from the long tradition of quasi-pacifist internationalism which had formed a persistent minority dimension of the Labour left from the early years of the ILP onwards. The ILP opposition to the 1914–18 War stands out as the most famous and significant example of this ILP internationalism. And yet this tradition embodied also a moral *nationalism*, a position stemming from the nineteenth-century radical ideological framework, emphasizing the importance of national sovereignty, parliamentary democracy, and the rights of free individuals and free nations to determine their own futures. It is from within this tradition, for example, that both Aneurin Bevan and Michael Foot have drawn their definitions of socialism, and its order of priorities.

In some respects, then, this Labour left perspective has been contradictory, advocating both an internationalist, and often pacifist, policy, and yet failing to move beyond the national ideological framework, with its stress upon the actions of the nation State rather than the international working-class socialist movement.

It is outside the scope of this study to analyse in any depth either the historical or the theoretical aspects of this ideological stance. Two observations may be made, however, which have direct relevance for the relationship between the Nuclear Disarmament Movement and the various sections of socialist opinion (including the New Left as well as the more orthodox formations). The first is

[69] Parkin, op. cit., 131.

that the inconsistencies and ambiguities of the Labour left/ILP attitude and policy towards the central issue of socialism and nationalism have been characteristic of the overall inability of the socialist tradition in all its forms to deal satisfactorily in either theoretical or actual political terms with this relationship. Socialism has failed manifestly to transcend nationalism and national consciousness: and the only 'International' to forge some disciplined, international, socialist movement—the Third International —suffered quite other, and far more dramatically unsocialist, problems. The second observation is that the Labour left/ILP internationalist perspective was based ultimately upon the moral socialism which formed the basis of the ILP's overall socialist framework, and took insufficient account of a structural analysis which could explain the connections between the capitalist system, class struggle, and the phenomenon of war between modern nation States. Because it was in this sense 'under-theorized' the Labour left has always tended to see all problems discretely. Thus, in the context of nuclear weapons, there was no attempt to make the structural links between the struggle for nuclear disarmament, the class struggle, and the international structure of capitalist dominance. The upshot of this incomplete ideological framework was thus an inability to break from the dominant culture and the processes and institutions that inhered within it: the nation State, the orthodox institutional structure, etc. Hence, too, it could be argued that the Labour left adopted the 'great power' morality, and translated it into its own quasi-pacifist moral framework. The result was thus to espouse both the morality of internationalism and the nationalism of the 'Britain must lead' position.

Be this as it may, there is no doubt that this 'moral imperialism' was a major force throughout CND—not least in the 'apoliticals', like Jacquetta Hawkes—but it found its strongest and most politically consistent expression in the Labour left. *Tribune* in particular took a consistently strong and strident position on this aspect of CND policy from the beginning, as was to be expected given the paper's close association with Bevan and Foot. The need for Britain to reassert her importance on the world's stage—following her rapid demotion from great power status after 1945—was seen as important on the left as well as on the right. Psychologically and politically the desire for Britain to 'lead again' was a powerful motivating force—and on both the Labour left and the New Left there were repeated calls for Britain to lead a new grouping of predominantly Commonwealth countries in a neutralist third force. David Ross in *Tribune,* for example, argued:

the neutral segment is growing all the time and all that it lacks is an advanced, highly industrialised Western European country. That role could belong to us. As leaders of the new force, we would have a function that would restore greatness to our country; as also-rans in an American Alliance, we must degenerate.[70]

These sorts of arguments go a long way to justify George Clark's claim, that the new chauvinism 'really arose from "political thinkers" on the left, who tried to define a role which they had no expression for anyway—so they literally had to retreat into "we can make Britain Great again"!'[71]

CND AND THE LABOUR MOVEMENT 1961–1964

The CND leadership had based its whole strategy, as has been seen, on winning over the Labour Party to a unilateralist policy. Having apparently succeeded in capturing the Party in 1960, and then having lost the vote so heavily and disastrously in 1961, what alternative strategy could now be adopted? As Peggy Duff wryly observed, 'they decided to go on doing the same thing.'[72]

Although the immediate effect of the Blackpool conference was to confirm Gaitskell's position as party leader—he was never again challenged seriously—the debate on nuclear weapons and defence policy in the Labour Party was by no means over. The resentment and anger felt by the left at the Blackpool decision, and the arbitrary way in which it had been taken, manifested itself in demonstrations against Gaitskell (most notably at the Glasgow May Day rally), and in condemnations by *Tribune*[73] and others of his public support for the American Government's decision to resume nuclear tests in response to a similar announcement by the USSR. Gaitskell was acting in flat contradiction of a unanimous conference decision opposing nuclear tests by any country. Through 1962, *Tribune*

[70] David Ross, 'The Politics of Neutralism', *Tribune,* 16 Sept. 1960.
[71] George Clark, in conversation with the author, Jan. 1978.
[72] Duff, op. cit., 193.
[73] *Tribune,* 2 Mar. 1962; Michael Foot pointed out that on this occasion Gaitskell was not defying 'a resolution passed by some narrow majority composed of "pacifists, unilateralists and fellow-travellers", but one sponsored by himself'.

fought with increasing vehemence against Gaitskell's leadership: by May 1962 the Gaitskellite leadership is referred to as 'Labour's Officers—only the most perverse joker would now describe them as the leadership'.[74]

But, despite its vigour, the campaign against Gaitskell had a hollow ring: the political left may have been just as solid for CND (or perhaps even more so—certainly the Campaign as a whole was attracting more and more support through 1962) but the battle in the Labour Party had been lost, and everyone, Tribunites as well as Gaitskellites, realized this. The debate in the Labour Movement was over, and did not arise again until 1973.[75]

Support in the trade unions subsided as quickly as it had arisen, and for the same combination of factors that have been discussed earlier. Those in and around the CND leadership who were most closely associated with the perspective of 'victory through the Labour Party' joined forces with the *Tribune* left through 1961, 1962, and into 1963 to put pressure on the Labour Party at conference time and, where possible, at parliamentary and local levels.[76] But in this period the 'Labour Party perspective' lost its central place, and in the overall Disarmament Movement's thinking the Labour Party became merely *one* area of activity, and not the central area.

As the Disarmament Movement developed in diverse directions so it became ever more difficult for the *Tribune* left, in the Labour Party and in CND, to hold together the remnants of the Labour

[74] *Tribune*, 11 May 1962.

[75] Thus the only motion debated on nuclear weapons at the Labour Party conference of 1962 was that moved by Cousins calling for a reiteration of the 1961 condemnation of all nuclear weapons tests by the Party. After a short debate this was passed unanimously (LPACR, 1962).

In 1973, conference carried a unilateralist resolution by a 704,000 majority. However, the resolution was 'virtually ignored. It says much about the lack of salience of defence policy in this period that the resolution could have passed the Conference without any of the rumbustious repercussions of thirteen years previously. And it says much about the priorities of Left-wing trade union officials during this period that the resolution could be supported then left aside. It was the industrial and economic issues which increasingly preoccupied their attention' (Minkin, op. cit. (book), 347). It was not until 1979–80 that unilateralism again became one of the key political issues in the Labour Party and Labour Movement.

[76] The New Left and CND Tribunite officers (e.g. Stuart Hall and Peter Worsley from the New Left, and Peggy Duff and David Boulton from CND) joined forces and produced *Focus* the CND bulletin for conference delegates at Scarborough in 1962, and at successive Labour conferences thereafter. For further details, see Duff, op. cit., 197 ff.

Movement/CND link. Indeed, just as many people in CND had joined the Labour Party in the 1957–61 period on the issue of unilateralism itself, so many Labour unilateralists began gradually to leave the Party or became inactive CLP members following the 1961 reversal of policy. In part cause and in part effect of this distancing of CND from the Labour Party, the Disarmament Movement as a whole moved in political directions radically at odds with the traditions and practices of the parliamentary democratic Labour Party. Two developments in particular widened considerably the political gap between the Disarmament Movement and the Labour Party: the attempt, unsuccessful as it transpired, to establish a new and separate political organization to contest elections (INDEC—the Independent Nuclear Disarmament Election Committee); and the dramatic growth, and increasingly militant ideological stance, of the Committee of 100 from late 1960 onwards, committed to civil disobedience and extra-parliamentary direct action in pursuance of its goals.

Following Gaitskell's death in January 1963 the Labour left showed a decreasing interest in CND. To quite a large extent the issue of unilateralism and support for CND had been bound up with the personal and ideological animosity which the left had felt, and shown, for Gaitskell. With Gaitskell gone and a new leader, Harold Wilson, whose political record and attitudes were far more attractive to the left, there was a decrease in incentive for the left's involvement in CND. However, this was not the only reason for the fairly rapid withdrawal of Labour left leaders from active support for CND.[77] The first and most important reason was the style of Wilson's leadership. Whatever may have been the subsequent disillusionments for the left in the 1964–70 Labour Governments and beyond, there can be no doubt that in 1963 Wilson seemed to represent a new and more radical socialism.

Wilson's foreign and defence policy was in all essentials the same as Gaitskell's, but the conciliatory and at the same time radical way in which he expressed the commitments created a quite different ethos in the Movement. Moreover, most of those on the left who had suspicions or reservations about his ability and/or will to deliver the 'socialist goods', reasoned that they would be able to exert left-wing pressure once the Government had been elected.

[77] Michael Foot, Judith Hart, and Anthony Greenwood did not stand for re-election to the CND executive in 1963.

And, anyway, it was argued, Wilson was a leader as far to the left as could be hoped for, given the balance of forces in the PLP (the alternatives had, after all, been James Callaghan or George Brown).

There were, however, other factors which also contributed to the slackening of the ideological and organizational ties between CND and the Labour Party. The increasing division in the Disarmament Movement—over INDEC and the Committee of 100, and the subsequent extra-parliamentary orientation of much of the Movement—led to a distancing between CND and the Labour left. Moreover, by 1963, many of the initial leaders of CND had themselves resigned, and the Labourist and élite nature of the leadership had decreased considerably. The trade union involvement in CND had also been steadily decreasing since 1961, not least because of the increasingly militant politics of a substantial section of the Committee of 100. Finally, on the domestic scene, the moral appeal of defence issues had declined, as noted earlier, since the cancellation of Blue Streak in 1960 had made all the issues concerned so much more complex and technical than the fundamental call for Britain to 'ban the bomb'.

Internationally, both the Cuban crisis and the Partial Test Ban Treaty of 1963 had, in their different ways, a profoundly negative effect on the Nuclear Disarmament Movement, and tended to downgrade the issue's importance in the eyes of the Labour left (and other former activists and supporters).

These developments of course affected the Movement as a whole—not just the Labour left; but the combination of these factors with the replacement of Gaitskell by Wilson, plus the approach of an election and the need to close ranks, all contributed to the fairly rapid exodus, and by 1964 few if any prominent Labour left figures remained actively involved.

CND AND THE LABOUR MOVEMENT: SOME CONCLUSIONS

Three distinct groupings saw the relationship between CND, unilateralism, and the Labour Movement as of crucial importance: the dominant group within the CND leadership and a substantial section of CND's supporters; the Labour left; and the Gaitskellite right.

Within CND itself there was a large body of opinion, including the bulk of the leadership, which saw the only way of advance for

CND's cause as being through the Labour Party. The left of the Labour Party saw the relationship as important too. It was, in its eyes, in the grand tradition of morally inspired Labour peace movements—from the 'No Conscription Fellowship' of the First World War, through the Lansbury and Peace Pledge Union campaigns of the 1930s, to CND, there was, it was argued, a clear moral and political continuum: the socialist commitment to 'peace and brotherhood'.[78] Reference has already been made to the Labour left's tendency to adopt 'Little Englander' attitudes. There was a sense in which the concept of unilateralism satisfied the ideological, and perhaps psychological, need of the Labour left to believe that 'Britain still has the power to change its destiny at will'.[79] There was a refusal to acknowledge that Britain had declined from being a major force in the world to being a second-rate or even third-rate power. The adoption of CND's policies was also seen by the Labour left as central to the achievement of the socialist society it was aiming for, not only in the much-discussed tactical sense of using CND and the issue of unilateralism as a means of deposing the Gaitskellite leadership,[80] but also because of the intrinsic link that the Labour left saw between a commitment to peace and a commitment to progressive 'socialist internationalism'.[81]

There was, too, an ideological rejection—or more often suspicion bordering on rejection—of the NATO alliance and the so-called American/British 'special relationship'. Over and above the 'Little Englander' dislike of American domination, there was on the Labour left a very strong antipathy towards both American imperialism and American capitalism.

On the Labour left the combination of these quasi-socialist objections, with the 'Little Englander' mentality, resulted in a strong and

[78] Hugh Brock, from the pacifist rather than the Labour Movement, confirmed this. 'The left and the Peace Movement have always been together in these upsurges' (in conversation).

[79] Alastair Buchan, 'The Odds Against Gaitskell', *Reporter*, 22 Dec. 1960, vol. 23, pp. 30–3.

[80] As Ian Mikardo has pointed out, if the Labour left had been intent only, or even primarily, upon deposing the right-wing leadership, giving support to CND 'wasn't the way to do it, we'd have done it in the Labour Party, not joined an outside organization' (in conversation).

[81] Frank Allaun put this left viewpoint succinctly. 'The whole of my object was really to influence the Labour Party, to make the Party the "Peace Party" ' (in conversation with the author, Jan. 1978). This commitment to 'internationalism' has coexisted rather uneasily with the 'Little Englander' tendencies of the Labour left, as was discussed earlier in this chapter.

continuing opposition to American bases in Britain. (Thus the
Labour Party conference in 1961, and for several years thereafter,
carried resolutions rejecting Polaris etc., after the CND case for
unilateral nuclear disarmament had been voted down.)

On a more prosaic level the Labour left always argued strongly,
too, that the social and economic policies that it saw as being essential to the creation of a democratic socialist society were being
dismissed or disregarded by the leadership, at least in part because
of the assumption that so large a proportion of government expenditure should be devoted to defence, and especially to nuclear
weapons. There were thus strong economic motivations for the
Labour left's support of CND, in addition to the moral and political considerations.

On a slightly different tack, both the Labour left and CND were
insistent on the issue of conference supremacy following the 1960
decision. Obviously, both had a vested interest in seeing the
unilateralist decision upheld and Gaitskell replaced by what, in
their view, would be a more enlightened leadership. But there was
also a commitment on the part of the Labour left to the concept of a
democratically controlled party structure: Michael Foot, in particular, wrote extensively and with consistency and conviction on this
theme.[82]

On the other side, as it were, the CND/Labour Movement
relationship was just as important to the Gaitskellite right. Again,
both the substantive issues connected with unilateralism and
NATO, and the questions concerning the ideological direction of
the Party and the leadership, were intertwined. There is no doubt
that, having lost the battle over Clause IV, Gaitskell made a tactical
as well as a principled stand on the issue of defence policy. And
again it cannot be denied that tactically he enjoyed a dramatic
success in snatching victory from the seemingly conclusive defeat
of 1960.

Both tactically and ideologically he read the situation accurately

---

[82] See *Tribune,* throughout late 1960 and early 1961, following the Scarborough
decision. There are numerous articles and editorials, and a sharp correspondence
between Michael Foot and Christopher Mayhew, at that time one of the most
outspoken of the Gaitskellites. (Mayhew was subsequently to join the Liberal Party.)

It is instructive to compare the debate over conference supremacy and party
democracy in the early 1960s with that of the early 1980s. In particular, the role and
perspective of Michael Foot in the two party debates illustrates the complexities of
the problem, as well as the specific changes in his personal attitudes.

and, in the crucial area of the trade unions, his appeal to back the
duly constituted leadership in order not to threaten party unity was
an astute and successful move (though it was considerably helped
by the changes in the defence situation which had occurred quite
independently of CND, or indeed of the Labour Party). But it
would be a mistake to underestimate the extent of Gaitskell's
principled commitment on the issues: as he made abundantly clear
in 1960 and 1961 he had a clearly held and, within its own terms of
reference, logical belief in NATO, nuclear deterrence, and multilateral disarmament. In the post-war context the emphasis in
foreign policy had been very much on building up the anti-
Communist alliance in NATO and strengthening the Anglo-US
relationship. As Gaitskell was fond of reminding the Labour Party
and the trade unions, it was Ernest Bevin who had been one of the
chief architects of NATO, and the 1945–50 Labour Government
which had been responsible for the overall creation of the
peacetime economic and political alliance between Britain and the
USA. Gaitskell was determined to protect this 'heritage', and he
never wavered in his uncompromising support of the USA, and of
the collective security policy of NATO. His opposition to
unilateralism was thus wholly consistent with his past attitudes,
and with the tradition of a pro-American foreign policy which had
dominated the Labour Party (and of course the Conservatives) ever
since the Second World War.

The CND/unilateralist issue needs to be seen in the wider context
of Gaitskell's commitment to an overall revisionist perspective, and
he saw the struggle against the left as the price that had to be paid if
the Labour Party were to be 'modernized'. This modernization he
saw as crucial if the Labour Party were to appeal to the new,
supposedly increasingly classless electorate. This problem became
particularly acute after Labour lost its third successive general
election in 1959. Central to this revisionism was the eradication of
the old 'pacifist/neutralist' image of the Labour Party. And a further
facet of the process was to bring the Labour Party firmly into the
parliamentarist fold and to remove trade union control through
conference. So, in this context again, there was a mixture of tactical, political, and ideological motivations underlying Gaitskell's
attitudes and actions.

These, then, were the basic dimensions to the CND/Labour
Movement relationship. The specific problems and political and

ideological developments that characterized the stormy interaction between the two organizations relates to the wider determinants of Labourism itself.

In this context the overriding characteristic of CND's alliance with the Labour left was, in practical political terms, the seemingly permanent minority position in which the latter found itself. Despite having a unity of purpose with the CND leadership, it could not make the pressure of this huge mass movement count in the Labour Movement. Despite the dramatic successes of 1959–60, and the prominence of the issue during 1959–61 in the Labour Movement, CND and the Labour left failed to hold the Labour Party to the unilateralist policy of the 1960 conference. This was a major factor, from 1961 onwards, in the Disarmament Movement's decline, and in the 'right of centre' consensus in the Party that developed around Harold Wilson from 1963 onwards.

7

MARXISTS AND NUCLEAR DISARMAMENT

ALTHOUGH playing a far lesser part in the Peace Movement than the mainstream CND, the radical direct actionists, and the orthodox Labour Movement activists, the Marxists had a distinctive and significant role in the 1958–65 period.[1]

Marxists presented a structural analysis of the H-bomb issue and the political questions surrounding it which was fundamentally incompatible with many of the assumptions on which the mainstream Movement was based. For all Marxists, whatever their differences in orientation, the issue of the bomb was inseparably linked to the structure of existing society, and for them the unilateralist Movement was intimately involved with the struggle to create a socialist system.

THE COMMUNIST PARTY AND THE PEACE MOVEMENT

The Communist Party (CP) saw CND as part of an ongoing and variegated Peace Movement which had been steadily growing since the end of the Second World War. The concerted international drive for disarmament conducted by the World Peace Council in the 1950s (including a campaign by the British Peace Committee which obtained over one million signatures for a peace petition in Britain), the Stockholm Appeal, the Campaign Against German Rearmament—all these were seen by the CP as a part of an internationally based peace campaign to reduce international tension and, ultimately, to lead to international agreement on disarmament.

This campaign and the related objective of securing Britain's withdrawal from NATO and the closure of American bases in Britain were the CP's priorities. Thus, whilst the CP (and in

---

[1] In other periods Marxists have played a considerably more prominent role in the Peace Movement. This applies particularly to the 1930s and the 1980s. See Martin Shaw, 'War, Peace and British Marxism, 1895–1945', and Richard Taylor, 'The Marxist Left and the Peace Movement in Britain since 1945', in Richard Taylor and Nigel Young (eds.), *Campaigns for Peace: British Peace Movements in the Twentieth Century*, Manchester, 1988.

particular its paper, the *Daily Worker*) gave considerable coverage to CND, it saw its activities and its policy of unilateralism as *ancillary*. Whilst it is true that the CP 'always supported CND—right from the outset',[2] this support was qualified. CND's increasing concentration upon unilateral action was seen as at best a diversion. Moreover, the CP regarded as reactionary those in CND who advocated renunciation by Britain of the bomb but adhered to the theory of the deterrent and, above all, wanted Britain to remain a loyal member of NATO. Such advocates merely took the view, it was argued, that America could defend the West alone, and that Britain's best contribution to the Western alliance would be through conventional armaments. For the CP this was tantamount to support for imperialism and had to be opposed.[3] And the CP was critical of what it saw as the 'moral defeatism' which characterized CND and was typified in Priestley's *New Statesman* article.[4]

Above all, though, the CP felt CND was *tactically* incorrect because the 'maximalist' unilateral policy would divide the wider Peace Movement. An editorial in the *Daily Worker* of 28 February 1958 put the point bluntly: 'to raise instead the question of unilateralism, against which the [Labour] Conference decided by a seven to one vote and which the later Gallup Poll shows is supported by only a fifth of the British people is likely to divert attention from the main job.'

The policy of 'unity' over a minimum set of demands is indicative of the whole CP philosophy in relation to the Peace Movement (and to later 'single-issue' campaigns). In this the Party agreed far more with Canon Collins and the CND leadership than it did with other more radical Disarmament Movement political activists, who saw the campaign, in one sense or another, as part of a wider social and political struggle. As Matthews said, the CP has always 'been prepared to co-operate, on the question of peace, with *anybody*, including Tories—who want peace. Whereas that is regarded as "betraying the revolution" and so on by some of these ultra-Left sects.'[5]

Related to this focus on 'unity', the CP argued at a more general

[2] George Matthews, formerly assistant secretary, CPGB; formerly editor, *Daily Worker*, now *Morning Star*, in conversation with the author, Jan. 1978.
[3] George Matthews, 'Unilateralism and the Fight for Peace', *World News*, 14 Mar. 1958.
[4] J. B. Priestley, 'Britain and the Nuclear Bombs', *New Statesman*, 2 Nov. 1957.
[5] Matthews, in conversation.

level that the degree of support for any progressive campaign should depend centrally upon its having a base in the working class and in the organized Labour Movement. Given its adherence in the 1950s and 1960s to orthodox Marxist–Leninist ideology, this was a logical position to adopt.[6] By these criteria CND did indeed appear to fall short of the mark: not only was the call for unilateralism 'maximalist' and 'diversionary': in 1958 it showed little sign of attracting trade union support. Equally, CND was quite clearly a predominantly middle-class movement. As Parkin rather spitefully has put it: 'CND . . . presented Marxists with the puzzling and somewhat disturbing spectacle of a radical movement with an absentee proletariat.'[7]

The CP, however, has good grounds for maintaining that it never *opposed* CND. The publicity given to the 1958 Aldermaston March by the *Daily Worker*, was, for example, fuller and more enthusiastic than the coverage of any other national newspaper:

It is one of the greatest Peace Marches ever known in this country . . . the column was four deep and nearly two miles long. . . . There were men, women and children of all religious denominations and none, of various parties and the non-committed, from different peace organizations, and also hundreds of ordinary folk who were doing something active for the first time to prevent the mass suicide of nuclear war . . . the accent throughout the procession was on young people. . . . The Aldermaston March ended in triumph yesterday. It was a most impressive demonstration by a representative cross-section of the British people and expressed the conviction that something must be done to stop tests and to ban all nuclear weapons.[8]

This general relationship—supportive but distanced—continued through 1958 and early 1959. All major CND and DAC demonstrations were faithfully reported, and repeated and largely unsuccessful attempts were made to arouse enthusiasm for various BPC demonstrations and rallies, all of which aimed at securing the

[6] This orthodoxy has been modified considerably since the late 1960s with the development of Eurocommunist perspectives.

[7] Frank Parkin, *Middle Class Radicalism: The Social Bases of the British Campaign for Nuclear Disarmament*, Manchester, 1968, p. 92. (Such radical middle-class involvement has, of course, become much more prevalent since the 1960s.)

[8] *Daily Worker*, 5 and 8 Apr. 1958. (But note the CP 'gloss' put on CND's demands. The reports also gave undue emphasis to the British Peace Committee's involvement.)

elusive Labour Movement unity behind the peace campaign. A special effort was made to boost the British Peace Committee's 'March for Life' held in London on 28 May 1959. For several weeks preceding this rally a relentless public relations exercise was undertaken by the *Daily Worker*: new celebrities were brought forward day by day, all declaring their fullest support for the March, and extravagant claims were made for the extent of its support: 'A Million Now Backing March!'[9] The event, from which CND carefully distanced itself, proved somewhat of an anticlimax: the *Daily Worker* bravely claimed that Trafalgar Square was packed 'with over 30,000 people. . . . This was a March mainly of working people',[10] but it was generally agreed, even in CP circles, that the 'March for Life' had failed to capture the numbers or the enthusiasm of the ever-growing CND, and it is significant that the Party never again attempted seriously to compete with CND.

At this stage the CP modified its policy. In the text of the resolution adopted in Trafalgar Square, the emphasis was still upon stopping nuclear tests and campaigning for a Summit Meeting, but there was also a commitment to asking Britain '*to take the initiative for agreement to end the manufacture of nuclear weapons*, to destroy stocks, and to renounce their use, *being prepared if necessary itself to set the example*' (my emphasis). This is the first tangible sign of the change of attitude to CND and its policy of unilateralism which was to follow later in 1959 and 1960.

It is inaccurate to claim, as Parkin has,[11] that 'in May 1960 . . . a sudden switch . . . was made directly by the Executive Committee without any internal Party discussion'. The 'full change' was accomplished then; but it was begun, almost imperceptibly, by the change in policy implied in the May 1959 'March for Life' declaration, and substantially spelled out in a major policy statement by the British Peace Committee, reported in the *Daily Worker* of 7 July 1959, which reaffirmed the BPC's opposition to British nuclear weapons, and welcomed the demand for an end to the manufacture of the bomb in Britain, but pointed out that, for this to be effective, it must be coupled with the withdrawal of US rockets and H-bomb bases from Britain. Immediately after this the TGWU at its conference carried a resolution which, although somewhat complicated in its expression and implications, was effectively unilateralist and

---

[9] *Daily Worker*, 26 May 1959. (This refers to trade union and similar representative bodies which pledged their memberships in support.)

[10] *Daily Worker*, 29 May 1959.   [11] Parkin, op. cit., 81.

clearly opposed to the Labour Party's official policy. The CP reacted swiftly and, in a special report of 12 July 1959, the Party came out firmly in support of the TGWU policy. The *Daily Worker* editorial next day reflected a change of emphasis towards unilateralism: 'only when the British government breaks with nuclear strategy, stops tests and stops manufacturing the bomb will it be in a position to influence events and to secure the banning of the bomb on an international scale.'[12] And, following this, the *Daily Worker* indulged in a concerted campaign in support of the TGWU and against the Labour leadership over nuclear weapons policy.

The CP's two most basic objections to full support for CND had thus been neutralized by events. With the TGWU (and other trade unions during 1959) moving towards a unilateralist stance—and combining this with a heavy insistence on a test ban, the removal of US bases and the need for a summit to secure international agreement—there could no longer be any doubt about the increasing involvement of the organized working class in the general unilateralist Movement. Even more important was the related point of 'unity': far from the TGWU package resolution being regarded as 'maximalist', the CP, rightly, took it as a unifying call around which, during 1959 and 1960, all the forces within the Labour Movement opposed to the bomb could be gathered.

In the aftermath of the decisive Labour Party defeat in the 1959 general election, the conflict between the right-wing leadership and the left increased rapidly. In the meantime, too, CND's support grew apace. By mid-1960, with the cancellation of Blue Streak and the consequent change in the context of the whole defence debate, the divisions and the level of feeling had intensified. From the point of view of 'left unity' and the possible capture of the Labour Party by the putative 'left alliance', it was essential to have both maximum trade union support for the TGWU resolution and maximum CND/Labour left support in the constituencies. In order to achieve this and to bring 'left unity' fully to fruition, the CP came out four-square behind CND in May 1960, encouraging its members to participate fully and actively in the Campaign.[13]

[12] *Daily Worker*, 13 July 1959.
[13] Secretary Gollan's statement to the executive committee of the CP (reported in the *Daily Worker* on 16 May 1960) outlined in some detail both the contents of the 'new policy' and the reasons for its adoption. The policy was officially adopted by the political committee in June 1960. The policy placed at the head of its list of demands the unilateral renunciation by Britain of the manufacture and use of nuclear weapons and the closure of all the American bases in Britain.

The CP thus achieved its initial political objective in 1960, when a united left faced the right-wing leadership at the Labour conference—and won the day. Secretary Gollan, in his report to the twenty-seventh congress of the CP in 1961, stressed the strategy of 'left unity' and its success. But, like others with a Labour Movement/parliamentarist perspective, the CP had no alternative strategy to propose when it became clear in 1961 that the Gaitskellite leadership had finally triumphed on the nuclear issue. The CP's policy and strategy was based absolutely upon the 'left unity' principle and the need to mobilize the organized working-class movement behind its policy demands. Thus the CP had even less in common with the direct action wing of the Peace Movement than had the CND leadership. At no stage did the CP consider giving *active* support to the Committee of 100. Indeed, it was always particularly ill at ease with the DAC and Committee of 100: full coverage was given to Committee of 100 activities in the *Daily Worker* but little attempt was made to come to grips with the nature and objectives of the direct action wing of the Movement. As George Matthews later recalled, 'we were never terribly keen on the Committee of 100. We would have felt happier to have had developments through the CND.'[14]

The CP has always seen the Disarmament Movement in a dual role: first, as a single-issue campaign in its own right, to be steered within the parameters outlined; and second, as a part of the 'grand design' of left unity—a part of the generalized campaign of the left against the control of the right.

This second objective rapidly faded as the right re-established its political control over the Labour Party following the reversal of the Scarborough decision in 1961. The CP's involvement in the Peace Movement, and hence its commitment to CND, became increasingly one of many commitments to left-orientated pressure groups, and not *the* major concern. The first role remained, however: once fully committed to CND as a single-issue campaign, the CP, whether or not for the overall benefit of CND, has remained remarkably consistent and diligent in its support.[15]

---

[14] Matthews, in conversation.

[15] Although of course differing markedly in their own perspectives, almost all the other major strands of opinion in the Movement were deeply critical and suspicious of the CP. As far as the leadership of CND was concerned, views on the CP ranged from outright hostility and opposition to a resigned tolerance. (This was confirmed

THE COMMUNIST PARTY AND CND: SOME CONCLUSIONS

During 1958–65 the CP never wielded decisive influence in CND—both critics and supporters are agreed about that at least[16]—but after 1960 the CP claimed, with some justification, to have had a significant impact in bringing about the more comprehensively left political climate of opinion in CND. The CP was not decisive in bringing about the 1960 Labour conference decision, but it helped. Similarly, the Party was not instrumental by any means in bringing CND around to the notion of a formal commitment to withdrawal from NATO in 1960—this was due far more to a combination of New Left and Labour left pressure—but its political perspective did add weight in that direction.

The CP's was thus rarely if ever the decisive voice, but its influence was felt. However, CND policies, even after the change to active CND support by the CP in 1959–60, were not always in line with those of the CP. On the contrary, as Parkin and others have pointed out, decisions such as the 1964 CND conference resolution to call upon 'the Soviet Union and the United States to disarm unilaterally, and urging internal resistance to the Bomb in these two countries'[17] were clearly at variance with the CP's own stance. But the overall tenor of the Campaign—a more politically orientated Movement committed to an anti-NATO, anti-American policy, and intent (at least as far as the leadership was concerned) on working

by several leading CND figures in conversation with author in 1978: Jacquetta Hawkes, Canon Collins, Peggy Duff, and Arthur Goss, amongst others.)

The views of the other Marxist groups on the CP's policy in relation to CND were, as might be expected, more hostile, and more central to their own conception of the Disarmament Movement as a whole. For the International Socialists, for example, the CP's change of line in 1959–60 to support for CND was 'just a further example of its unprincipled policy on the Bomb. . . . This is not because the CP has changed its position fundamentally on the H-Bomb. It merely means that they saw the mounting support throughout the country for CND and thought, for opportunist reasons, it would be a good thing to get on the fast-moving bandwagon.' CP policy on the bomb had, it was argued, been determined since 1945 by the perceived interests of the Russian rulers. 'The Communist Party has reeled to and fro like a drunken man. But the poison has not been alcohol—it has been Stalinism' (Raymond Challinor, 'Zigzag: The CP and the Bomb', *International Socialism*, 3, winter 1960–1).

[16] However, Nigel Young has claimed that the CP, whose build-up of influence had begun after 1963, had, by 'the mid-1960s, virtual control over the CND national office, its newspaper and its major committees' (Nigel Young, *An Infantile Disorder? The Crisis and Decline of the New Left*, London, 1977, p. 155).

[17] Parkin, op.cit., 84.

through and with the Labour Movement—was very much in keeping with the CP thinking and ethos.

Although the CP had had a somewhat ambivalent attitude to nuclear weapons in the 1940s, from the early 1950s the Party campaigned consistently for peace through international disarmament via summit meetings between the major powers. But there is substance in the familiar claim that the CP has always been dominated, in its Peace Movement activities as elsewhere, by its marked pro-Soviet stance. To some extent the CP has not denied this: it has not claimed to be 'neutralist' in the sense that the New Left so claimed.[18] In the context of the CND campaign this made the CP always uneasy about the uncompromising condemnation by CND of *all* tests and *all* nuclear weapons. The CP's left unity tactics for the Peace Movement were thus tempered to a considerable extent by its own ideological parameters.

As argued earlier, the fundamental reason for the CP's decision to give full backing to CND's unilateralism was the decisive shift of opinion towards unilateralism within the Labour Movement during 1959 and 1960. In particular, the decisions of the trade unions in support of unilateralism convinced the CP that, tactically, unilateralism was the issue around which to mobilize left unity within the Labour Movement. This was thus a tactical decision rather than a principled conversion to unilateralism, but, given the ideological assumptions of the CP's position, it was a perfectly justifiable, genuine, and legitimate policy development.

The CP saw CND as essentially another branch of the Peace Movement that needed to be brought more closely into the mainstream of Labour Movement politics. The CP saw no useful role for *any* organization in the social and political field outside this context: and it withheld its full support from CND during its early years precisely because, on various criteria, it failed to match up to these requirements. The CP thus had, despite its superficially eclectic world view of politics and the struggle for peace, an essentially restricted and static view of CND's role. Because it was unwilling, and probably unable, to break out of its orthodox strategic and ideological framework, the CP never really understood those important dimensions of the Disarmament Movement which were characterized by a commitment to direct action as the central

---

[18] George Matthews made it quite clear that the CP did not favour the neutralist approach of the New Left (Matthews, in conversation).

organizing concept, and to the mass, extra-parliamentary Movement as the vehicle for achieving radical change. Despite its rather earnest support, and the willingness of its members to undertake a lot of the routine CND work, the CP thus made a relatively modest impact on the Movement. In many ways the Movement was too big and too wide—both numerically and ideologically—for the CP to hope to dominate it. The fact that the CP never managed in the 1958–64 period to assume dominance of the Movement, and never really appreciated its full potential, was indicative perhaps of the ideological and strategic conservatism that has characterized the Party's overall political approach for many years.

THE SOCIALIST LABOUR LEAGUE

The Socialist Labour League (SLL) in its early days (and, before it came formally into existence in February 1959, its predecessor the *Newsletter* group) gave full support to CND.[19] This was of course linked to the political struggle: *Newsletter* worked within the Labour Party for the overthrow of the right-wing leadership, and it was in fact a Trotskyist, Vivienne Mendelson, who moved the unilateral disarmament resolution at the 1957 Labour Party conference. The paper was deeply critical of Bevan and all that he stood for, placed no reliance on international diplomacy, and consistently opposed the CP policy of 'summit talks'. Rather, emphasis was placed upon 'the British working class [using] its industrial and political strength' to bring about 'the immediate cessation of the [H-bomb's] manufacture'.[20]

As orthodox Trotskyists, the *Newsletter* group, and later the SLL, was highly critical of the Soviet Union: 'The Soviet leaders, following the basic line of Stalinism in foreign policy, have abandoned working-class internationalism and rely on the H-Bomb and diplomacy, not working-class struggle, to defend the USSR against imperialism.'[21] On the other hand, accepting Trotsky's categorization of the Soviet Union as a 'degenerated workers' state', the group argued that the USSR, despite its manifest shortcomings, had to be defended from the 'imperialist powers' and had the right to maintain nuclear weapons.

[19] Indeed, in terms of specific policy concerns the nuclear issue had been predominant in the *Newsletter* from its beginnings: the first issue carried the headline 'H-Bomb Tests: The Scientific Facts' (*Newsletter*, 10 May 1957).

[20] Ibid., 25 Jan. 1958   [21] Ibid., 1 Mar. 1958.

Trotskyists had no faith whatever in the potential for reformist change in Western society, and they despised and opposed the CP both for its reformism and for its adherence to the USSR. All efforts had therefore to be directed to building the alternative, revolutionary socialist, political party, concentrating upon rank-and-file trade unionist, working-class activists rather than on the trade union bureaucracies and the élite groups which, the Trotskyists maintained, were the CP's 'bureaucratized' points of contact with the working class.

Within this context the *Newsletter*/SLL group saw the unilateralist campaign of CND as a major opportunity for mobilizing political forces *outside* the conventional political arena on an issue which could command substantial support. From the outset the SLL emphasized that only the organized working-class movement, engaging in direct action industrially and politically, could bring success to CND's campaign. Thus, whilst supportive of CND's initiative, the *Newsletter* pointed out that 'one element is missing from the "moral lead" of the CND. That element is working-class internationalism.'[22]

The SLL conducted a consistent campaign around the slogan 'Black the H-bomb! Black the bases!' Only through industrial action could the movement against the bomb really begin to bite. Thus Peter Fryer, in a speech to Aldermaston marchers in 1959, reported in the *Newsletter*, exhorted the Campaign to adopt a more militant approach. 'Is Aldermaston to become a yearly catharsis for the middle-class conscience, an act of ritual mortification and sacrifice, till one day good miraculously triumphs over evil?'[23]

Unlike the CP, then, the *Newsletter* group, and the SLL in its early days, was drawn towards the DAC, despite a fundamental division over ideology: the idea of appealing, over the heads of trade union and right-wing Labour bureaucracies, directly to the workers to take action themselves to oppose nuclear weapons, was attractive to the militants of the Trotskyist movement.

On the specific question of the DAC, Peter Cadogan, at that stage an SLL activist, had strong views.

The DAC has gone so far, but can go no further on its own . . . CND and DAC are both led by the very best type of middle-class people—they see protest as essentially an individual matter. The Quaker tradition of

[22] Ibid., 22 Mar. 1958
[23] Ibid., 4 Apr. 1959.

individual protest and suffering is strong among them. They are moved by silence, the struggle within the soul, and against any tyranny from without ... of necessity the working-class has a different outlook. Its values are those of mass organization and the need to free society from the isolation between individuals. . . . If Pat Arrowsmith and the DAC are to continue to set the pace in the anti-H-bomb fight, they must understand the impossibility of appealing to the working-class by middle-class methods.[24]

But, from early 1959, the SLL in fact began to move away from close involvement in the Disarmament Movement, for political reasons related neither to CND nor to DAC but rather to internal Trotskyist ideology and strategy.[25] From the relatively tolerant, eclectic, and quasi-libertarian interpretation of Trotskyism espoused by Peter Fryer and the early *Newsletter*, the SLL, under Healy's control, rapidly assumed a rigid, vanguardist structure and sectarian ideology. A part of the process of turning the SLL into a more disciplined and 'hard-line' political force was the toughening up of the attitude to CND and the DAC/Committee of 100. Thus, for example, on the occasion of the Soviet resumption of nuclear tests in 1961 when the Committee of 100 held a demonstration outside the Soviet Embassy, the SLL took a very critical line. In September 1961, Gerry Healy wrote:

it took three years for the leaders of CND to become 'respectable'; it has only taken a little over three months for the Committee of 100. Their marches and demonstrations outside the Soviet Embassy are typical reminders of the age-old fact that during a critical period pacifism, which rejects the class struggle, always helps imperialism to mobilize the working-class for war.[26]

[24] Peter Cadogan, ibid., 17 Mar. 1959. Cadogan was expelled from the SLL in November 1959, and Peter Fryer resigned shortly afterwards. For details of the dispute see the *Newsletter* during Nov. and Dec. 1959 and Jan. 1960. Cadogan was, later, an important figure in the Committee of 100 (see ch. 5).

Although the DAC and the SLL had a certain amount in common in assumptions and analysis (mainly negative critiques of various bodies and strategies), there was a quite unbridgeable *ideological* gap. With very few exceptions the activists of the DAC did not link their campaign to any wider socialist strategy. More specifically, the DAC activists rejected entirely the concepts of class conflict and the vanguard party which were at the heart of the Trotskyists' ideological framework. It would not be a great exaggeration to say that the politics of the SLL were as alien to the DAC as the politics of the Conservative Party.

[25] Principally the determination of Gerry Healy, the SLL's leading figure, to create a new political force for Trotskyism in the SLL following the proscription by the Labour Party of both the *Newsletter* and the SLL in early 1959.

[26] *Newsletter*, 9 Sep. 1961.

By 1963 this attitude had hardened still further, and Jack Gale could write: 'to call today for the "utmost unity" in the Peace Movement, as the *Daily Worker* does, is totally wrong. Without a decisive break with all forms of pacifism, the movement against nuclear weapons will fizzle out.'[27]

The SLL was thus an isolated force in the Disarmament Movement: it had a policy and perspective diametrically opposed to both the CND leadership and the CP; despite some initial common ground with direct actionists there was in reality little, if anything, in common between the SLL and DAC/Committee of 100—and the debate between them soon turned to mutual acrimony; and its advocacy of the 'workers' bomb' put the SLL in an isolated, incongruous, and somewhat ridiculous position, providing a heaven-sent opportunity for the anti-Communists to point to what 'all Communists really wanted'. Most important of all, the SLL's consistent and dramatic appeals to the rank-and-file workers to take unofficial action to stop arms production failed totally (the only success in this whole campaign, and that was marginal, must be credited to the DAC's Pat Arrowsmith). The SLL campaign to win round CND, or even a substantial section of CND, to its policy thus failed almost totally.

Over and above its involvement in the Young Socialists, was the SLL important in the Movement? There are several reasons for asserting that the SLL had some significance in this context, albeit ancillary to the mainstream Movement. Despite all its manifest shortcomings, the early SLL did represent one of the first attempts to break with prevailing Cold War orthodoxies. And the SLL was the only one of the Marxist groups[28] to make a serious attempt in the early days to link main-line Marxism with the direct action militancy of the Campaign's radical wing. With hindsight the attempt can perhaps be seen as doomed to failure from the outset: the ideological gulf was too wide. But the clarification of perspectives that resulted from the interchange of polemics was important both for an understanding of the Movement at the time and for the attempt at subsequent analysis. Finally, the concerted attempts by the SLL (and the DAC) to stimulate *working-class* direct action provided a unique dimension to the

[27] Ibid., 20 Apr. 1963.
[28] *Solidarity* is excluded: although Marxist in origin and in its analytical framework, it was so heavily libertarian in its approach that it is best considered in the context of the Committee of 100 (see ch. 5). IS also made some attempt to make links with the Committee of 100 in 1960–1 (see below).

Campaign. In the virtual absence of CP advocacy of working-class industrial action, it was the SLL activists who took the lead in trying to instil nuclear campaign militancy amongst the rank-and-file workers. Their failure in this aim did not render the attempt unimportant, but rather underlined the wider problems inherent in involving the working class in the Movement.

INTERNATIONAL SOCIALISM

In many ways there were similarities between the SLL and IS in their attitude to the Disarmament Movement. Both organizations based their unilateralist campaigns on attracting the working class; both were highly critical of the CND leadership for its non-political stance; both were Trotskyist in orientation and origin[29]—and as a consequence of this general perspective both were deeply hostile to the CP.

IS was highly critical of the Labour leadership, and of the belief prevalent in Labour left circles that CND's aims could be achieved through Party conference resolutions, and this paralleled the SLL's critical attitude to the Labour Party. But IS, in relation to CND, always placed emphasis on developing a *political* movement against the bomb, whilst the SLL, as has been argued, concentrated upon the *industrial* struggle and the central role of the industrial working class. 'The heterogeneous coalition which comprises CND makes it impossible to commit itself to a political issue outside defence unless it can be approached *through* the question of the bomb.'[30] Such an ideological stance, it was argued, distorted the proper analysis of capitalism, making the bomb the cause of the situation rather than the product of a particular socio-economic system. What was the function of the arms establishment within the capitalist system?

It was in relation to this point, perhaps, that IS made its most important contribution to the theoretical analysis of the relationship between capitalism and the bomb. All Marxists accept that

[29] IS (since 1977 the Socialist Workers' Party) has highly unorthodox ideological origins and policies, from a Trotskyist point of view. The original defining characteristic of the *Socialist Review* group, the forerunner of IS, was the adherence to the analysis of the USSR as a 'State capitalist' society. (See Tony Cliff, *Russia: A Marxist Analysis*, London, International Socialism, 1970.

[30] Dave Peers, *International Socialism*, 12, spring 1963.

there is a *structural* link between the capitalist system and the development of nuclear weapons. With the CP this has been couched in traditional Leninist categories of imperalist competition, and with the SLL the assertion of the connection was made with little or no attempt at analysing the nature of the connection in any depth. However, IS developed the theory of the 'permanent arms economy' to explain *structurally* the phenomenon of nuclear weapons and the huge increase in armaments spending, by East and West, since the War. Essentially the theory, couched within orthodox Marxist economic concepts, held that the development of the armaments industry was at base a response by the State to the inherent economic instability of capitalism. 'Arms production while decreasing productive capacity mops up unemployment and offers outlets for investment and in so doing stabilises the economy.'[31] The struggle against nuclear weapons was therefore inextricably linked to the struggle against the economic system *per se*: without the destruction of this system, nuclear disarmament could never be achieved. And this linkage between 'the State and the Bomb' applied to the communist East as much as the capitalist West. The permanent arms economy theory thus added further weight to IS's contention concerning the 'State capitalist' nature of the USSR, and the need for socialists to divorce themselves entirely from identification with the USSR's position in the Cold War struggle.

Subsequent analysis, and indeed political events and processes, have resulted in a considerable modification of the theory in its pure form, and Michael Kidron himself has revised his view of the centrality given in the theory to arms production within the contemporary capitalist structure. Nevertheless the theory made a lasting impact, and its influence was felt not only at the time and subsequently in IS, but in wider and later socialist conceptions of the nature of the arms race and the Cold War.[32]

Most Marxists would perhaps agree with Stuart Hall's judge-

[31] David Yaffé, 'The Marxian Theory of Crisis, Capital and the State', *Economy and Society*, 2. 2, May 1973. The full version of the theory, formulated by Michael Kidron, is to be found in his *Western Capitalism Since the War*, London, 1970. For a discussion and explication of the theory, and critiques of it by Yaffé and others, see Richard Taylor, 'The Permanent Arms Economy Theory', appendix to ch. 5, *The British Nuclear Disarmament Movement of 1958 to 1965 and its Legacy to the Left*, Ph.D. thesis, University of Leeds, 1983, pp. 448–53.

[32] E. P. Thompson's theory of 'exterminism', for example, owes something to the notion of the 'permanent arms economy'. See E. P. Thompson *et al.*, *Exterminism and Cold War*, London, 1982.

ment that, although subsequently shown to be fundamentally incorrect, the theory may well have 'played a pivotal part in thinking about those essentially *war*-orientated economies becoming essentially *peace*-orientated ones . . . it's not that it's not important, but he made it the single, central explicator for everything, which I think was not true.'[33]

This is not to say that IS had any real light to shed upon the basic strategic problem of the Disarmament Movement: that is, how to get its policies adopted and put into practice. Given its Marxist perspective, IS was firmly wedded to a Labour Movement orientation; given also its minuscule size in the early 1960s, it had no alternative to offer, at least in the short term, other than working through the Labour Party. And it was this advice—for CND supporters to join the Labour Party *en masse*—that was indeed offered, albeit with less than total enthusiasm and commitment, by IS in 1961.

IS was, though, in practice more interested in and hopeful about the development of the civil disobedience campaign of the Committee of 100. Although never so closely involved with the specifically industrial campaign as the SLL, IS, in common with the New Left, took a more optimistic and eclectic view of the Committee of 100 as a radical organization, and of civil disobedience as a tactic.[34]

This view of civil disobedience was indicative of the links, in the early years, between IS, the New Left, and the Peace Movement. There was a considerable overlap of both ideology and people between these three groups: it would in fact be a mistake to view the small IS organization at this time as a completely separate force. In these years (although not later) IS was not a sectarian organization: it was relatively open, and relatively unconcerned with 'discipline' and 'organization'. Thus, although it would be wrong to suggest that IS was ever anything other than a firmly committed Marxist group, there was something of a shared ethos between IS and the Disarmament Movement, and their relationship was therefore of a different order from that of other Communist and Trotskyist groupings.

---

[33] Stuart Hall, in conversation with the author, Mar. 1978.

[34] See e.g. Notes of the Quarter, *International Socialism*, 5, summer 1961, where it was noted that, despite some disadvantages, civil disobedience reminded people 'that politics is not all talking', and that the State is not neutral (and that the South Wales miners had been involved in the Ministry of Defence 'sit-down'). 'The moral for socialists is clear: sit-down—without illusions.'

On specific policy issues two distinctive themes stand out: the analysis of Soviet Russia and the attitude to positive neutralism. Both policy stances had direct relevance to IS's perspective on the Disarmament Movement. The original dinstinguishing feature of IS had been its attitude to the Soviet Union. Under Stalinism there had developed, it was argued, a new ruling class, the party bureaucracy, whose power base resided in its control of both the political machine and the collectivized economy. The USSR was thus accurately described neither as socialist (as by the Communist Party), nor as 'degenerated workers' state' (as by the SLL) but as 'State capitalist'.

IS shared with other Marxists a belief in the imperialist threat of a nuclear America, and wished to see Britain unilaterally disarm and withdraw from NATO. But, unlike both the CP and the SLL, IS had no hesitation in condemning the USSR, its military policy, and its possession of the bomb. The IS slogan 'neither Washington nor Moscow but International Socialism', although resulting from a very different background of analysis, did represent the 'plague on both your houses' attitude that was central to the mainstream ethos of the Disarmament Movement, and which linked IS's socialism to the 'positive neutralism' concept of the wider Movement.[35]

IS had very little political strength or importance in relation to the Disarmament Movement: *all* the leaders of the Movement who were interviewed for this study regarded IS as an unimportant, almost non-existent influence on CND. However, its *theoretical* contribution to the debate on the bomb was considerable. Both in terms of its permanent arms economy theory and in terms of the formulation of the positive neutralist approach, IS attempted to achieve some genuine fusion between the Disarmament Movement and the far left. And, in its willingness to accept civil disobedience as a positive and legitimate development, it illustrated a more flexible and realistic political attitude than was the case with the other Marxist groupings.

Nevertheless, the interrelationship between the Peace Movement and the Trotskyist left as a whole in this period was minimal. Not until the resurgence of the Peace Movement in the 1980s, when such groups—and in particular the Socialist Workers' Party (formerly IS)—had become far stronger, did the Trotskyist left have

---

[35] And from this came IS's commitment to a 'positive socialist neutralism'. See e.g. *International Socialism*, 5, summer 1961, for a delineation of this position.

any significant impact on the politics and policies of the Peace Movement.

THE NEW LEFT

The New Left (hereafter NL)[36] was a major influence on the thinking of the Disarmament Movement. 'More than any other element in the politics of unilateralism this group belonged to its time.'[37] Unlike any of the other political groupings considered (including the Labour Party as well as the Marxist groups), the NL put unilateralism as a policy and CND as a Movement at the centre of its political programme. The NL had no formal membership, no constitution, no official 'party' programme (and no aspirations to become the Leninist vanguard party). The NL was thus very much like CND in its organizational format—or perhaps more its *lack* of organizational format. It was as much a generalized ethos, an attitude, as it was a set of specific political theories and policies.[38]

Of what did this 'ethos' consist and how did it relate specifically to the Disarmament Movement? The explanation lies in the two mainsprings of NL development: the group of ex-CP members around the *New Reasoner* (NR) and the 'unattached' young radicals of the *Universities and Left Review* (ULR). The *NR* evolved from *The Reasoner*, a duplicated journal published by two university lecturers from Yorkshire, Edward Thompson and John Saville, both members of the CP. *The Reasoner* was published (first issue July 1956) following correspondence in the CP journal *World News* and the *Daily Worker*, with the intention of linking up those

[36] It is important to define the New Left. In the late 1960s and early 1970s a second New Left, concentrated initially around the Vietnam and student movements, came into being, and some of the revolutionary groups involved grew relatively quickly. But this 'New Left' was a quite different phenomenon from the movement of the late 1950s and early 1960s and lies outside the scope of this study. Nor is it intended to consider the *New Left Review* group of Anderson, Nairn *et al.*, which assumed dominance of the journal in 1962–3, and developed it as a major forum for the discussion and articulation of contemporary Marxist theory and analysis. The New Left which will be analysed here consisted of the groupings around the *Universities and Left Review* (ULR) and *New Reasoner* (published from 1957 to 1960) and their successor, the *New Left Review* (NLR) between 1960 and 1963.
[37] Christopher Driver, *The Disarmers*, London, 1964, p. 73.
[38] This is not say, of course, that the NL was concerned only with generalities— far from it. It became 'the think-tank' of CND, with Stuart Hall in particular producing major policy statements.

in the CP who were critical of the rigidities of 'Stalinist democratic centralism . . . our objective, until the repression of the Hungarian insurrection, was to *change the Party*: to which we had an intense (if diminishing) loyalty.'[39]

The editors refused a request from the CP to cease publication, and were suspended. When the Hungarian insurrection was suppressed many members left the Party. 'Since more than half our readership had now left the Party, we decided not to fight our suspension but to leave with them.'[40]

The *NR*, although now published by *ex*-CP members, was very much in the 'old left' mould—at least at the beginning. The fact that Thompson and Saville were both Labour historians is almost as significant as the fact that both had been until 1957 CP members. The insistence that the NL must not jettison the relationship— theoretical and practical—with the Labour Movement was as much due to a 'sense of history', and to their commitment to the radical, working-class tradition embodying the values of democratic socialism, as it was to any rigid application of orthodox Marxist analysis. Nevertheless, until its merger with *ULR* to form *New Left Review* (NLR) in 1960, the *NR* 'maintained a dissident-Communist identity of sorts . . . with the merger the *NR* gave up certain formal attributes of ex-Communism, for instance its tendency to lapse into roll-calls of the Marxist great'. This Communist tradition 'brought into the fusion far more than it shed: an explicit commitment to class-struggle, an iteration of the role of human agency as against impersonal historic process',[41] *and* an adherence to a Labourist strategy.

From the beginning the *NR* was in favour of British withdrawal from NATO, unilateral nuclear disarmament, and the adoption of a neutralist foreign policy. In an editorial of spring 1958, Saville and Thompson argued that 'all talk of sweeping socialist advances in the next few years is unrealistic unless it starts from this premiss: there is no way forward until the international deadlock is broken'. The international theme—the need to end the Cold War and develop a neutralist bloc—was linked to the international role of British Labour—the opportunity for Britain to take the lead

---

[39] E. P. Thompson in a letter to Mr Risher, 18 Nov. 1976, in reply to an article in *FS Newsletter*.

[40] Ibid.

[41] Peter Sedgwick, 'The Two New Lefts', in David Widgery, *The Left in Britain 1956–1968*, London, 1976, p. 135.

through unilateral nuclear disarmament, a withdrawal from NATO, and the espousal of a neutralist foreign policy. NATO was always seen as central. 'The fig-leaf which Mr Bevan holds on to so desperately turns out to be—not the H-bomb at all—but NATO and the American alliance. . . . We must make a choice between NATO and the unmapped policy of positive neutrality.'[42]

A further dimension to the *NR*'s advocacy of neutralism was its conviction that through a unilateralist initiative 'Britain could again lead the world'. It will be recalled that this was one of the keynotes of J. B. Priestley's *New Statesman* article, which was the immediate cause of CND's coming into being. The *NR* group's commitment to Britain's 'moral lead' was based on not altogether dissimilar assumptions. Thompson argued in the *New Reasoner* in 1958 that it was essential that 'our destiny should not be left indefinitely in American or Russian (or Polish or Hungarian) hands. It is now our turn to move . . . our turn because the world waits for someone to move.'

It was the guiding principle of moral revolt, in which the 'struggle for democratic and social rights has always been intertwined', that brought together Thompson's and the *NR*'s belief that the essentially *moral* campaign of the Disarmament Movement could be fused with the radical tradition of the British Labour Movement, to produce a major innovative force on the radical left. The actual *form* of neutralism advocated by the *NR* and, later, by others in the NL was, as can be seen now if not then, all too sanguine in its implicit assumptions of the good (socialist) faith of many regimes, subsequently seen to have been anything but progressive, let alone dedicated to humanistic Marxism.[43] Nevertheless, the NL was close

[42] *New Reasoner*, spring 1958. The NL was of key importance in persuading CND to adopt as policy, in 1960, withdrawal from NATO. However, it is significant that, whereas the NL's main reason for demanding withdrawal was its ideological commitment to positive neutralism, most CND and Committee of 100 supporters were motivated to give support to such a policy because of the perceived illogicality of a unilaterally disarmed Britain remaining within a nuclear alliance.

[43] The fullest statement of the NL position on 'positive neutralism' is contained in Peter Worsley's 'Imperialism in Retreat': [Britain could] generate immense pressure, in alliance with India, Ghana, Yugoslavia and backed by the uncommitted countries, for world peace and active neutrality. And most of these uncommitted nations are countries which could, under such stimulus, move towards socialism . . . India, Austria, Israel, Indonesia, Ghana to name a few . . . not forming another frozen bloc, but trading and communicating freely, gradually breaking down the barriers on both sides'. Worsley, 'Imperialism in Retreat', in E. P. Thompson (ed.), *Out of Apathy*, London, 1960.

in spirit to CND—or certainly its more radical elements—and there were links to the ideology of the DAC. As Thompson claimed, the NL 'champions a new internationalism which is not that of the triumph of one camp over the other, but the dissolution of the camps and the triumph of the common people'.[44]

If the *NR* was still firmly within the Marxist tradition, albeit emphasizing a 'new' humanistic, non-aligned interpretation, the early *ULR* group was not of such orthodox lineage. Peter Sedgwick has characterized the *NR* as the representative of the 'political' concerns of the NL 'as against the pretensions of its chief rival, which may be called Socio-Culture'.[45] The *ULR* activists, who were largely students or radical intellectuals,[46] had close links—politically, personally, and in terms of age and outlook—with the DAC. They were part of the 'Aldermaston generation' to which Thompson referred: those who

> never looked upon the Soviet Union as a weak but heroic Workers' State; but, rather, as the nation of the Great Purges and of Stalingrad . . . their enthusiasm is not for the [Labour] party, or the movement, or the established political leaders . . . they prefer the amateur organization and the amateurish platform of the CND to the method and manner of the Left-Wing professional.[47]

If the *NR* provided the Labour Movement and Marxist experience and, substantially, the bedrock of *political* theory for the NL, the *ULR* fulfilled the equally central role of providing a bridge to non-Marxist but left-orientated students and radicals, and to the rapidly growing radical pacifist movement. It was the *ULR* group that thus provided 'the English NL [with] a conscience during its short early life'.[48]

It is also important to note that not all those involved in these early *ULR* activities were Marxists, orthodox or otherwise. Many of the people who flocked to the 'Partisan' coffee-house and to the NL clubs in the early days were drawn, not to Marxism, humanistic or otherwise, but to a new kind of politics.

However, Stuart Hall has stressed too the very real *political* orientation of the *ULR* group.[49] The aim was to dominate CND

---

[44] *New Reasoner*, summer 1959.   [45] Sedgwick, op cit., 136.
[46] Its editorial board was exclusively student/academic and included Stuart Hall, Gabriel Pearson, and Chuck Taylor.
[47] *New Reasoner*, spring 1958.   [48] Young, op. cit., 145.
[49] Hall, in conversation.

politically and intellectually rather than organizationally: there was in fact a quite deliberate tactic of 'entrism', not with the intention of 'subverting' the Movement but rather with the open and declared aim of winning over CND to NL ideas and policies. As Hall pointed out, NATO was in many ways the key practical political issue for the *ULR* group, and it was symbolic of the wider politics which the whole NL stood for. British membership of NATO was the major link between the predominantly *moral* campaign against nuclear weapons, and the predominantly *political* analysis of the left which argued for a change to socialism and a rejection of the entanglement of Britain in the American system of alliances. Moreover, the NATO issue, and its positive corollary, the commitment to an active neutralist politics, brought the two wings of the NL movement into close agreement, both ideologically and practically. Both the *NR* and the *ULR* groups were thus of one mind in their commitment to the primacy of the NATO/positive neutralist issue. (In this sense, therefore, it would be mistaken to conceive of the ULR group as being politically softer, more naïve, and outmanoeuvred by the older, more politically experienced ex-CP members of the *NR*.)

Given this increasing liaison and co-operation of both ideology and short- to medium-term political goals, plus the different constituencies that the two groups had the potential to mobilize for political involvement, it was almost inevitable that some more formal collaborative structure should emerge. The merger came in late 1959, following discussions initiated by the *NR*, and the first issue of *NLR*, under the editorship of Stuart Hall, appeared in January 1960.[50]

The concern with 'conventional' politics as exemplified by the *NLR*'s neutralist policy, contrasted with the *ULR*'s earlier and less structured approach, not in the sense of supporting conventional political policies and objectives (NATO and so on), but in the more fundamental sense of the conceptual framework of political thought within which policies were formulated: in this context, thinking in nation State, diplomatic, and international relations terms, and in the orthodox organizational forms of parliamentarism

---

[50] In 1963, after disagreements within the NL and the subsequent sale of the journal, the editorial personnel was changed radically. Henceforth Anderson, Blackburn, Nairn *et al.* took over the journal, and it changed rapidly from an activist orientation to more abstract and intellectual concerns.

and party politics. The legacy of the CP perspective on foreign policy, and politics generally, was writ large in the NL: again, the political arguments, whilst not acceptable to all on the Labour left, were couched in the same political context. For very different reasons, both the far left and the Committee of 100 rejected the suppositions of the argument, as well as the specific policies themselves.

This drift back to a more orthodox politics was evident in the discussion and policy documents produced by the *NLR* in the early 1960s on the specific problems and orientations of CND itself.[51] Although the *ULR* group had been close to the DAC, the early 1960s saw a fragmentation of the New Left/direct action axis. As the NL became, through 1961 and 1962, more and more wedded to a Labour left perspective—and the Committee, after the relative failure of the Wethersfield demonstration, and the Offical Secrets trial, came more and more under neo-anarchist influence—so the distance between the two formations grew and became unbridgeable.

As the Committee of 100 and the NL drew further apart, so the relationship between the NL and CND—or rather those socialists at or near the centre of CND policy-making who were sympathetic to NL thinking—became ever closer. The rejection by the Labour Party conference in 1961 of the previous year's unilateralist resolution resulted in a whole range of alternative strategies being put forward. The credibility of the traditional CND policy of 'working through the Labour Party' had been severely, if not fatally, weakened by the reversal of the Scarborough decision. The NL provided the theorists in this situation, and this modified, more orthodox Labour left, central sector of the NL became 'CND's think-tank'. But it was a very different NL from the old *ULR* group: it had become more uniform ideologically, and much more influential in the Movement, but it had become also smaller, narrower, and arguably less radical.

As the Disarmament Movement began to disintegrate after 1963, so the NL lost both interest and influence. The decline of CND and of the Committee of 100 as mass movements came coincidentally with the 'take-over' of the *NLR* by Perry Anderson *et al.* in 1962–3.

[51] See e.g. John Rex, 'Britain without the Bomb', NL pamphlet, London, 1960; see also Stuart Hall, 'NATO and the Alliances', pamphlet, London, (?1960–1).

The originators of the NL 'dispersed to catch up on their research, emigrate, help run CND, or just vanish'.[52]

There are several aspects of the make-up of the two movements which go some way towards explaining the ultimate failure of the NL. First and foremost, the NL never developed a mass base of its own. Initially the NL movement, largely through the *ULR*, had created a promising network of regional and local New Left clubs and groups. But the early emphasis on youth—'the bureaucracy will hold the machine; but the New Left will hold the passes between it and the younger generation'[53]—produced few results. 'The only section of young people among whom the movement made any progress was its own further-educated juniors . . . among the thousands of youngsters who marched with CND the New Left never established an independent socialist presence.'[54] Why was this? The rarefied 'University language' in which NL perspectives were transmitted certainly did not help: much of what the NL was saying was both complicated and to some degree alien (because couched in unfamiliar Marxist concepts), especially to those young people in the Disarmament Movement not involved in higher or further education. Ironically, there was a communications failure by the NL. Moreover, it is perhaps the case that not enough of the NL activists committed themselves to the hard political grind of building up a new mass movement. Outside the universities, for example, little attempt was made to recruit a mass membership. And in the most crucial area of all for a Marxist movement, the attraction of working-class support, the NL made virtually no progress at all.

Equally important, the NL, for all its theoretical sophistication, had ambivalent attitudes to the Labour Movement, to the Labour Party, and to Labourism. Eventually, as both Sedgwick and Young[55] have pointed out, the NL opted for a tactic of pressurizing the Labour Party into pursuing socialist policies. With some prescience Segdwick wrote in 1964, 'what is particularly staggering is [the NL's] failure to imagine that it might be outmanoeuvred; pursuing a tactic of total theoretical entry, all its eggheads have marched into the single basket of Left reformism.'[56] The complete

---

[52] Sedgwick, op. cit., 145.   [53] Cited in ibid., 140.
[54] Ibid., 140–1.
[55] Ibid., 144–53; and Young, op. cit., 144–53.
[56] Sedgwick, op. cit., 151.

failure of this tactic, from a Marxist viewpoint, during the 1964–70 period of Labour Government has been all too obvious to those on the left in subsequent decades.

Earlier, the NL had been 'perfectly prepared for a break in that Party . . . but it had to be a maximal break'; there was no point in 'hiving off a few Trotskyist militants in each place—what we really wanted was two major Unions to say "Hey—unless you move it", as it were, "you will lose the bloc vote." That's the kind of language the Party understands.'[57] But, of course, this never happened—and the right time for the 'maximal break' never arrived.

The upshot of the failure of this NL strategy was a gradual but steady shift in emphasis away from the 'non-Labour Movement', extra-parliamentary aspects of action, and towards an ever more moderate and compromising policy with the Labour Party. Ultimately, the NL's strategy hinged on Labour Movement rather than direct action support: the more the Labour Movement seemed to be moving away from CND (and the NL), the more the NL suggested compromise to try to win them back into the fold.

In the end, the NL became in part creator and in part victim of the strategically orientated left Labourism that came to dominate CND's politics by 1963–4. However, although it failed to fulfil its objectives—and was indeed a numerically small-scale and certainly a short-lived movement—its legacy of humanistic, socialistic, and libertarian political ideas and practices has been of considerable significance in subsequent decades, and not least in the revivified Peace Movement of the 1980s.

[57] Hall, in conversation.

POSTSCRIPT
Nuclear Protest and Radical Change

THE intention of this book has been to analyse a particular and crucial period in the development of the Peace Movement in Britain, rather than to polemicize or indicate the 'lessons to be learned'.[1] Nevertheless, in this brief conclusion some general issues may be noted, and the relationship to the later Peace Movement of the 1980s may at least be broached.

The Movement's objectives were certainly ambitious. All sections of the Movement were agreed that their first objectives were to achieve unilateral renunciation of nuclear weapons by Britain, the removal of American nuclear bases, and the cessation of H-bomber flights over British territory. The more radical branches of the Movement were aiming, of course, to achieve far more than that: in the case of the direct actionists, the 'non-violent society', and in the case of the left in its various forms, some version of the socialist commonwealth. In all these aims, both large and small, the Movement failed. Not only has Britain, even in the 1980s, and at immense cost, retained at least a quasi-independent nuclear deterrent, but the arms race has escalated, and nuclear weapons proliferated, to a degree that was not imagined by most activists in the 1950s and 1960s. Moreover, in the specifically British context, the prolonged period of extreme right-wing Conservative Government in the 1980s (preceded by ineffectual 'centrist' Governments in the 1970s) has hardly been indicative of a long-term radicalization of the political culture in Britain.

Yet all this is not to argue that the Movement and its politics were unimportant. On the contrary, their significance for subsequent political development has been very great indeed. And before returning to an analysis of the failure and some of the reasons for it, we should summarize the areas of significance (which

---

[1] For my own more polemical views in this area see Richard Taylor, 'The British Peace Movement and Socialist Change', in Ralph Miliband and John Saville (eds.), *The Socialist Register 1983*, London, 1983. And, for a sharp attack on these views, see Michael Randle, 'Non-violent Direct Action in the 1950s and 1960s', in Richard Taylor and Nigel Young (eds.), *Campaigns for Peace: British Peace Movements in the Twentieth Century*, Manchester, 1988.

have been implicit, of course, in the whole of the foregoing discussion of the Movement). At the most obvious level, the Movement was a part of the process that broke the post-war consensus and took politics and political concerns outside the exclusive confines of Westminster and the professional politicians. For the first time since the 1930s a mass extra-parliamentary movement emerged onto the political scene. And the rapidity of that growth, the size of the Movement, and the intensity of feeling on the issues involved was something quite new. This whole ethos of involvement and concern—and of ordinary people's *right* to be heard on centrally important issues—has been a continuing theme in British politics (and indeed in Western politics generally) ever since. In particular, the concepts and practices of NVDA, whilst not widely adopted in their 'pure' forms, have become almost commonplace techniques of protest in campaigns ranging from the parochial to the international.

Similarly, the Movement was centrally important in creating a 'culture of protest' which grew and flourished from the late 1960s onwards.[2] This had direct political manifestations: as in the growth of the Trotskyist groupings following the anti-Vietnam War movement, many of whose leading activists had cut their political teeth in the Nuclear Disarmament Movement a few years earlier; and in the various libertarian, 'community' movements of the 1960s and 1970s (the campaigns for the homeless, and the development of 'community politics', for example). But perhaps the most significant of all has been the rise of the Women's Movement in the 1970s and beyond. Experiences, both negative and positive, within the earlier Nuclear Disarmament Movement and the post-1968 Trotskyist New Left had a profound influence upon the content, the style, and the whole approach of the Women's Movement, as Sheila Rowbotham, for example, has testified.[3] The libertarian political mode and the critical approach belongs unquestionably to the New Left culture of protest rather than to the old left orthodoxy.

And, of course, the Nuclear Disarmament Movement was identified with, and supported by, the proponents of radical cultural attitudes in less directly political areas. Many of the leading radical playwrights of the late 1950s and early 1960s, for example,

---

[2] See e.g. David Widgery, *The Left in Britain 1956–1968*, London, 1976.
[3] Sheila Rowbotham, Lynne Segal, and Hilary Wainwright, *Beyond the Fragments*, London, 1979.

were involved with the Movement—mostly in the Committee of 100 (John Osborne, John Arden, and Arnold Wesker, for instance).

In all these ways, then, the Movement was a catalyst for later, often more generalized protest movements and the culture of protest in which they developed. Such movements have generally been characterized by radical middle-class involvement. As Parkin has noted, the Nuclear Disarmament Movement of the 1958–65 period was a prime example of 'middle-class radicalism';[4] but this constituency has expanded enormously since the 1960s, and so have the political and social movements with which it has been associated. (There have been three major groupings within this expanded substratum: white-collar trade unionists; 'new artisans' —that is, those denied entry to suitable professional or bureaucratic occupations who have turned to petty commodity production; and welfare bureaucrats—that is, those involved professionally in schools, hospitals, social work, and so on.[5])

Whilst the Movement of 1958–65 was characterized by its insularity and by its fundamentally nationalistic view of Britain's importance, and the potential significance of *British* action over weapons, there were also radical middle-class elements in the Movement which stressed the importance of Third World and international perspectives. Some of them lay within the Marxist tradition—in both the orthodox Trotskyist groups (small though they were) and in the New Left, with its concept of positive neutralism. But most notable among those engaged in international peace activism was the DAC, as was discussed in Chapter 4. Arguably, it is from these roots that has grown the greater awareness amongst the radical left of the importance of *transnational* links in both the Peace Movement and other related areas (Greenpeace, War on Want, etc.). The linkages between the arms race, arms industry, neo-colonialism, and world poverty—within the overall context of the North/South division—have become commonly accepted on the left as a crucial issue, or series of issues. But in the 1950s and 1960s the DAC's emphasis, in practice as well as theory, on those linkages was both new and in sharp contrast to the established orthodoxies of the left.

[4] Frank Parkin, *Middle Class Radicalism: The Social Bases of the British Campaign for Nuclear Disarmament*, Manchester, 1968.
[5] See David Coates, *The Context of British Politics*, London, 1984, for further discussion.

As was argued in Chapters 4 and 5, however, there were grave weaknesses at both the practical and ideological levels in the DAC's position. A more coherent (though in the short term no more effective) ideological stance was that formulated by the New Left (as discussed in Chapter 7). The New Left's overall perspective has had a sustained relevance. In the developing Cold War atmosphere of the 1950s the parameters of choice appeared to be either 'the free capitalist, bourgeois individualist creed of the West' (the 'Natopolitan culture', as E. P. Thompson termed it),[6] or the thoroughgoing Stalinist Communism of the Eastern bloc. The fundamental achievement of the New Left was to rediscover a genuinely humanistic socialism which adhered to neither orthodoxy, and which placed positive neutralism and the abandonment of nuclear weapons not only at the emotive heart but also at the logical centre of its politics.

The New Left's politics thus inspired afresh the radical socialist tradition whose parameters of debate lay within the boundaries of rejection of both Labourist and Stalinist orthodoxy. In all its variants—from Trotskyism to the libertarian radicalism of the Women's Movement and the Peace Movement of the subsequent decades—it has been this tradition that has predominated on the radical wing of British politics.

Both in the Nuclear Disarmament Movement of 1958 to 1965 and in subsequent radical movements, the majority of activists (certainly in the more militant and innovative wings of the various campaigns) have been in the youth sections. Whilst this study has not analysed the 'youth involvement' separately, it is important to note that the youthful radicalism—again, largely of the middle classes—was an important part of the Movement. And it was the first time in post-war Britain that a new generation had rejected the politics and questioned the morality of its elders. (Interestingly, Parkin has argued that, far from being normatively deviant, the youthful protesters were contending that the liberal idealism expressed but not practised by the orthodox culture should be adopted in terms of political policy decisions on nuclear issues.[7]) All this was, of course, part of a much wider growth of youth culture,

---

[6] See E. P. Thompson, 'Outside the Whale', in E. P. Thompson (ed.), *Out of Apathy*, London, 1960. Reprinted in Thompson, *The Poverty of Theory*, London, 1978.

[7] Parkin, op. cit.

resulting primarily from the new economic independence in the post-war era of full employment. To a large degree, the cultural independence in terms of teenage music, fashion, and so on flowed from this economic context. Youthful radicalism, as expressed in the Nuclear Disarmament Movement, was only a part of the process. But it acted, again, as the catalyst for many subsequent campaigns of youthful protest on social and political issues, and, as higher and further education expanded, so the numbers involved grew in the 1960s and 1970s.

The empirical survey of Movement activists and their subsequent involvements that Colin Pritchard and I undertook in the late 1970s showed that, politically, most activists had continued to adhere, with varying degrees of enthusiasm, to a Labourist position.[8] Over and above this, however, the degree of political involvement (on the far left, for example) was negligible—but the one exception was the environmentalist movement.[9] The realization that nuclear testing carried with it such appalling dangers to the health of both present and future generations was one of the key precipitants of CND, as we have seen. This environmental concern over radiation, and the catastrophe that would occur in the whole ecosystem if nuclear war were ever to take place, was combined with the moral opposition to nuclear weapons to form the core of the Movement's ideological position. Since the 1950s not only have the means of destruction become more sophisticated and considerably more powerful, but the knowledge of the ecological seriousness of nuclear war has grown; hence the concern over nuclear power and its effects (wholly unforeseen in the 1950s and 1960s) and the nightmarish predictions of the 'nuclear winter'. Given these developments, and the associated questioning of the whole technological and industrial culture, posited on the assumption of humanity's ever-increasing domination of the environment, it is hardly surprising that the Greens and other linked movements— such as Friends of the Earth and Greenpeace—have expanded in the 1970s and 1980s (though less in Britain than elsewhere). In

[8] See Richard Taylor and Colin Pritchard, *The Protest Makers: The British Nuclear Disarmament Movement of 1958–1965, Twenty Years on*, pt ii, Oxford, 1980.

[9] For discussion of the linkage between the Greens and the Peace Movement in the 1970s and 1980s, see Richard Taylor, 'Green Politics and the Peace Movement', in David Coates, Gordon Johnston, and Ray Bush (eds.), *A Socialist Anatomy of Britain*, Cambridge, 1985, pp. 160–70.

Britain, the origins, core beliefs, and libertarian ethos of this development—as well as some of its personnel—can be traced back to the Nuclear Disarmament Movement of the 1958 to 1965 period. Nuclear weapons are, after all, the greatest of all environmental threats.

Finally, the Movement of 1958–65 had an unquestionably important role in developing people's awareness of the nuclear issues themselves. The educative effect of the Movement's activities did have a profound impact on 'ordinary people's' consciousness. Before 1958 few were aware of the importance and nature of nuclear weaponry—and fewer still of its awesome implications. With the coming into being of the mass Movement, no Government, then or since, could continue to rely on public ignorance (though from the late 1960s to 1979–80 public *apathy* again became widespread). This 'political education' has been achieved by the Movement despite massive and persistent counter-propaganda by the Government. And it is a lasting testimony to the earlier mass Movement that its political education on the issues provided a bedrock of both strategic and defence knowledge and political sophistication which paved the way for the more formidable Movement of the 1980s.

In all these ways, then, the Movement was of great significance and acted as a catalyst in a whole series of contexts. And yet it was, in another sense, a failure. Most obviously, of course, it failed to achieve nuclear disarmament, either by Britain or by other nations. (Indeed, the proliferation and escalation of nuclear weaponry in subsequent decades, already noted, has been one of the most dramatic and depressing aspects of international politics.) *Why* did the Movement fail? On the international scale, after all, 'humanity' as a whole is agreed that disarmament is desirable, and that nuclear weapons in particular are a moral abomination, a political liability, an economic waste on a grand scale, and above all lethally dangerous. Internationally, the answer has lain within the realms of superpower politics—of diplomatic and political manoeuvring to outwit the 'other side' and protect the interests of the West/East. This is a game that is as old as history itself; but the stakes are now species survival—or species extinction. E. P. Thompson's notion of 'exterminism'—of the super-powers locked into a logic of bureaucratic and military escalation beyond the power of reason and orthodox human, political intervention—has presented a frightening new development of this process.[10]

On the domestic British scene such issues have proved equally intractable. Despite the Movement's huge impact, the major political parties, the media, and public opinion have remained predominantly hostile to its policies and overall objectives. Whilst the sincerity of activists, and their idealism, was recognized and, for the most part, respected, the Movement's politics were dismissed as either naïve or subversive.

As has been discussed in some detail, the various political strategies of the Movement were all inadequate.[11] The apolitical moralism of a large section was unrealistic because it side-stepped the essentially political issues; the direct actionists had neither ultimate ideological coherence nor sufficient human and material resources for their ambitious objectives; and the extra-parliamentary left, in all its guises, proved too weak to harness the Movement to its politics (though the New Left was, perhaps, potentially better placed than any to provide a fusion of the Movement and the 'socialist constituencies' of the left). A large part of the problem resided in the nature of the wider political culture: in our profoundly conservative society, radical change of any sort has been extraordinarily difficult to achieve.[12] Moreover, the main radical political party of the twentieth century—the Labour Party —has acted more as a 'manager of discontent',[13] as a 'safety valve' for channelling protest safely through the existing system, rather than as an agency for transformation.[14] Thus, over and above the *specific* problems the Movement encountered in working with and through the Labour Party, there was the general problems of the Labour Party's inability (or perhaps unwillingness) to press for genuinely radical advance.

The Movement's central link with Labourism was in this sense at the heart of its flawed strategy; and the ambivalence of the New

[10] E. P. Thompson *et al.*, *Exterminism and Cold War*, London, 1982 (esp. the chapters by Thompson and Raymond Williams).

[11] For further discussion, see Taylor, 'The British Peace Movement and Socialist Change'.

[12] See David Coates and Gordon Johnston (eds.), *Socialist Strategies*, Oxford, 1983.

[13] The phrase was originally coined by C. Wright Mills.

[14] As has been argued by many analysts, pre-eminently Ralph Miliband *Parliamentary Socialism*, 2nd edn., London, 1973.

Left over Labourism was also a key factor in its own 'crisis and decline'.[15]

All this is not to argue that the Movement, had it pursued other methods and strategies, would have succeeded. It may indeed have stood a better *chance* of success, as I have argued elsewhere, had it adopted a more radical strategy:[16] but this must remain conjecture. The relevant point here is that, in addition to its substantive failure, it failed to solve the inherent *political* problems common to all mass, single-issue movements. Reduced to their essentials, the problems can be summarized as: how to maintain unity and momentum in a disparate campaign; how to devise strategies which effect progress both in the tactics and in the objectives of the movement; and how to link into existing 'cultural' strengths on the left without becoming incorporated into Labourism.[17]

Important though it was, the Movement thus acted primarily as a foundation and a catalyst for subsequent movements. It changed the face of radical politics in Britain; but it left the fundamental problems unresolved. The 'new' Movement of the 1980s is larger, and more politically sophisticated, than the earlier Movement; moreover, its composition and outlook reflects the experiences and the lessons of the 1950s and 1960s. The Greens, the Women's Movement, and the successors of the New Left (and the direct actionists) all have central influence in the 1980s Movement, which has, in addition, a genuinely *international* ethos. To the extent that these perspectives have their roots in the 1958–65 Movement, this earlier Movement is of profound importance. Older, wiser, and more international the new Movement may be: but whether it can surmount the political problems encountered by the Nuclear Disarmament Movement of 1958–65—which has been the primary focus of attention of this book—will be the ultimate test of its efficacy.

[15] See Nigel Young, *An Infantile Disorder? The Crisis and Decline of the New Left*, London, 1977.

[16] See Taylor, 'The British Peace Movement and Socialist Change', and *The British Nuclear Disarmament Movement of 1958 to 1965 and its Legacy to the Left*, Ph.D. thesis, University of Leeds, 1983, ch. 9.

[17] See Richard Taylor and Kevin Ward, 'Community Politics and Direct Action: The Non-aligned Left', in Coates and Johnston, *Socialist Strategies*.

BIBLIOGRAPHY

There is a voluminous amount of material on the general question of nuclear weapons in book, article, and pamphlet form. There is also a very large number of articles, etc. on British foreign policy since the Second World War, and on the related defence and strategic issues. Included here are only those books, articles, and pamphlets which are of revelance either to the Nuclear Disarmament Movement of 1958 to 1965 *per se,* or to the political considerations with which this study is centrally concerned. The Bibliography is divided into four sections: primary sources; unpublished theses; journals; and books. (A fuller bibliography is given in Richard Taylor, *The British Nuclear Disarmament Movement of 1958 to 1965 and its Legacy to the Left,* Ph.D. thesis, University of Leeds, 1983.)

I. PRIMARY SOURCES

(a) Private collections of papers

Direct Action Committee archive. These papers were loaned by Hugh Brock and April Carter.

National Council for the Abolition of Nuclear Weapons Tests archive. These papers were loaned by Arthur Goss.

Committee of 100 archive. These papers were made available for consultation by Peter Cadogan.

(b) CND papers

CND archive at the British Library of Political and Economic Science, London School of Economics and Political Science, University of London.

CND minutes and journals at the Modern Records Centre, Library, University of Warwick.

Commonweal Collection, housed in the J. B. Priestley Library, University of Bradford.

(c) Interviews conducted with leading Movement figures

Frank Allaun MP, Pat Arrowsmith, Hugh Brock, April Carter, George Clark, Canon L. John Collins, Diana Collins, Peggy Duff, Michael Foot MP, Olive Gibbs, Arthur Goss, Professor Stuart Hall, Jacquetta Hawkes,

Alan Lovell, George Matthews, Ian Mikardo MP, Dick Nettleton, J. B. Priestley, Michael Randle, A. J. P. Taylor, and Arnold Wesker.

All interviews were tape recorded and transcripts made of the recordings. The transcripts were then checked with the interviewees, and their agreement obtained for quotation. The taped interviews are in the possession of the author.

II. UNPUBLISHED THESES

Edelstein, S. J., *The Failure of Consensus: The British Labour Party and Unilateralism, 1957–1961*, Ph.D. thesis, University of California, 1966.

Edwards, D. Van Deusen, *The Movement for Unilateral Nuclear Disarmament in Britain*, BA thesis, Swarthmore College, 1962.

Exley, R. A., *The CND: Its Organization, Personnel, and Methods in its First Year*, MA (Econ.) thesis, University of Manchester, 1959.

Holden, D. R., *The First New Left in Britain 1956–1962*, Ph.D. thesis, University of Wisconsin–Madison, 1976.

Minkin, L., *The Labour Party Conference and Intra-Party Democracy*, Ph.D. thesis, University of York, 1975.

Myers, F. E., *British Peace Politics: The Campaign for Nuclear Disarmament and the Committee of 100, 1957–1962*, Ph.D. thesis, Columbia University, 1965.

Parkin, F., *A Study of the CND: The Social Bases of a Political Mass Movement*, Ph.D. thesis, University of London, 1966.

Rigby, A., *The British Peace Movement and its Members*, MA dissertation, University of Essex, 1968.

Taylor, R. K. S., *The British Nuclear Disarmament Movement of 1958 to 1965 and its Legacy to the Left*, Ph.D. thesis, University of Leeds, 1983.

III. JOURNALS

(a) Main journals, newspapers, periodicals, etc., containing articles relevant to the Nuclear Disarmament Movement

Anarchy, Bulletin of the Atomic Scientist, CND Bulletin, CND Scientist, Direct Action, Freedom, Guardian, Inside Story, International Socialism, Labour Monthly, London Committee of 100 Newsletter, New Left Review, New Reasoner, Newsletter, New Statesman, Observer, Peace News, Resistance, Sanity, Solidarity, Socialist Review, Socialist Standard, The Times, Tribune, War and Peace, War Resister, Universities and Left Review, War Resistance, World News, Daily Worker, Young Guard, Youth Against the Bomb.

As many of these journals contain a very large number of articles on the Movement, only those of central importance are listed in the following section.

(b) Journal articles and pamphlets

Alexander, H., 'Resisting Evil Without Arms', *Northern Friends Peace Board,* n.d. (?1956).

Allaun, F., 'Disarmament Hopes Rise: New Moves in the Struggle', *Views,* 3, autumn–winter 1963.

—— 'New Moves in the H-bomb Struggle', *Union of Democratic Control,* n.d. (1960).

—— 'Stop the H-bomb Race: Before It's Too Late Let Britain Give the Lead', *Union of Democratic Control,* 1958.

Amis, K., 'Socialism and the Intellectuals', Fabian Tract 304, *Fabian Society,* 1956.

Anarchy, 'The Spies for Peace Story', *Anarchy,* 29, July 1963.

Arnison, J., 'Peace in our Time', *Labour Monthly,* Apr. 1960.

Association of Scientific Workers, Atomic Sciences Committee, 'Nuclear Nightmare', ASW, 1958.

Aylmer, G., 'Labour and the Bomb', CND, n.d.

Bartlett, P., 'Deterrence and Retaliation or Christianity', Friends' Peace Committee, 1958.

Beaton, L., 'Would Labour Give up the Bomb?', *Sunday Telegraph* pamphlet, Aug. 1964.

—— 'Labour's Defence Policy: Learning to Love the Bomb', *Statist,* 187. 4530.

Beswick, F., 'The Hydrogen Bomb—What Shall We Do?', Cooperative Union, 1964.

—— 'When We Renounce Nuclear Weapons', London Cooperative Society, n.d. (?1961).

Birkett, S., 'Humanity v. the H-bomb', Independent Labour Party, 1955.

Blank, S., 'Britain: The Politics of Foreign Economic Policy, the Domestic Economy, and the Problem of Pluralistic Stagnation', International Organization, 31.4, autumn 1977.

Bolt, R., Manifesto, Committee of 100, n.d. (?1962).

Booth, A. R., 'Christian Theology and Modern Warfare', *Brassey's Annual,* 1962.

—— Edwards, D., and Jenkins, D., 'Christians and Nuclear Disarmament', *Theology,* 64, June 1961.

Boulton, D., 'CND in 1964', *Views,* 3, autumn–winter 1963.

Brinton, M., 'Danger! Party Hacks at Work', *Solidarity,* 2.10.

British Atlantic Committee, 'Nuclear Disarmament: Questions and Answers for Those who Want Facts', 1961.

British Council of Churches, 'Christians and Atomic War', *Survival,* July–Aug. 1959.

—— 'The British Nuclear Deterrent', 1963.

—— 'The Pattern of Disarmament', 1962.

Brock, H., 'The Century of Total War', *Peace News,* 1961.

Buchan, A., 'Britain and the Bomb', *Reporter,* 20, 19 Mar. 1959.

—— 'Britain and the Nuclear Deterrent', *Political Quarterly,* 31, Jan.–Mar. 1960.

—— 'The Odds Against Gaitskell', *Reporter,* 23, Dec. 1960.

Bull, H., 'The Many Sides of Unilateralism', *Reporter,* Mar. 1961.

Cadogan, P., 'Committee of 100: What Is It?', *Resistance,* 2.4, 1961.

—— 'Non-violence as a Reading of History', *Anarchy,* 20, Oct. 1962.

—— 'The Politics of Direct Action', *Anarchy,* 13, Mar. 1962.

Calder, R., 'The Non-nuclear Club', *Bulletin of Atomic Scientists,* 16, Apr. 1960.

Callow, P., 'Letter to a (Aldermaston) Marcher', *New Statesman,* 63, 20 Apr. 1962.

Cameron, J., 'One in Five Must Know', *Peace News,* n.d.

Cameron, J. M., 'The New Left in Britain', *Listener,* 8, 15, 22 Sept. 1960.

Campaign Caravan Workshops 'A Sense of Urgency', CND Workshops, 1963.

Campaign for Nuclear Disarmament, 'Civil Defence and Nuclear War', n.d. (1963).

—— 'In Ignorance, Refrain!', 1959.

—— 'Let Britain Lead', n.d. (1960).

—— 'New Three Point Programme' (incorporating 'Steps Towards Peace'), 1962.

—— 'Questions and Answers for Christians on Nuclear Disarmament', n.d.

—— 'Sanity or Suicide', n.d. (1959).

—— 'Six Reasons why Britain Must Give up the Bomb', n.d. (1962).

—— 'Tell Britain', 1963.

—— 'The Bomb and You', 1962.

—— 'The CND', basic policy leaflet, 1958.

—— 'The CND', n.d. (?1962).

—— 'The Economic Case for Nuclear Disarmament', n.d.

—— Tomorrow's Children: A Pamphlet for Women, n.d. (1959).

—— 'Women Ask Why', n.d.

Carter, A., 'Direct Action', *Peace News,* Mar. 1962.

—— 'Disarmament: A Question of Unilateralism', unpublished MS.

—— 'The Common Market: A Challenge to Unilateralists', *Peace News,* n.d. (1962).

—— (ed.), 'Unilateralism', special issue of *Our Generation Against Nuclear War,* 3.3, Apr. 1965.

Catlin, G. E. G., 'On Unilateralism', *Contemporary Review*, 199, Jan. 1961.

Chalfont, Lord, 'The Next Ten Years: A Review of British Defence Policy', *Hawk*, Dec. 1962.

—— 'The Politics of Disarmament', *Survival*, 8.2, Nov. 1966.

Challinor, R., 'Zig Zag: The CP and the Bomb', *International Socialism*, 3, winter 1960.

Christians on Nuclear Disarmament, Christian CND pamphlet 1, 1960.

Clark, G., 'For Freedom and Survival', Campaign Caravan Workshops, *Views*, 5, summer 1964.

—— 'Second Wind', CND, 1963.

Clark, H., 'Making Non-violent Revolution', *Peace News* pamphlet 1, 1981.

Collins, D., 'Can Christians Accept the Nuclear Deterrent?' Christian CND pamphlet 4, n.d.

Collins, Canon L. J., 'Forward from Aldermaston', *Labour Monthly*, 44, Apr. 1962.

Crane, P., 'Catholics and Nuclear War', *Month*, Oct. 1959.

Crosland, C. A. R., 'British Labour's Crucial Meeting', *New Leader*, Oct. 1960 (USA).

—— 'The Mass Media', *Encounter*, Nov. 1962.

Crossman, R. H. S., 'The Nuclear Obsession', *Encounter*, July 1958.

—— 'Western Defence in the '60s', *Royal United Services Institution Journal*, Aug. 1961.

Davies, H., 'Bull's Eye's Island', Union of Democratic Control, n.d. (?1960).

—— 'Why NATO?', *Victory for Socialism*, 1960.

De Weerd, H. A., 'British Unilateralism: A Critical Review', *Yale Review*, 1962 (USA).

—— 'The Labour Party and Unilateralism', RM-2914-PR, Santa Monica, California, The Rand Corporation, Feb. 1962.

Doncaster, L. H., 'Personal Action and Public Demonstration', Friends Peace Committee, 1964.

Encounter, 'The British Press During "the Week of Cuba" ', *Encounter*, 20.1, Jan. 1963.

Epstein, L. D., 'Who Makes Party Policy: British Labour 1960/61', *Midwest Journal of Political Science*, 6.2, May 1962 (USA).

Evans, Canon S., 'The Nuclear Deterrent and Christian Conscience', CND, n.d.

Farley, C., 'CND after the Election', *New Left Review*, 1, 1960.

Fawcett, G. C., 'The Uphill Way', Friends' Peace Committee, n.d. (1962).

Fay, S., 'The Late New Left', *Spectator*, 21 Sept. 1962.

Fletcher, R., 'Military Thinking and Unilateralism', Union of Democratic Control, 1962.

Fletcher, R., 'The Suicide Race', *Twentieth Century*, 170, winter 1962.

Foot, M., 'Bevan and the H-bomb', *Tribune*, 11 Oct. 1957.

Fox, A., 'The Unions and Defence', *Socialist Commentary*, Feb. 1961.

—— 'Trade Unions and Unilateralism', *Socialist Commentary*, Feb. 1961.

Frankau, P., 'Letter to a Parish Priest', CND, n.d.

Freeman, J., 'The End of Labour's Nightmare', *New Statesman*, 10 Feb. 1961.

—— 'Why Should We Ban the Bomb?', *Peace News*, 1962.

Gale, G., 'The Workers and the H-bomb Fight: A Reply to Michael Randle', *Newsletter*, 4 July 1959.

Gollan, J., 'Gaitskell or Socialism?', Communist Party, 1960.

—— 'Labour and the Bomb', Communist Party, n.d. (?1960).

Goodman, G., 'The Economic Consequences of Staying Alive', CND, n.d.

Goold-Adams, R., 'Those Against the Bomb', *Brassey's Annual*, 1958.

Gordon-Walker, P., 'The Labour Party's Defence and Foreign Policy', *Foreign Affairs*, 42.3, Apr. 1964.

Gough, K., 'When the Saints Go Marching In: The Ban the Bomb Movement in Britain', Correspondence Publishing Company (Detroit, USA), 1961.

Greer, H., 'Tremble Dammit', *Spectator*, 12 Apr. 1963.

Hall, S., 'Breakthrough', CUCaND, 1958.

—— 'NATO and the Alliances', London Regional Council of CND, n.d. (1960).

—— 'The Cuban Crisis: Trial Run or Steps Towards Peace', *War and Peace*, 1, 1963.

—— Rustin, M., and Clark, G., 'The Condition of England Question', *People and Politics*, special issue, Easter 1967.

—— and Whannell, P., 'Direct Action: A Discussion with Alan Lovell', *New Left Review*, 8, Mar.–Apr. 1961.

Harris, T., *et al.*, 'Labour and the Bomb', *International Socialism*, 10 autumn 1962.

Hartley, A., 'The British Bomb', *Encounter*, May 1954.

—— 'The British Bomb', *Survival*, 6.4 July–Aug. 1964.

Heelas, T., 'Balance of Risks: Communism or Nuclear War', CND, n.d.

Henper, V., 'Russell and the Anarchists', *Anarchy*, 109, Mar. 1970.

Hindell, K. and Williams, P., 'Scarborough and Blackpool: An Analysis of some Votes at the Labour Party Conferences of 1960 and 1961', *Political Quarterly* 33.3, July–Sept. 1962.

Hollis, C., 'Catholics and the Nuclear Dilemma', *Spectator*, 26 Nov. 1965.

Howard, M. L., 'Not East—Not West', London Regional Council of CND, discussion pamphlet, 1960.

Huddleston, T., 'Meet Fear with Faith', in New Age for Peace pamphlet, Fellowship of Reconciliation, n.d. (?1959).

Hughes, E., 'Bomb over Britain', Civic Press, 1954.

Hughes, E., 'Polaris and the Arms Race', Housmans, n.d. (1961).

Hughes, J., 'Socialism for the 1960s', *Tribune*, n.d.

Independent Labour Party, 'The 100 v. The State: Trafalgar Square, Wethersfield, The Trial', ILP/*Solidarity* pamphlet, ILP, n.d. (1962).

Independent Nuclear Disarmament Election Committee, 'Statement of the Aims of the Independent Nuclear Disarmament Election Committee', INDEC, n.d. (1962).

Inside Story, 'The Spies that Got Away, pts. 1 and 2, *Inside Story* 8 and 9, May–June 1973.

Johnson, P., 'Will Wilson Keep the Bomb?', *New Statesman*, 13 Dec. 1963.

Jones, F., 'Can Britain Deter?', *Crossbow*, Jan. 1961.

Jones, M., 'The Flowing Tide', CND, n.d. (1960).

—— 'Freed from Fear', CND, 1962.

—— 'Labour's Defence Policies', *War and Peace*, 1, Jan.–Mar. 1963.

Jude, F., 'Christians and Nuclear Disarmament', *Theology*, 64, Aug. 1961.

Kenny, A., 'Catholics Against the Bomb', *Blackfriars*, 42, Dec. 1961.

Kettle, A., 'The New Left', *Marxism Today*, Oct. 1960.

Labour Party, 'Disarmament and Nuclear War', Mar. 1958.

—— 'Disarmament and Nuclear War: The Next Step', 1959.

—— 'Disengagement in Europe', Apr. 1958.

—— 'Foreign Policy and Defence', 1960.

—— 'The Great Defence Scandal', 1960.

—— 'Let's Go with Labour for the New Britain', 1964.

—— 'Policy for Peace', 1961.

Labour Peace Fellowship, 'NATO or Neutralism', Labour Peace Fellowship and UDC, 1962.

Labour Research Department, 'Facts on the Nuclear Arms Race', 1958.

Laski, M., Mitchinson, N., Hunter, E., and a Doctor, 'Survivors', CND, n.d.

Lehmann, J., 'Radicalism Then and Now', *Listener*, 9 Aug. 1962.

Levy, B., 'Britain and the Bomb', CND, 1958.

Lindop, P. and Matthews, P. T., 'A Poor Man's Guide to Nuclear Weapons', Today and Tomorrow Publications for the Socialist Medical Association, n.d.

Lonsdale, K., 'Can the Use of Atomic Weapons Ever Be Justified?', Friends Peace Committee, 1949.

—— 'Christian Pacifism and the Hydrogen Bomb', Friends Peace Committee, 1954.

Lort-Phillips, P., 'Towards Sanity', Radical Publications, n.d.

Lovell, A., 'Where Next for the Campaign?', *Universities and Left Review*, 1.6, 1959.

Mac an Fhaili, C., 'From Arrows to Atoms: A Catholic Voice on the Morality of War', *Peace News*, n.d. (?1960).

McCabe, H., 'Morals and Nuclear War', *Blackfriars*, 42, Nov. 1961.

MacFarlane, L. J., 'Disobedience and the Bomb', *Political Quarterly*, Oct.–Dec. 1966.

Martin, K., 'The Future of CND', *New Statesman*, 4 Oct. 1963.

—— 'Outlook for CND', *New Statesman*, 15 Dec. 1961.

—— 'Where to from Aldermaston?', *New Statesman*, 27 Apr. 1963.

—— and Howard, A., 'Where Have All the Flowers Gone?', *New Statesman*, 27 Mar. 1964.

Marquand, D., 'Bombs and Scapegoats', *Encounter*, Jan. 1961.

—— 'England, the Bomb and the Marchers', *Commentary*, May 1960.

—— 'The English Labour Party and its Discontents', *Commentary*, 20, Dec. 1960.

Mason, D., 'A Pacifist Look at Politics', Fellowship of Reconciliation, n.d. (1964).

Matthews, G., 'The Hydrogen Bomb', *World News*, 14 May 1955.

—— 'Unilateralism and the Fight for Peace', *World News*, 14 Mar. 1958.

Middleton, D., 'The Deeper Meaning of British Neutralism', *New York Times Magazine*, 11 Dec. 1960.

Mikardo, I., 'Labour and Peace', *Tribune*, 15 Sept. 1961.

Milford, T. R., 'The Valley of Decision: The Christian Dilemma in the Nuclear Age', British Council of Churches, n.d. (1961).

Moncrieff, A., 'The Rise and Fall of CND', *Listener*, 23 Mar. 1967.

Morris, S., 'Peace Pledge Union (Great Britain)', *War Resister*, pt. 89, 1960.

Multilateral Disarmament Information Centre, 'The British Peace Movement', 1963.

Myers, F. E., 'Civil Disobedience and Organizational Change: The British Committee of 100', *Political Science Quarterly*, 86.1, Mar. 1971 (New York).

National Council for Civil Liberties, 'Public Order and the Police: A Report on the Events in Trafalgar Square, Sunday 17 to Monday 18 September, 1961', NCCL, n.d. (1961).

Nettleton, D., 'The Case for Nuclear Disarmament Today', CND, n.d. (1968).

—— 'If You Want Peace . . . The Case for Nuclear Disarmament', CND, 1975.

New Left Review, 'What is the New Left?', *NLR*, n.d.

New Reasoner, 'Beyond the Bomb', *New Reasoner*, 1.4, 1957.

Newsletter, 'Black the A-bomb and Rocket Bases', *Newsletter* pamphlet, 1958.

Overy, B., 'How Effective Are Peace Movements?', Peace Studies Papers 2 Housmans 1980.

Parkin, B., 'Multilateral Disarmament', Union of Democratic Control, n.d. (1961).

Peace News, 'The Black Paper: H-bomb War—What It Would Be Like', n.d. (1963).

—— 'From Protest to Resistance: The Direct Action Movement against Nuclear Weapons', *Peace News* pamphlet 2, 1981.

Peace Pledge Union, 'Pacifism', 1957.

—— 'Report of the Second Non-violence Working Party of the PPU 1958–1960', n.d.

—— 'What is Pacifism: A Declaration of Policy and Principles', 1958.

Peers, D., 'The Impasse of CND', *International Socialism*, 12, 1962.

Petch, G. H., 'Civil Defence and CND', *Anarchy*, 17, July 1962.

Powell, C. F., 'The Hydrogen Bomb and the Future of Mankind', London Co-operative Society Education Department, 1955.

Priestley, J. B., 'Britain and the Nuclear Bombs', *New Statesman*, 2 Nov. 1957.

—— 'CND's Future', *New Statesman*, 15 Oct. 1960.

Radcliffe, C., 'The Last Aldermaston', *Anarchy*, 26, 3.4, Apr. 1963.

Raison, T., '*The Missile Years*', Conservative Political Centre, 1959.

Randle, M., 'The Committee of 100', *Views* 1, spring 1963.

—— 'Is It Revolution We're After?', *Peace News*, 10 Mar. 1961.

Rees, D., 'The March to Nowhere', *Encounter*, 24, Feb. 1965.

Rety, J., 'Anarchists and Nuclear Disarmers', *Anarchy*, 62, Apr. 1966.

Rex, J., 'Britain without the Bomb', *New Left Review*, 1960.

—— 'The Sociology of CND', *War and Peace*, 1.1, Jan.–Mar. 1963.

Richardson, B., 'What Has It Got to Do with the Bomb?', *Anarchy*, 26, Apr. 1963.

Ricks, C., 'Last Things: "The Disarmers" by Christopher Driver', *New Statesman*, 69, 1 Jan. 1965.

Roberts, A., 'Nuclear Testing and the Arms Race', *Peace News*, 1962.

—— 'The Uncertain Anarchists', *New Society*, 27 May 1961.

—— 'War by Accident', *Peace News*, 1962.

Ross, D., 'The Politics of Neutralism', *Tribune*, 19 Sept. 1960.

Rothman, S., 'British Labour's New Left', *Political Science Quarterly*, Sept. 1961 (New York).

Russell, B., 'Bertrand Russell's May Day Message', London Committee of 100, 1962.

—— 'On Civil Disobedience', YCND, 15 Apr. 1961.

—— 'The Case for British Nuclear Disarmament', *Bulletin of the Atomic Scientist*, Mar. 1962.

—— 'Unilateralism', *New Republic*, 6 Mar. 1961.

—— 'Win We Must', Second Midlands Conference for Peace, 1961.

—— and Scott, M., 'Act or Perish', London Committee of 100, Oct. 1960.

Sampson, R., 'Society without the State', 2nd edn., Housmans, 1980.

Schaffer, G., 'Nuclear "Defence" is Suicide', National Peace Council, 1970.

—— 'Peace in your Hands', British Peace Committee, 1961.

Schoenman, R., 'Civil Disobedience to Halt Polaris', *Peace News*, 17 Feb. 1961.

Schoenman, R., 'Resistance in Mass Society', *Peace News*, 25 Aug. 1961.

Scots Against War, 'How to Disrupt, Obstruct and Subvert the Warfare State', SAW, 1963.

Scott, M., 'Politics in the Nuclear Age', *War Resistance*, 40–1, 1972.

Sedgwick, P., 'The Direction of Action', *Socialist Review*, May 1961.

—— 'NATO, the Bomb, and Socialism', *Universities and Left Review*, 1.7, 1959.

Seed, P., 'The Psychological Problem of Disarmament', Housmans, n.d.

Sharp, G., 'Creative Conflict in Politics', Housmans, 1962.

—— 'Gandhi on the Theory of Voluntary Servitude', *Anarchy*, 14, Apr. 1962.

—— 'Tyranny Could not Quell Them', *Peace News*, n.d.

Shelley, D., 'Influx or Exodus? Anarchists and the Committee of 100', *Anarchy*, 50, 5.4, Apr. 1965.

Slaughter, C., 'Non-violence or Class Struggle?', *Newsletter*, 30 Dec. 1961.

Smythe, T., 'The Radical Protest at Harrington', *War Resister*, 1960.

Solidarity, 'Against All Bombs', *Solidarity*, 2.5, 1962.

—— 'Beyond Counting Arses', *Solidarity*, 2.11, 1963.

—— 'Canon Balls', *Solidarity*, 2.10, 1963.

—— 'Civil Disobedience and the Working Class', *Solidarity*, 1.9, 1961.

—— 'The Death of CND', *Solidarity* pamphlet 28.

—— 'From Civil Disobedience to Socialist Revolution', *Solidarity*, 1.8, 1961.

—— 'To Sit or Stand: INDEC?', *Solidarity*, 2.5, 1962.

Solidarity Scotland, 'The Way Ahead for a New Peace Movement', *Solidarity Scotland* pamphlet 1, 1966.

Southall, T., and Atkinson, J., 'CND 1958–1965: Lessons of the First Wave', *Socialist Challenge*, 1981.

Standing Joint Pacifist Committee, 'Unarmed: A Discussion on the Consequences of Total Disarmament', Standing Joint Pacifist Committee, 1957.

Steck, H. J., 'The Re-emergence of Ideological Politics in Great Britain: The CND', *Western Political Quarterly*, 1965 (USA).

Stein, W., 'Christian Attitudes to War', *War and Peace*, 1, Jan.–Mar. 1963.

—— 'The (Vatican II) Council and the Bomb: Casuistry or Witness', *New Blackfriars*, 47, Nov. 1965.

Stoke Newington Eight Defence Group, 'If You Want Peace, Prepare for War', SNEDG. n.d.

Strachey, J., 'The Pursuit of Peace', Fabian Society Tract 329, Dec. 1960.

—— 'Scrap All the H-bombs', Labour Party, n.d. (1958).

Sweet, C., 'Nuclear Plot in Europe', British Peace Committee, 1962.

Syndicalist Workers' Federation, 'The Bomb, Direct Action and the State', SWF, n.d.

Tatum, A., 'Reflections on the H-bomb', *War Resister*, 80, 1958.

Taylor, A. J. P., 'Campaign Report', *New Statesman*, 21 June 1958.

—— 'The Exploded Bomb', CND, n.d.

—— 'The Great Deterrent Myth', CND, 1958.

Thomas, H., 'Disarmament, The Way Ahead', Fabian Society Tract 307, 1957.

—— 'Dream or Reality?', *Political Quarterly*, Jan.–Mar. 1960.

Thompson, E. P., 'Commitment in Politics', *Universities and Left Review*, 1.6, 1959.

—— 'NATO, Neutralism and Survival', *Universities and Left Review*, 1.4, 1958.

—— 'Notes on Exterminism, The Last Stage of Civilization', *New Left Review*, 121, May–June 1980.

Vernier, A., 'British Defence Policy under Labour', *Foreign Affairs*, 42.2, Jan. 1964.

Victory for Socialism, 'How to End the Cold War: A VFS Broadsheet', VFS, n.d. (1958–9).

—— 'Let Britain Lead', VFS, n.d.

—— 'Policy for Summit Talks: How to End the Cold War', *Tribune*, n.d. (1958–9).

—— 'This Changing World', VFS, n.d. (1961).

Wainwright, W., 'Close All U.S. Bases', Communist Party, n.d.

—— 'Nuclear Weapons and the Communist Party', *World News*, July 1959.

—— 'Who Is to Blame?' Communist Party', n.d. (1962).

Walter, N., 'Book Review: *The Disarmers: A Study in Protest*', *Solidarity*, 3.7, 1964.

—— 'Damned Fools in Utopia', *New Left Review*, 13–14, Jan.–Apr. 1962.

—— 'Direct Action and the New Pacifism', *Anarchy*, 13, Mar. 1962.

—— 'Disobedience and the New Pacifism', *Anarchy*, 14, Apr. 1962.

—— 'The RSGs 1919–63', *Solidarity* pamphlet 15.

—— and Walter, R., 'The Committee of 100 and Anarchism', *Anarchy*, 52, June 1965.

War Resistance, 'Greek Demonstration', *War Resistance*, 22, 1967.

War Resister, 'World Peace Brigade', *War Resister*, 1962.

Ward, C., 'Industrial Decentralisation and Workers' Control', *Anarchy*, 10, Dec. 1961.

—— 'The State and Society', *Anarchy*, 14, Apr. 1962.

Weaver, A., 'Schools for Non-violence', Committee of 100, n.d. (1961).

—— 'War Outmoded', Housmans, 1960.

Webbe, H., 'Scarborough and After', *Quarterly Review*, 628, Apr. 1961.

Welfare Group, 'Committee of 100 Prisoners Against the Bomb', London Committee of 100, n.d.

Williams, R., 'The Politics of Nuclear Disarmament', *New Left Review*, 124, 1981.

Wilson, G., 'War and the Christian Witness', Prison Publications, n.d.

Wilson, H., 'Britain's Policy if Labour Wins', *Atlantic*, 162.4, Oct. 1963.

Winter, E., 'Tooling for Inhumanity', Union of Democratic Control, n.d. (1961–2).

Worsthorne, P., 'Britain and the Bomb', *Reporter*, 23 July 1959.

—— 'Dare Democracy Disengage?', Conservative Political Centre, 1958.

Yaffé, D., 'The Marxian Theory of Crisis, Capital and the State', *Economy and Society*, 2.2, May 1973.

Young Fabian Group, 'NATO or Neutrality: The Defence Debate', Fabian Society, 1961.

Young, W., 'An Abolitionist's Position', *Encounter*, Nov. 1958.

—— 'The Nuclear Disarmers', series of articles, *Guardian*, 12, 16, 17 Sept. 1959.

—— and Young. E., 'Disarmament: Finnegan's Choice', Fabian Society Tract 333, Sept. 1961.

Younger, K., 'Britain's Role in a Changing World', Fabian Society Tract 327, 1960.

Zilliacus, K., 'Anatomy of a Sacred Cow', CND, 1960.

—— 'Arms and Labour', CND, n.d. (1965).

—— 'Four Power Talks: For Peace or War?', Union of Democratic Control, 1955.

—— 'Mutiny Against Madness', Housmans, n.d. (1957).

—— 'Our Lives and Cuba', *New Gladiator*, 1963.

IV. BOOKS

(*Note:* place of publication is London unless otherwise stated.)

(a) Centrally concerned with the Movement

Boulton, D. (ed.), *Voices from the Crowd: Against the H-Bomb*, 1965.

Clark, G., 'Remember Your Humanity and Forget the Rest', in R. Benewick and T. Smith (eds.), *Direct Action and Democratic Politics*, 1972.

Collins, Canon L. J., *Faith Under Fire*, 1966.

Driver, C., *The Disarmers: A Study in Protest*, 1964.

Duff, P., *Left, Left, Left*, 1971.

Greer, H., *Mud Pie: The CND Story*, 1964.

Groom, A. J. R., *British Thinking About Nuclear Weapons*, 1974.

Minnion, J., and Bolsover, P. (eds.), *CND Story*, 1983.

Parkin, F., *Middle Class Radicalism: The Social Bases of the British Campaign for Nuclear Disarmament*, Manchester, 1968.

Randle, M., 'Non-violent Direct Action in the 1950s and 1960s', in R. Taylor and N. Young (eds.), *Campaigns for Peace*, Manchester, 1988.

Taylor, R., 'The British Peace Movement and Socialist Change', in R. Miliband and J. Saville (eds.), *The Socialist Register 1983*, 1983.

—— and Pritchard, C., *The Protest Makers: The British Nuclear Disarmament Movement of 1958–1965, Twenty Years On*, Oxford, 1980 (2nd edn., extended, 1982).

—— and Ward, K., 'Community Politics and Direct Action: The Non-aligned Left', in D. Coates and G. Johnston (eds.), *Socialist Strategies*, Oxford, 1983.

—— and Young, N. (eds.), *Campaigns for Peace: British Peace Movements in the Twentieth Century*, Manchester, 1988.

(b) Secondarily concerned with the Movement

Acland, Sir R., *Waging Peace: The Positive Policy We Could Pursue if We Gave up the Hydrogen Bomb*, 1958.

—— *Why So Angry?*, 1958.

Anderson, A., *Hungary 56*, A Solidarity Book, 1964.

Anderson, P., and Blackburn, R. (eds.), *Towards Socialism*, 1965.

Arnold, G. L., 'Britain: The New Reasoners', in L. Labedz (ed.), *Revisionism*, New York, 1962.

Barker, R., *Political Ideas in Modern Britain*, 1979.

Benewick, R., and Smith, T. (eds.), *Direct Action and Democratic Politics*, 1972.

Bennett, J. C. (ed.), *Nuclear Weapons and the Conflict of Conscience*, 1962.

Bevan, A., *In Place of Fear*, 1952.

Bigelow, A., *The Voyage of the Golden Rule: An Experiment with Truth*, Toronto, 1959.

Birnbaum, N., 'The CND' in R. Theobald (ed.), *Britain in the 1960s*, New York, 1961.

—— 'Great Britain: The Reactive Revolt', in M. A. Kaplan (ed.), *The Revolution in World Politics*, New York, 1962.

Bondurant, J. V., *The Conquest of Violence: The Gandhian Philosophy of Conflict*, Princeton, NJ, 1959.

Brock, P., *Pacifism in the United States*, Princeton, NJ, 1968.

Bunyan, T., *History and Practice of the Political Police in Britain*, 1976.

Butler, D. E., *The British General Elections of 1955, 1959 and 1964* (three separate studies, each published after the relevant general election, and co-authored in 1959 with R. Rose and in 1964 with A. King).

Buxton, J., and Turner, M., *Gate Fever*, 1962.

—— *Inside Story*, 1963.

Carter, A., *Direct Action and Liberal Democracy*, 1973.

—— *The Political Theory of Anarchism*, 1971.

—— 'The Sahara Protest Team' in P. A. Hare and H. H. Blumberg (eds.), *Liberation without Violence*, 1977.

Carter, A., Hoggett, D., and Roberts, A., *Non-violent Action*, 1970.

Ceadel, M., *Pacifism in Britain, 1914–45*, Oxford, 1980.

Clark, R. W., *The Life of Bertrand Russell*, 1975.

Cliff, T., *Russia: A Marxist analysis*, 1970.

Coates, D., *The Context of British Politics*, 1984.

—— *The Labour Party and the Struggle for Socialism*, Cambridge, 1974.

—— and Johnston, G. (eds.), *Socialist Strategies*, Oxford, 1983.

—— Johnston, G., and Bush, R., *A Socialist Anatomy of Britain*, 1985.

Cox, J., *Overkill: The Story of Modern Weapons*, 1977 (3rd edn., revised, 1981).

Cranston, M., *The New Left*, 1970.

Crick, B., and Robson, W. A., *Protest and Discontent*, 1970.

Crosland, C. A. R., *The Future of Socialism*, 1956.

Davidson, B., *What Really Happened in Hungary?*, 1956.

Dunn, T., (ed.), *Alternatives to War and Violence*, 1963.

Edwards, D. L., *Withdrawing from the Brink*, 1963.

Foot, M., *Aneurin Bevan: A Biography* (2 vols.), vol. 1, *1897–1945*, 1962; vol. 2, *1945–1960*, 1973.

Fryer, P., *The Battle for Socialism*, 1959.

—— *Hungarian Tragedy*, 1956.

Glasgow, G., *Child of Terror: The Peace Born of the Thermonuclear Menace*, 1958.

Gregg, R. B., *The Power of Non-violence*, 1959.

Grigg, M., *The Challenor Case*, 1965.

Hall, R. T., *The Morality of Civil Disobedience*, 1971.

Harris, N., and Palmer, J. (eds.), *World Crisis: Essays in Revolutionary Socialism*, 1971.

Harrison, M., *Trade Unions and the Labour Party since 1945*, 1960.

Haseler, S., *The Gaitskellites: Revisionism in the British Labour Party 1951–64*, 1969.

Henderson, I. (ed.), *Man of Christian Action, Canon John Collins: The Man and his Work*, 1976.

Hentoff, N. (ed.), *The Essays of A. J. Muste*, New York, 1967.

Hersey, J., *Hiroshima*, 1946.

Hyams, E., *The New Statesman: The History of the First Fifty Years, 1913–1963*, 1963.

Jenkins, M., *Bevanism, Labour's High Tide, the Cold War and the Democratic Mass Movement*, Nottingham, 1979.

Jones, M., *Today the Struggle*, 1978.

Jungk, R., *Brighter than a Thousand Suns*, 1958.

de Kadt, E., *British Defence Policy and Nuclear War*, 1964.

Kennan, G., *Russia, The Atom and the West*, Oxford, 1958.

Kidron, M., *Western Capitalism Since the War*, 1970.

—— 'Capitalism: The Latest Stage', in Harris and Palmer.

King-Hall, Sir S., *Defence in the Nuclear Age*, 1958.

—— *Power Politics in the Nuclear Age,* 1962.

Krug, M., *Aneurin Bevan: Cautious Rebel,* New York, 1961.

Lloyd, L., and Sims, N. A., *British Writing on Disarmament from 1914 to 1978,* 1979.

McAllister, G. (ed.), *The Bomb: Challenge and Answer,* 1955.

McKenzie, R. T., *British Political Parties,* 1959.

McMahan, J., *British Nuclear Weapons, For and Against,* 1981.

Martin, K., *The Vital Letters of Russell, Khrushchev, Dulles,* 1958.

Meehan, E. J., *The British Left Wing and Foreign Policy,* Rutgers, NJ, 1960.

Middleton, D., 'The Deeper Meaning of British Neutralism', in R. Theobald (ed.), *Britain in the 1960s,* New York, 1961.

Miliband, R., 'Moving On', in R. Miliband and J. Saville (eds.), *The Socialist Register 1976,* 1976.

—— *Parliamentary Socialism,* 2nd edn. 1973.

Minkin, L., *The Labour Party Conference,* 1978.

Morrison, S., *I Renounce War: The Story of the PPU,* 1962.

Moss, N., *Men Who Play God: The Story of the Hydrogen Bomb,* 1968.

Nairn, T., 'The Nature of the Labour Party', in P. Anderson and R. Blackburn (eds.), *Towards Socialism,* 1965.

Nakhnikian, G. (ed.), *Bertrand Russell's Philosophy,* 1974.

Noel-Baker, P., *The Arms Race,* 1960.

Nuttall, J., *Bomb Culture,* 1968.

Pelling, H., *The British Communist Party,* 1958.

Ramsey, P., *War and the Christian Conscience,* Cambridge, 1961.

Reid, B., *Ultra-leftism in Britain,* 1969.

Reynolds, E., *The Forbidden Voyage,* 1962.

Richards, V., *Protest without Illusions,* 1981.

Roberts, A., *The Strategy of Civilian Defence,* 1967.

Rolph, C. H., *Kingsley: The Life, Letters and Diaries of Kingsley Martin,* 1973.

Rotblat, J., *Science and World Affairs: History of the Pugwash Conferences,* 1962.

Rowbotham, S., Segal, L., and Wainwright, H., *Beyond the Fragments: Feminism and the Making of Socialism,* 1979.

Russell, B. (Earl Russell), *Autobiography,* 3 vols., 1967, 1968, and 1969.

—— *Common Sense and Nuclear Warfare,* 1959.

—— *Has Man a Future?* 1961.

—— *Unarmed Victory,* 1963.

Ryle, M. H., *The Politics of Nuclear Disarmament,* 1980.

Schoenman, R. (ed.), *Bertrand Russell: Philosopher of the Century,* Boston, Mass., 1967.

—— 'Bertrand Russell and the Peace Movement', in G. Nakhnikian (ed.), *Bertrand Russell's Philosophy,* 1974.

Scott, M., *A Time to Speak,* 1958.

Scott, M., *Pacifism is Not Enough*, 1964.

Sharp, G., *The Politics of Non-Violent Action*, Boston, Mass., 1973.

Shaw, M., 'War, Peace and British Marxism, 1895–1945', in R. Taylor and N. Young (eds.), *Campaigns for Peace: British Peace Movements in the Twentieth Century*, Manchester, 1988.

—— 'The Making of a Party?', in R. Miliband and J. Saville (eds.), *Socialist Register 1978*, 1978.

Shipley, P., *Revolutionaires in Modern Britain*, 1976.

Snyder, W. P., *The Politics of British Defence Policy 1945–1962*, Ohio, 1962.

Stein, W. (ed.), *Nuclear Weapons and the Christian Conscience*, 1961.

—— *Peace on Earth: The Way Ahead*, 1966.

Taylor, R., 'George Orwell and the Politics of Decency', in J. A. Jowitt and R. K. S. Taylor (eds.), *George Orwell*, Bradford Centre Occasional Papers 3, Leeds, 1981.

—— and Ward, R., 'Community Politics and Direct Action', in D. Coates and G. Johnston (eds.), *Socialist Strategies: A Socialist Primer*, vol. 2, Oxford, 1983.

Thayer, G., *The British Political Fringe*, 1965.

Theobald, R. (ed.), *Britain in the 1960s*, New York, 1961.

Thompson, E. P., *Beyond the Cold War*, 1982.

—— *The Making of the English Working Class*, 1963.

—— 'Peculiarities of the English' in R. Miliband and J. Saville (eds.), *The Socialist Register 1965*, 1965.

—— (ed.), *Out of Apathy*, 1960.

—— *et al.*, *Britain and the Bomb*, New Statesman, 1981.

—— *et al.*, *Exterminism and Cold War*, 1982.

The Times, *The Nuclear Dilemma* (collected letters to the editor on the nuclear issue), 1959.

Tonybee, P. (ed.), *The Fearful Choice*, 1958.

Vincent, J. J., *Christ in a Nuclear World*, 1962.

—— *Christian Nuclear Perspective*, 1964.

Watkin, E. I., 'Unjustifiable War', in Charles S. Thompson (ed.), *Morals and Missiles: Catholic Essays on the Problems of War Today*, 1959.

Widgery, D., *The Left in Britain 1956–1968*, 1976.

Williams, P. M., *Hugh Gaitskell: A Political Biography*, 1979.

Williams, R. (ed.), *The May Day Manifesto*, 1969.

Windlesham, Lord, *Communication and Political Power*, 1966.

Wittner, L. S., *Rebels Against War: The American Peace Movement, 1941–1960*, Columbia, 1969.

Wood, A., *Bertrand Russell: The Passionate Sceptic*, 1957.

Wood, N., *Communism and British Intellectuals*, 1959.

Young, N., *An Infantile Disorder? The Crisis and Decline of the New Left*, 1977.

INDEX